Figurae

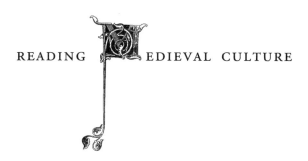

READING MEDIEVAL CULTURE

THE
AMBIVALENCES OF
MEDIEVAL RELIGIOUS
DRAMA

Rainer Warning

Translated by Steven Rendall

Stanford University Press, Stanford, California, 2001

Stanford University Press
Stanford, California
© 2001 by the Board of Trustees of the Leland Stanford Junior University

The Ambivalences of Medieval Religious Drama was originally published in
German in 1974 under the title *Funktion und Struktur:*
Die Ambivalenzen des geistlichen Spiels
© 1974 Wilhelm Fink Verlag.

Printed in the United States of America on acid-free, archival-quality paper.

Library of Congress Cataloging-in-Publication Data
Warning, Rainer.
[Funktion und Struktur. English]
The ambivalences of medieval religious drama / Rainer Warning ;
translated by Steven Rendall.
p. cm. — (Figurae)
Originally published: Funktion und Struktur. München : W. Fink, 1974.
Includes bibliographical references (p.   ) and index.
ISBN 0-8047-3791-6 (alk. paper)
1. Mysteries and miracle plays, German—History and criticism.   2. German
drama—Middle High German, 1050–1500—History and criticism.
3. Christian drama, German—History and criticism.   I. Title.
II. Figurae (Stanford, Calif.)
PT694. W313 2001
832'.051609—dc21   00-057320

Original printing 2001

Last figure below indicates year of this printing:
10   09   08   07   06   05   04   03   02   01
Typeset by Keystone Typesetting, Inc. in Adobe Garamond

Contents

Foreword by Hans Ulrich Gumbrecht

PUSHING THE LIMITS OF UNDERSTANDING

Rainer Warning's Book on Medieval Theater Recontextualized

Rainer Warning's book on medieval religious theater is very demanding reading by any standards. As for any other work of undoubted excellence, it is trivial to mention that it should have been made available to a broader readership a long time ago—rather, it needs to be said that this (that is, translating Warning's book into English, say, ten years earlier) would not have made the challenge of reading less intense. For there are at least two dimensions in which the book is not synchronized with its potential present-day readers outside Germany. Written between the late 1960s and the early 1970s as a *Habilitationsschrift* at the University of Konstanz, Warning's text was part of a specific intellectual moment from which we all are now separated by more than three decades. When it first appeared in 1971, "Funktion und Struktur: Die Ambivalenzen des geistlichen Spiels" immediately earned its author the admiration of some of Germany's most eminent humanists. Even among those colleagues of Warning's own generation who had considerable difficulties with the book's complex argument, quite a few began to acknowledge the author as a potential leader in the German world of cultural and historical studies (about a year before its publication, this work had already earned Warning a prestigious appointment at the University of Munich). Seen from today, the book indeed became the starting point for the intellectual trajectory of one of the most interesting (and yet also one of the most internationally under-discovered) German critics in the second half of the twentieth century.

All of this, however, does not mean, as one might think, that "the right moment has now arrived" to read Warning's book in English. How should one identify "the right moment" anyway? To use this phrase would presuppose that the book, when it first appeared, was "ahead of its time," and that we, the common readers, have now finally "caught up" with it. Such a premise would indeed imply too one-dimensional a vision for the history of scholarship. After all, Warning's book was not only the product of a specific moment in intellectual history, a product of the turning between the 1960s and the 1970s—which happened to be, on a truly international scale, a moment of intense experimentation and ambitious innovation. This work was also shaped—and very much so—by the specific intellectual style of the German academic tradition that today, having undergone many profound transformations, is about as far away from other academico-intellectual styles as it used to be 30 years ago. Because there is no strong reason to believe that these different traditions are now finally in a process of convergence, the publication of Warning's book in English, some quarter century after its first appearance, requires a double recontextualization—one historical and one cultural. Warning's own epilogue to this English translation of his book does a perfect job of mediating between the book's intellectual past and the author's intellectual present. Yet the intellectual present from which the author rereads his work is of course a specifically German intellectual present. It is a present that, in many of its implications, may be as unfamiliar for an Anglo-American reader as the book's—German—past. Warning's epilogue thus beautifully intensifies the intrinsic complexity of his book by integrating it into a new present—but, in doing so, he certainly does not make it more accessible for non-German readers. The double task for my brief introductory remarks is obvious then. I want to recontextualize Warning's book for its new readers, paying attention, above all, to its (academico-)cultural otherness. However, because we are no longer convinced that there is any deep historical logic determining the "adequate" or even "ideal" moments for translations or for fresh reception-processes regarding individual books, it will also be appropriate to suggest why—in absence of such a logic—it might still be a good (albeit not a "historically necessary") idea to read Warning's book *now*.

For those who participated in the intellectual moment around 1970 and for those interested in the history of literary scholarship, the name of the University of Konstanz, where Rainer Warning was then a *Wissenschaftlicher Assistent*, may be remindful of "reception history" and "aesthetics of receptions" as claims for an academic "paradigm change" that, at least for a few years, seemed to set the future agenda for research and teaching within literary studies in Germany. Though Warning was a student both of Hans Robert Jauß and Wolfgang Iser, the school heads of the reception-movement, his project only tangentially participated (if at all) in this relatively short-lived intellectual fashion. For while it is true that his book tried to retrieve the "social functions" and the "effects" ("*Wirkungen*") of the texts in question, Warning was neither particularly interested in the documentary traces of their reception ("*Rezeptionsbelege*") nor did he ever pretend to derive a heightened democratic legitimacy from the so-called "turn to the reader." For a book of literary scholarship written in Germany around 1970, it is astonishingly text-focused and almost arrogantly (or should I say, refreshingly?) nonpolitical. The way, however, in which the historical and cultural moment of its origin made itself present in this book is the sharp dichotomy that it constantly and almost obsessively draws between "traditional" presuppositions of research and "new," promising, more intellectually powerful paradigms. Intellectual innovation as a quest for higher complexity was the goal by which Warning was driven—and it was this goal (more than the wish to make a contribution to "medieval studies") that determined his choice of an obscure—that is, difficult—textual body from a remote—that is, challenging—historical period.

But what did Warning's innovation consist of, where and how did he hope to beat "traditional scholarship"? His bet seemed to be that, through a combination of different "theoretical paradigms" (to use a phrase that was eminently popular in the German academic language of the 1970s), it was possible to push further the reach of historical understanding. In other words, Warning's book was an attempt at maximizing the powers of hermeneutics, an attempt, however, that departed from Hans-Georg Gadamer (whom Warning nevertheless frequently quotes) by trying to develop a "method" of understanding, rather than relying on the interpreter's intuition. In this sense, Warning's book is parallel both to Jürgen Habermas's contemporary effort to strengthen the self-reflexive component—and, with it, the political pertinence of Gadamer's hermeneutics—and to the then much-debated claim of a German psychoanalyst (also quoted by Warning), Alfred Lorenzer, who set out to "reconstruct," "systematize," and thus ultimately "improve" Freud's technique of interpretation. If "maximizing the reach of hermeneutics"—into the "depths" of the preconscious or into the "dark spaces" of remote periods of the past—if maximizing the reach of hermeneutics by giving interpretation the systematic rigor of a "method" was the most ambitious goal for the younger German humanists in the early 1970s, it is also important to take into account that the intellectual style and gesture by which different scholars wanted to achieve this goal was deliberately and often daringly eclectic (in the best sense of what French intellectuals used to call "*éclecticisme éclairé*"). Here we may indeed hit upon a—seldom-mentioned—cultural specificity of humanistic scholarship in Germany. Frequently, if not regularly, German scholars seek for higher intellectual complexity by means of a combination (and why not say with Lévi-Strauss: by means of an intellectual *bricolage*?) of different theories, philosophies, and epistemologies. One could indeed write a comprehensive history of Jürgen Habermas's or of Niklas Luhmann's lifeworks by distinguishing the different paradigms that, over the years, they have tried to combine with their primary (Hegelian or phenomenological) premises. The same eclectic gesture (although with different epistemological and ideological contents) has characterized Rainer Warning's writings ever since his book on medieval theater, and this is why it would be inadequate to ask into which of the then-existing intellectual genealogies he tried to inscribe himself.

If optimizing the powers of historical understanding was the self-defined assignment, Warning brought together at least four different paradigms to reach his goal: the "social anthropology" of Arnold Gehlen, structuralism (mainly in the tradition of Claude Lévi-Strauss), Niklas Luhmann's "systems theory," and elements from different theories of play and of laughter. What the German tradition subsumes under the name of "social anthropology" are different theories of culture whose common denominator lies in the premise that human life, compared to the life of all other species, is characterized by the lack (or by the atrophy) of those innate instincts that otherwise guarantee individual and collective survival. All kinds of cultural artifacts are seen as devices that compensate for this lack. Social anthropology thus provides a first and basic hypothesis for the interpretation of any cultural artifact, and, as a common point of reference, this hypothesis suggests a comparison of the different specific functions through which different cultural artifacts with their different structures contribute to the general need of compensation. It was this theoretical framework that gave Warning a map on which to place and on which to compare different kinds of religious practices, rituals, and texts: they would all contribute to the institutional stability of a transcendental horizon surrounding everyday life, a horizon that gave legitimacy to whatever everyday life turned out to be.

Structuralism, Warning's second theoretical paradigm, was still very much alive around 1970 as a method of analyzing texts and other cultural artifacts. At the same time—and perhaps most intensely so in Germany— this was also the intellectual moment when structuralism had already incurred the critique of being "unhistorical," that is, of tracing and reconstructing, over and again, the same structures in all different cultures and times. This very frustration with structuralism is one of the historical circumstances that help us understand the shape of the earliest versions of Niklas Luhmann's theory of social systems. For, instead of being interested in recurrent structures, Luhmann wanted to show how the different structures of different social systems would depend on the different functions that these systems fulfilled. Structural analysis of a system, in this context, would be subordinated to the formation of a hypothesis about the specific function of that system. While specific functions of specific systems thus needed to be identified individually, they were all based on the general hypothesis that social systems were producing sense ("Sinn"), that is, they were reducing the complexity of their respective environments by selecting among the components constituting these environments—and without deleting the nonselected elements. Somehow surprisingly, thus, the role that systems theory played in its coupling with structuralism was the role traditionally fulfilled by hermeneutics. Systems theory would confirm and differentiate the very broad hypotheses about the functions of cultural artifacts and social systems provided by cultural anthropology, and it would thus initiate and guide individual analysis and interpretation. From today's perspective, we can say that, by bringing together structuralism and systems theory in this way, Warning's approach was truly visionary. For he had systems theory fulfill the role of hermeneutics at a moment when readers rather tended to see hermeneutics and systems theory as occupying opposite positions. In the meantime, however, it has become apparent that, based on the concept of sense and constantly searching for functions of the systems in question, systems theory can indeed be seen as a new version of hermeneutics, a version that replaces the subject and his intentions through the system and its functions. Finally, the theories of play and laughter that Warning integrated into his picture of medieval theater allowed him to state that, very often, the plays and texts in question were undoing selections operated by the "official" social systems and brought back into the picture components that had already been eliminated.

In the concluding chapter of his book, Warning is the first to admit that he is not interested in offering a fully developed mediation between all the different theoretical paradigms that he had brought together (although it must be said that his awareness of the problems involved went far beyond the standards even of his more ambitious colleagues in literary studies). At any event, it is fair to state that Warning's way of optimizing the powers of historical understanding was that of combining a style of analysis (structuralism) with an eclectically built configuration of multiple theories, theories that attribute different functions to the cultural phenomena in question (that is, social anthropology, systems theory, and theories of play and laughter). And what was the outcome of Warning's so richly grounded reading of medieval texts? How did the specific hermeneutic power of his approach manifest itself? The main point of this book, a point that comes back in an infinity of always interesting and surprising variations, is the observation of a nonconvergence between medieval Christian theology, on the one hand, and on the other hand, the specific form of experience staged and offered by the Passion plays. The key point of this intrinsically complex difference between theology and play has to do with presence and distance. As the main ritual of Christian religion, the Eucharist promises to produce the "real presence" of God. But theology has always tended to tame this strong claim by surrounding God's presence in the world and the "real" repetition both of Christ's Last Supper and of his sacrifice, with a halo of absence and distance (Warning uses the theological concept of "kerygma" for this paradoxical concomitance of presence and absence). The Passion plays, according to Warning's then most innovative and still most important hypothesis, undermine the precarious balance of kerygma; they play religion back into archaic, mythological presence—and in doing so they often transform the official theological monotheism into scenarios of potentially violent dualism. In this dualism, Christ can become over and again (at least temporarily) the victim of his archenemy, the devil.

Today, it may be hard to fully appreciate how far Warning's exercise in historical understanding went beyond the then-prevailing interpretations of medieval religious theater. He indeed seems to have been the first student of medieval theater who did not just read the theologically problematic passages in the Passion plays as "concessions" that orthodox playwrights and actors made to their popular audiences. Nobody before Warning had seen, at least nobody had seen as sharply as he did, the precarious oscillation between the production of presence and the production of absence as the basic pattern of medieval Christian religiosity; nobody before him had understood that, quite often, these plays had run out of theological control; and that, therefore, the Church had to be concerned with taming (if not with prohibiting) them. This observation may have been the one where our present view of medieval literature has indeed caught up with Warning's book—we are much more aware than we were only twenty years ago of the importance that the idea of "real presence" had for medieval culture. But rather than privileging just one feature of the text-corpus in question, we should realize that Warning's own main concern (and his main merit) may well have been the complexity of the picture that he offered, a complexity that, almost automatically, brought him into conflict with some more cautious readings of the texts in question.

The thesis that certain genres of medieval religious theater would "bring back" archaic, mythological, and potentially dualistic elements that theological orthodoxy had excluded was the point where, as I already said before, several theories of play and laughter came into the picture. Warning interpreted situations of play as an opportunity to reintegrate, at least temporarily, forms of experience that the seriousness of everyday institutions needed to exclude. Laughter would be the most typical way of reacting to such reintegration of the excluded—at least for those who could afford to welcome it. But if we trust the epilogue that Warning wrote for the English translation of his book, this aspect of "reintegration" is the one position among the range of theories that he originally used in which he is the least interested today. In reevaluating his own theory-construction almost 30 years later, Warning is specifically interested in establishing a *new* connection between the archaic, mythological, presence-oriented side of his analysis and the concept of the imaginary that did not play a role in the book's original version. Rather than in the transgression of well-established social limits and taboos, he now discovers the cultural energy of the Passion plays—and, ultimately, their social function—in their capacity to enhance, through drastically sexual and drastically violent detail, pushes of imagination that would ultimately undermine and destabilize the socially established sphere of the "symbolic" (if we want to use this more or less Lacanian terminology). By replacing, today, the paradigm of "recuperating what was excluded" by that of "imagination as cultural energy," Warning becomes part of a general shift, in literary studies, from a style of analysis focused on the thematization of ideological contents toward a theory of imagination that, at this point, may be considered to be in the status of a collective intellectual work in progress.

What can scholarly readers today learn from this book? For those specifically interested in medieval culture, Warning certainly offers a picture of its staging phenomena whose complexity and innovative power are far from being completely absorbed. Different from what we tended to presuppose (or, at least, to hope) around 1970, however, I want to emphasize how unlikely it is for any contemporary scholar to take Warning's approach as a recipe. Who would necessarily want to bring together today, in a single approach, social anthropology, structuralism, systems theory, and play theory? And if ever somebody wanted to do so, he or she would probably not refer to a more-than-two-decades-old book as a model and as a source of intellectual legitimation. The inspiration we can gain from this book (and from the way in which Warning engages with his own previous positions in the newly written epilogue) is that of a specific "theory style," of a highly subjective, daring, and eclectic use of different theories; of an approach also that, rather than caring too much about "doing justice" to other scholars, tries to maximize the intellectual capital that they have left us, often by "wounding" (as Harold Bloom would say) and by contaminating them in the coupling with other, heterogeneous approaches.

Perhaps it would indeed be a good thing to read, like Rainer Warning does, our favorite theory authors strictly in relation to our own interests—instead of endlessly reinterpreting them as "classics." How entertaining and complicated such an intellectual style can be is one experience that makes spending time on this demanding book an absolutely worthwhile investment.

Acknowledgments

This book goes back to the 1970s. Suggestions to have it translated into English came from friends of mine living and teaching in the United States. On the Continent the book inaugurated a new view of medieval religious drama. It is quite natural, however, that theoretical issues have changed in the meantime, and so I would like to refer the reader to the Afterword, in which I say what I would perhaps stress somewhat differently if I wrote the book today. The translation project took its course, headed by a number of very competent people, to whom I am greatly indebted. My thanks go, first of all, to Hans Ulrich Gumbrecht, who initiated the project and gave me useful advice whenever required. They go to Steven Rendall for his conscientious translation. He had to cope with a complex subject matter and a no less intricate German text. They go to Helen Tartar and Elizabeth Berg of Stanford University Press. They saw to it that things went on in an atmosphere of effective and amiable cooperation. They go finally to the Editorial Board of Stanford University Press for an invitation that I regard as a great honor.

R . W .

THE
AMBIVALENCES OF
MEDIEVAL RELIGIOUS
DRAMA

Introduction:
Function and Structure

I

At first glance, it is not clear that medieval religious plays can be approached in any way other than with a historical, not to say antiquarian, interest. This impression appears to be confirmed by a cursory survey of research to date, which seems until very recently not to have been able to tear itself away from an unreflective, positivistic erudition in order to achieve a historico-hermeneutic point of view—not to mention a systematic perspective. To be sure, one can take the easy path and refer to everything that still requires "further exploration." For although research on religious drama goes back to the beginnings of philology as a discipline, it would be easy, even in fundamental areas such as textual criticism and textual history, to draw up a whole catalog of topics for investigation. However, this kind of investigation avoids a task of the most basic kind, which the discipline of literary history is now taking up: articulating its place within the framework of a systematic conception of literary studies. This idea holds for medieval studies as well: scholars should recognize the opportunity presented by a methodological re-conception that has as its goal not to bring the antiquated into a merely apparent proximity but rather, when necessary, to provide a grounding for an interest in the antiquated as antiquated. However, this goal can no longer be achieved through an unmediated access to the texts; rather, it requires a theoretical problem formulation that finds exemplary answers in these texts and thereby allows us to recognize and actualize them in their inescapability.

Thus it is not enough to show how interesting medieval studies can be,

or how one can bring well-deserved recognition to something that has allegedly been neglected. There has been no lack of this kind of research. As an
example, we can mention the "re-evaluation"—connected, in the realm of
English studies, with E. Prosser, G. Wickham, and O. B. Hardison[1]—that
has argued against the tendency to assess religious drama solely as a precursor to Shakespeare. While this critique has made a significant contribution, particularly with regard to the Darwinian-evolutionist approach
associated with E. K. Chambers, the solution cannot consist in comparing
the plays to a standard of "good drama" still normatively defined by reference to Shakespeare and excluding as "bad drama" everything that does not
meet this standard (Prosser), or in substituting structural continuity for the
continuity of evolutionary history, in order to see actualized in religious
drama the same "archetype" that is actualized in Shakespeare (Hardison).
If Shakespeare remains the focus, then it seems almost more logical to
pursue prehistory further, now in the form of a "marxist-leninist reception
of the heritage,"[2] and—with R. Weimann—to place religious plays in a
"folk drama" tradition leading up to Shakespeare. Then we would have
immediately to ask how it happened that it was precisely in the cycles
shaped by the urban bourgeoisie that the "peasant and plebeian world first
achieved aesthetic consciousness of its historical existence."[3] However, if we
assume that through a "comparison of past values and present valuations"[4]
it is possible to arrive at a consensus regarding these values and valuations,
then we could bring into such a perspective even what investigations like
Prosser's have to let fall through the cracks. Nevertheless, one thing remains
common to both approaches: the question about the meaning of our concern with religious plays is obscured by the variously grounded reception of
what Chambers called the "Shakespearean moment."

The general hermeneutic helplessness with regard to religious drama
first becomes directly apparent at the point where this focus is absent, where
prehistory cannot be studied in either an acknowledged or an unacknowl-
edged way. In France this has led to scholars being apparently unable to get
anywhere at all in this field of medieval studies, except in the case of the
Adam play. G. Frank's study, published in 1953, is currently the only comprehensive survey of the available materials. As an introductory overview it
is certainly helpful, but methodologically it remains within the positivistic
perspective of his earlier studies relating primarily to the establishment of
texts and their history.[5] These studies, which are no less significant contri-

butions in their own kind, were for a long time not followed up by other researchers: the great Passion plays by A. Greban and J. Michel, which are central to the present study, were not made available in critical editions until 1965 and 1959, respectively. Nothing more had been said about them since the days of L. Petit de Julleville, E. Roy, and G. Cohen—that is, for more than half a century—at least nothing that could be said to result from a methodological reinterpretation.

The situation in Germany is much the same, if we set aside the fact that from the outset the texts were more available in Germany than in France. H. de Boor's masterly *Textgeschichte der lateinischen Osterfeiern* towers over the massive production of recent decades as the only work that, by rejecting evolutionary-historicist positivism of its predecessors, presents itself as guided by an explicit methodological interest. While the other studies that have been written may be useful and even indispensable for any further investigations of this subject,[6] they can hardly awaken new interest in such research, because they do not represent a methodological advance beyond the work of W. Creizenach, E. Hartl, and R. Froning.[7] It is as though scholarship were still crippled by the shock created in the 1930s by E. Stumpfl's research on Germanic religious drama (*Kultspiele der Germanen*). His focus is well known: the heritage of a folk-Germanic continuity, which he tried to prove was the central driving force behind Shrovetide (*Fast-nacht*) and Easter (*Oster*) plays. In the first part of our study we will have to look into the controversy ignited by Stumpfl's book—not simply in order to pursue further the debate that then took place under oppressive circum-stances and was more broken off than concluded, but rather because an investigation that is guided by an explicit, even if problematic, interest always produces more than an unreflective addition to current research.

Stumpfl's opponents drew on authors such as H. Brinkmann, who had published in 1929 and 1930 two fundamental and still important articles on liturgical and vernacular drama. Thirty years later, in 1959, Brinkmann published a brief overview of medieval religious drama, for which he com-posed a noteworthy introduction. In the latter he remarked that:

> "Humane" drama, as it has developed in the West since Humanism, de-riving first of all from Roman comedy, seems to have become problem-atic today. After the shattering experiences of our century, we no longer assume that people have the unquestioned ability to understand symbols that earlier periods took for granted. On stage, new modes of play con-

struction are appearing that cannot be considered simply continuations of earlier traditions. Drama (*Drama*) is once again taking on the characteristics of play (*Spiel*); it makes use of procedures that were common in the theater of the Middle Ages. To see this, it suffices to think of the role of the stage manager (*Spielleiter*) in Thornton Wilder's *Our Town* and Jean Anouilh's *Antigone*. He is the one who knows, who calls the characters to life and explains the meaning of the proceedings to the spectator—and in this respect he is comparable to the role of Augustine in the Benediktbeuern Christmas play and in the St. Gallen and Frankfurt Passion plays. It remains only to ask how this role can be justified on the modern stage. Theater is seeking in various ways to emerge from its self-inflicted isolation in order to establish a new connection with the spectator, so that it can fulfill its mission of being our play, in which the actor represents us on stage, the play of our life, in which our existence is illuminated, so that we have the feeling that we could stand where the actor stands, and that the fate of the character he plays could also be our fate. In this regard medieval drama has a new relevance to our own situation. If we recognize its essence, we can hope to open our horizon to possibilities that cannot be derived from the "humane" tradition.[8]

I have quoted these remarks because they demonstrate very clearly an ongoing hermeneutic incapacity. For they do not ground any interest but only a mode of research that is conceptually still wholly modeled on the historical positivism of the earlier articles and only secondarily legitimated.[9] However, medieval studies cannot be cured by continuing along the same path and then claiming that one's subject of research is fundamentally very relevant to current concerns. Let us assume for a moment that religious drama can be seen as anticipating Brechtian epic theater (for this seems to be what Brinkmann is suggesting); it is unlikely that those concerned with Brecht will become interested, on that ground, in religious drama, for they would surely be disappointed. They would identify with things other than Mary's earthly life and her Assumption and would hardly be inclined, as Brinkmann hopes, to reflectively acknowledge that "I am like that—that is how I should be."[10] That might still be the case for some of the visitors to Oberammergau. However, what is staged in Oberammergau is a degenerate baroque Jesuitical drama, in which the specific nature of the medieval religious play is no longer recognizable. Neither have the productions of individual cycles that have been mounted in England since the 1950s rediscovered or revitalized medieval religious plays; rather, they have been exhibitions in imaginary museums, deriving their interest not from renewed relevance but from the archaic foreignness of what is irretrievably past. The religious plays are dead, and nothing will ever bring them back to life. We can attempt to understand them, but we cannot make them our contemporaries. Gadamer's conception of a "fusion of horizons" (*Horizontverschmelzung*),[11] Benjamin's demand that we "become conscious of the critical framework within which precisely this fragment of the past is juxtaposed with precisely this present"[12]—such hermeneutic categories of self-mediation through manifestations of past experience cannot be retained here.

This situation need not be disadvantageous for anyone who has come to regard as problematic the premises of the philosophy of history or a Heideggerian, "existentially" hypostatized "historicity of understanding" (Gadamer). If literary history wants to establish its claims in the present scholarly situation, it will do well to distance itself from substantialist concepts of teleology and tradition and see history as "suggestions for solving problems," as N. Luhmann has proposed for the social sciences.[13] Historicity—that of the object as well as that of the analyst—cannot become an excuse for not attempting to work out generalizable descriptive models. A good systematics will in any case reflect its models as idealizations of its objects, replete with assumptions, but assumptions about the history of scholarship, not about the history of being or the philosophy of history. The hostility to methodology that characterizes Gadamer's influential hermeneutics cannot be replaced by the opposite extreme of a hermeneutically unenlightened structuralism, which thinks it can systematically "work off" the individuality of historical patterns, with no residue. The present discussion of theory in literary studies seems rather to require that we reflect on the possibilities as well as on the limits of such processes of "working off" and then formulate research interests with them in mind. Thus reflection on the status of hermeneutics means rationalizing, through a preliminary ordering of systematic interests, an interest in hermeneutical "application" that in Gadamer remains explicitly linked to the paradigm of the classical and its "expressive power" [*Sagkraft*].[14] And it is just this preliminary ordering of systematic interests that permits us to actualize objects not open to historical mediations. In this respect, religious drama can be compared with the usual "dead" objects of structuralist analysis, such as myths and folk-

tales, which became hermeneutically relevant again only through systematic interests.

If we are looking for a first approach to our subject, we must ask where
the problematic and structural handicap in question is to be seen. What
distinguishes religious drama from all other forms of modern theater is its
proximity to worship. It emerged in the framework of Christian liturgy, and
it never fully severed its bonds to religious ritual. However, it is in this same
proximity to worship that its irreplaceability resides. For drama's rootedness
in religious ritual, which, because of a highly fragmentary tradition, remains largely a hypothetical reconstruction so far as antiquity is concerned,
can be persuasively demonstrated and proved with regard to the Middle
Ages because we have many more sources to rely on. Religious drama is an
indigenous new departure for dramatic representation in historical time,
and viewed from this perspective it could have become the privileged object
of a line of research that not only makes the relation between literature and
its origins, substrates, or analogues in ritual and myth into a central point
of its program but also draws its conception of literature from this relationship. I am referring here to so-called archetypal structuralism, which
has for some time been a domain of Anglo-American literary studies in
particular, is mainly represented by Northrop Frye, and sees itself as the
decisive opponent of the formalist aesthetics of the New Criticism. However, this kind of discovery has only recently begun,[15] and the attempt has
not exploited the possibilities of the subject: in the name of an unprob-
lematized concept of structure, it ignores the hermeneutic foreignness of
these plays and thus lays itself open to the objections that hermeneutics
makes against structuralism, which the present work seeks to pursue con-
structively with a view to possible mediations. It seems necessary to stake
out first the methodological framework of relationships within which this
endeavor will proceed.

II

Archetypal criticism is a specifically Anglo-American variant of literary
structuralism. Although in its homeland it has a rich, highly diversified
tradition, up to this point it has not really had any impact on the Continent.
This statement holds true in France, where Parisian semioticians have approached Frye's work hesitantly,[16] and particularly in Germany, where,
although archetypal criticism has been developed in English departments,

the methodological self-examination of the differing schools and especially of hermeneutics has not yet been affected by this development, and thus archetypal criticism could not be subjected to a long overdue critique from the point of view of hermeneutics.

There are historical reasons for this failure to connect. Archetypal literary criticism starts from a position explicitly opposed to that of hermeneutics. Whereas the latter was constituted in the wake of the secularization of theological hermeneutics, the former was based on Darwinian anthropology. Thus on one side stand Friedrich Schleiermacher and Wilhelm Dilthey and on the other the so-called Cambridge school, with W. R. Smith, J. G. Frazer, and J. E. Harrison as its chief representatives. Harrison formulated, in the framework of an investigation into the origins of Greek mythology, three theses that go beyond an anthropological research program:

1. A myth arises out of a ritual and not vice versa.

2. A myth is the oral correlate of the ritual performed, the *legomenon* as opposed to the *dromenon*.

3. A myth is nothing more than this and hence has no other origins.[17]

These origins are, however, hidden from us. In the course of time, myths detach themselves from the rituals through which they are institutionalized, and their structures become available for other contents. For instance, they take on etiological functions and enter into religion and customs, into literature and art. With the help of certain structural recurrences, the Cambridge school members sought to reconstruct the original on the basis of the so-called "survivals." Within this framework, G. Murray and F. M. Cornford undertook such attempts at reconstruction for epic, tragedy, and comedy, that is, for the main genres of Greek literature.[18] Murray's anchoring of the central categories of Aristotelian poetics such as *agon, pathos*, and *anagnorisis* in the Dionysian cult has outlived the anthropological origins of this mode of literary research. His "Excursus" is still cited whenever tragedy is subjected to archetypal analysis. Much the same can be said of Cornford. The way psychoanalysis has drawn on the Cambridge school has undoubtedly greatly contributed to its prestige. It is well known that Freud did not regard the archaic rituals brought together in Frazer's monumental work as worn-out, magical forms of religion and art but rather as substitute-formations that pointed toward a great, aboriginal Oedipal tragedy and saw their recurrence as exercising a universal power in all periods.[19] His competitor C. G. Jung saw this omnipresence not as neurotic—that is, in relation to the repression-recurrence schema—but rather as a collective unconscious identical in all human beings. The content of this collective unconscious was supposed to consist in primeval figures or types, that is, as what Jung called "archetypes" in his systematic use of the concept.

In the course of its history, archetypal literary criticism has drawn in significant ways on anthropology and psychology.[20] In so doing, it has often burdened itself with these other disciplines' problems, and in particular those of Jungian depth psychology, and this burden caused it to be viewed with justifiable skepticism. Frye acknowledged this skepticism when he insisted on separating works like those of Jung and Frazer from their anthropological roots and annexing them as structural paradigms for literary criticism. The latter were to show that what had been analyzed in terms of sources, origins, and influence could be used to demonstrate literary analogies and affinities:

> To the literary critic, ritual is the *content* of dramatic action, not the source or origin of it. The *Golden Bough* is, from the point of view of literary criticism, an essay on the ritual content of naive drama: that is, it reconstructs an archetypal ritual from which the structural and generic principles of drama may be logically, not chronologically, derived. It does not matter two pins to a literary critic whether such a ritual had any historical existence or not. It is very probable that Frazer's hypothetical ritual would have many and striking analogies to actual rituals, and collecting such analogies is part of his argument. But an analogy is not necessarily a source, an influence, a cause, or an embryonic form, much less an identity. The *literary* relation of ritual to drama, like that of any other aspect of human action to drama, is a relation of content to form only, not one of source to derivation.[21]

Frye's effort to secure the autonomy of literary criticism in opposition to what he calls the determinism of anthropology and psychology finds its clearest expression in the definition of his central concept: an archetype must no longer have anything to do with the collective unconscious, any more than with a worn-out, archaic past; rather, it is nothing other than "a literary symbol, or cluster of symbols, that are used recurrently throughout literature, and thereby become conventional."[22] Consequently, Frye sees his *Anatomy of Criticism* less as a systematic poetics than as a "schematic construct": "The reason it is schematic is that poetic thinking is schematic."[23]

With this definition of the archetype as a literary universal, recurrent, structuring pattern, points of contact and agreements between Frye's structuralism and that of the Paris semioticians emerge.[24] In both cases, the goal is to transform structural analytical procedures originally developed in anthropology or folklore studies into universal structural models of text production. The ways of going about this task differ. Whereas Frye seeks to verify anthropological hypotheses by reference to literary texts considered as a similarly reconstructed mythology, the Paris school, following Vladimir Propp's example, usually starts out from a finite corpus of texts (for instance, myths, folktales, story collections), using it as a matrix for constructing invariants. The claim to universality made for the models employed is the same in both cases. One important difference is that the Paris school occasionally tries to ground its models in linguistics, even though up to now this has produced only somewhat questionable results.[25]

The so-called structuralist controversy cannot be summed up as merely asking in what way universal models can most effectively be employed and whether they can or cannot be linguistically grounded. Alongside this more or less internal debate there is an external one that problematizes in a transcendental way the categories of invariance and universality themselves and thereby the structuralist enterprise in general. Frye is at the center of this critique in the Anglo-American arena;[26] in France, the debate has been more fundamental.[27] This critique was not always constructive. It often took as its point of departure the positions that lie behind structuralism and simply opposed its own one-sided positions (hermeneutics, Marxism) to those of its opponent. If we want to achieve progress rather than mere confrontation, then we must resolve to carry out both a mutual problematizing of basic assumptions and systematic attempts at mediation.

Within sociological systems theory are reflections that might prove fruitful in such attempts at mediation. With respect to the structural-functional theory of social systems like that of Talcott Parsons, Niklas Luhmann has suggested that it is a secondary question "whether what is seen as structure and is not problematized is taken from empirical reality or derived from the theory of action, that is, whether we are dealing with concrete or analytical systems." A progressive critique should begin by inquiring, not into the status of structures but rather into the primacy of the concept of structure itself, since this primacy evades certain stages in the meaning of the problematization.[28] The suggestion that follows logically from this seems to me of greater significance for the meaningful continuation of the structuralist controversy: to transform structural-functionalist theories into functional-structuralist theories, that is, to consider the concept of function as prior to the concept of structure rather than the other way around. The reference point of functional analysis would thus no longer be the internal order of structured systems but rather the question of the environment to which a certain mode of system-formation significantly replies: "Functional theory is system-environment theory."[29]

The subordination of the concept of function is in fact characteristic of the Paris semioticians. This subordination is always particularly evident in cases in which—following Propp—the recurrent units are explicitly described as "functions" (as in R. Barthes, C. Bremond, T. Todorov), and thereby the internal order of the system is shown to be the reference point and not the problem to which system-formation responds. In this respect, Frye's archetypes can be compared with functions. The archetypal pattern does not bring the meaning of structure-formation into view, and Frye is therefore incapable of problematizing it: the loss of a pattern, no less significant functionally-structurally than its retention, is for him unquestionable. To illustrate this briefly with a particularly striking example: Frye describes the archetype of comedy as a "ternary action," in which a solid and harmonious order is disturbed by conflict between the younger and the older generation and is finally restored through an unexpected turn of events.[30] This pattern in fact governs comedy up to the eighteenth century. However, then it becomes problematic for obvious reasons: the sociological identity of the (bourgeois) public and of the world represented on stage no longer allows bourgeois domestic conflicts to be selected as subjects for comedies. Thus it becomes necessary to neutralize the conflict between young and old either in a sociological manner (Beaumarchais's Bartholo, for instance, is represented as a character-type, not as a bourgeois), or by abandoning it, as Marivaux does. Frye does not mention Marivaux and does not say why the pattern functions in Molière. It is evident that his models depend on not inquiring into certain questions.

When he argues in a functional-structural manner, Frye implicitly contradicts himself. Thus his basic definition of literature as the emancipation of nature in culture, as a vision of the goal of human work, as ritual freed for play, adheres to the same Cambridge-school genetic model that was supposed to be overcome in the basic structuralist definition of the archetype.[31] In fact, the official formalization of the archetypes, through which "poetic thinking" is attributed to them as their dimension, finds its unofficial counterpart in the evolutionary derivations of literature from myth and in depth-psychology derivations of both in Freud's and even Jung's sense.[32] Frye operates on one hand with the concept of "total form" as a synopsis of all literary works that does away with historical sequence and on the other with the categories of dream, return, and wish-fulfillment, which do not disown their Freudian provenance;[33] what is denied in one place is presupposed in another. Archetypes are supposed to be nothing more than schematic models, myths nothing more than stories organized with the help of such models, and yet what is supposed to be organized in this way is the return of an archaic condition: the golden age of a classless society. According to Frye, literature in its totality is the utopian vision of this return. Here is restored to the archetype what it connotes semantically: something aboriginal, in which ritual returns, and in which ritual finds its representation [*Wiedervergegenwärtigung*]. However, insofar as return implies discontinuity in this way, it is not derivable from mere recurrence and clearly cannot be made equivalent to it.[34] No path leads from pattern to return, so the passage must be by way of the institution of the ritual. However, Frye defines ritual only structurally, not institutionally, and thus remains, when he takes the concept of function as his starting point, in the grip of a "subjectless transcendentalism."[35]

The same can once again be said about the Paris school and first of all about Lévi-Strauss. The latter does with myths themselves something very similar to what Frye does with literature as a reconstituted mythology. In place of Frye's schematisms of "poetic thinking" we find in Lévi-Strauss the classificatory power of "the savage mind": with the help of a universal logic operating through unconscious structures, myths present solutions to aporias of social practice. Wherein does this logic reside, wherein is its subject? In no case can it be in concrete social institutions. They are precisely what is abstracted from in the interest of the structures of the "savage mind" that determine them. However, this de-institutionalization, which Lévi-Strauss carries out in an exemplary way precisely with regard to the phenomenon of totemism, also characterizes the central problematic of his approach, and it has been the primary target of criticism of his work. Lévi-Strauss can show that cannibals have an amazingly subtle classificatory logic, but he does not indicate how we get from this logic to anthropophagy. Thus Anglo-American anthropology in particular, which owes much to the functionalist school of A. Radcliffe-Brown and B. Malinowski, has objected that Lévi-Strauss merely presents long-familiar and uncontested facts in a new and interesting light but does not explain the conventional aspects as the essentially relevant aspects of archaic institutions, instead merely ignoring them.[36]

Lévi-Strauss's selection of his materials is already characteristic of the structural-functional approach. Detailed analysis would almost certainly lead to the conclusion that in the great majority of cases these are etiological myths, which first arise with the function of a "logical tool." However, etiological myths, as A. E. Jensen in particular has noted, differ from genuine myths in that they usurp the latter's narrative schemata for pseudo-explanatory contents that are in fact redundant. They are secondary formations, concerning which it is assumed "that a meaningful appearance loses its authentic meaning and yet continues to exist, because it has not lost all meaning."[37] At the same time it becomes clear, however, that the problem of mythical thinking cannot be approached structurally-functionally by way of etiological myths (Jensen explicitly stresses their formal similarity to genuine myths) but only functionally-structurally, that is, by way of structural formations. To the latter category belongs the repetition-structure of ritual, which once again has no systematic place in Lévi-Strauss's work. Rituals are brought in as interpretants for myths and also interpreted by means of myths. They are not grasped categorically, however. The strict opposition between the synchronic "structure" and the diachronic "event" that threatens the structure excludes the category of ritual. Ritual is precisely not one of the contingent events that disturb the structure, but rather in it the structure itself becomes an event. In the same process of representation, the diachrony that distinguishes the "now" of ritual from the "formerly" of myth is conceived as transcended, and thus synchrony is conceived not as destroyed but as consolidated. One of the fundamental insights of empirical myth research in the tradition of Malinowski is that this repetition-structure decides whether or not the obligatory content of a founding, aboriginal event will be attached to a story.[38] In other words, structures do not characterize stories as myths but rather their institutionalization in a ritual that guarantees an ongoing actuality.

The present investigation seeks in that measure to mediate between the objectivist concept of structure typical of current myth-criticism and an anthropological theory of institutions. Therefore it relies primarily on the broadest and most influential attempt at such a theory, A. Gehlen's *Urmensch und Spätkultur.* At first glance Gehlen's work seems unsuitable for such a mediation, but he accompanies his "philosophy of institutions," which he describes as empirical-analytical, with an expressly antihermeneutical polemic. Thus he opposes Dilthey's "horrifying proposition" that the experience of one's own condition and the indirect experience of an alien condition are basically similar events, the postulate of a quasi-objective categorical analysis of social behavior and the institutions that support it.[39] Quasi-objective, because even an anthropology that thinks of itself as an empirical-analytical discipline "must formulate its propositions about human beings with an awareness that it is interpreting them on the basis of those who are living under the very unique conditions of the present."[40] It is equally necessary to objectivize the historicity of these propositions in categories whose claim to describe essential characteristics of archaic cultures remains verifiable by the "abundance of the insights that can be derived from them."[41]

In fact, the present study is conceived as being, among other things, a test of what can be derived, and even of the derivability of the institution of religious drama from a range of anthropological categories. However, it can in no way deny hermeneutical status to such a venture: the analysis's arsenal of instruments does not determine in advance the questions to which its application may lead. The hermeneutic logic of question and answer remains in force even when we are no longer inquiring ontologically into truth but rather functionally into the constitution of meaning through system references.[42] This Luhmannian concept of the constitution of a system of meaning, for instance (as a meaning-constituting system) coincides in large measure, according to the subject, with Gehlen's concepts of institution and release.[43] However, methodologically Luhmann seems to argue more realistically when he sees in the progress from a structural-functional to a functional-structural systems theory an "abandonment of positivism and a shift to a quite different, more or less hermeneutic methodological postulate."[44] The task of the logic of question and answer would thus be to articulate the (specific historical) problem of relation, that is, the environmental functions on the basis of which structural formations can be explained. Consequently, we will have to analyze recurrent structural formations within the textual corpus of "religious drama" as indices of certain interests, as solutions to problems but not as a matrix for structural universals. The guiding model that emerges in this way, that of the "inclusion of the excluded," the "positivizing of negativity," has a functional status and may be generalizable as a functional class of equivalences, "play." In any case, the goal-models of functional-structural analysis no longer have the status of structural universals but rather of functional equivalences. Thus at the same time the value of structural models like those of the Paris semioticians or of archetypal criticism is determined: a functional-structural procedure will put them to work as "heuristic fictions" (H. Vaihinger[45]). Thus Barthes's functions or Frye's archetypal patterns lead us to the points at which structural-functional constants are to be functionally-structurally dissolved. Then the concept of the archetypal can, however, no longer or not already qualify structures but rather functions, and we will use it in precisely this sense. By it we designate a certain "orientation" toward biblical stories, a certain selection of these models that gives their repetition in the play a mythical-archetypal meaning. The concept will thus be seen neither substantialistically as in Jung, nor structurally-functionally as in Frye, but rather functionally-structurally, that is, in relation to the meaning-constitution of the play.

III

Here we have arrived at the point where the hermeneutic path that leads to these functions must be indicated. They are far from obvious, and at first it is not at all clear just what religious drama has to do with myths, rituals, and archaic institutions. What it stages in accord with its articulated self-understanding is a story that constituted itself as an exact antithesis to myth and its eternal return: a salvation history that derives its life from the kerygma, from the announcement of a fulfillment still to come. Thus at first glance it seems to make no sense when Malinowski draws on Christian belief in order to characterize myth:

> Myth in a primitive society, that is, in its living, original form, is no mere narrated tale but rather a lived reality. It is not a kind of invention, such as we read in our novels today, but rather living reality, which is believed to have taken place in the earliest times and to have influenced the world and the fate of men ever since. For primitives, myth has the same role as for Christians the biblical account of creation, fall, and redemption through Christ's sacrifice on the cross. Just as our sacred history lives on

in our ritual and in our ethics, so the sacred history of primitive peoples lives on in their myth.[46]

This analogy can be applied only to the psychological stage of belief in a story, not to the view of reality that underlies both forms of belief. For here one can imagine no greater opposition than that between the mythical piety that turns its back on the future and looks back toward archaic origins by revisualizing them in ritual and, on the other hand, the kerygmatic, salvation-history anticipation of a future fulfillment, which was guaranteed in an event that is historical or at least believed to be historical. The fact that Christian liturgy understands this past event not as something that is revisualized in an identical repetition but rather as its merciful perpetuation *in effectu* is an expression of this salvation-history tension between past guarantee and future fulfillment. The Venerable Bede's sermon on the Sacrifice of the Mass as a *pascha perpetuum* very relevantly indicates the Christian antithesis to a form of worship that does not perpetuate but rather leaps over the hiatus between an original beginning and what is revisualized in ritual and is thus essentially based on discontinuity.[47]

However, I have not quoted Malinowski to oppose to him something of which he was also surely aware. For him the important thing was first that myth not be prematurely identified with the forms that have come down to us from classical antiquity, the sacred books of the East, and other sources "without the context of living belief." For myth "is not an idle tale, but rather a renewed, effective power; it is neither an intellectual explanation nor an artistic fantasy, but rather, for primitives, a fundamental law of belief and ethics, and in this respect effectiveness in the life-world seems to Christian belief a possible way of initially interpreting mythical piety by means of experience in a post-mythical age."[48] However, as we will show here, this belief produced for a few centuries forms of worship that also brought it a decisive step closer, in its implications as regards content, to mythical piety—forms concerning which one may say, adapting Malinowski's words, that in them "our sacred history lived, as for primitives their myth lived": the religious plays of the Middle Ages. Superficially, these plays are didactic illustrations of what Christian liturgy celebrates symbolically. This symbolics is, however, as the epitome of a different way of repeating the past, indispensable for the salvation-history kerygma. When it is relinquished, this kerygma is put in question, and the salvation-history tension between a past act of salvation, a present guarantee in liturgical ritual, and a future fulfillment is dissolved. This suggests that we should see in such shortcomings nothing more than the unavoidable price to be paid for concrete illustration. Nevertheless it will be shown that the didactic stage cannot be prematurely equated with the play impulse. It is a secondary rationalization at least in the sense that the shaping of just such a form of didactic communication is itself already borne by a highly ambivalent understanding of Christian salvation history: the mythical type of identical repetition brings the biblical past into the dimension of an archetypal myth, which is revisualized in the play. In this sense the ambivalence of kerygma and myth will be the main thesis of the present study. This ambivalence implies that the questions to which the religious play is the answer are not to be found, or at least not primarily, in this dimension of the concrete mediation of salvation in which it articulates its official self-conception. Its primary relational problems are latent, lying in the dimension in which Gehlen locates what he calls "unconscious categories of cultural anthropology": "undetermined obligation," "stabilization," and "release" through "representation."[49] The archetypal structural formations of the plays are to be related to them.

The way problems are framed in this work owes a great deal to W. Pannenberg's discussion in "Späthorizonte des Mythos in biblischer und christlicher Überlieferung." Pannenberg inquires into the positive function of the retention or reintroduction of mythical ideas in the motivational context of the heritage of Israel, and in doing so he uses as one example among others an institutional area that particularly clearly preserved mythical modes of thought: worship. Referring to festivals such as Passover or the renewal of the covenant, he points out that in these cases mythical modes of thought not only function as interpretants for historically grounded institutions but also themselves indicate a mythical meaning for such festive celebrations:

> The salvation-history grounding of festivals and rituals that characterizes the Jewish conception of worship offers no argument against the mythical meaning of such worshipful celebrations, insofar as historical and allegedly historical events themselves take over the function of original, grounding events. Where this function is not grounded in the historical meaning of the corresponding event but rather appears directly as its essential content, there the mythical conception is no longer only an interpretant of the historical event; it has repressed its historical meaning.[50]

The most important criterion here will be the kind of repetition of the redemptive event that grounds the form of worship in question. So long as this repetition does not seek identity with what is repeated, the initial event on which worship is based is preserved as part of salvation history. However, this is not the case in the mythical form of identical repetition. It seeks to overleap the historical distance and return to the beginning, and in that respect it is the surest indication "that the salvation-history grounding had not only the meaning of a worship-etiology, but also functioned as a regular worship-myth."[51]

It is easy to show the applicability of such questions to medieval religious plays. The task will be to analyze salvation-history foundations on the basis of a form of identical repetition, with a view to a truly mythical meaning. Beneath the salvation-history foundations we must first of all take into consideration, of course, the typological-figural interpretation of history that Erich Auerbach and others showed to be one of the most important components of medieval notions of reality and of history. In fact, it is also a structural element in religious drama, whether because Old Testament prefigurations are invoked before New Testament events or because in the plays about Old Testament occurrences the antitype is already present, for example, when Adam and Eve foresee their future salvation through Jesus Christ. However, the problematic does not begin here. Interpretation first runs into difficulties when history that has been constructed figurally is presented in a peculiar, apparently timeless actuality that seems to us anachronistic. Auerbach considered this presentation as well the manifestation of a figural interpretation of events, of transposing them into a "perspective of eternity" [*Jederzeitlichkeit*].[52] This concept is perhaps unfortunate, since the figural interpretation of a salvation history event, that is, the determination of its allegorical meaning within the system of fourfold meaning, is directly concerned with its temporal and spatial uniqueness. No one has stressed this more than Auerbach himself, and his formula of a figural omnitemporality is comprehensible only from his insistence on the "concrete historical reality" presupposed in figural interpretation as opposed to the "abstract allegorical spiritualism" of the doctrine of fourfold meaning.[53] We will need to discuss this attempt, with its difficulties and limits, in relation to the Adam play. With regard to the actualization of the past in religious drama, it is in any case less misleading to speak of a moral rather than a figural omnitemporality—in the sense of the moral or tropological meaning that, precisely by blurring salvation-history and figural aspects, relates the object of interpretation to the fate of the individual soul.

To be sure, this moral sense—that is, the timeless moral validity of the redemptive event—covers what seems to us its anachronistic representation, not only in religious drama but also in medieval religious art in general. However, precisely in the case of drama we must not be satisfied with this representation alone. For drama does not simply offer an image of salvation history, does not conceive itself simply as its living illustration or as concreteness at a higher degree of reality but rather links itself in its whole history back to its ritual sources in liturgy: as late as the Easter and Passion plays of the fifteenth and sixteenth centuries, vernacular drama retains a liturgical substratum. And in just this respect the identical representation of the past in Pannenberg's sense becomes analyzable in a truly mythical sense. To the extent to which drama modeled on liturgy seeks to be a sacred activity, a ritual drama, it passes under theological cover not only through the timeless moral meaning but also through the timeless "today" of liturgy: just as the latter refers to a mercifully offered presence of the past *in effectu*, it must be asked of drama whether its "today" does not indicate the return to a "mythical instant of the beginning."[54]

Alongside the identity of repetition are two further factors that will be important to us here. The first is the periodicity of this identical repetition. Even if plays are not performed every year—the conditions differ from play to play, and, on the basis of the archival sources catalogued to date, can in every case be reconstructed only inadequately—there was still only one time for plays each year, and an attempt was made, by flexibly adapting the church calendar, to bring it into conjunction with other religious holidays. As a result of the concordance of the annual cycle and the periodic repetition of the birth, Passion, death, and Resurrection of Christ, the historical development of the church year arrived at a peculiar symbiosis of the kerygmatic and the natural-archetypal, which need not detain us here. For at the same time there were safety devices that prevented a short circuit connecting pagan sun and year-god myths with the "true son" Jesus Christ.[55] One of these safety devices was non-identical repetition. However, it dropped out in drama, and the Easter play in particular shows how, as a result of this loss, the kerygma of the Resurrection of Jesus was played back into the naturalness of a pagan *ōstarūn*.

However, this playing back—and here I come to the second factor—

must also be seen in a temporal dimension: religious drama is essentially a latter-day product. Identical and periodic representation cannot alone bring acts of salvation into the dimension of an archetypal myth. In addition, the mythifying distance of a millennium and a half lies between the biblical events and their representation in the play. Vernacular drama no longer reads the biblical stories historically but rather mythically, if not as an original, then as a "foundational" beginning in Eliade's sense, and it confirms the insight proceeding above all from research on epics and ballads, "that the recollection of a historical event or an authentic character does not remain in popular memory for more than two or three hundred years. This has to do with the fact that popular memory is able only with difficulty to hang on to 'individual' events and 'authentic' characters. It functions with the help of entirely different structures: categories instead of events, archetypes instead of historical characters. The historical figure is associated with its mythical model (hero, etc.), while the event is put into the category of mythical actions (battle against the monster, hostile brothers, etc.)."[56] Thus the fall into sin and the descent into hell appear as the beginning and ending points of a dualistic battle, the appearance of Christ before Mary Magdalen is played out as a metamorphosis, and the Passion play sacrifices Jesus as a scapegoat. In all this the play kindles the archetypal-natural substratum of this story, whose overcoming, repression, or negation it deals with in itself: in the Adam play dualistic creation myths, in the Easter play the *katabasis*-mythologeme and the rebirth of the year-god, in the Passion play the sacrifice of the year-god. Religious drama thus tends toward the establishment of a monumental remythification of salvation history. It plays this history back into the dimension in opposition to which it had once constituted its kerygma: in it the biblical acts of salvation are mythically-archetypally present.

In its very conception, the present study intends to take this subject matter into account. Thus it begins with tenth-century liturgical Easter festivals and ends with fifteenth- and sixteenth-century Passion plays. However, its structure already makes it clear that it does not pretend to be in any way a genre history. Rather it seeks to mediate between the historical development and a systematic unfolding of the archetypal structure within which the plays grasp salvation history and play it out. When this mediation encounters difficulties because of the state of the texts, the diachronic aspect will be subordinated to the synchronic-systematic aspect. Thus, for example, the Easter plays that were first fully preserved from the fourteenth century onward will be analyzed before the Old French Adam play of the twelfth century. The Easter play marks—with the "end" including the descent into hell, that is, an "end" that fades out into a future fulfillment—the vanishing point, whose dualistic arrangement structurally determines and thus dualistically transforms the function of the history leading up to it from the beginning in the fall into sin, by way of the "middle" of the sacrifice on the cross. Salvation history appears as a kind of battle between God and the Devil, carried out in a mythical past, and the play opposes to the continuing earthly power of its opponent, whose metaphysical impotence has already been revealed, not the kerygma of a future final victory— the Corpus Christi play will require special comment here—but rather a return to the beginning, the identical representation of battle and victory in the sense of an archetypal model. In this way salvation history becomes myth, and drama becomes its ritual representation.

The plan of the present work makes one further point clear. If on one hand the salvation-history grounding of these plays is analyzed on the basis of the mythical repetition-type, on the other hand the immanently achieved results of such an analysis are constantly checked against the corresponding stage of liturgical and dogmatic history. Such checkpoints appear in the first part in the debate between Amalarius of Metz and Florus of Lyons, in the second part in Anselm of Canterbury's doctrine of Christ's death on the cross as an act of "satisfaction," laid out some 50 years after the Adam play, and in the third part the high Scholastic reception of this doctrine, with special emphasis on the theory of sacrifice. These plays will thus not be seen, as they sometimes are, against the background of unselectively assembled dogmatic determinations. Such enterprises always succeed only insofar as we always find what we are looking for. In reality they lead to cognitive abdication. To illustrate this with one example: in the English *Ludus Conventriae* elements not only of the patristic doctrine of redemption (that is, the doctrine of the outwitting of Satan through Christ's death on the cross) but also of the Scholastic doctrine of a specific satisfactory performance of this death (one that restores God's injured honor) have been recognized and the ways in which both these traditions merge in a dramatic unity have been investigated.[57] Such comparisons become meaningful, however, only when one has formulated a series of questions. Such questions can in this case be formulated only if we discern systematic interests in historical dogmatic positions and compare these interests with those of the drama. We must also consider at the same time that the doctrine of satisfaction does not simply supersede the doctrine of redemption; rather, the doctrine of satisfaction derives from the doctrine of redemption its central impulse to separate off the latter's mythological-dualistic relics, through a systematic exclusion of the Devil's authority. The appearance of patristic ideas in the plays thus shows the recurrence of something dogmatically outdated. This allows us to inquire into the motivating interest of the plays as well, and only someone who does so can be guaranteed access to the problematic that proceeds from the simultaneous presence of both traditions and leads to truly irreconcilable contradictions. If drama is measured against official doctrine in this way, that is, against the corresponding stage of dogmatic reflection, then a fundamental and insurmountable divergence of interests is produced, which consists, as will be shown in detail, in the fact that drama always incorporates and perpetuates exactly what dogmatic purism diagnoses as a mythological watering-down of doctrine and tries to exclude. In this sense the "inclusion of the excluded" and the "positivization of negativity" will turn out to be the functional model of our analyses, corresponding to the main thesis.

This model is valid not only for the relationship between drama and the Scholastic doctrine of satisfaction, which will be central to the investigation of the vernacular tradition. Florus of Lyons's critique of Amalarius of Metz's (ca. 780–850) liturgical allegory already has the same background. This controversy will also have to be explored in greater detail, since liturgical allegory has long and rightly been seen as being in a causal relationship with the rise of liturgical celebration, and O. B. Hardison has recently claimed that it is a fundamental harmonization of religious drama and church doctrine. The previously unexplored criticism of Florus and his successors nevertheless makes it clear in which direction the switch was moving. Amalarius's *Liber Officialis* is a first-rate document for a mythically-archetypally oriented approach to the *historia passionis*; it is a latter-day product in the sense described above and insofar as religious drama is conceived as the unfolding of what has been put into it, it also shows that the mythification of salvation history is not first of all a product—unavoidable and to be taken into account—of its identical repetition in drama but that a highly ambivalent understanding of the biblical acts of salvation is already a condition of the emergence of drama itself.

The structure of the work cannot make it clearer how we can see the ambivalence of kerygma and myth in the plays themselves, that is, by the respective standard of an immanent theological self-verification. These forms of voluntary self-verification will nonetheless not only provide a further confirmation of our thesis but also probably count among the most stimulating details of that epochal effort to supplement the official church institutions with a further one—with an institution that would never escape the odium of contraband of which Léon Gautier already spoke with regard to liturgical tropes, and which, even though it was tolerated for a few centuries, remained only an episode.[58]

IV

In opening its object to questions arising from the intersection of anthropological and theological perspectives, the present investigation could rely on only a few previous studies. A more detailed discussion of research will be necessary only in the first part, and above all with regard to the liturgical celebration. For in this case every investigation necessarily led to the problem-complex just sketched out. However, since it has hardly ever been recognized in its whole extent and in all its implications, the answers remain partial and open to revision. The discussion of these answers thus cannot adopt the limited perspective on liturgical celebration that is proper to them. Rather, it is necessary already in this early phase to develop the main thesis, which will then determine the analysis of the vernacular tradition.

In considering the liturgical and vernacular tradition together, the present study also has no predecessors, insofar as it is not limited to a single vernacular. This openness again has to do with its way of formulating questions, which not only does not demand such a limitation but rejects it. What it requires is a synoptic view of all the relevant plays, with the goal of explaining, on the basis of the ways in which the kerygma is inhibited, the various forms in which archetypal structures are played out, and thus to pursue the emergence of religious drama against the background of theological exclusions. The author was thus free to choose his examples in each case according to their potential for clarifying the problem. This freedom explains the special attention given, particularly in the third part, to the French Passion plays, which were far more committed to trying to deal with the doctrine of satisfaction and thereby became ideal objects for demonstration. The same can be said of the German Easter plays in the first part, and of the French Adam play in the second part, although because of the state of the texts in the other vernaculars the choices were limited from the outset.

Thus only one limitation must be justified: the limitation to the German, French, and English vernacular traditions. If, with the exception of two Spanish plays that are also brought in, the whole of European religious drama is represented by only these three traditions, that is because they are in fact sufficiently representative for a complete development of the problem outlined. The claimed completeness is thus—within the three indicated traditions as well, moreover—related to the problem and in this sense entirely independent of the question of the continuity of genre-history. Nor does the present study result in a pure filling in of gaps in genre-history but rather in the inclusion of further plays both inside and outside the traditions discussed in the perspective of the questions developed here. This study seeks among other things to be assessed on the basis of whether this kind of inclusion appears to be worthwhile and meaningful.

The same can be said with respect to a meaningful continuation of investigations into text history. Here we are hindered, as was stressed at the outset, by gaps in research on religious drama. It is nevertheless in the nature of a functional-structural analysis to establish comparisons not with regard to sources and influences but rather to functional standpoints, and to that extent in the present case as well the distinguishing traits of a specifically archetypal reading of biblical patterns had to be worked out through a synoptic survey of the plays. Structural similarities as well as differences result from this archetypal orientation of the drama toward the salvation-history beginning and the respective perspectivisms produced by its encounter with kerygma. For that reason however the chosen approach could not only largely forgo studies on text history but does not take its lead from them. On the contrary, the questions formulated here provide a significant guide for future studies on text history as well but mark out the limit within which the ambivalence of kerygma and myth is played out and through in the most diverse possibilities. This approach seemed to the author both more appealing and more far-reaching, and so he entered, fully aware of the problematic character of this step, into areas where he cannot always claim to be competent.

Rather to be sought here is leniency, and especially further criticism on the part of the disciplines with whose help these questions were developed.

This is true for theology, which has not yet discovered religious drama as its subject, although it would seem to fall within its domain at least as much as within that of literary studies. This statement is also especially true for anthropology in the narrower and in the wider senses, that is, including sociology, psychoanalysis, social psychology, and folklore. They not only all prove to be indispensable at particular points in the argumentative context developed here but become fundamentally significant to the extent that literary studies abandon naive claims to autonomy. Historically, such claims proceed from the Romantic aesthetics of genius and its assumptions about the uniqueness, superiority, and irreplaceability of poetic "statement." The structuralist demolition of this tradition emerges in a new metaphysics of structural universals: wherever attempts are made to set forth structures in relation to invariants instead of problematizing them, embattled substantialism comes in again through the back door. Not structures but first of all functions that determine structures can resolve thoughts into substances. However, the functional relational problems this kind of problematization makes possible can be articulated only within the framework of a general hermeneutics of the social sciences.

PART I

The End Brought Near:
The Liturgical *Visitatio Sepulchri* and
the Vernacular Easter Plays

Liturgical Celebration and Allegorization of the Mass: The *Visitatio Sepulchri* Between Kerygma and Myth

I

The dialog *Quem queritis in sepulcro*, with which the liturgical celebration began, appeared in the Easter liturgy of the tenth century, primarily in two places: in the introit to the Easter Mass and at the end, and occasionally also at the beginning, of Easter matins.[1] In the Mass it has the character of a trope playing on the first antiphon, *Resurrexi et adhuc tecum*, about whose performance in most cases we can only conjecture. It is certain that it came only by gradual extensions to be a representation of the Marys on one hand, and of the two angels at the sepulcher on the other, more or less in this way: a priest at the altar spoke the angel's words and two choir members spoke those of the Marys. The dialog did not undergo textual or subject-matter expansion in this place. In the matins, however, it was organized into a liturgical "scene." It represents the pious women going to the sepulcher, where they learn that the one whom they had come to anoint has arisen. They are represented by groups of priests, who step forward from the choir and, in a place designated as the *sepulcrum* (which for the most part can be identified with the altar), act and sing *in persona mulierum* or *angelorum*. It is here, in the texts of the so-called *visitatio sepulchri*, that first appear textual expansions (the way-stanzas [*Wegestrophen*], the Easter sequence [*Ostersequenz*]) and subject-matter expansions (the disciples' race to the sepulcher [*Jüngerlauf*], the epiphany of Christ [*Christophanie*]). The scene is arranged to provide a celebratory closure not only of the matins but also of a preceding series of cross-celebrations. The latter begin with the *Adoratio* on Good Friday and continue through the *depositio* to the *elevatio*, which commemorates before the matins the mystery of the Resurrection, and with the *visitatio* as a confirmation of this event, undergoes a dialogic-dramatic continuation and intensification. In this sequence only the *Adoratio* is strictly liturgical. The rest is unknown in Roman Catholic liturgy. These extraliturgical ceremonies must have arisen in the ninth or tenth centuries. The *Regularis Concordia* (965–75), the product of an Anglo-Saxon monastery reform carried out under King Edgar, speaks of a *usum quorundam religiosorum imitabilem ad fidem indocti uulgi ac neofitorum corroborandam.*[2]

Although in this passage the *Concordia* itself mentions only the *Depositio*, the formula had long before been adopted for the *visitatio* as well. In the discussion of the liturgical origins of religious drama it became one of the documents most often cited and most productive of conflicting interpretations. In Germany it was above all J. Schwietering who, in 1925, leveled the charge of positivistic complacency and "solid rationalism" against all those who saw a didactic-missionary intention as a sufficient answer to the question of origins and demanded an "interpretation in accord with the human sciences." He himself immediately pointed to the commemorative interpretation of the liturgy, which "was able to lead to a new liturgical tendency more in keeping with experience and to transform arbitrary allegorization into living symbolism."[3] A short time later H. Brinkmann, acting on this suggestion, interpreted liturgical drama as the expression of a spiritual attitude that had produced liturgical allegory as well, especially as the latter was developed by Amalarius of Metz. In both cases he recognized an "overpowering yearning to experience the procedures of the Mass in a concrete manner."[4] This yearning could not be simply reduced to "goal-oriented reflections," that is, to the search for ways of strengthening belief, but rather it points to a very much deeper need that Brinkmann expressed in the formula "dogmatic experience": "The Easter play is created far more out of joy in the certainty of belief, after the peripeteia from lamenting fasting to Easter joy was experienced. It seems to me that this is the spiritual origin of medieval drama. The time was ripe. The formation of the liturgy in the ninth and tenth centuries speaks eloquently of the dramatic longing that was awakened."[5]

According to Brinkmann, E. K. Chambers "subtly observed the stirrings of this longing."[6] If Chambers did so, it was certainly not in the sense of a "dogmatic experience." For him liturgical celebration had indeed arisen in the framework of church ritual, however not as a genuine product of ritual but rather as a clever attempt "to wrest the pomps of the devil to a spiritual service," or even as an "ironical recoil of a barred human instinct within the hearts of the gaolers themselves."[7] Thus was the didactic function of religious drama analyzed here as well, and indeed in a way that was no less consequential than the specific intellectual-history answer that thought it could be satisfied with the reference to liturgical allegorization. For Chambers, religious drama is a manifestation of the "mimetic instinct" of the "people," which finally finds a way to break through despite long-standing repression. According to him, religious drama's liturgical beginnings did not proceed from the Christian doctrine of salvation but rather emerged in opposition to the latter, and its history is marked, particularly in its postliturgical, vernacular phase, by increasingly prominent comic and realistic elements; that is, through the accumulation of a persistent pagan substratum.

In 1936, R. Stumpfl transformed this folkloric answer into a *völkisch* one, in that he denied the liturgical celebration's priority. For him, the latter is a product of the "amalgamation strategy" of Christian missionary politics, through which heathen Germanic religious plays were to be suppressed. His frequently fantastic reconstruction of these religious plays, which does not lead to any recognizable competing analogue in the decisive case—namely the two Marys scene as the keystone of the *visitatio*—discredited his whole line of research no less than did the numerous ideological premises upon which he relied.[8] Ideologically unprejudiced students of English literature were the first to pursue the inquiry further. However, their attempts also led nowhere, because they were unable to move beyond familiar hypotheses. Thus R. Pascal described the sociological implications of the Germanizing of Christendom, in particular the entry into monastic orders by men associated with the Germanic elite, and from this point of view he tried to present the *visitatio* not as immediately derived from pagan initiation rites, as Stumpfl had claimed, but as channeling and preserving their emotional potential.[9] Finally, the whole arsenal of the arguments developed since Chambers was mobilized again by B. Hunningher: pagan fertility rites, the survival of ancient mime, the church's polemic against contacts between clerics on the one hand and *histriones* and *joculatores* on the other.[10] His main evidence has since been demolished by H. M. Gamer: the St. Martial-Tonarium miniatures do not show mimes singing tropes but rather King David's musicians.[11] The suggestion is so seductive, and the refutation so clear. Stumpfl's fate seems to be repeated wherever his approach is adopted. One ought to think twice before trying it again.

At the same time, I believe we are making things too easy if we settle the matter simply by arguing that such attempts begin by denying the clearest evidence.[12] There is such a thing as a bad answer to a good question. All those who, confronted with a centuries-long Christian polemic against *ludi theatrales*, are not satisfied with the claim that in the ninth century "the time was ripe" for Christian drama (Brinkmann) and look instead for heterogeneous impulses leading to its emergence will undoubtedly have grounds for their questioning. Hardison rightly argued against Chambers's organic-evolutionary thinking.[13] The history of literary forms cannot be dealt with by means of a concept of biological growth. But anyone who in contrast points to medieval clerics' well-known will to shape and form has a long way to go to make the problem of a Christian *ludus* less acute. In his debate with Scheunemann, Stumpfl fell back on the claim that for him it essentially boiled down to the "proof of a Germanic continuity in drama as the origin of our mimic-dramatic art in the Middle Ages."[14] While this proof has been shown to be unacceptable, the question that prompted it remains. Hunningher formulated it very clearly: "Hymns like the tropes which in question and answer were alternatively sung by choir parts, do not turn into drama simply because they were given opportunity to expand."[15]

Hardison himself indirectly confirms that here a solid core of the so-called folkloric question becomes visible. His lengthy discussion of liturgical allegorization can only be understood as a reply to a doubt that must be quite strong to require such extensive refutation.[16] But against this enterprise still stands the argument that Stumpfl had already deployed against Schwietering and Brinkmann: the emergence of allegories of the Mass coincides temporally and spatially with the Christianizing of the Germanic peoples. To what extent this Christianizing of the Germanic tribes also resulted in a Germanizing of Christian religious ideas is a question that does not concern literary historians alone. Theological research on the Carolingian period is still engaged in an unresolved debate as to whether and to what degree the new tendencies that arose in dogmatics and especially in liturgical studies in that age can be traced back to a specifically Germanic reception and reinterpretation of early Christian beliefs. No less a figure than A. Kolping has viewed the debate between Amalarius and his theological opponent Florus of Lyons in this perspective and interpreted liturgical allegorization as product of a "Germanic theology" foreign to the early Christian conception of mysteries—an interpretation supported by the work of well-known liturgical scholars such as J. A. Jungmann, O. Casel, and I. Herwegen.[17] But if the possibility of a "Germanic theology" is seriously weighed, the literary historian should not see his task as producing hasty eliminations. The problem of the pagan role in Christian drama is not resolved just because Stumpfl ideologized it.

On the other hand, the Stumpfl example shows precisely how we should not approach this question. It is absolutely not to be resolved through a rigid opposition between research oriented toward intellectual history and research oriented toward folklore. Experience has shown that the "proof of a Germanic continuity in drama" always ends in hypotheses. It must be conducted *per negationem*, that is, in every case we must start from the texts, and before we attach these to a Germanic tradition we have to investigate their place in the known Christian traditions. Intellectual history makes its task too easy when it is satisfied with taking drama under its wing as a conscious structuring in opposition to the irrationalism of indigenous and folkloric elements. But research on the substratum also prematurely resolves the problem when it takes refuge in hypothetical reconstructions instead of first examining more closely the material intellectual history has contributed to the field under investigation. For if something is supposed to have developed that in fact should not have developed, then it will leave behind traces of its problematic existence.

In the case of liturgical allegorization, such traces are clearly evident in the already mentioned controversy between Amalarius of Metz and Florus of Lyons. Up to this point it has been generally believed that this controversy was of minimal importance, since it was not Florus who was victorious at the synod of Quiercy (838) but rather the condemned Amalarius, who ultimately prevailed and determined the medieval conception of the liturgy. However, this belief does not take into account the fact that this controversy was reignited at the height of Scholasticism and that allegorization of the Mass, as it unfolded in Amalarius's wake, remained on the whole an episode that came to an end with the Council of Trent—an end that coincided with that of the liturgical celebration and vernacular drama. Harmonizations often conceal the price that has to be paid to produce them. Indicating this price could be the first step out of a dilemma in which research has been imprisoned for decades.

II

Quae aguntur in caelebratione missae, in sacramento dominicae passionis aguntur, ut ipse praecepit dicens: "Haec quotiescumque feceritis, in mei memo-

riam facietis. "[18] Isn't this "memory" supposed to be relevant not only to the specific consecration but also to the whole course of the Mass? Isn't this also the key to many other submerged ceremonies that it has been difficult to explain? Weren't their apparently buried historical origins in fact obvious and visible to everyone in the evangelical reports on the life, sufferings, death, and Resurrection of the Lord? Amalarius was not the first to find himself confronted by such questions. They arose to the extent that with the spread of Christendom the rapidly growing clergy came to need instruction. Allegorical explanations of the Mass were worked out in both the Eastern and Western churches as early as the seventh century, and Amalarius probably used not only Gallic but also Oriental sources. His teacher was Alcuin, and Amalarius's retrospective allegory drew its central impulse from the tradition of the Carolingian reform of spiritual instruction. He looked into the instructive potential of ritual, projecting each of its phases onto a period in the life of Jesus, and, in interpretations that changed from one passage to another, made the priests into representatives of Christ, the disciples, the apostles, Joseph of Arimathea, or the women at the cross, and moreover tried to explain allegorically every detail, every position and every change of position of those concerned, each of their actions, every time they fall on their knees, stand up, nod their heads, or raise their voices. Thus, to give only a few examples drawn from the Consecration and Communion, the deacons who stand behind the officiating priest represent the apostles who fearfully hid themselves; the subdeacons, who stand with the officiating priest on the other side of the altar, indicate the women waiting at the cross; the raising of the voice at the *Nobis quoque* stands for the centurion's confession of belief at Jesus' death; in the concluding doxology the officiating priest and the archdeacon figure as Nicodemus and Joseph of Arimathea, who took the Lord down from the Cross; the *sudarium* thus becomes the shroud, the altar becomes the sepulcher; in the Communion the subdeacons appearing at the altar are the Marys at the sepulcher; the *fractio* indicates the supper at Emmaus, the final blessing of Christ the last blessing of his disciples before the Ascension.[19]

Difficulties already arise with Amalarius's account. On the basis of his way of conceptualizing the matter, it is not possible to see just how these references are to be more precisely understood. Most frequently he speaks of *monstrare,* (*de*)*signare* and *in memoriam ducere,* and also of *praesentare, figurare, typum gerere* or *in typo gerere,* or else, substantively, of *imitatio* and *similitudo* (or *similis esse*). Amalarius's opponents did not have to bear him any ill to recognize a very serious danger in this way of describing liturgical anamnesis. In the retrospective projections of the allegorical segmentation of the ritual according to the details of the story of the Passion, he saw a direct challenge to his own conception of the sacrifice, which was representative of the early church tradition. These projections necessarily emptied out the mystery, making it into shadowy "figures," which instead of pointing toward a sacramentally guaranteed future salvation instead seemed to find their fulfillment in the past alone. In the complaint he prepared for the synod of Quiercy, Amalarius's method reminds him of the antipodes, and yet gives the impression that the *figura* follows the *res ipsa*, whereas in truth with the incarnation the world of shadows came to an end.[20] *Tu semper vis esse in umbra*, reads one of his marginal notes to the *Liber Officialis*, and this central objection runs throughout his whole polemic.[21] He also sees very clearly what makes the salvation history dimension fade away: not the commemorative retrospective connection of the ritual with story of the Passion—a connection that seems self-evident to him as well—but rather above all its segmentation, the many *fatuas divisiones*, by which he sees the invisible, self-producing mystery of salvation, the *plenitudo sacramenti* torn apart.[22]

This objection becomes very clear in the *Opusculum de causa fidei*, where Florus—who is certainly not impartial—reports the results of the synod. Once again, he attacks—now with the backing of the synod, and in a much sharper manner—the peculiar inversion of typology. Shadows and figures existed in the Old Testament alone. No one can be allowed, now that with Christ light has come into the world, to establish "new kinds of figures," *nova figurarum genera vel mysteriorum sacramenta.*[23] The fulfilled truth in its complete *puritas* and *simplicitas* is the object of the church ritual, *non figuras aliquas vel mysteria vanitatis.*[24] But Amalarius, who had the effrontery to appeal to Augustine in support of his fantastic discoveries, is now compared with the true Augustine by means of the distinction between the *visibile sacramentum* and the *virtus sacramenti. Sed quid,* Florus asks, *pertinent ad virtutem sacramenti, quod pertinet ad visibile sacramentum? . . . ideo autem dicuntur sacramenta, quia in eis aliud videtur, aliud intelligitur. Quod videtur, speciem habet corporalem; quod intelligitur, fructum habet spiritualem. Manet igitur in mente fidelium incorrupta venerabilis mysterii virtus, et efficacissima potentia, purgans delicta, emundans consciencias, perficiens gratiam redemptionis et salutis.*[25] Florus thus also accepts the *aliud videtur*, but what it "means" here is not the historical steps in Jesus' suffering in Amalarius's sense but rather the *fructus spiritualis* of this suffering: the salvation mercifully transmitted in the sacrament.

What Florus wants to establish in opposition to Amalarius is the true figural interpretation of the Eucharist, as it was usually understood in the Middle Ages. It is connected with a synthetic view of salvation history, as a consequence of which the figures of the Old Testament find their fulfillment with the coming of Christ but in themselves remain preliminary with regard to the new promises of the end of the world and the Last Judgment. *Umbra in lege, imago in evangelio, veritas in caelestibus*—thus we find in Amalarius the tri-level typological fulfillment Augustine had elaborated and which precipitated in the medieval view of the Eucharist, above all in the concept of the *pignus*, or pledge: the Sacrifice of the Mass prolongs the preliminary fulfillment given with the incarnation, and it is a symbolic pledge of the real if still concealed presence of what is to come.[26] In his own explanation of the Mass, Florus also expressly states that in the sacrifice of the Mass it is less the suffering Christ than the *Christus jam passus* that is present, and with it the *tempora venturi Christi* are simultaneously already assured.[27]

Amalarius's deviation becomes most clearly visible here. For him all interpretation leads toward a detailed illustration of a history that has a "beginning" (the entry into Jerusalem), a "middle" (Passion and Resurrection), and an "end" (the Ascension), in contrast to which Florus sees in the visible ceremony of the Mass only the repetition of the middle, the event of the Last Supper. He does not regard the visible ceremony as in any way problematic or requiring interpretation. Restoring the historical origin, it is merely the spatial substratum of the true ceremony that escapes certainty, of the sacramental effectiveness of the sacrificial atonement, which is mercifully granted anew in every celebration of the Mass. Thus the difference can be conceived most simply in this way: for Florus and the tradition he represents, the ritual repeats and structures an event (the Last Supper), whereas for Amalarius it repeats and structures a history.

Formulated in this way, the difference points to implications that cannot be grasped in Florus's critique. Judged by the standard of his understanding of the Eucharist, Amalarius's "figures" remain shadowy evacuations of the *plenitudo sacramenti*, mere images of a history rather than the continuation of its *fructus spiritualis*. Nevertheless, for Amalarius as well it is still a ritual that structures this history, and he does deny the event-like nature of the ritual ceremony. He assumes that Christ's body lingers on the earth even after the Ascension, he believes that through the Eucharist this body is "poured out" (*diffundere*) into our limbs and veins, and he is concerned with the question as to what happens to it in our bodies after it is consumed: whether it is breathed out with the air, whether it can flow out with the blood, or is even excreted in the usual way.[28] It is chiefly on the basis of these remarks drawn from Amalarius's correspondence that scholars have concluded that Amalarius belongs to the so-called realistic-metabolic trend in pre-Scholastic eucharistic doctrine, from which the doctrine of transubstantiation emerged, and his contemporaries even already accused him of stercorianism.[29] This accusation is also made by Florus, whose criticism thereby seems to claim sometimes too much, sometimes too little, and thus loses credibility. But it could just as well be the case that Florus felt that in this he was so fully in the right that he had to interpret Amalarius's "new figures" as mere shadows in comparison with the *plenitudo sacramenti*, while on the other hand he probably saw—and here he sensed the true danger—that as returning events reality would be attributed to these shadows of Amalarius's themselves. If that is so, Florus would be the first to have recognized the true impulse leading to allegorization of the Mass that was hidden behind the didactic function: a latent, pagan understanding of ritual and its grounding of the history of the Passion and death of Jesus Christ.[30]

In fact, he not only recognized this impulse but also gave it a name. He reacts particularly strongly when naturalistic rather than historical explanations appear in Amalarius's allegorization. That happens above all in the first two allegories, on the liturgy of the church year and on the books of the *Liber Officialis* devoted to ordinations. In these allegories, Amalarius connects, for instance, the celebrations on the first day of each quarter with the four elements, and the two readings on the first Wednesday in the quarter with the sun and the moon, which for their part once again retain heathen names, Phoebus and Phoebe—*ut paganis ejus verbis utar*, as Florus expressly adds.[31] Heathen gods are suspect, then, even when they appear metonymically. *David bellicosum fuisse et valde arsisse in marte* is, according to Florus, a diabolical assertion, since David was courageous in the Lord and was not serving Mars.[32] The exegesis of Luke 11:1–12 (where Amalarius, commenting on the great litany, interprets the bread, fish, and egg for which the Son asks the Father as being connected with the prayer for the treasures of the earth and air and the two-gendered animals) strikes Florus as an *insanissima falsitas que multum aberrat*.[33] At first, all these examples seem to bespeak only a peripheral carping that merely draws attention to details, especially when, as in the last case cited, it is not mentioned that Amalarius interprets morally as well as naturalistically insofar as he sets the *tria temporalia* alongside Faith, Hope, and Charity, the *tria spiritualia*. But the *temporalia* appear in the first place and are broadly elaborated. The *spiritualia*, on the other hand, are disposed of in a single brief sentence that does not succeed in further explaining how the fish is supposed to indicate faith and the egg, hope.[34]

This kind of ambivalence is typical of Amalarius's way of proceeding, and it is quite clear that in the examples he criticizes, Florus hit upon something symptomatic. For although expressly naturalistic-pagan interpretations are limited, so far as I can see, to the cases mentioned, it remains that they only make explicit what characterizes Amalarius's method in general: an exhaustion of the *plenitudo sacramenti*, an intentional dissolution of the salvation-history tension between historical event, mercifully granted continuation, and future revelation of the invisible fulfillment already achieved. The difference between historical event and ritual repetition—between the *passio Christi* and the commemorated *Christus jam passus*, between the bloody sacrifice and the bloodless repetition—is essential to this tension. Christian ritual maintains precisely this difference in the salvation-history dimension, allowing ritual to become, not the celebration of an eternally returning original event but rather the prolongation of a historical or rather historically believed occurrence and the act of salvation effected in it: this ritual does not celebrate a magical return but rather, to use a term of Beda's that is very illuminating in this context, a merciful *pascha perpetuum*.

The fundamental tendency of allegorization of the Mass is, by means of a return to the beginning, to break out of the salvation-history progress from the act of salvation toward a future fulfillment. Paradoxically, it is thus precisely the overloading of the ritual with the "historical" that exhausts its kerygmatic historicity. For with this overloading, ritualistic repetition no longer takes place in relation to the difference but rather to the identity with the beginning that grounds it. Here we see already how it becomes possible to connect religious drama with the "performance" of the allegorization of the Mass but also at the same time the problematic nature of both. With Amalarius's allegorization of the Mass, a process of unnoticed mythification of the salvation events begins that continually increases and marks the whole history of religious drama, reaching its apex in the superficially typological announcement of the *historia passionis* that we will examine at length later on. In this case as in the other, the interest in the "historical" indicates that the kerygma is being played back into a mythical-archetypal dimension. So one can in fact say that everything began with the allegorization of the Mass, but not in the manner that either Brinkmann or Stumpfl claimed. For the mythical paradigm of identical repetition clearly shows that the allegorization of the Mass must be seen not only as a product of proselytization in the spatial dimension but also as a particular late product in the temporal dimension. Even if the processes of mythification were first set in motion by allegorization of the Mass, its advent nevertheless already presupposes those ten centuries that lent the biblical history the dignity, if not of an origin, at least of a foundational beginning. The allegorizers regarded this history as having mythical dignity, and it seemed to them the most enlightening thing about the world only because the mythical image is, in the eyes of the believer, once and for all more plausible than the unreasonable demands of Christian salvation history.

It can be taken as a sign of the polemical hardening of his position that Florus, at those points where the allegorization of the Mass arrives at such unreasonable demands, insists on the *puritas* and *simplicitas* of the Christian truths of faith. In the end, he cannot have failed to note that Amalarius, along with all those to whom a clear warning is addressed (*Unde nemini omnino licuisse aut licere*),[35] saw enormous difficulties in the communication of these "pure" and "simple" truths of salvation. Florus registers the rapid spread of the new doctrine but not the difficult situation of the lower levels of the clergy. This unwavering refusal to understand the pedagogical impetus behind the allegorization of the Mass may also have been determined by the controversy's background in church politics. But fundamentally Florus could not allow himself to make any concessions with regard to this kind of teaching. He saw the true impulse driving this praiseworthy effort, and certainly it was against this impulse that he set out to do battle, in his spontaneous marginal annotations to the *Liber Officialis*, through a series of attacks: *insana dictio, rabida locutio, rara insania, stultissimum men-*

dacium, execrabilis dementia, demonica locutio. And in fact Amalarius's production of *nova genera figurarum* probably looked to him like the work of the Devil.

Thus the synod of Quiercy's condemnation of Amalarius cannot be seen as simply a dogmatically disguised act of revenge on a political opponent.[36] Allegorization of the Mass overcame this condemnation and dominated the medieval liturgy. Among its representatives are found illustrious figures such as Cardinal Lothar, who was later to become Pope Innocent III. His *De Sacro altaris mysterio*, written shortly before he was elected pope, became the primary source of the compendium of allegorizations of the Mass in the high Middle Ages: the *Rationale divinorum officiorum*, which Wilhelm Durandus composed while he was the papal deputy in Romagna.[37] But in spite of all that, the claim made by H. de Lubac and others, that the Lyons clergy's opposition remained without any echo, is valid only for liturgy history considered in isolation, and even then only up to the Council of Trent.[38] The efforts made, in post-Tridentine theories of the sacrifice of the Mass, to provide a new foundation for the sacramental *commemoratio* signal the end of allegorization but thereby only make visible a tense relationship that had also existed before Trent. As early as the thirteenth century Albertus Magnus had polemicized almost as violently as Florus against all interpretations that were not legitimized by the literal meaning of the text. To see Judas's treacherous kiss in the kiss at the altar during *Supplices,* and in the subsequent blessing of the offering the rope with which Jesus was led away to Annas, seemed to him *ominino profanum et omnibus fidelibus abominandum.* He even describes similar interpretations of the blessing during the *Consecratio* as *deliramenta et hominum illiteratorum.*[39] It is interesting that a series of these *deliramenta* can already be found in Lothar and later in Durandus as well. Thus Scholastic dogma rejected what was taught with papal approval. But it is also interesting, and this confirms our analysis, that Albertus objects precisely to the details of the genuine story of the Passion. For here he must most resolutely maintain, in accord with his own orthodox interpretation, the difference between the bloody sacrifice and the bloodless repetition. He did not live to see what could happen when this dam broke and the connection between allegorization of the Mass and identical repetition also came to an end. The Passion plays will reveal this to us. But the history of the liturgical celebration, for which legitimation had been claimed appealing to the allegorization of the Mass as a genuine product of Christian liturgy, in fact already allows us to clearly recognize the impossibility of such a reconciliation.

III

If tropes do not develop into drama simply because they (in matins in contrast to the introit of the Mass) have the potential for expansion, what then is the impulse behind this process? Anyone who thinks this question can be resolved through an unmediated connection of the liturgical celebration with the allegorization of the Mass has failed to notice that the latter was at least superficially a product of the lower clergy's educational needs. To that extent the allegorization of the Mass found its true "place in life" (*Sitz im Leben*) in this group and in its activity of caring for souls. Its opponents also speak of *simpliciores*, about whose histrionic celebration of the Mass they complain.[40] The liturgical celebration, in contrast, developed and remained in the closest association with monastic, and particularly Benedictine, ceremonial—which could be opened to a non-monastic community as well—but whose self-concept was certainly not dominated by a didactic point of view. All attempts to analyze this alleged didactic function encounter here a resistant core. A relationship between the celebration and allegorization first emerges after the didactic phase—which cannot be excluded in either case but is not at all decisive: the celebration makes explicit the allegorization's implicit interest in (the mythical form of) identical repetition. It produces as a concrete image what liturgy can only evoke in the individual phases of the ritual.

However, the celebration in no way takes the place of the sacramental rite itself; indeed, it does not enter immediately into association with the rite but rather in connection with the readings, homilies, and responses of matins, in the case of the *visitatio sepulchri*, that is, in connection with the biblical announcement of the Resurrection. The images of the celebration are thus shifted in relation to the sacramental core of the canonical office, of the Mass; their place is on the periphery. The history of the celebration is therefore not, like that of the allegorization of the Mass, merely an episode in liturgical history but rather runs alongside it at the same time, on a parallel track, without ever putting in question the fundamental invisibility of the true sacramental rite. The relationship between the Mass and the celebration thus cannot be described with the help of an anthropological model of emancipation derived from archaic religions, as consequence of which a rite does not survive the self-intensification brought about by institutionalization and repetition and discharges itself in the image; such a liberation of the representative is fundamentally denied to Christian liturgy.

This denial alone, however, already invalidates the repeated attempts to establish an analogy between the religious origins of ancient and Christian drama. Hardison, drawing on Murray's *Excursus* regarding the development of Greek theater out of the Dionysian cult, ultimately made this analogy his thesis and then also attempted to put the celebration into an immediate genetic relationship with the rite of the Mass, by proposing a new hypothesis about their origin. Thus the *visitatio* is supposed to have developed, not in the framework of matins but rather in that of the Easter vigil, in which it was performed between the baptism of catechumens and the Mass, or more precisely, when the neophytes return from the baptistry to the high altar. Then in the course of the tenth century, when the vigil took place earlier, a temporal discrepancy with the commemoration of the visit to the sepulcher in the early morning developed, and as a result it was moved up to the end of matins, so that it once again took place at the same time as the event commemorated. The trope of the introit to the Mass, on the other hand, long regarded as the original form of the *visitatio*, is supposed to be only a secondary abbreviation of the introit itself.[41] Those who elaborate such clever hypotheses by neglecting the most obvious evidence reveal their own extremely deductive way of proceeding. To harmonize the Mass and the celebration in the formula "Christian rite and Christian drama," Hardison has first to shift the *visitatio* from the periphery to the center of the sacramental rite, and then—in accord with the model of emancipation he borrows from Murray—interpret it as a mimetic play that is supposed to have been introduced first in the instruction of neophytes and later in the general instruction of the laity. Up to the end of the Middle Ages, however, monasteries—and here again almost exclusively the Benedictine monasteries[42]—remained the chief places where the celebration was practiced, and even a brief glance at its history shows the truth about its alleged emancipation into a mimetic play.

The most striking characteristic of this history is the persistence of the *visitatio* at the so-called first stage. About 400 texts remain from that stage, as opposed to only 80 from the so-called second stage (with the arrival of the disciples), and only 12 from the so-called third stage (with the appearance of

Christ). The concept of stages supporting an emancipatory "development" is thus highly misleading, and for this reason de Boor replaced it with a distinction between three types of celebrations. Type I, the simple celebration involving the Marys, with the angel's question, the Marys' answer, the angel's announcement that Christ is risen, and the Marys' subsequent announcement of the same to the disciples, must therefore be the basis for a description of the characters in the celebration. Even while the third response, *Dum transisset Sabbatum* (drawn from Mark 16:1) is being sung by the choir, the participating priests appear at the altar to present what follows in a scenic-dialogic fashion. In the rubrics for this presentation appear concepts that are familiar to us from the allegorization of the Mass: *(agere) ad imitationem, ad similitudinem, in significatione, in persona, in specie, in figura, sub typo.*[43] And here again these concepts alone are not sufficiently informative. *Imitatio*, for instance, does lead directly to costumes but only to cautious symbolizations by means of the priestly vestments at hand and the vessels of liturgical ceremonial. The Marys do indeed cover their heads *ad modum mulierum* but only with liturgical paraphernalia (*amicta, humerale, capitagia*). In the rubrics, mention is made of the neutral *parare* or *induere*, and sometimes also of *ornare* (*more muliebri ornatis*).[44] The priests are not "playing" something they are not but rather remain in their priestly "roles" and as such are the performers of a liturgical celebration. The clearest expression of this integration of the *visitatio* into the liturgical framework is found in the music. The scenic dialog is still sung. This is probably the most important clue for determining the character and goal of the celebration.[45]

The *visitatio sepulchri* thus transfers the *Dum transisset* antiphon not into a biblical dramatic play but rather into a celebratory, dialogically enriched, and thus delayed and all the more effective announcement of the Resurrection. As such, that is, as a liturgical kerygma, it remains the foreground of the sacramental, and its place in the canonical office precisely corresponds to this. In his exegesis of Luke 24, Bede had interpreted Jesus' sepulcher, which the Marys approach, as a *figura altaris, in quo carnis ejus ac sanguinis solent mysteria celebrari.*[46] When Amalarius, drawing on Bede, interprets Communion as a reminder of this biblical scene and situates it in a series of similar images, what is invisibly already fulfilled is visibly possessed.[47] This is not the case in the celebration. It is a "figure" in a theologically much less problematic sense than the *nova genera figurarum* of allegorization. For instead of reducing the sacramental presence of the resurrected Christ to a "shadow," and thus, as Florus complained about Amalarius, reversing the relationship between *figura* and *res ipsa*, there develops an opposing tendency in the liturgical visualization, not of the resurrected Christ but less problematically of the proofs of the Resurrection. The *visitatio* is an organized celebration announcing the Resurrection; it is a *repraesentatio*, that is, a liturgical renewal of the early announcement to the Marys.

Fundamentally, this kerygmatic character of the *visitatio* can be maintained only in a pure celebration of the Marys. However, the orientation toward the kerygmatic goal of the concluding *surrexit* jubilee also characterizes Type II and Type III celebrations, and this can be illustrated in detail by comparing them with their respective biblical models. Thus, in John 20:1–10, when the bewildered Mary Magdalene's report leads the disciples to rush to the sepulcher, this event does not result in an announcement: *Nondum enim sciebant Scripturam, quia opportebat eum a mortis resurgere* (20:9). The *visitatio*, in contrast, associates it with the scene in Mark 16:1–7, and thus allows it to appear as a result of the annunciatory mission given the women by the angel: *Non est hic quem queritis, sed cito euntes nunciate discipulis eius et Petro quia surrexit Jhesus.* The disciples learn more than they do in John, and their race to the sepulcher takes place against the background tense expectation, which finds its resolution in the *surrexit*-response of the choir to the empty shroud that is displayed. The Type III celebration also stands in opposition to the biblical model, insofar as it places the Lord's appearance to Mary Magdalen after the coming of the disciples, whereas in John 20:11–18 His appearance precedes their coming.[48] This change makes it possible, on one hand, for the two Marys scenes (the *visitatio* and Christ's appearance) to follow one another, and on the other hand the model is once again "corrected," in that what is reported in John 20:11–18 is moved to the place of John 20:1. The sequence of scenes thus produces, in contradistinction to the model, a highly effective intensification of the kerygmatic event: the annunciatory mission given by the angel, its carrying out by the Marys walking back to the choir, the Lord's appearance to Mary Magdalen, the announcement of the Resurrection to the disciples, the disciples' arrival with a further announcement on seeing the empty sepulcher.

Although in the interest of a compositional crescendo relatively free use of the announcement is thus made, still Type II and Type III simultaneously raise new event-complexes, and this modification inevitably puts in question both the way the Marys celebration distinguished itself with respect to biblical reality, on one hand, and with respect to sacramental fulfillment on the other. In this way the coming of the disciples brings into the celebration a turbulence that is unsuited to its liturgical dignity and disturbs the economy of its kerygmatically arranged composition. That this was seen as a danger is made clear by a series of celebrations that apparently belong to Type I but that, as de Boor has demonstrated in a convincing, detailed analysis, are in fact secondary, abbreviated forms of Type II celebrations that omitted the coming of the disciples and sought to return to a pure celebration of the Marys.[49] Similar concerns probably also explain the fact that the Type II *visitatio* is extant in only 80 texts, and yet is relatively widespread compared with Type III, although limited to Germany. The Anglo-Norman celebrations do not include the coming of the disciples. In only two cases (Dublin and Fleury-Orléans) was it later incorporated into a Type III celebration.[50] Nor was it able to establish itself in the French vernacular tradition.

The appearance of Christ became no less problematic, though in another way. Here the priest, who appears before Mary Magdalene *in persona Domini*, had to adumbrate Him whom the Mass would later complete *in persona Christi*.[51] Liturgical visualization of the biblical account is pushed so far here that it coincides with what Amalarius's interpretation of the Communion in the Easter vigil evokes in the mode of memory: *Sacerdos, vicarius Christi, implet officium suum. Dubitantibus apostolis de sua resurrectione, timentibus mulieribus et nihil dicentibus, angelorum concentus clamat Christum resurrexisse a mortuis. Christus ipse per suam gloriosam apparititionem manifestum se facit quibuscumque vult.*[52] A man who sits with his back to the sun, we read in Florus, can recognize someone coming up behind him by looking at the shape of his shadow, but a man who has the person in question standing in front of him and still looks at the shadow instead of at the *veritas corporis* at hand is a fool whom one will rightly find annoying.[53] Amalarius may have ultimately won out over Florus, but the authors of the liturgical celebrations were not willing to follow him unhesitatingly, even along the parallel track of matins: the appearance of Christ was incorporated into only about a dozen celebrations. Thus while the celebration, like the allegorization, tends toward visibility, it nevertheless makes room for this impulse only in a very controlled way. Its history makes explicit not only the allegorization's implicit interest but also its theological problematics. It shows clearly that the anthropological emancipation model based on archaic ritual cannot be applied to Christian liturgy without the previously mentioned shift of the image to the periphery of the ritual, and that even here the allegorization of the Mass is not simply brought to an end: two-thirds of the more than 400 celebrations extant belong, as we saw, to Type I; we still find it in manuscripts from the fourteenth and fifteenth centuries,[54] and not even this type survived the Council of Trent.

It is important to emphasize this autonomy of the tradition of the liturgical celebration and the theological self-control that characterizes it, particularly because it also involves significant preliminary decisions regarding the vernacular Easter plays. At least in Germany, this Easter drama is connected directly with the ceremony, and more precisely with the Type III ceremony, that is, the one that includes the appearance of Christ and the coming of the disciples. It builds the Latin scaffolding of the *visitatio* scenes in all the Easter plays going back to the so-called Rhenish "original play,"[55] and this coupling of the vernacular play with the most complex form of the liturgical celebration seems to offer a further confirmation of the emancipation model. However, precisely because this most complex form of the liturgical celebration—which is basic to all the aforementioned Easter plays—is itself the exception in the liturgical tradition and does not represent a sort of endpoint in a developmental history, the vernacular tradition shows that in this "coupling" it is operating under heterogeneous conditions. Thus even if, adopting a specifically German point of view, we proceed as though the vernacular tradition began in the fourteenth century along with the Easter plays, there appears at this point as well a discontinuity between the liturgical and the vernacular traditions that we will discuss in detail later on in connection with the Old French Adam play from the twelfth century. In actuality the Type III liturgical *visitatio* is no more the ritualistic substratum of the Easter plays than it found in the sacramental ritual its own "archetype" in Hardison's sense. The Easter drama responds to needs different from those to which the liturgical *visitatio* responded.

From the *Visitatio Sepulchri* to the *Descensus Ad Inferos*: Jesus' Descent into Hell As Cardinal Function

I f the liturgical celebration represents one extreme on the spectrum of the possibility of rationalization and analysis from the point of view of intellectual history and theology, then the vernacular Easter drama represents the other. The apparently quite unholy way in which most of these plays structure the Marys' purchase of the ointment, Jesus' meeting with Mary Magdalene, and the disciples' race to the sepulcher is among the most enigmatic and strangest aspects in which religious drama presents itself to us. What is stimulating about it is not so much all the "obscenity," "dirt," and "coarseness" that Hartl considers "a rather unfortunate way for religious poetry to appear in history" and a "vivid example of the decline and inner dissolution of the genre."[1] What is stimulating is, first of all, the immediate juxtaposition of this "dirt" with the Latin liturgical elements of the ceremony. Here we can scarcely speak of contradiction, since clearly nothing of the kind was experienced. It seems more appropriate to speak of secularization: the ceremony abandons the sacred realm, the *fanum*, and finds its new place in the *profanum*, where it is freed of the shackles that bound it. However, at least since Stumpfl's investigation, we can no longer talk about a secularization conceived in this way. For if Stumpfl's work made one thing clear, it was the religious implications of the alleged obscenities and vulgarities. This demonstration was not given sufficient weight in E. Scheunemann's critique. The attack—a rather courageous one in 1936–37— on the ideologically preliminary thesis of the general priority of a Germanic springtime drama must not be allowed to obscure the fact that the "secondary growth of the folkloric" acknowledged by Scheunemann also poses a problem that cannot be resolved merely by the recognition that this sort of thing "fits well into the alternative picture of late medieval literature."[2]

German studies have not taken up this problem since that time. Although Stumpfl's hypothesis concerning the origin of the Easter plays may be regarded as refuted, the debate it elicited remains unresolved. In reopening it and pursuing it further, we can hope to succeed only if we abandon in the case of vernacular drama, just as we did in that of liturgical celebration, the assumptions underlying the debate for the past 30 years, and adopt instead a new methodological approach.

This new approach is instigated no less by Scheunemann than by Stumpfl. Both proceed as though the vernacular play consisted, just like the Type III *visitatio*, of the Marys scene, the epiphany of Christ, and the race of the disciples. However, this comparison ignores the most striking difference between these two types. In contrast to the celebration, the plays do not begin with the Marys scene but rather with a guardian scene framing the Resurrection of Jesus and his descent into hell. The fact that neither Stumpfl nor Scheunemann bring this elementary structural change into their analyses shows the extent of their fixation on origins and developments. Even this change does not provide the decisive argument against Stumpfl's hypothesis about origins, but it does allow us to see in its real function what can be salvaged from his analyses. However, let us first turn to the descent into hell itself.

II

The moving forward of the *descensus ad inferos*, which can already be assumed in the earliest extant Easter play, the Anglo-Norman *Seinte Resurreccion* from the twelfth century, is a constant of the vernacular drama, whose significance for the latter's heterogeneous character in contrast with the liturgical *visitatio* cannot be too greatly emphasized.[3] A quick glance at the unfolding of the first fully extant Easter play, the one from Innsbruck, suffices to show this significance.[4] The play begins with the deployment of the tomb guard for which the Jews asked Pilate. While the soldiers are sleeping, Jesus is awakened by an angel. After a brief intervening scene in which the soldiers are reprimanded, the *descensus* begins. As the *Canticum triumphale* is sung (251 ff.), the resurrected Christ approaches the gates of hell, the angel accompanying him thrice calls out *Tollite portas* and thrice asks Lucifer who the King in Glory is, until finally, while the evil spirits howl, Jesus breaks through the barred gate and frees the righteous patriarchs. Lucifer, burning with wrath, commands Satan to make up for the loss, and this episode leads to the scene of the capture of souls. The Marys scene follows with the consequence familiar from the liturgical tradition. A broadly conceived merchant scene is followed by the *visitatio*, the appearance of the Lord to Mary Magdelene and Thomas, and finally the coming of the disciples.

The bipartite nature of the type represented by the Innsbruck play, with the descent into hell and the *visitatio* as the two basic scenes, is clearly evident. Since H. Rueff's study, it has been common to contrast the concluding Marys play with the first part, as "play" and "counterplay."[5] That is appropriate insofar as the sepulcher at the center of the event divides the two parts: on the right is the world of the faithful, on the left that of the deniers. However, this opposition suggests a balance between the two parts that is not evident in practice. The dramatic dualism is not worked out between the play and the counterplay but rather in the descent into hell, and thus in the "counterplay" itself. Bringing the descent into hell into the image means, however, allowing the not-yet-resurrected Jesus to appear once again in bodily form. This difficulty will be overcome both simply and cleverly, as the Innsbruck play already shows: the awakening is merely moved forward, so that the already resurrected Jesus can make the assault on hell. The result is that the play's character is totally different from that of the liturgical *visitatio*. For since the play broadens the event-character of the ceremony manifest in the *surrexit* announcement, it immediately brings into the picture what the ceremony only attests to: the mystery of the Resurrection itself. This alteration allows a shift of emphasis to the first part, however, which dramatically weakens the testimony to the Resurrection in the second part, to the point of depriving it of a function: something that has happened in front of everyone's eyes no longer needs further proof. This shift of emphasis can be so radical that the Marys play is left out altogether. Thus the Redentine Easter play consists solely of the guard scene, the Resurrection, and the descent into hell, together with a concluding scene of soul-capturing. This is, it is true, an isolated case, but it is characteristic of the tendency of the vernacular Easter play. For in the cases in which the Marys play is retained, the "counterplay" nevertheless determines the character of the whole. Thus the prologue to the Innsbruck play, for instance, refers only to the Resurrection and the descent into hell—as if the following *visitatio* sequence did not exist at all:

wir wullen uch lassen kunt werden
wy unser herre ist entstanden
von dez bittern todes banden
allem menschlichen geschlechte czu troste,
da mit (er) alle erloste,
vnd wy er fert vor der helle tor
cnd wil nemen ervor,
dy sinen willen haben gethan,
beide frawen vnd man,
wy er dy helle czustost,
vornichtet vnd enplost
wan in funff tusent jaren
keyn mensche so wol mochte gebaren,
iz mûste (spate adir fru
iedoch) der helle czu
vnd mûste dy pin liden,
dez mochte ez nicht vormyden:
daz wil got hüte brengen wider. (Innsbruck, 6–23)

We want to tell you
how our Lord arose free
from the bonds of bitter death
for the consolation of the whole human race
whereby (He) all redeemed,
and how He goes before the gate of hell
and seeks to bring out from there
those who did His will,
both women and men,
how he closed up hell,
destroyed and emptied it
which in five thousand years
no man had tried to do,
he had to (late or early, still)
close up hell
and suffer pain
that he did not try to avoid:
God wants to do that again today.

If the Marys play nevertheless concludes in this way, it seems reasonable to suppose that it will be able to take on new functions. The next chapter will be devoted to a discussion of these new functions. However, a preliminary decision concerning this modification is already made in the *descensus*, and if we first examine this shift of emphasis a little more closely, we can see in it an exemplary case of how little a hermeneutically unenlightened structural description is able to account for the implications and consequences of such a way of proceeding.

The play, we said, broadens the kerygmatic event-character of the ceremony manifest in the *surrexit* announcement. It therefore presents a selected moment in salvation history, for which a rough preliminary segmentation can be made with the help of Barthes's distinction of "functions" into "cardinal functions" and "catalysers":

> The cardinal functions are the risky moments of a narrative. Between these points of alternative, these "dispatchers," the catalysers lay out areas of safety, rests, luxuries. Luxuries which are not, however, useless: it must be stressed again that from the point of view of the story a catalyser's functionality may be weak but not nil. Were a catalyser purely redundant (with relation to its nucleus), it would nonetheless participate in the economy of the message; in fact, an apparently merely expletive notation always has a discursive function: it accelerates, delays, gives fresh impetus to the discourse, it summarizes, anticipates and sometimes even leads astray. Since what is noted always appears as being notable, the catalyser ceaselessly revives the semantic tension of the discourse, says ceaselessly that there has been, that there is going to be, meaning.[6]

The *descensus* would thus be a cardinal function, and the Marys play a catalyzer. However, difficulties immediately arise. The *visitatio* sequence can still be added as a catalyst to the descent into hell (and the play will spin it out in this sense: as boisterous celebration of the victory over the Devil), but it does not adumbrate another cardinal function, since the *descensus* concludes the story of Jesus' battle with the Devil. If a "semantic tension" exists here, it is not between functions that are immanent to the system but rather between the text and the addressee, between the kerygmatic *surrexit* and the person who is to "hear" it. Here the application of a structural model of description encounters the sort of difficulties encountered by a series of articles published in the journal *Langages* (volume 22, 1971) under the general title *Sémiotique narrative: récits bibliques*. Particularly instructive for our purposes is Louis Marin's analysis of the pious women's search for the sepulcher, that is, of the biblical model of the Marys play. His analysis leads to the conclusion that the analytical methods the Paris semioticians originally developed on the basis of myths and folktales can no longer be regarded as adequate to the "event-structure" of biblical texts. Thus Marin maintains that in the case of the *surrexit* announcement and the reporting mission assigned to the Marys, the "object of desire" (Jesus' corpse) is replaced by a message (from the angel) that refers, through its nature as an announcement and call to action, to a non-narrative dimension. Within the manifest tale is embedded a "prophetic discourse" that obliterates the referential relationships in favor of a self-thematization of the message as "a sign to be believed." Marin therefore sees the structural law of biblical texts as consisting in a constant "permutation of the constative and performative modalities," of which the treatment of the mystery of the Resurrection offers striking evidence:

> The Gospels make Jesus' resurrection something that cannot be repre-
> sented: they remove it from the fiction (the fable) of narrative in order to
> entrust it to discourse. By refusing to narrate this worldly event, this fact
> that must be the evidence and truth of all subsequent preaching, they
> make it expressible, that is, they constitute it as a fundamental proposi-
> tion of discourse: this is, in the text itself, the *reality* of the glad tidings.[7]

If we here refer back to Barthes's conception of the function, we can see that the Marys play is clearly more—or rather, ought to be more—than a mere catalyzer, and that, seen from the point of view of the Marys play, the moved-up *descensus* just as clearly would not deserve the status of a cardinal function but remains in precisely that dimension of narrative visibility in which Christian salvation history does not take place. Therefore we can already hypothesize that Christian theology will endeavor to play down the salvation-history significance of the *descensus* and to not acknowledge just what the play grants: that it is a cardinal function. We can further hypothe- size that this theology will endeavor to make the *surrexit* announcement a "cardinal function," that it will reject all attempts to reduce this announce- ment to what it actually is in the play: a catalyzer, which no longer refers to the salvation-history future of Christ's return but rather boisterously cele- brates the "end" already achieved in the *descensus*.

Thus it is entirely possible to operate with Barthes's functions, but one must be clear about what is segmented in this way: a history or rather a selection from a history that can no longer be seen as an unequivocally

Christian salvation history. For this salvation history has not already come to an end in the past, does not precede its repetition in the play, but rather is essentially unfinished, open to its future fulfillment, that is, open to an end that will at the same time be the end of time. System-immanent functions can be problematized in this way only by someone who moves beyond the opposition, characteristic of the Paris school, between "sense" and "function" on one hand and "interpretation" on the other,[8] to develop a "transcendental theory of the intersubjective constitution of sense"[9]—that is, someone who inquires into the interests lying behind system-constructions, in short, someone who analyzes structures as solutions to problems, as answers. Fundamentally, of course, no segmentation can do without such a hermeneutic logic of question and answer. This insight is, however, all too often sacrificed to an objective self-conception that does not recognize the associated sacrifice of knowledge. It hardly needs to be emphasized that this sacrifice of knowledge increases to the degree that an attempt is made to resolve the segmentation problem through system-immanent procedures of refinement and analysis alone, as some linguists strive to do.

The methodological alternative is to subordinate structures to functions, that is, to compare different systems, not in order to expose some sort of structural invariants but with precisely the opposite goal: to problematize the non-identical, to trace differing structural constructions back to differing interests. Our whole investigation will proceed by such comparisons: comparisons of the drama with the celebration, with other plays, with biblical models, with dogmatic positions. The structuralism that is interested in establishing invariants is, through this very interest in the identical, still bound up with ontological thinking. The true alternative to thinking in terms of substances is a functional-structural comparative technique that juxtaposes beings with other possibilities and thus makes them ontologically incapable of truth.[10]

Religious drama is such an exposition of other possibilities. It constantly runs counter to theology's interest in the unambiguous, in the exclusion of non-being from being. This is absolutely clear first of all in the *descensus*. The play is constituted by setting up oppositions and playing these out and through. Opposition, however, implies theological dualism, and thereby a fundamental divergence of interest with respect to theology emerges, since theology constantly endeavors to construct a sequence of events presented as an outcome of divine acts alone and not as the mediation of oppositions. Thus we can expect theology to segment the biblical narratives differently from the way they are segmented by drama; it will emphasize what the latter neglects, namely the performative units, and neglect what the latter emphasizes: the constative units. Drama, as we will see, generally tends toward the integration of what theology excludes. In the case of the descent into hell, which reaches in the Easter play its high point and endpoint as a conclusive cardinal function, we can immediately speak of such an integration with respect to three such excluded elements: the liturgical celebration, the canonical books of the Bible itself, which do not refer to the *descensus*, and finally the history of dogma, which includes the mythologeme only by denying its dualistic self-evidence. We will have to examine this matter at length when we discuss the relationship between the descent into hell and the preceding death on the cross.[11] In the present connection we will limit ourselves to the observation that by including the *descensus*, the Easter play breaks out of the kerygmatic dimension of the liturgical celebration, insofar as it brings the salvation-history "end" forward into the victory over the Devil and thereby presents in a phenomenally saturated form what should remain essentially invisible. This tendency becomes explicit wherever the Resurrection is moved forward, as it is in most of the German Easter plays, so that the already resurrected Christ attacks the Devil. The salvation-history future fades away, and the play repeats a story that was already concluded in the past.

III

One could argue that all these shifts of emphasis could still be adequately explained by drama's specific interest in visibility, and the resulting theological problematics would then be precisely the unavoidable price to be paid for this kind of visibility. However, if we characterize as kerygmatic the segmentation of the biblical model that stresses the performative units and as mythical-archetypal the one that stresses the constative units, then we cannot regard the interest in visibility specific to drama as a sufficient explanation, since our concept of the mythical-archetypal in the previously defined sense is not concerned with the images of a didactic drama but rather with the representation in religious drama of a past considered in its mythical dignity.

Now in fact the text allows us to show that the play no more makes use of the *descensus* mythologeme as a mere image-dispenser than it seeks itself to be a mere image of salvation history. At first glance, it even appears that only such images, or, as they are called in the rubrics and prologues, imitative *figures*, are involved. When, for instance, a Tyrolean Easter play is described as a *frölich figur* (merry figure),[12] or the Passion scene in the Donaueschingen Passion play is described as a *gar meng schön andächtig figur* (a very beautifully commemorative figure),[13] in such cases—related to the New Testament, it should be noted—*figure* can no longer indicate the prototype of a future fulfillment but rather the imitation of a past act of salvation, that is, what already appears in the liturgical ceremony's rubrics in connection with concepts such as *similitudo* or *imitatio*.[14] However, just as in Amalarius's *nova genera figuraram* a ritually observed event-character was not rejected, the play now always wants to be more than a mere didactic show. When for example in the previously cited prologue to the Innsbruck play it is written that God wants to save us "today" (*daz wil got hüte brengen wedir*, 23), it is immediately clear that the "shown" images of the play remain connected with a religious self-concept. The play, like the celebration, has an event-like "today," in which what is shown in the image becomes present again. Thus in the Redentine play:[15]

> Wi willen ju ein bilde geven
> Wo sik van dode heft upgeheven
> Gades sone Jesus Krist,
> De vör ju gestorven ist. (3–6)

> *We want to show you an image*
> *In which arises from death*
> *God's Son Jesus Christ*
> *Who died for you.*

And shortly afterward:

> Vrouwet ju an desser tit,
> Gi mögen werden van sünden quit.
> got de wil in desser tit lösen
> De dar laten van dem bösen.
> De dar hüten mit gad upstan,
> De schölen vri van sünden gan.

> *Rejoice in this time,*
> *You may be redeemed from sin.*
> *God will in this time free*

those who forsake evil.
Those who rise today with God
Can go free from sin.

What the image will show (the Resurrection of Jesus and the redemption of evil) happens "in this (Easter) time," happens "today," and the biblical witnesses to this redemption deliver their message to the fourteenth-century audience. In the Erlau Easter play Peter complains:

owe wo warn all mein sinn,
das ich nicht gelauben wolt,
als ich von recht solt?
das mûs mich heut und immer reuen!
da von, îr christen getreuen,
helft zu piten Jhesum Christ,
der durch unsern willen gemartert ist,
das er unser sûnd vergeben well. (1492–99)[16]

Alas! where were all my wits
that I did not want to believe
as I should rightly believe?
This must I now and ever rue!
Therefore, you Christians true,
help us pray to Jesus Christ
who by our will was martyred
that he might forgive our sin.

The biblical Peter sorrows "today" and still "today" Christ is martyred "by our will." The play thus also has an event-like, timeless "today," and the ambivalence of its "figures" is very similar to that of Amalarius's *nova genera figurarum.* One must therefore ask whether the play does not also take on the obligation with which the celebration was already burdened and even whether this obligation does not now become even heavier. For the play's timeless "today" does not occur, like that of the liturgy, against the background of an "effective" present that outdoes the past, that is, not against the background of the difference but rather against that of the identity with the past acts of salvation. This submerging of the past in the contemporary actuality is supposed to document the continuing presence of the act of redemption in the midst of a world that has fallen to the Devil, but this does not alter the fact that this continuing presence in the most stringent salvation history sense can be only a presence *in effectu.* On this point we cannot be generous if we want to lay bare the true impulse behind this kind of play.[17] Just as we can understand a myth as being in its own way "salvation history," Christian salvation history can definitely be understood as myth. The conscious entry into the tension between past act of salvation, effective presence, and future fulfillment, or else an unnoticed escape from this tension, are the only criteria here. Thus if the drama is to be examined with regard to the past's ability to produce effects, a power that is presupposed in its identical repetition, it must also be asked whether its timelessness does not in reality point toward a "mythical moment of the beginning."[18]

IV

Structurally regarded, as we saw, the self-constitution of the drama signifies a narrative broadening of the liturgical kerygma. The celebration presents salvation history in the performative mode: the Lord is arisen, we are redeemed. The play brings this kerygma into an oppositional relationship, moves the message back into what H. Weinrich called the "narrative sequence" of myth:[19] the Lord arose and attacked the Devil—now we are redeemed. Empirical myth research, especially as it is represented by Malinowski and his school, has however made it clear that a story is not identified as a myth by having such a narrative sequence but rather first of all by anchoring this "narrative" religiously and institutionally. Weinrich has rightly described Lévi-Strauss's structural analysis of myth as one that tends toward a demythologizing approach. In Lévi-Strauss's analysis the paradigmatic oppositional models are supposed in fact to show "that the same logic is at work in mythical and scientific thought, and that human beings of all eras have thought in much the same way."[20] However, to legitimate myth once again it does not suffice to bring a syntagmatic narrative sequence to bear in opposition to this paradigmatics. We can grasp the mythical element in a story neither through its paradigmatics alone, nor through a syntagmatics supplementing the paradigmatics, but rather through anchoring these structures in a religious "place in life," in an institution.

For this purpose a structural detail becomes important that with few exceptions marks the arrangement of the descent into hell in the plays: three times the antiphonal demand *Tollite portas* and the Devil's counter-question are heard before the gates of hell are broken open. This triplet, which the play may have borrowed from the B-version of the Gospel of Nicodemus,[21] is a virtually classical example of the controversial "three with admonitory weight" in which A. Olrik sees the "most notable characteristic of folk poetry"[22] and which is known primarily for its action-constructing function in folktales. It is usually regarded as a play-form, concerning whose embedding in original mythical tales there are the most diverse theories.[23] It appears that religious drama can make an important contribution to the solution of this problem. It allows us to study precisely what in all other relevant cases of "simple forms" (A. Jolles) can at most be hypothetically reconstructed or only assumed: nascent play-forms that have not yet been completely emancipated from their ritualistic function. Here we come back to our example. So long as we compare the play solely with the Gospel of Nicodemus, we will not be able to discern a possible ritualistic character of the triplet in either the play or the prototype. This triplet is encountered, however, not only in the play's scene of the descent into hell but also in a liturgical ritual: in the elevation of the cross that precedes the visitation. The reaction to the difficulties characterizing the dialog nonetheless leads to this ceremony, which we will have to discuss here briefly.

In an *elevatio* from St. Gallen, for instance, while the antiphon *Tollite portas* is being sung three times, the cross is struck against the door of the choir *In signum redempcionis animarum ex limbo*, the door opens, and the cross is laid before the altar of the mother of God. The dialog has thus not taken place, the counter-question *Quis est iste rex gloriae?* is omitted.[24] In Barking, the *elevatio* offers a similar picture. There the abbess and the nuns go into the Magdalene chapel *figurantes animas sanctorum Patrum ante adventum Christi ad inferos descendentes*. Then a priest approaches the chapel and knocks with the crucifix on the locked door, *figurans dirupcionem portarum inferni*. After the *Tollite portas* has been repeated three times, the priest goes in and leads the prisoners out of the chapel, *id est de limbo Patrum*.[25] Thus the counter-question is again omitted. This kind of inconsistency is characteristic: Satan, the questioner, can no longer appear in the space once it is consecrated. He is probably to be encountered outside instead, and a Würzburg *elevatio* tries to take advantage of this. In this case the priest carrying the crucifix approaches the locked church door from within, and a person who is *foris ianuam* asks *Quis est iste rex gloriae?* Presumably the doors are opened after the dialogue, in order to let the people in, since the following rubric mentions the worship of the cross *ab omni clero et populo.* This solution is a fairly clever one, which makes the whole outside world into hell and the church into the place of redemption.[26] Two celebrations from Bamberg and Augsburg are related to this Würzburg text. In these cases the person representing Satan is inside the church, but it should be noticed that when leaving the church the procession seeking to come in had carried out with it not only the cross but also the Blessed Sacrament. If the procession—and thus also the Blessed Sacrament—is not taken out of the church, the person representing the Devil is explicitly expelled *extra templum.*[27]

What the liturgical ceremony excludes to this extent, the play includes. The play brings to an end what is rejected by the ceremony, it represents *in vivo* Satan, whom the ritual concerns but who cannot appear in the sacred space. In so doing, however, the play intersects with a further ritual that has heretofore been considered solely as a dramatization of the *descensus* but has not been put into an immediate relationship with the play:[28] the ceremony consecrating the church. In Young, we find an example of this from the ninth century.[29] The procession moves through the church three times; each time, it stops before the door, and the bishop, thrice calling out *Tollite portas, principes, vestras, et elevamini, portae aeternales, et introibit rex gloriae,* knocks on the door with his staff, whereupon the cleric representing Satan calls out from within the church the counter-question, *Quis est iste rex gloriae?* After this dialogue has been repeated three times, the bishop answers *Dominus virtutum, ipse est rex gloriae,* whereupon the doors open and the cleric within hurries out, *quasi fugiens,* and then joins the procession. Thus here the dialogue that was broken off in the *elevatio* is carried out in full. The Devil can reply from the still unconsecrated church; thereafter it is forever closed to him. In this ceremony, which is part of a long tradition of ecclesiastical and apocryphal exorcism formulas,[30] the ritualistic character of the triplet is quite obvious—and also in the (Innsbruck) play:

ADAM CANTAT "ADVENISTI":
*[Advenisiti, desiderabilis,
*quem expectabamus in tenebris,
*ut educeres hac nocte
*vinculatos de claustris.
*te nostra vocabant suspiria,
*te larga requirebant lamenta.
*tu factus es spes desperatis,
*magna consolatio in tormentis.]

ANGELI CANTANT "A PORTA INFERI":
*[A porta inferi eripe nos, domine!]

Lucifer clamat:
Stoz den regel vor dy tor!
ich weiz nicht, waz da rouschet davor!

ANGELI CANTANT "TOLLITE PORTAS PRINCIPES VESTRAS":
*[Tollite portas principes, vestras,
*et elevamini portae aeternales,
*et introibit rex gloriae.]

LUCIFER CLAMAT:
*Qui est iste rex gloriae?

ANGELI:
*Dominus fortis [et] potens,
*dominus potens in proelio.

ITEM ANGELUS PERCUTIENS DICIT:
Ir hern, selißet uff dy tor,
der konnig der eren ist hy vor!

LUCIFER DICIT:
Wer ist der konig lobelich,
der da stost so geweldiglich
mir an myne helletor?
her mochte wol bliben da vor!

ANGELI CANTANT "TOLLITE PORTAS PRINCIPES VESTRAS":
*[Tollite portas, principes, vestras,
*et elevamini portae aeternales,
*et introibit rex gloriae.]

LUCIFER "QUIS EST ISTE REX GLORIAE?" (UT PRIUS):
*[Quis est iste rex gloriae?]

ANGELI "TOLLITE":
*[Tollite portas, principes, vestras,
*et elevamini portae aeternales,
*et introibit rex gloriae.]

LUCIFER "QUIS EST ISTE REX GLORIAE?" (UT PRIUS):
*[Quis est iste rex gloriae?]

IHESUS DICIT:
Ir hern vz der finsterkeit,
vwir rufes sit ir gar vngemeit.

balde schliset vff dy torr:
der konnig der eren ist da vor!

LUCIFER DICIT:
Stoz den regel vor dy tor,
der konnig der eren ist da vor!
her schriget vns czu den oren:
werlich, er mag wol toren,
so vil kan her klaffen!
waz hat her hy czu schaffen?
balde heiz en enweg gen,
anders en wert eyn boße weter besten!
ly mir crewel vnd kelle,
ich wil en sencken in dy helle!

ET SIC IHESUS FRANGIT TARTARUM, DAEMONES ULULANT. IHESUS DICIT:
Nu kumt, myne vil liben kint,
dy von mynem vater bekomen sint! (258–304)

ADAM CANTAT "ADVENISTI":
*[Advenisiti, desiderabilis,
*quem expectabamus in tenebris,
*ut educeres hac nocte
*vinculatos de claustris.
*te nostra vocabant suspiria,
*te larga requirebant lamenta.
*tu factus es spes desperatis,
*magna consolatio in tormentis.]

ANGELI CANTANT "A PORTA INFERI":
*[A porta inferi eripe nos, domine!]

LUCIFER CLAMAT:
*Bar the door!
*What is that noise out there!

ANGELI CANTANT "TOLLITE PORTAS PRINCIPES VESTRAS":
*[Tollite portas principes, vestras,
*et elevamini portae aeternales,
*et introibit rex gloriae.]

LUCIFER CLAMAT:
*Qui est iste rex gloriae?

ANGELI:

Dominus fortis [et] potens,
dominus potens in proelio.

ITEM ANGELUS PERCUTIENS DICIT:

You men, open up the door,
The King of Ages stands before!

LUCIFER DICIT:

Who is the praiseworthy king
Who is knocking so powerfully
on my hellsgate?
He can just stay out there!

ANGELI CANTANT "TOLLITE PORTAS PRINCIPES VESTRAS":

[Tollite portas, principes, vestras,
et elevamini portae aeternales,
et introibit rex gloriae.]

LUCIFER "QUIS EST ISTE REX GLORIAE?" (UT PRIUS):

[Quis est iste rex gloriae?]

ANGELI "TOLLITE":

[Tollite portas, principes, vestras,
et elevamini portae aeternales,
et introibit rex gloriae.]

LUCIFER "QUIS EST ISTE REX GLORIAE?" (UT PRIUS):

[Quis est iste rex gloriae?]

IHESUS DICIT:

You men of darkness
Our call displeases you.
Quick, open up the door:
The King of Glory stands before!

LUCIFER DICIT:

Bar the door,
the King of Glory stands before!
he cries in our ears:
truly, he can just go mad
he can shout so much here!
what is he doing here?

quick, tell him to go away,
otherwise he'll get foul weather!
give me my fork and scourge
I want to throw him into hell!

ET SIC IHESUS FRANGIT TARTARUM, DAEMONES ULULANT. IHESUS DICIT:
Now come, my dear children
Who proceeded from my father!

The comparison of the play with ecclesiastical rituals does not prove any sources or influences, since that would in any case be possible only in a very limited way. The priority of the ceremony consecrating the church is clear, but in the *elevatio* this holds only for the *Canticum triumphale* (which in the play introduces or frames the dialog), which has been shown to be part of this ceremony as early as the beginning of the tenth century.[31] On the other hand, it was late in opening itself up to the *Tollite portas* dialogue. The first evidence of this appears in the fourteenth century, that is, coevally with the play, which suggests mutual influence.[32] Far more important than the question of sources is the distance separating this ceremony from the sacramental rite. This holds true for the formula of church consecration as well as for the *elevatio*. For even if the question of the priority of the *descensus* in the play and in the *elevatio* ritual cannot be answered without ambivalence, it remains first, that the *elevatio* emerged very late, scarcely before the tenth century,[33] and is thus unknown in the Roman liturgy; second, that it opened itself up to the truly dualistic moment in the *descensus* thematics—that is, the *Tollite portas* dialogue—only five centuries later; and third, that even this late opening up still took place entirely against the background of the inhibitions analyzed above. The fact that the Devil's reply was pushed out to the periphery of the sacramental rite reveals the latter's essentially antidualistic character. Thus it is precisely the proximity of the play to the *elevatio* that once again demonstrates that its "archetype" in Hardison's sense is not to be found in the broader surroundings of the sacramental rite, and still less at its very heart. It does not take off from the sacramental rite but rather from peripheral church rituals, in which the apocryphal tradition of the Gospel of Nicodemus is continued. However, what is thus brought from the periphery of the liturgy into the heart of the play was clearly of central interest to the latter. The shift of emphasis from the *visitatio* sequence to the descent into hell is not a mere broadening into a dramatic climax but rather a shift of interest from the kerygma of the Resurrection to the exonerating function of a represented exorcism. If we consider that the basic framework of the *descensus* in most plays consists either in whole or in part of the Latin *Canticum triumphale* and the Latin *Tollite portas* dialogue, which is sometimes translated but seldom wholly repressed by the translation, then this retention of the arcane Latin even in the vernacular play makes clear how powerful the church exorcisms remained in the play as its "latent function."[34] The play about the Lord's Resurrection has the latent function of a ritual release from the fear of the Devil.

V

Ritualizings of the descent into hell are not peculiar to the German play. They are also found in France and in England. It is even hard to find exceptions. Thus in German we can name the Augsburg Passion, which has only two *Tollite portas* demands (following lines 2402, 2411). Here it is clear that only the Gospel of Nicodemus, and more precisely the A manuscript, has served as a model. The same can be said of the English Chester cycle (324 ff., 145, 177, 181–82). In the Hegge cycle even this model is cut back to a single demand (306, following line 993).

These exceptions are, as I said, highly unusual. Since the *descensus* ritual in the Easter plays touches the very heart of religious drama, it is something like its *raison d'être*. Only when regarded in this perspective is the entire distance separating the ceremony from the play revealed. In order to recognize it, we must not compare the liturgical *visitatio* with the play's *visitatio* sequence observed in isolation, but rather the latter must be set back within the overall development of the Easter play. Then it becomes clear, however, that the Easter play, which is essentially a Devil play, does not secularize the ceremony but just like the latter has its own religious "place in life." Just as the ceremony receives its law from the liturgical rite surrounding it, the ritualistic structure of the play has the character of a religious answer. The liturgical-kerygmatic "place in life" is thus not abandoned without a substitute but rather exchanged against a mythical-archetypal "place in life." Here we should recall the previously analyzed Würzburg *elevatio*, in which the priest with the crucifix approaches the church door from within and defeats the Devil *foris ianuam*.[35] "Out there," however, in the space the ceremony thus characterizes as hell, is where the vernacular play takes place.

The ceremony receives its law from the *terribilia sacramenta*,[36] which do not tolerate the image of God and refuse the Devil entry, whereas the play receives its law from the one whose realm is "outside." The play occurs not in a neutral space but rather in a terroristically occupied one, and its popularity becomes understandable only when we relate it to the terroristic reality of the Devil's omnipotence, which it acts out and away.

We do not know in what way the people of the Middle Ages believed in the Devil. We can only attempt, using the extant historical documents and literary testimony, to gain access to this phenomenon, which will remain forever closed to us in its full complexity. This testimony is usually gathered together and interpreted in relation to the period's predominant obsession. Recent investigations, in particular concerning late medieval folk belief and superstition, have shown that possession and belief in magical powers did not appear at the same time or in the same place, and thus not at all so constantly as their literary reflections in manuals of confession and treatises on preaching might lead one to think.[37] Hence one will do well to be careful with the assumption that obsession was a characteristic of the period. The Devil was a reality but nonetheless one that humans had the freedom to "play." Conversely, however—and this fact seems no less significant—this freedom of the play is understandable only against the background of the terror that is overcome through it.[38] If the play was able to become expressly vernacular, that was apparently because a need was encountered and articulated that found no satisfactory answer in the sacramental communication of redemption and guarantee of salvation. The popularity of a play that, no matter what its particular thematics is, constantly celebrates the defeat of the Devil, can never be adequately explained so long as we fail to discern behind its represented "figures" the exonerating function of an archaic ritual. As we know, legends were sometimes attached to those who acted the part of the Devil, legends that told of subsequent poverty, death on the gallows, and suicide.[39] The mere possibility of forming such legends shows that the play does not take place in a monotheistically reduced and non-religious space but rather in a world of sympathetic relationships, in which negative beings definitely continue to exist and must be constantly driven away through play. This interpretation is confirmed, in another context, by no less a figure than Geroh von Reichersberg. His often-cited polemic against priests taking part in plays culminates in the suspicion that those who put on the *larvus daemonum* are not merely playing the Antichrist but actually incorporate him and appear in his service: *Quid ego mirum si et isti nunc Antichristum vel Herodem in suis ludis simulantes eosdem non, ut eis intentioni est, ludicro mentiuntur sed in veritate exhibent, utpote quorum vit ab Antichristi laxa conversatione non longe abest? (. . .) Et quis scire potest, an et cetera simulata Antichristi scilicet effigiem, daemonum larvas, herodianam insaniam in veritate non exhibeant.*[40] If Geroh's polemic had the political relationship to the Tegernsee play that it is commonly assumed to have had, his argument would be an even more powerful proof in our context. For precisely in order to be politically effective, it could not attempt just a crude demonizing of a mere play; rather, it would have to formulate something that was obvious and considered thoroughly possible.

On the other hand, we know that the Devil's role was sought after by (lay) actors. The challenge of the terroristic—and thus omnipresent and yet invisible—adversary was assumed, his mask was put on. In his article on the comprehensibility of magic, Gehlen speaks about "the decision to accept the existence of horrors."[41] This phrase seems to me of heuristic value with regard to the phenomenon in question here, and the same should hold for the other central categories in Gehlen's anthropology. Religious drama gains ritual as a mimic answer to "provocative data" whose terroristic significance did not admit of any construction of meaningful "spheres of action" but could only be bridged by "stabilized tensions." By accepting and confirming the existence of horrors the play brought about their "transcendence in the immanent."[42] Herein lies the specific archaic character of religious drama's "place in life," or, as we shall henceforth say with Gehlen, of this "institution." Herein also lies the only chance for the play to constitute itself at all. Christian liturgy stands in contradictory opposition to the archaic ritual and its "stabilized tensions." Essentially, it is not a "representation,"[43] not an imitative "transcendence in the immanent." Its repetitive elements are only an anamnestic reconstruction of the spatiotemporal substratum of a historical or would-be historical event and produce effects on their own, that is, as repetition, and nothing else. This ritual comes to an end not in the image but rather in the internalization of the belief in an invisible presence of the God who deigns to have mercy on us. Or conversely: wherever this ritual becomes an image, its specificity is lost, and degeneration appears instead of the supposed emancipation.

The play must thus go back beyond the kerygma, in order to procure representation as an anthropological category. However, what it gains anthropologically is gained at the cost of its theology. In actuality, religious drama, although composed without exception by clerics, was never officially and expressly acknowledged by the church as a theological institution. It could claim to have a didactic function, and therefore achieve the church's good will and even its encouragement, but that is something quite different. Defenders of the drama as a genuine product of church doctrine commonly point out that no prohibition was ever handed down by the Holy See. In fact, encouragement as well as criticism and prohibition remained a matter for the diocese, but this only shows that the church eschewed official institutionalization of this supposedly "most effective instrument of propaganda."[44] To be sure, the drama "showed" images of salvation history, but our foregoing analysis has already made it clear that one always does well not to identify prematurely these didactic potentialities with the interests and impulses that support the plays.

From the *Visitatio Sepulchri* to the Mythical *Ōstarūn*: The Marys Play As Catalyzer

I

The liturgical *visitatio* opened itself only hesitantly to the figure of the ointment-seller. In a thirteenth-century celebration in Prague, only a mute *ungentarius* appears, while another ceremony grants him just a single antiphon.[1] The first purchase scene occurs in the Latin Easter plays, and here we must already reckon with back-formations from the vernacular tradition. Stumpfl was the first to operate systematically with the possibility of such back-formations, not only with regard to the Latin plays but also with regard to the *ungentarius* figure who had already appeared in the celebration. He was therefore completely misunderstood by Scheunemann, whose criticism was prejudiced by a commitment to developmental history. If text historians such as de Boor and Hardison have recently taken back-formations into account as well, this amounts to a methodological rehabilitation of Stumpfl that ought not to pass unnoticed.[2]

For Stumpfl himself the vernacular merchant scene is in fact already, if not a back-formation, at least an epiphenomenon, which points to a pagan raising-from-the-dead ritual that precedes it. His main argument for this is the identification of the ointment-seller (*mercator*) with a physician (*medicus*) that characterizes most of the vernacular plays. The origin of the religious merchant scene is supposed to be a pagan physician-play in the manner of the comparable Shrovetide [*Fastnacht*] plays or of the Bohemian *Mastickar*, into which the Marys purchase-scene is assumed to have been later interpolated.[3] In fact, not only German plays but also many French ones contain the merchant's or physician's claim, which is characteristic of these "worldly" examples, that his ointment can bring the dead back to life. However, this fact does not resolve Stumpfl's fundamental dilemma, namely, that whatever might have constituted a Germanic-ritual dramatic continuity *before* the aforementioned late medieval plays has to be reconstructed from the Christian Easter play tradition alone. However, anyone who, in dealing with the Latin Easter plays of the eleventh and twelfth centuries,[4] draws on back-formations from the ritual physician plays has to postulate, without a single bit of evidence, a centuries-long tradition for the latter. No one will seriously doubt that the vernacular play provided the *ungentarius* of the liturgical ceremony with the traits of the "extremely ancient" figure of the quack. This quack, however, cannot be regarded as original with the play but only the ointment-seller, who became necessary at that moment, since the account in Mark 16:1 (*emerunt aromata, ut venientes ungerent eum*) had to be made into a scene. In the illustration of biblical models lies the primary impulse that first grounds the continuity of the play. However, a merchant peddling ointment was already included in the quack, that is, in the man who "prattles" (Middle Netherlandish *kwaken*, "to prattle, to boast") about his wonder drugs. The biblically promoted figure thus was ritually taken over but the other way around: the ritual figure, who at the outset was not mythologically super-elevated, is now incorporated into a represented "story," and only then is he guaranteed what outside the Christian domain remains a pure postulation: a real dramatic continuity.

In view of all that, the existence of something like a ritualistic physician's play should not be simply contested. I consider it important to show that the question as to what may have existed in such a substratum is not the decisive one. For whatever this may have been, it was brought into a demonstrable continuity through the Christian drama. Thus something entirely different becomes decisive: the question as to the self-concept of this "Christian" Easter play that so willingly included elements stemming from heterogeneous contexts. This question cannot be answered, however, so long as we act as though the Marys scene was in fact the central dramatic complex. Anyone who along with Stumpfl makes this assumption can only set against the projection onto a postulated ritualistic play the projection onto the liturgical *visitatio* and thus inevitably falls into the dilemma of having to consider the Easter play as a degradation that is completely inexplicable when seen against this liturgical background. Things look quite different, however, if we extricate the ointment purchase from this polarity between the liturgical *visitatio* and the ritualistic physician play and see it as a response to what already preceded: the ritual of the *descensus*. Here lay the concluding cardinal function and everything that follows it is shaped by it, is—again in Barthes's terminology—a redundant catalyzer. We must therefore not see the ointment purchase from the point of view of the *visitatio*— then it can only appear as an inexplicable amplification—but rather recognize it as virtually constituted by the Devil play. Only with the victory over the Devil is the free space won that can now, in the turbulence of a merry annual fair atmosphere (Rubin: "Men, today is the fair!" Innsbruck, 811), be truly acted out. "What I say is not true," the Erlau *medicus* and his servant Rubin say (103, 467), thereby unmistakably indicating the freedom and uninhibitedness of the play in contrast with the ritual rigor and compulsory nature of the *Tollite portas* in the *descensus*.

However, what especially suggests that we should approach the merchant play from the *descensus* and not from the *visitatio* is a structural aspect. What is acted out in the triangular relationship between the merchant/ physician, the merchant's wife, and Rubin is once again an opposition. Thus we can connect this with what, as the goal of the *visitatio*, can only appear as an unmotivatable amplification. That the servant leads the Marys to the merchant's shop is an unnecessary function. And that the merchant's wife spares her husband the actual haggling scene regarding the price is a purist back-formation of the Benediktbeuren play unknown in the vernacular tradition. The Benediktbeuren play represents the merchant as "an agent of the representation of a substance regarded as sacred"[5] and tries to persevere in this. In opposition to the assumption of an original "discovery" of this figure, Stumpfl was thus able to point out effectively the figure's ritualistic background. This argument is generally persuasive in the case of the Rubin-figure, in spite of occasionally problematic affiliations (to the English Robin Hood, the ghostly Hobby-horse, Rupprecht, Wotan, the Hosts of the air, etc.).[6] In the case of the *uxor mercatoris*, on the other hand, a difficulty—not mentioned—already arises. To be sure, the stereotypical fighting between husband and wife that may have fertility-magic significance, along with the equally stereotypical motif of the "new clothes," indicates extra-Christian ritualistic practices.[7] However, a ritualistic *uxor mercatoris* cannot be discerned here. There is the ritualistic physician and there is the Easter squabbling between a husband and wife, but there is no Easter squabbling between a ritualistic physician and his wife. Stumpfl can prove ritualistic ancestry for each individual figure or for each individual motif but not for the dramatic constellation *mercator-uxor mercatoris-Rubin.* The ritualistic motifs and figures enter into a new and different tradition and only then achieve what Stumpfl already postulated as the substratum, namely dramatic continuity; still more important, it is only then that they come together in a ritualistic springtime play.

The Rubin of the Easter play appears with a function that is not connected with any of the figures with ritualistic ancestry listed by Stumpfl: he represents the sexual demands of youth and their victory over the impotence of the old. The Rubin in the Innsbruck play considers himself best suited for "serving women" (549); he knows all about "young women," among whom he also counts Antonia, the merchant's wife. To pass time with her by the fireside in the evenings is the condition of his service (555, 590, 694). The merchant lets it happen—he is an old man who can no longer take care of his wife's needs. However, behind the motif of the impotent "old man" stands the dying year-god. In the scene of the fight over the purchase of the ointment, in which the wife curses the old man's love as "devil's love," this is made explicit:

Ja, ja, leider,
sin daz dy nuwen cleyder,
dy du mir czu desen ostern hast gegeben?
daz du daz jar nymmer must vbirleben! (1017–20)

Yes, yes, unfortunately,
are those the new clothes
that you gave me for Easter?
May you never survive the year!

The fact that the Devil is referred to in precisely this context is neither unique nor an accident. In all, this happens seven times in the Innsbruck merchant play, and indeed it is usually Rubin who wishes old women to go to the Devil (820 ff., 884 ff., 1035 ff.), just as the merchant's wife wishes her husband the same fate. Old people are precisely good enough for him who has himself been conquered: just as the *descensus* confirmed the character of what R. Reitzenstein called "dogmatic myth," which from the outset lacks any connection with specific natural processes, so here in the merchant play the opposition is acted out in a naturalistic manner.[8] The marriage breakup caused by Rubin fulfills the curse on the old man, who is not supposed to survive the year, and thereby makes it evident which Easter is involved here: the pagan springtime festival that culminates in a ritualistic marriage ceremony (1063 ff.) The Erlau Easter play is even clearer on this point; the whole physician play takes place against the background of the motto announced *ad populum* by Rubin's servant Pusterpalkch:

> ir jungen maid, ir merkcht mich recht
> und nempt euch all jung chnecht
> zu disen ostern frei:
> habit ir an ainem ze wenig, so nempt ir drei! (522–25)

> *You young girls do listen well*
> *and take all the young fellows*
> *who at this Eastertide are free:*
> *if one fellow's not enough, you take three!*

And in the concluding marriage breakup, the motif of the old and young man appears once again but this time with a clarity that unmistakably emphasizes the ritualistic character of what Hartl considered "dirt" and "obscenity":

> Nů merkcht, ir herrn wolgemůt
> und auch ir fraun gůt,
> ein gůten wechsel hab ich getan,
> das ich ein alten man
> han geben umb ein jungen,
> der vert dort her von sprungen,
> mit dem ich mich tůmern wil,
> unz (an) meins leibs zil;
> wen ich nicht enleug:
> er růrt es in dem zeug
> nach meins herzen gir;
> des entet nicht der alte stir. (967–78)

> *Now pay attention, my merry men,*
> *and also you good women,*
> *I've made a good trade,*
> *an old man I've given*
> *against a young one,*
> *who comes here as a stud*

with whom I want to romp in bed
until my body is satisfied
if I'm not mistaken:
he moves it in my thing
the way I like it;
the old man cannot do this even.

Rubin, according to the following rubric, *ducit dominam ad locum cantando*:

Nächten da was ich siech,
do macht ains in das ander nicht;
heut wil uns got bewarn,
und můz ains in das ander varn. (981–84)

At night I was sick
so one did not fit into the other;
today may God protect us
for one must go into the other.

Thus the Christian Eastertide is celebrated with an "Easter-like" return of fertility—admittedly in only one play, which ironically cancels itself in Pusterpalkch's final words:

habt ir von uns icht nucz genommen,
es mag euch wol ze reun chomen.
ir habt groß geschäfft:
mich tunkcht, wir haben euch geäfft
mit unserm großn tant. (1015–19)

if you've not profited at all from us,
you may well come to regret it.
you've had a big time:
I think we've made fools of you
with our crude display.

Cancellation does not, however, mean judgment: the display (*tant*) is not condemned. The old man who sold the Marys the ointment ends up being laughed at, and Rubin, who has told the Marys to go to the Devil (Innsbruck, 1053–54; Erlau, 905), goes unpunished, as does his ritualistic bride. The merchant play thus follows its archetypal logic very consistently through to the end.

This structure could be interpreted as suggesting that the visit to Christ's grave and the celebration of the true Easter event were preceded by all that this Easter event has overcome and that the audience recognizes as overcome. Even this interpretation, however, would be an expression of that retrospective view whose inappropriateness I am trying to demonstrate here. For in contrast to the liturgical *visitatio*, here the central dramatic event occurs not at the end but at the beginning; it has already happened in the victory over the Devil. Consequently, the ritualistic boisterousness of the merchant play is not the moved-forward, negative background of a self-announcing kerygmatic *surrexit* jubilee but rather an expression and brimming-over of Easter joy that from the outset began in another, mythical-archetypal dimension and is now acted out in naturalistic terms. Certainly, the merchant play remains bound up with the purchase of ointment and therefore with the Marys play that provides the occasion for it. Occasion and impulse are different things, however, and the play draws this impulse from the dimension in which Easter joy, which the Marys are supposed to be the first to experience, has long since been achieved.

From this impulse results the peculiar heterogeneity of the Latin verses about the way traveled and the purchase of the ointment. Unlike the liturgical-ecclesiastical rituals of the *descensus* play, the elements of the liturgical ointment-purchase are not included in the play and produce no substratum, as occurs in the case of the *Tollite portas* dialogues. The Marys who come to the merchant's shop come from a different world and return to it, and although here in the ritualistic play, they bought the ointment for the dead Jesus, in truth no contact between these two worlds has taken place. The Marys lose none of their holiness, and conversely the play shows no sign of becoming holy. It follows its own archetypal logic opposing young and old and brings it to an end in the way described. Herein lies the true duality of value, the ambivalence of the merchant play, in which the Christian Easter and the pagan *ōstarūn* are simultaneously present, without either of them being explicitly denied. In the play, kerygma and myth overlap, both of them persisting in their own dimension and never encountering one another. After the ritual wedding of Rubin and the merchant's wife, the play leaves the archetypal dimension opened up in the *descensus* and shifts over into the kerygmatic dimension. However, here essentially nothing can be "played," and so the play quickly seeks to break out of this dimension, in Jesus' appearance to Mary Magdalene as a gardener after the scene at the tomb.

Before we turn to this encounter, however, we must once again come back to Stumpfl. His claim that the Marys' purchase of the ointment is a later interpolation into a ritualistic physician's play is based on, among other grounds, the argument that the salvation motif "is not at all appropriate to the ecclesiastical sequence of events," and thus could only be "amalgamated."[9] This claim is typical of his thinking about the Germanic substratum. What it does not take into consideration is the self-conception of a "Christian" play that was inclined not to reject such pagan elements but rather on the contrary to "amalgamate" them fully and thoroughly. Obviously this "amalgamation" is thus in truth a mode of reception and is supported by a highly ambivalent concept of Easter that oscillates between Christian resurrection and pagan rebirth. Thus it is once again characteristic of Stumpfl's fixation on the continuity of the substratum that he pays almost no attention to the scene in which this ambivalence first becomes evident: the descent into hell.[10] The ritualistic substratum of the play lies not in hypothetical physician plays but rather in the ecclesiastical exorcisms analyzed above, with their oppositional structure going back to the katabasis mythologeme, and the merchant play acts out this opposition in naturalistic terms. The thematic affinity between Christian resurrection and pagan rebirth appears in Stumpfl solely with regard to what it presupposes, namely that one of them can be avoided by the other. However, what is acted out and not judged is clearly not something that those involved sought to avoid. On the contrary, the affinity's effect tended in precisely the opposite direction: in its mythical-archetypal repetition of the Easter event, the play was opened to motifs and elements of the pagan *ōstarūn* that thus not only entered into a demonstrable dramatic continuity but also achieved, from the point of view of "Christian myth," a new, Christian-ritualistic significance.

This fact must therefore be emphasized because it adumbrates the tendency in current research on popular drama to extend the critique of the Germanic thesis carried out by the Vienna school (R. Much and O. Höfler), on the basis of which Stumpfl also proceeded, into a general denial of a determining relationship between dramatic development and religious ritual. Thus H. Bausinger objected to Stumpfl's having in principle rejected the "initially unassociated theatrical element."[11] It seems to me that this attempt to liberate research on popular drama from a "peculiar suspicion with regard to the theatrical" falls into the opposite extreme. It is perhaps justified—I claim no competence here—with regard to the Shrovetide play [*Fastnachtspiel*], although even in this case it may not be fully satisfactory to give up tracing back the sexual to the ritualistic substratum on account of its hypothetical character and instead to speak simply of "real motifs." The uncontested entertainment function of this play does not suffice to explain why this entertainment acts out precisely these motifs, and Bausinger himself thus cannot completely exclude ritualistic implications from Shrovetide customs and their dramatic development.[12]

The situation is quite different in the Easter play. In this case we cannot in fact speak of an "unassociated theatrical element" since here is available and proven what is missing in the Shrovetide play: a "Christian" myth, drawn from the biblical and apocryphal gospels, that is revisualized in the ritual play. A highly ambivalent understanding of the event of Resurrection leads to such a "Christian" ritualistic play, in which Easter and *ōstarūn* peacefully coexist and which brings already exhausted ritualistic figures such as the quack physician into a new, ritualistic dramatic significance. The latter is on one hand the contemporary annual fair figure, a drunkard, a thief, a gallows-bird, but he is still good enough to sell the Marys the ointment for the Lord's body.[13] Stumpfl is right: the quack is not really suitable for the ecclesiastical sequence of events. In the "Christian" ritualistic play, however, which already presents this ecclesiastical sequence of events in an archetypal dimension, it seems to suit it very well—indeed, so well that the resurrected God himself is sometimes able to slip into the ritualistic figure's cloak and play practical jokes on Mary Magdalene.

II

In John 20:14–16 we read that Mary Magdalene suddenly saw Jesus standing in front of her (*vidit Jesum stantem*) and took him for a gardener (*illa existimans quia hortulanus esset*), whence arises the initial misunderstanding: *Domine, si tu sustulisti eum, dicito mihi ubi posuisti eum.* John does not make it clear whether this mistaken assumption was based on the appearance itself or only on the place where it occurred (the garden of Joseph of Arimathea). The appearance itself is not interesting; the recognition is not achieved through it but rather through language: *Dicit ei Jesu: Maria. Conversa illa dicit ei: Rabboni (quod dicitur, Magister)*. The scenic representation does not have this kind of room for play. It has to be perfectly open and explicit: the misunderstanding has to be motivated immediately thereafter by the figure that appears at the altar. In fact, in the celebration at Fleury the priest appears *preparatus in similitudinem Hortolani*.[14] Hence it has already gone a step beyond the biblical account, which left this interpretation open, and finds itself confronted by the question as to why Jesus should have presented himself as a gardener. What is set in motion by this question is shown by a celebration from Coutance. Here as well Christ first appears *in habitu Ortolani* but does not present himself as such.[15] As soon as Mary Magdalene has made her request, *Domine, si tu sustulisti eum, dicito mihi, et ego eum tollam*, he disappears and immediately returns (presumably two priests shared the role) dressed in liturgical vestments and holding a cross in his hand, and only then reveals himself by calling out: *Maria!* Hence in contrast to the Fleury ceremony something very decisive occurs: whereas in the Fleury ceremony Mary Magdalene recognized the divine voice in spite of the gardener's clothing, in this case the correct hearing brought about by the change of garments is associated with the latter. The language in which the Christian God alone makes himself recognized is deprived of its revelatory power. The shift into visibility has released the sequence of events centering on the salvation-history moment of the God's call and has suddenly passed over into the dimension of metamorphosis.

It is characteristic of the tendency of the liturgical celebration that it was obviously uneasy about this solution, which is first found in the Klosterneuburg *Ordo Paschalis*.[16] The later Coutance celebration (fifteenth century) represents an exception and must have been influenced by the Latin play and perhaps also by the vernacular play.[17] The liturgical tradition is concerned to preserve the specifically salvation-history character of the scene and thus either leaves Christ's appearance as a gardener unexplained, as in the Fleury example, or else—and this is the case in all the remaining texts—immediately confronts Mary Magdalene with a *Dominica Persona*, without referring to the garden or the gardener. And even this solution seems still to have appeared problematic; scarcely a dozen celebrations include it. This shows, as we have already seen, the subordination of the *visitatio* in principle to sacramental presence of the Lord and thus subordination to the *pascha perpetuum* of the Mass following matins. The identity of its repetition remains the (salvation history) identity of the glad tidings, not that of the theophany itself.

Things are altogether different in the play. Strictly speaking, it operates in the kerygmatic dimension in only one place: the scene at the sepulcher, which preserves the *Quem quaeretis* that is at the heart of the *visitatio*. What then follows in the celebration in only a few exceptional cases—that is, the appearance of Christ—cannot be avoided in any of the plays. Thus it reenters the mythical-archetypal dimension of identical repetition of the mystery itself, in which the *descensus* already operated. The appearance of Christ has however already detached the *descensus* from its testimonial function, as it documents visibly what remained invisible in the framework of the celebration. The construction of the Mary Magdalene scene in the vernacular play thus also shows clear signs of de-functionalization. Its inclusion within the dimension opened up by the *descensus* first makes it possible to explain what must once again appear, in direct comparison with the ceremony, as an incomprehensible degeneration.

Therefore the German Easter plays, which like the merchant scene appear in the context of such a supposed degeneration, are the best object for investigation. Not only do they include the appearance of Christ, as does the vernacular tradition in general, but in every case Jesus also appears as *hortulanus*, in order to later reveal himself as *salvator*. Thus they eagerly seize on what is shown only once in the *visitatio*: the dramatic possibility of metamorphosis. This metamorphosis will now be acted out in the most diverse ways, most impressively in the dramatic form of the triplet already familiar to us: the *hortulanus* twice approaches Mary Magdalene, asking her about the cause of her grief; only on the third occasion does he reveal himself as *salvator*.[18] Here what is important is not the triplet as such but rather the way in which it is used. This usage can once again be clarified by comparing it with the liturgical ceremony. In the Nuremberg *visitatio* III there is a similarly structured scene of the Lord's appearance. In the antiphonal exchange with the choir, Mary Magdalene's complaint *Heu! redemptio Israhel* rings out three times before the empty tomb. Shortly thereafter appears a *Dominica Persona* (that is, not a gardener), and the recognition is achieved in strict accord with the dialogue in John 20:15–16. Following the transfigured Christ's *Noli me tangere*, Mary Magdalene sings her song of worship, emphasizing it by kneeling three times, thus rounding out the second triplet in the sequence of events.[19]

This symbolic marking is, however, no longer unambiguous in the play, where the triplet structures the event itself. The thrice-repeated *Heu! redemptio Israhel* in the ceremony is, as the rubric clearly indicates, a reference to the Trinity, the symbolic apotheosis of the *Sepulchrum de sublatione Corporis Domini*, and finds its fulfillment in the sublation of the *Dominica Persona*. In contrast, by associating the triplet with the metamorphosis, the play desymbolizes the sequence of events, making it into a ritualistic dramatic form. In contradistinction to the *descensus*, however, in this case there is no preexistent homologous, synchronic ritual. This triplet was realized in the play itself. The terroristic reality is clearer than in the *descensus*, where it was still much nearer and had to be played away; here, it is assumed to have already been played away: the acted-out ritual has already become a ritualistic play, as it did in the case of the ointment-purchase scene.

The ritual thus shares in the merchant play's ambivalence concerning the conception of Easter. For not only the misunderstanding is acted out, since Jesus, intentionally misinterpreting Mary Magdalene's question, suggests that she is looking for a lover,[20] but also the gardener role is acted out, since Jesus is furious about the trampled grass and plants in his garden; he then turns to Mary Magdalene:

> Ich kan deyn jo nicht gewartin:
> ich muß graben meynen garten,
> ich bereyte meynen pastarnag
> vnd stose den yn meynen sag
> vnd wil do mete czu margkte loffin
> vnd mir des brotis kewffin,
> das ich irnere meynen leib
> keyn desir osterlichen czeit.
> nu gang engelich von mir:
> dy Juden werden kommen schir!
> wer weys, wy dyrs mochte betayn,
> worden sy dich sichtig an!
> dor vmb sage ich dir yo:
> suche deynen herren andirswo! (Vienna, 904–17)

> *I cannot wait for you,*
> *I have to cultivate my garden,*
> *I'm picking my salsify*
> *and putting it in my sack*

and want to take it to the market
to buy myself some bread,
to nourish my body
in this Easter time.
Now leave me quickly:
the Jews are coming soon!
Who knows what may happen to you
if they lay eyes on you!
Therefore I say to you:
Look elsewhere for your Lord!

Here the resurrection is associated with the garden, that is, with the naturalistic, in a very special way. At Eastertide [*osterlichen czeit*] Jesus nourishes his body with bread he has gotten at the market in exchange for salsify from his garden. One might be tempted here to interpret this allegorically, connecting the bread with the Eucharist or the garden and the gardener with the Song of Songs. A clear reference to the latter appears in Mary Magdalene's subsequent complaint about the loss of her "friend": "I cannot find my cherished Jesus Christ, who is my friend and my Easter day" (920–21). Here the author is obviously appealing to an exegetical tradition probably founded by Hippolytus of Rome, which relates the beginning of the third hymn (Song 3:1–4) to the pious women at the sepulcher and to Mary Magdalene in particular. However, in that case there is no mention of a friend, or even of the gardener.[21] The garden allegories in the exegesis of the Song of Songs are connected with 4:12, where the bridegroom's bride is compared with a *hortus conclusus,* and of course this tradition concerns not Mary Magdalene but rather Mary, mother of God.[22] In contrast, Christ's garden in the Easter play is not a product of the exegesis on the Song of Songs[23] but rather of the dramatic development of the gardener's speech in John 20:14–16, and this development cannot be interpreted coherently in an allegorical manner either as a whole or in detail. Jesus has not, as it were, prepared his garden—that is, his kingdom—for Mary Magdalene; on the contrary, he sends her away, has no time for her, because he has to buy bread for himself. However, eucharistic bread would be bread provided by him, and that nourishes the faithful, not himself. It is obvious that here, and especially in the details of his activity as a gardener and its results, appear the dramatically specific motifs that tinge the Resurrection with a naturalism that is not allegorically reduced. The Song of Songs tradition mentioned in connection with the "friend" remains heterogeneous to this context. Mary Magdalene's Easter day [*ostirliche tag*] does not connote the same thing as the Eastertide [*ostirliche czeit*] in the gardener's speech. Like the merchant play, this scene takes place against the background of an ambivalence between the Judeo-Christian *pascha* and the pagan *ōstarūn*.

The starkest and for us most alien example of this ambivalence occurs in the Sterzing Easter play. Here the encounter begins with the *Mulier quid ploras, quem queris* (John 20:15) familiar from the liturgical celebration, and then falls immediately into the crude tone of the merchant scene:

Salvete salvete! sprach der wolf zu dem stier
Got grüß euch schone frau schier
Und sag mir zu dieser stund:
wen suchstu so weinund,
Oder was hast du verloren?
Des sag mir an zoren.
Es ist aber nit frommer frauen recht,
Daß sie laufen als die knecht
Des morgen in den garten,
Als si der knaben wellen warten.
Ich kan dir nit sagen,
hastu icht zu klagen,
Das verfür anderswo.
Ei du meinst ich sei dein gar fro,
Daß du mir niedertritst das kraut?
Get resch ir bose haut,
Und get aus dem garten
In die schul zu den gelarten,
Oder ich smier euch eure glieder,
Daß euch in drei tagen nit lust herwider. (pp. 152–53)

Salvete salvete! *said the wolf to the bull*
God's greetings to you, pure lady,
And tell me now
whom you seek weeping so
Or what you have lost?
Say it in my ear.
It isn't right for pious women

To run like young men
into the garden in the morning
as if they were expecting a boy.
I can tell you nothing,
If you have something to complain about
do it somewhere else.
Hey, do you think I'm happy
that you are trampling my plants?
Quickly take your vile body
And go out of the garden
To the wise men's school
Or I'll grease your limbs
So you won't want to do it again three days hence.

In this scene the *hortulanus* episode already known to us (it is recognizable in the assignation motif) is actually contaminated by the equally familiar ointment-purchase scene.[24] Jesus himself grows all the plants in his garden that will be offered for sale in the merchant scene and whose foremost qualities will also be fully described here:

Auch wil ich mit euch teilen die wurzen,
Die langen und die kurzen,
Die wol fugen den alten weiben
Do mit sie die runzen vertreiben,
Daß sie sich mit waschen,
So werden sie glitzen als die betlertaschen.
Auch fugen sie wol zu dem har,
Das sag ich euch fürwar,
Daß es werd rau als ein entensnabel
Und gelb als ein rabenzagel.
Auch wer indert ein man,
Da für ich wol kan,
Der do hiet ein boses weib,
Das nit fuget seinen leib:
Der nem der wurzen ein lat
Und aus eichen knittel ein quintat,
Und salb sie allenthalben
Mit der guten prügelsalben,
Und hor nit e auf:
Ir sei dann der ruck so weich as der bauch,

Und schau dar nach dar zu,
Ob sie nit gern seinen willen tu. (pp. 155–56)

I also want to share with you the herbs
The long ones and the short ones,
That are suitable for old women
who use them to get rid of wrinkles,
when they wash themselves with them,
they glisten like a beggar's purse.
They are also suitable for the hair,
And there I'm telling you the truth,
it becomes as rough as a duck's bill
and as yellow as a raven's.
Also if there's any man
I can help out,
Whose shrewish wife
Doesn't like his body:
Let him take the herbs
And pour a fifth of oat-seeds
And rub himself all over
With the good ointment
And not stop doing it:
His back will be as soft as his belly,
And then just see
If she doesn't willingly do what he wants.

Like the *mercator*, the gardener also has a servant, who also is modeled on Rubin:

Ich wil auch hinter dem zaun liegen,
Wenn die dirnen austreiben die ziegen.
Begreif ich dar in eine
Sie seit groß oder klein,
Ich wil ir scheren den bart,
Daß sie meint, ich heiß Eberhart.
Nun ge wir von dannen
Und lassen Maria hie zannen. (p. 157)

I also want to lie behind the fence
When the girls drive the goats out.

If I can grab me one there,
Whether she's big or little,
I want to shave her beard
So she'll think my name is Everhard.
Now let's get out of here
And let Mary jaw a bit.

These passages all stand in an apparently unbridgeable contrast with Mary Magdalene's liturgical-ceremonial antiphons and laments, and right after Rubin's obscenity, it passes over once again, without the slightest transition, into the highly ceremonial recognition scene. However, the concept of contrast may not be the right one in view of the archaic strangeness of such a scene. For us, a contrast always implies a new dimension of meaning introduced in and through it; the most obvious example is, of course, Shakespeare, where the clownish perspective complicates and relativizes the noble event by bringing it into contact with another reality. In the Easter play, however, this relativization is missing. To be sure, the illusory nature of the metamorphosis is used to act out the naturalistic Jesus-*hortulanus*. However, as we already saw in the case of the merchant play, here as well the pagan in no way develops into a self-consistent inversion or negative background against which the *salvator* stands out as the Christian overcoming of the year-god. Rather, in the *hortulanus* figure naturalistic graphicness and the Christian notion of redemption are immediately juxtaposed:

Gut weib! ich wil dir sagen,
Den du suchst, der was begraben,
Und er ist erstanden froleich
Und fert in seines vaters himmelreich. (p. 154)

Good woman! I want to tell you:
The man you're looking for, he was buried,
And he rose up again gladdened
And is going to his father's heavenly kingdom.

That is the beginning of the speech that ends with the praise for the ointment (*prügelsalben*). Here no significant contrast is in evidence, but rather we simply find something Christian interpreted in a pagan way and something pagan meant in a Christian way. As in the ointment purchase, the liturgical substratum of the *visitatio* breaks out of another dimension into ritualistic play, without being incorporated by the latter, but also without in the end forcing it to come under its own truth. This Jesus-*hortulanus* remains bi-valued, ambivalent, he is the Christian resurrected Christ and at the same time the pagan year-god, whom the garden in which he was buried brings forth again at Easter, at the time of the springtide *ōstarūn*.

III

How much this ambivalence is a very specific product of the play can be shown by a quick glance at the exegesis of John 20:14. In one of Ambrose's homilies there is an allusion to the garden of Joseph of Arimathea:

> Ergo in hortulo Salvator redivivum corpus assumit et inter florentes arbores et candentia lilia carne iam mortua reflorescit, et ita germinat de sepulcro, ut germinantia et nitentia cuncta reperiat. sic enim post hiemalis rigoris frigidam quodammodo sepultaram pullulare elementa omnia festinarunt, ut resurgente Domino et ipsa consurgerent. nam utique ex resurrectione Christi aer salubrior est, sol calidior, terra fecundior, ex eo surculus in fruticem, herba crescit in segetem, vinea pubescit in palmitem. sic igitur cum reflorescit Christi caro, omnia floribus vestiuntur.[25]

Very characteristically, no relationship whatever with the *illa existimans quia hortulanus esset* (John 20:15) is recognized here. This reference first becomes virulent when Jesus appears visibly before Mary Magdalene, that is, when the encounter is represented *in vivo* and, as we have already shown in detail, the misunderstanding is motivated by and in the appearing figure. The hymn, on the contrary, does not deal with the figure himself but rather with the garden blooming anew as the backdrop for the Resurrection of the Savior, under which nomination Jesus is immediately and exclusively addressed. Indeed, with a formula such as *germinat de sepulcro* even the Resurrection itself comes dangerously near to being a naturalistic conception— H. von Campenhausen speaks of the "trusting, innocent disregard of this historical meaning" in Ambrose[26]—but the whole thing remains within the framework of a patristic tradition that interpreted the revival of nature as a reflection of the Resurrection of Jesus, just as his death was associated with sunset.

How the exegesis proceeds when it also explicitly comments on this misunderstanding can be very clearly seen in a homily discovered by Abbé

Bourgain (he attributes it, probably erroneously, to Anselm of Canterbury).[27] I must quote in full both the passages relating to John 20:14–15:

Cum Maria sic doleret et sic fleret, et cum hec dixisset, conversa est retrorsum et vidit Jhesum stantem et nesciebat quia Jhesus est, et dicit ei Jhesus: Mulier quid ploras? Quid queris?

Ipsa paulo ante occulos suos, cum magno dolore tum cordis sui, viderat speciem suam [tuam] suspendi in ligno, et tu nunc dicis: Quid ploras? Ipsa in die tercia ante unxerat manus tuas, quibus sepe benedicta fuerat, et [viderat] pedes tuos, quos deosculata fuerat et quos lacrimis irrigaverat, clavis affigi, et tu nunc dicis: Quid ploras? Nunc insuper corpus tuum sublatum estimat, ad quod ungendum, ut se quoquo modo consolaretur, veniebat, et tu dicis: Quid ploras? Quem queris? Dulcis magister, ad quid, queso provocas spiritum hujus mulieris? Ad quid provocas animum ejus? Tu scis quia te solum querit, te solum diligit, pro te omnia contempnit, et tu dicis: Quid queris? Tota pendent in te, et tota manet in te, et tota desperat de se, ita querat [querit] te, ut nichil querat, nichil cogitat [cogitet] preter te. Ideo forsitan non cognoscit te, quia non est in se, sed pro te est extra se. Cur ergo dicis ei: Cur ploras? Quem queris? An putas quia ipsa dicat: Te ploro, te quero, nisi tu prius inspiraveris et dixeris in corde suo: Ego sum quem queris et quem ploras? An putas quia ipsa cognoscat te, quamdiu volueris celare te?

Ut ipsa extiminans quia ortolanus [hortulanus] esset, dixit ad eum: Domine, si tu sustulisti eum, dicito michi ubi posuisti eum, et ego eum tollam. O dolor innumerabilis! O amor mirabilis! Mulier ista, quasi densa dolorum nube obtecta, non videbat solem qui mane surgens radiabat per fenestras ejus, qui per aures corporis jam intrabat in domum cordis sui! Sed quoniam languebat amore, isto amore sic occuli cordis caliginabant, ut non videret quoniam videbat: [non] videbat enim Jhesum, quia nesciebat quia Jhesus est. O Maria, si queris, cur [non] agnoscis Jhesum? Ecce Jhesus venit ad te, et quid queris querit a te, et tu ortholanum [hortulanum] eum existimas! Verum quidem est quod existimas. Sed tamen tu in hoc erras dum eum, si ortholanum [hortulanum] eum existimas, non Jhesum non agnoscas. Est enim Jhesus, et est ortolanus [hortulanus], quia ipse seminat omne semen bonum in orto [horto] anime sue [tue] et in cordibus fidelium suorum. Ipse omne semen bonum plantat et rigat in animabus sanctorum, et ipse est Jhesus qui tecum loquitur. Sed forsitan eumdem non agnoscis, quia tecum loquitur. Mortuum enim queris et viventem non cognoscis. Nunc in veritate comperi hanc esse causam pro qua a te recedebat et pro qua tibi non apparebat. Cur enim tibi appareret, quoniam non querebas eum? Certe querebas quod non erat, et non querebas quod erat. Tu querebas Jhesum et non querebas Jhesum, ideoque videndo Jhesum, nesciebas Jhesum.

This text is a model example of getting rid of a biblical problem, as theological rigorism seeks to do. The problem is addressed in the first part: how could Jesus, who after all knew very well whom Mary Magdalene was grieving for and whom she was seeking, nevertheless play dumb and ask her precisely these questions? The author does not really discuss the fact that Jesus plays dumb but rather says that he concealed (*celare*) himself, and in the following passage he tries to show why. Mary Magdalene has sought Jesus, but she has not sought him in the right way: not with the mystical *occuli cordis*. She has tried to find with her bodily eyes the man who was on the point of penetrating her heart *per aures corporis*, that is, through the word, and so the regrettable happened: *Ecce Jhesus venit ad te, et tu ortholanum eum existimas!* The reason for the misunderstanding must thus be sought in Mary Magdalene and not in the resurrected Christ's appearance. The *hortulanus* is a product of seeing with the wrong eyes, and it is not asked whether perhaps it could be brought about by a sensory gardener-appearance. To be sure, Jesus is also a gardener, but as a mystical gardener who sows the good seed in the heart of the faithful,[28] he reveals himself only in the word, and is identical with the *Jhesus qui tem loquitur*. Mary Magdalene's heart is thus the (allegorical) garden: once again we see in this now explicitly mystical interpretation of the encounter how alien to it is the *hortulanus's* garden in the Easter play, out of which Mary Magdalene is driven. Nevertheless the questions remain: Why then did this mystical gardener not immediately speak openly with Mary Magdalene? Why did he not immediately make himself recognized by speaking to her in his divine person? Why did he ask when he already knew the answer? And once again the reasons are sought in Mary Magdalene: perhaps she did not at first recognize him because he spoke with her, because she was seeking him as a dead man, and thus, once again, seeking him with the wrong eyes: *Cur enim tibi appareret, quoniam non querebas eum?* Why should Jesus show himself to her as alive, when she was not seeking him as a living man at all?

These reasons do not really suffice to set aside the problem, either. For if Jesus knew that Mary Magdalene was, so to speak, on the wrong track, he could have logically either withdrawn altogether or else immediately allowed her to recognize him. Yet he plays dumb and thus brings about the misunderstanding. However, the interest of our text lies less in the fact that the reply is omitted than in the way it is sought. The argumentation sets out logically to absolve the Godhead of any share in the blame for the misunderstanding. This absolution consists above all not in rejecting the explanation suggested by the biblical text itself, which is in fact obvious, but rather in ignoring from the outset the fact that Jesus could appear to Mary Magdalene as a gardener at all. The author must have recognized the *skandalon* concealed, or at least discernible here, involving a Jesus who plays dumb and toys with Mary Magdalene as if he were a metamorphosed god in the pagan manner, for only in this way does the radical displacement of the whole event into mystical imagelessness become comprehensible.[29] However, this interpretation is possible only because the homily does not need to take a position with regard to the simple *conversa est retrorsum et vidit Jhesum stantem.* The visible presentation of the scene cannot fail to ignite the *skandalon* and must bring the latent metamorphosis "into (the) play." And although, theologically regarded, it should not exist, one of the play's most original inherent possibilities thus imposes itself: the "information gap" between the audience who knows and Mary Magdalene who doesn't.[30] What it does with this possibility can be seen as a measure of its theological reflectedness. The examples analyzed thus far represent one extreme. Jesus appears in these examples just as the author of our homily did not want him to appear: disguised as a gardener, playing dumb and toying with Mary Magdalene, playing a practical joke. Moreover, it is precisely the naturalistic components of this gardener-metamorphosis that are acted out. Herein lies, after the ritualistic graphicness of the merchant play, a further indication of a mythically-archetypally shaped conception of the Easter event. This thematizing of the naturalistic is no longer a mere image-like reflection of the resurrection, no longer a mere expression of "joy at Christ's triumph over hell," as it is described in one of Fortunatus's Easter songs;[31] rather, here, as already in the merchant play, the "dogmatic myth" of the descent is once again explained naturalistically: Jesus himself appears in the ambivalence of the resurrected Christian God and the reborn year-god. In the mythical-archetypal dimension into which the play moves with the metamorphosis, there is obviously already a basic dramatic impulse. A world lies between our homily and these two examples.

There are also other examples, however. Plays like those in Innsbruck, Erlau, Vienna, and Sterzing are representative of only one tendency of the German Easter play as it moves from its home in the Rhineland toward southern Germany and not of German Easter plays in general. The plays from Trier, Wolfenbüttel, and Osnabrück, for example, include neither an ointment purchase scene played out in naturalistic graphicness nor a *hortulanus*.[32] We find a similar situation in England. In the Hegge plays Mary addresses the Lord as if he were a gardener, thereby strictly adhering to the biblical presentation, but that Jesus also actually appears as a gardener is not clear from the rubrics. The recognition is at least wholly geared to hearing in the right way, not to seeing, to which the manuscript orthographically refers by using capital letters:

MARY:
but jentyl gardener I pray to the
if þou hym took out of his graue
telle me qwere I may hym se
þat I may go my lorde to haue

JESUS:
M.A.R.I.A. (33–37)

Not only the usually theologically purist Hegge plays, however, but also the English plays in general are in this case just as conscientious as the liturgical ceremony. Digby (95, following 1060) and Chester (347, following 432) forgo the gardener altogether, Towneley (323, following 562) probably had him, York (422, following 22) surely had him, but the recognition still takes place in both cases independently, Mary understanding by herself.[33]

In the French plays we also find hardly a single example. When they allow Jesus to appear as a gardener at all, he also presents himself as such.[34] Far more interesting is the attempt made in a Spanish Resurrection play to mediate theological interest by means of the play's own interest.[35] As Mary complains to the gardener, she is said to be "full of love/for the best man who has ever been" (*llena de amor/del mejor que nunca a sido*, 450 ff.), making this a marriage contract for her by taking up and carrying further the semantic ambivalence of a mystical language of love (455 ff.). Mary conceives the garden in a profane manner, points out that so far as she is concerned, she considers herself already the fiancée of the man whom she is seeking and also misunderstands the still insistent courting of the one she has refused:

Para que os llamais muger
del otro? Siendo finado,
que bien os puede hazer?
Yo soy bivo, y tengo padre

en las mas rrica majada;
tengo hazienda no pensada,
y soy higo de una madre
la mejor y mas honrrada.
Tengo ovejas quantas quiero
so una paloma sin yel,
y tengo un abrevadero
que no ay semejante a el,
y es una gloria mi apero.
Aosadas, si me mirais
con ojos del coraçon,
qu'en dos palabras digais
que soy pulido garçon,
y otro tanto me querais.
Çinco brancas os apuesto
que aunque me deçis de no,
que no es mas galan que yo,
ni de mas hermoso jesto,
ni mejor que yo lucho. (472–94)

Why do you call yourself the wife
of the other man? Being dead,
what good can he do you?
I am alive, and I have a father
in the finest sheepfold;
I have a farm unimaginable,
I am the son of a mother
who is the best and most honored.
I have as many sheep as I want,
under a dove without gall
and I have a trough
that has no peer,
and it's the glory of my sheepcote.
I'll bet if you'd look at me
with the eyes of the heart,
in two words you'd say
that I'm a polished fellow
and you'd like me as much as the other.
I'll bet you real money,

although you'd deny it,
he's no more gallant than I,
nor has a handsomer face,
nor fucks any better than I do.

Two interests are clearly evident here. Jesus asks Mary Magdalene to look at him with the mystical *ojos del coraçon*, the eyes of the heart, which we have already found in our homily, but he does not appear to her as the transfigured, resurrected Christ; rather, he identifies himself explicitly as a *hortolano* and is addressed as such by Mary Magdalen—as a gardener, whose request the sorrowing woman can only find clumsy and tasteless:

Mi alma no sufre oyr
un colloquio tan grosero (495–96)

My soul cannot endure hearing
Such a crude insulting speech.

Everything this gardener says about himself, everything he claims to possess, his riches as well as his bodily attractions, can be theologically associated, and yet in this case the misunderstanding is clearly blamed on God. This Jesus-*hortulanus* does not merely play with words, he also plays with Maria, he acts dumb: what she tells him about her heavenly spouse and about the Trinity, is *algarvia* (519), utterly incomprehensible chatter, which she might nonetheless explain in greater detail. In this way, however, the play still becomes a play with a good—that is, a didactic—intention. As Mary Magdalen enlightens the gardener and thus the audience, the gardener becomes increasingly explicit in his self-praise. However, it is only when he finally reveals himself as the mystical Gardener that Mary Magdalen is also able to see him with the right eyes:

CHRISTUS:
Ora, mirad si os engaño
en pediros por esposa
que yo's digo, qu'es preçiosa
mi cavaña, y el rrevaño
come mi fruta sabrosa.

MARIA:
Valame Dios soberano!
quien eres, o como as nonbre?

que yo te digo, hortolano,
que nunca vi en puro honbre
un rrenonbre tan loçano.
Desata la pena mia,
que me confunde el dolor.

CHRISTUS:
Alça tus ojos, Maria.

MARIA:
O mi maestro y Señor,
mi gloria, y bien, y alegria! (640–54)

CHRISTUS:
Now see if I am deceiving you
in courting you for my spouse
when I tell you that my shepherd's hut
is precious, and the flock
as sweet as my fruit.

MARIA:
Help me, O Sovereign God!
Who are you, or what is your name?
Let me tell you, gardener,
that I never saw a mere man
with such a shining reputation.
Let my pain break forth,
for grief confounds me.

CHRISTUS:
Raise your eyes, Mary.

MARIA:
O my Master and Lord,
my glory, good, and delight!

Although in the end the *hortolano* himself is drawn into the ambivalence of the mystical language of love, this conclusion alone does not suffice to obscure the fact that the appearance is at first acted out precisely in its phenomenality. Even if the gardener's crude and insulting speech (*colloquio grosero*) did not descend into the sexual but was instead brought under didactic control, the whole scene would still depend on the phenomenal deception, and thus the recognition, along with the following *no toques a mi* (*noli me tangere*) and the reporting mission, once again stand out against the background of a breach of consistency, that is, the shifting into another dimension—the kerygmatic dimension.

We have intentionally dilated somewhat longer on the Lord's appearance to Mary Magdalene, for it is particularly instructive with regard to the question we are pursuing. If we survey the whole spectrum of the possibilities that are sought, seized, or avoided in this scene, the tension and divergence between the interests of the play and those of theology once again become visible. They were already evident in our analysis of the liturgical celebration. However, the vernacular play allows us to fully recognize that it had to be constituted in direct opposition to the liturgical forerunner. And indeed it did so precisely where the ceremony rejected and excluded play-forms for theological reasons. It is the play that first clearly reveals where the analogy to the emancipation model that was developed in Murray's *Excursus* has to be abandoned. The *Christophany* suggests a parallel with the final phase of the Dionysus ritual, and thus with Murray's *theophany*, in which he sees the ritual prototype of the Aristotelian *anagnorisis*, and which he describes in the following way: "An *anagnoris*—discovery or recognition—of the slain and mutilated *daimon*, followed by his resurrection or apotheosis or, in some sense, his epiphany in glory. This I shall call by the general name *Theophany*. It naturally goes with a *peripeteia* or extreme change of feeling from grief to joy."[36] This definition can easily be applied to religious drama: such a change, such a transition from a lament (by the pious women) to an appearance of the resurrected God, is involved in the epiphany of Christ as well. The analogy can be evaluated in two ways: structurally-functionally and functionally-structurally. Frye takes the first path, since he assumes that *anagnorisis* is a universal archetype, a phase in the "quest myth." This assumption leads to the difficulties analyzed at the beginning of our discussion, the attempt to maintain the formalization of the archetypes against the threat of re-substantialization proceeding precisely from the claim to universality. Following Luhmann's suggestion, we have decided to follow the second path. And in fact giving precedence to the concept of function seems to be the only way to allow the problematizing of structural constructions that our analyses seek to produce. The ceremony and the play both appeal to an ambivalent biblical passage, and each of them reads it differently: the ceremony concentrates on the divine call and subordinates the *hortulanus*. The play, on the contrary, seizes on what should really not exist: the metamorphosis. It reads the passage no longer in an unequivocally kerygmatic manner but tends toward a mythical-archetypal interpretation and plays the epiphany of Christ back into the dimension of the phenomenal and naturalistic.

Thus the reference to a "three-day rhythm of dying, going out of the world, and resurrection, which is found in the myth of Attis and other dying gods, and found its way into our Easter celebrations,"[37] tells us nothing at all about the function of the *agon/pathos/anagnorisis* sequence in religious drama. On the contrary, situating the Christian Easter in the archetypal pattern in this way obscures the problem. For if an *anagnorisis* can be seen as archetypal, that is not because of the discovery of a homology; rather, it results from functional-structural comparisons such as we have presented here.

Thus archetypal functions are no longer reconcilable with the self-concept of the Christian Easter. The play uses them to fulfill needs other than those of the ceremony; it includes what the latter excludes. The relationship between the ceremony and religious drama is not an "emancipatory" one between "Christian rite and Christian drama" (Hardison) but rather a relationship of implicit mutual contradiction. Seldom does this tension become so clear as in the case of the *hortulanus* metamorphosis, for a play-form as explicit as this one can seldom be juxtaposed with a theological exegesis as expressly contradictory as that of our homily.

IV

The concluding scene of the vernacular Easter play, the disciples' race to the tomb, is also located wholly within the ambivalence of kerygma and mythos. The biblical account, according to which John was indeed the first to arrive at the sepulcher, but Peter was the first to enter it (John 20:1–10), leaves us with a remaining question regarding motivation, as does Christ's appearance as a gardener. According to Gregory the Great, Peter and John signify the pagan church and the synagogue; Jews were indeed the first to arrive at the tomb but nevertheless did not enter it, because they did not believe in the one who had died for them.[38] However, this exegetical rescue of a biblically unmotivated detail cannot be translated into visibility. On the other hand, it would be easy to translate another motivation, which the ceremony, as we have already shown in chapter 1, part III, finds for itself in deviating from the biblical presentation: since the disciples have already heard the glad tidings from Mary Magdalene, their going to the sepulcher takes place against the background of the eager expectation of another confirmation of what they have heard. The fact that John arrives first can thus be seen as the result of a "race" to the longed-for goal. With this new interpretation of the biblical account it may be possible to explain why only a few ceremonies insist on the point that John let Peter go in first.[39] Characteristically, the ceremony nevertheless acknowledges the "race" only with great hesitation. In only about a quarter of the texts collected by Young do the rubrics require strict adherence to the letter of the accompanying antiphon *Currebant duo simul, et ille alius discipulus praecucurrit citius Petro, et venit primus ad monumentum.* In most cases it is mentioned only that the two disciples go (*ire, vadere*) to the tomb while the antiphon is being sung or else arrive there (*ad Sepulchrum venientes*) and display the empty shroud. Here lies the kerygmatic *telos*, and everything that cannot be associated with this telos (such as the precedence accorded Peter) or might disturb it (such as the race) is for the most part excluded—exactly as in the Type III celebration the gardener is frequently omitted.

Once again, things are quite different in the play. What the ceremony at most admitted as a "race" to the desired goal is in the play introduced with a concrete wager:

JOHANNES:
Petre, ich wette mit dir vmb eyn phert:
ich loffe hewer zirrer wen vert!

PETRUS:
Johannes, ich wette mit dyr vmb eyn ku,
ich lofe sirrer wen du! (Vienna, 1139–40)

JOHANNES:
Peter, I'll bet you a horse
I can run faster than anyone.

PETRUS:
John, I'll bet you a cow,
I can run [faster than you!]

This wager[40] is still another good example of the fact that the sequence of events that the vernacular play takes over from the liturgical *visitatio* is governed by the dualistic structure provided by the preceding *descensus* and the archetypal dimension it opens up. As in the merchant play and in the epiphany of Christ, the disciples' movement is also acted out in that free space constituted by the ritualistic victory over the Devil. There the decisive event has already occurred—in contrast with the ceremony, where the decisive event occurs at the end: in the concluding *surrexit* announcement made by disciples arriving at the sepulcher. In the play, the kerygmatic telos is already achieved; it has lost its object through the visually represented resurrection and descent into hell. This de-functionalization of the kerygma nevertheless finds its most significant expression precisely in the race between the two disciples. This competition stands at right angles to the spontaneous "race" to the desired goal; it finds its motivation first of all in itself: it is an elementary play-form, as both disciples position themselves in a relationship of opposition and now carry, or rather run, it out. Of course, the disciples do not know what the audience knows, and for them such preliminaries can hardly make sense. However, this logic is sacrificed to the law of the drama. And because in this episode no one is on hand who—like Rubin in the ointment purchase scene and the *hortulanus* in the encounter with Mary Magdalene—could assume the true play-function, it is imposed on the disciples themselves, and although the latter should in principle be just as serious as the Marys, they are permitted to turn the glad tidings into a frolic.

So the play is also not without motivations for the outcome of the wager. Whereas the ceremony, when it insists on John's earlier arrival at all, makes Peter appear as the elder of the two, the play presents a whole range of reasons: Peter is stooped over, he has a tattered cassock, a bad knee, a limp, he has overslept that morning (Vienna, 1143 ff.). Once again, Stumpfl must be credited with pointing out the ritualistic background of this kind of "degenerations." In fact, they cannot be explained without reference to the rich and persuasively demonstrated background constituted by the pagan springtime races.[41] However, these races cannot be proven to be a component part of a more comprehensive springtime play. The provable is once again used to provide surreptitious support for what is merely postulated, in order to assert the epiphenomenality of the play in contrast to an originary Germanic dramatic continuity. A more plausible assumption seems to be that here as elsewhere no ritualistic springtime play was amalgamated and undermined; rather, a mythless ritualistic custom was incorporated into a comprehensive myth and only then became a component part of a (heterogeneous) dramatic continuity. If such a ritualistic race is described in Sebastian Franck's *Weltbuch*, or if an Eastertide dance is described by a Neithart imitator as an *osterspil*,[42] then these are only ritualistic customs, not the postulated ritualistic springtime play to which the Christian Easter play is supposed to have been a reply. One of Stumpfl's chief arguments is that the biblical pattern for constructing this scene drops out. The pattern is indeed "formally sound, as most Christian etiologies are, even though the perception of it as a race does not clearly emerge from the written text, since here *currere* is used in the sense of *exire*."[43] This last point is correct, but it ignores that in this case the scene cannot be judged by the biblical source. For wherever the trek to the sepulcher takes place against the background of tense expectation, as it already did in the ceremony, a (secondary) interpretation of John 20:4 as a "race" lies close at hand. Thus we are confronted by the paradox that along with the kerygmatically oriented interpretation is given simultaneously an assembly point for pagan-ritualistic occupations. Thus the motif of limping, which Stumpfl considers an "ancient ritual form" connected with ritualistic races,[44] can itself make its way into the ceremony, so far as it is involved in an explanation for Peter's lagging behind. However, when this limping turns up in only two late texts probably under vernacular influence[45] and is a stereotype in the vernacular drama (Sterzing, Vienna, Erlau, Munich, Eger), then we see here once again the contrast between the ceremony's purist self-conception and the play's highly ambivalent self-conception.

Here again the Sterzing play goes furthest. In John's view Peter is "lazy as a worn-out nag," and among all the complaints all he hears is call for a "little bottle." In fact, a powerful attraction is exerting its influence here:

> Jetzund was ich lam und krumb,
> Nun bin ich frisch und gesunt.
> Nun se hin lieber Johannes
> Und kost auch des weines,
> Und laß uns laufen zu dem grab,
> Ob Maria war hab. (p. 166)

> *A moment ago I was lame and crippled,*
> *Now I'm fresh and healthy.*
> *Now see here, dear John,*
> *You drink some wine too,*

And let's run to the tomb
To see if Mary is right.

However, when they arrive, fortified in this way, at the empty sepulcher they sing the liturgical *Cernitis, o socii.* Once again the kerygma is not destroyed in the contrast with "something lower," and the "lower" is not judged and overcome; instead, both are incorporated into a highly ambivalent "Christian" ritualistic play. Nonetheless, the kerygmatic moment is repressed here as in hardly any other play. For characteristically, John's announcement of the Resurrection does not represent the conclusion of the whole play but rather an epilogue—which is, so far as I can see, unique in the history of the Easter play:

PETRUS DICIT AD POPULUM
Ir herren, neue mer ich euch sag:
Heut ist der heilig ostertag,
Daß man masanzen wirt weichen,
Dar umb rat ich armen und reichen:
Hüt jeder seine taschen wol,
Wen ich red als ich sol;
Mein gesell stilt als ein rab,
Was er mir ankommen mag.

JOHANNES DICIT AD POPULUM
Nun hort, ir herren all gemein,
Beide groß und auch klein:
Wie gar ein lugenhaftige zungen
Treit Peter an seinem munde.
Ich mag nit recht lenger verdagen,
Ich muß im die warheit sagen.
Er hat unsers herren drei mal verholen
Un hat das lempretel aus dem osterlamp gestolen.
Er nimt hüner, gens all geleich,
Er ist halt nit entleich,
Und spricht: vender dich vender dich,
Kanst nit gen, so trag ich dich!
Secht, das mocht in mir nit beleiben,
Wen er wolt selber nit still sweigen.

PETRUS AD JOHANNEM
Treun lieber gesell Johann du hast recht!
Wer mir nur der ein fuß geschlecht!

Wen wer etwas wil haben,
Das ligt am zusamm tragen.
Dar umb laß wir davon
Und heben ein anders an,
Wen wir gnotigs haben zu schaffen.
Ich mag nit lenger hie klaffen,
Welt ir haben ein predinger
So get zu dem Jeckel hafner,
Er sagt euch ein Neitharten var,
Es meint es sei gelogen, so ist es war. (pp. 167–68)

PETRUS DICIT AD POPULUM
Gentlemen, I tell you something else new:
Today is the holy Easter day,
On which unleavened bread is soaked,
And so I advise poor and rich:
Keep an eye on your purse,
If I speak as I should;
My comrade steals like a raven,
Whatever may come of it for me.

JOHANNES DICIT AD POPULUM
Now hark, all you good men,
Both big and small as well,
I'll tell you what a lying tongue
Peter has in his mouth.
I can in justice no longer keep silent,
I must tell the truth.
He has thrice served our Lord,
And stolen the liver from the Easter lamb.
He takes hens, and geese as well,
He is simply not easy to get rid of,
And says: come along, come along!
If you can't walk, I'll carry you!
No dryness can remain in me
If he himself won't dry up.

PETRUS AD JOHANNEM
Dear, true comrade John, you are right!
Would that I only had one bad foot!

If you want to have something,
You have to work together.
So let us go away from here,
And get someone else to help us,
If we have something important to do.
I can no longer stay here gabbing,
People, if you want a preacher,
Go to the potter Jeckel,
He'll tell you a tale like Neithart,
It's meant to be a lie, and so it's true.

The "holy Easter day"—with the reference to the "masanzen," originally the unleavened Jewish bread—alludes to the paschal celebration of Judeo-Christian tradition. Even this interpretation is immediately complicated, however, when Peter warns the audience to be wary of John, likening him to a larcenous raven, and this warning seems explicable only—as Stumpfl suggested—as a reflection of the license to steal during ritualistic processions and pagan peregrinations.[46] This same ambivalence emerges in John's retort when he combines the Easter lamb with the motif of the stolen liver, familiar to us from folktales.[47] The Christian play has thus here gone over entirely into a pagan-ritualistic this-worldliness, into the general holiday joy; as in the Shrovetide play, the actors bid farewell to the holiday community and refer those who have not yet had enough of "preaching" to the dirty jokes of the potter Jeckel, no doubt a well-known character in the town. They themselves "have something important to do," they have to go put on their play somewhere else, or else, and this is very likely, they are off to the inn to put away a few more bottles. What they are presenting may well have been intended as "a merry figure" (*fröhlich figur*), but in truth it was a highly ambivalent play that drew no less on ritualistic laxity and a wholly pagan feeling for life than on Christian Easter joy.

How could the Christian holiday nonetheless be observed with such a play? Certainly, in the vernacular tradition the going of the disciples remained confined to Germany, and even here the restrictions mentioned in connection with the appearance as a gardener are once again valid. However, the explicit abandonment of this episode altogether (Trier) or a farcical version of it (Osnabrück, Rheinish Easter Play, and also Innsbruck) makes our question all the more urgent. Might it be no accident that the conclusion of the Sterzing play so strongly recalls the Shrovetide play? Could it be that the hustle and bustle of Shrovetide gave the Easter play a comparable license? Was laughter allowed not only just before but also just after Lent? Are we dealing in both cases with a tolerated exclave of carnivalesque laxity? The following analyses of the so-called comedy of the Easter play will offer an opportunity to discuss these questions.

CHAPTER 4

From Glad Tidings to the
Risus Paschalis: The Easter Play
and Ritualistic Laughter

I

omedy" derives from *komos*, from the Dionysian procession with
whose ritualistic laxity ancient comedy used to end. The model
for the first poetics of this genre was not provided by this archaic form,
however, but rather by the intermediate comedy of the fourth century. Only
with respect to the latter could Aristotle protect laughter against Plato's
condemnation. It is legitimate to laugh at its comic mimesis—as interpreted
by Aristotle—because it represents a flaw that, as a harmless, accidental
nature, "doesn't hurt," that is, cannot entail serious damage for either the
person who has it or for those around him. Thus what archaic comedy was
and wanted has already disappeared from view: liberation from social and
political reality as the epitome of the unreasonable, the unleashing of human beings' animalistic, entirely natural drives, which paradoxically help
them break through to their true humanity and the reasonableness most
proper to them.[1] Aristotle makes this comedy moral, literary, harmless. In
doing so, he burdened for centuries all understanding and theory of comedy. We are still under his spell today.

This view also holds true when we are concerned with the comedy of
the Easter play. In the terrible soldiers at the sepulcher Plautine *milites
gloriosi* have been seen; the ridiculous Devil in the *descensus* became an
example of a nay-sayer who is harmless, in precisely the Aristotelian sense
of the word, because he is metaphysically powerless and thus incapable of
doing damage; and what followed with the merchant play, the epiphany of
Christ, and the going of the disciples, was declared to be a "burlesque" in
which all questions remained open.[2] Stumpfl's reply was not satisfactory,
but although his critics may have been able to neutralize his hypotheses,

they were not able to develop a positive counterinterpretation. However, if our attempt to reopen the discussion instigated by Stumpfl and to reach a solution is to be proven also and above all by the phenomenon of the comic, then it is obvious that we must begin where the decisive failure of the preceding discussion first became evident: in the descent into hell that it neglected.

In reality, this scene offers the key to the comedy of the Easter play. In order to demonstrate this fact, we must clear the way with an illusion that is tempting because of its superficial plausibility: the discussion of the "comic" element in its powerless, ridiculous Devil. This discussion is superficially plausible because through this figure and its role in religious drama, it is apparently possible to explain the dogma of the created nature of the Satanic counterworld by reference to the "comic conflicts" analyzed by F. G. Jünger:[3] a discrepancy in the two parties' powers evidently becomes a disproportionate challenge and the subsequent reply—this is supposed to be the descent into hell—on the part of the already victorious interlocutor. What can be constructed in this manner is nothing less than a dogmatically founded theory of the comic, a theological appropriation of laughter. However, this remains only a construction, about which theology itself knows nothing and has never known anything. All attempts at interpretation tending in this direction must turn a blind eye to the fact that the church has at no time seen in the comic and in laughter a genuine mode of salvation, and what is more important, that at no time could the church provide a foundation for it.[4] Jesus never laughed, according to John Chrysostom, and as the evidence collected by E. R. Curtius shows, the model so conceived exercised an enduring influence on medieval discussions of laughter.[5] The twelfth-century compiler Petrus Cantor thought Jesus might have laughed but only because the God-Man took on not only all our guilt but also all our *defectus* as well. Laughter is the defining characteristic of fallen humanity—this topos persisted through seventeenth-century Jansenism up to Baudelaire's *On the Essence of Laughter*. *Verba vana aut risu apta non loqui*, we read in the Rule of St. Benedict, although with the restriction that this statement holds true primarily for a *risum multum aut excessum*. At most, moderate laughter, a *modesta hilaritas*, might be permissible. Similarly, Hugo of St. Victor believes that *aliquando plus delectare solent seriis admixta ludicra*. However, in such passages, which bespeak a "benevolent toleration of laughter" (E. R. Curtius) in the sense of a mixture of jest and earnestness, there is typically no mention of laughter itself. The mixture of jest and earnestness was tolerated in the interest of the doctrinal teaching that went along with it but not as a "didactic principle" in the sense of "an interweaving of doctrine and laughter."[6] Theologians certainly did not consider evil to be ridiculous because of its metaphysical negativity. Scholasticism, which sought to provide convincing proof of this negativity, nevertheless does not regard the Devil as laughable. And fundamentally there is nothing clearer than the fact that the metaphysical negativity of sin presupposes the earthly dimension of salvation needed, sought, endangered, and possibly lost, and even in this dimension, in which religious drama took root, the ridiculous cannot fail to have an extremely confusing effect. For wherever the sinful world is laughed at its need for salvation is ignored. The Devil is powerless only with regard to God. His activities on earth are marked by omnipotence and omnipresence—even if the latter are merely "allowed."

II

The Easter play makes this ambivalence unmistakably clear. In various ways it thematizes Satan's powerlessness with respect to God at the same time as his earthly omnipotence. This theme becomes evident precisely when it presents Satan as a clueless, stupid braggart and thus most unequivocally as a laughable figure: in the dialogue with Inferus or Lucifer, which is modeled on Nicodemus and triggered by the imprisoned patriarchs' joyful expectation of their liberator's arrival.[7] Lucifer, the Lord of the infernal city, already foresees what is to come, while Satan is still boasting about having crucified the man who claimed to be God. This doubling of the diabolic counterworld is first fully developed in the Passion play, where Lucifer appears as the one who plans, foresees, and even in defeat remains the true strategist of the antidivine powers, continuing to manifest evil's pride, whereas Satan commits one tactical error after another and is still bragging about his cleverness when it has long since been revealed as stupidity. The true effect of this doubling is nonetheless already present in a preliminary form in the Easter play: the ridiculousness, the "comic nature" of Satan is a compensatory phenomenon that points to the terroristic background of perennial evil. All the same, this laughable Satan is Lucifer's emissary on earth, lurking and threatening at all times and in all places, the cunning seducer, with regard to whom we know that we are in fact defenseless. However, in the play Satan, against whose wiles and tricks we can never be sufficiently protected, is at last for once the dumb one, whom we can overcome; this time he is in for a drubbing. Meanwhile, the conquered Lucifer goes on, and in the harrowing of hell scene Satan is already no longer the ridiculous fool but rather Lucifer's highly successful governor on earth, the representative of the infernal powers.

Our previous comments regarding the "acted out" Devil are confirmed by his "comic nature": the latter becomes comprehensible only against the background of the terror that is conquered through it and always remains visible through it.[8] This "comic nature" crystallizes around an acted-out ritual, as we demonstrated; it is essentially foreign to the models and theories of literary comedy, since it is a ritual and in this sense an archaic kind of comedy. Mikhail Bakhtin's criticism of Wolfgang Kayser's well-known book makes it once again possible to work with the concept of the grotesque here.[9] That is because Bakhtin's critique of Kayser also bears on Leo Spitzer's attempt—of which Bakhtin was not aware—to extend the romantic and modern grotesque, with which Kayser was solely concerned, back into the Middle Ages. According to Spitzer, the demonic in the Middle Ages is always aligned with and subordinated to an overall world picture, but one may nevertheless wonder whether in medieval art there was not already an alienating "play with the absurd," whether it is not the case that "the desire for plenitude and the play impulse combined with the tendency to represent a demonic-comic world unilluminated by belief, out of which the representations of the sublime elements of belief then arose all the more luminously."[10] Bakhtin very clearly shows what is not taken into consideration in this kind of retrospective projection of the Romantic dualism of the grotesque and the sublime: that in this dualism it is not always a question of an aesthetic counterfigurativeness [*Gegenbildlichkeit*]; sometimes it is a question of world-orders and life-orders. "The medieval and Renaissance grotesques are pervaded by the carnivalesque sense of the world, they free the world from everything upsetting and dreadful, and make it merry and light. Everything that brought fear into the everyday world is transformed in the world of carnival into an amusing bugbear. Fear is the extreme expression of the one-sided and foolish seriousness that is overcome through laughter."[11]

Bakhtin mentions medieval religious drama only in passing. For him, the carnivalesque object of laughter is manifested primarily in the ritualistic forms that since Chambers have been commonly connected with a pagan substratum: fool and donkey festivals, deviltry in the streets, etc. It seems, however, that here religious drama has equal if not superior demonstrative force, and indeed that the ambivalence—explicitly so called by Bakhtin—of "ritual laughter" is first fully achieved in religious drama.[12] The moment of fear overcome is far more easily seen in religious drama than it is in the always already reduced ritualistic forms of carnival, since here laughter concludes a ritual that, unlike the carnivalesque exclave, itself stands out against the background of salvation-history seriousness. What it achieves is not merely a grotesque "carnivalization of consciousness" but rather a carnivalization of religious consciousness itself.[13] The grotesque of religious drama exorcises the counterworld not as do the stone facades of gothic cathedrals or the moralistic-allegorical interpretations of epic grotesque but rather in an acted-out ritual. Herein lie its uniqueness and specific character and above all the hermeneutic difficulty of thinking one's way into it. Instead of the implicit self-interpretation of static ornamentation or explicit moralization in allegorical description, we find here the processlike course of the acted-out ritual itself; we find what is realized in each new performance of the ritual. We could speak of a ritualistic grotesque and in that way indicate quite clearly the distance that separates these plays from a moralistic-aesthetic dualism of sublime and grotesque. The ritualistic grotesque is not one included within a reliable order of salvation and an experienced certainty of salvation but rather one that in the certainty of salvation is indissolubly connected with a world-reliability that must be each time achieved anew. It plays the kerygma back into myth.

III

As we have seen, the merchant play, Christ's appearance as a gardener, and the disciples' race to the sepulcher all refer, in their self-constitution, to the space of freedom conquered in the *descensus*. They draw their life from fear overcome and act out the opposition between God and the Devil in a naturalistic way. They celebrate, like all forms of ritual laughter, the return of the life-force and fertility, and they are—in their mythical-archetypal dimension—"laughing rituals."[14] Stumpfl also spoke of the "magical power of laughter, of its purifying and fertility-providing power."[15] However, he did not succeed in deriving from this description any systematic outline that could be opposed to the rightly and conclusively criticized weak interpretation of the comic, and we can now see why he was not able to do so. His fixation on the postulated physician's play and his neglect of the descent into hell prevented him from discerning the moment when terror is overcome and therefore the point where the *visitatio* sequence, which he considers in isolation, begins and is connected to the rest. Thus against a weak interpretation of the comic he can draw attention to its ritual implications; conversely he cannot also establish the comic implications of the ritual dimension he demonstrates. This is never more evident than when he mentions the *risus paschalis*, Easter laughter, only in passing, and without any reference to the Easter play.

The *risus paschalis* was a custom that persisted into the eighteenth century and whose purpose was to loosen up the Easter sermon through amusing "Easter tales" and thus to cause the parishioners to laugh. Folklorists have succeeded in tracing it back as far as the fourteenth century, but it is certainly much older, for the earliest documents alluding to it already speak of it as something ancient and known to everyone. If one glances through these documents, especially those gathered together by H. Fluck, one quickly sees that the debates elicited by the *risus paschalis* are relevant to the comedy of the Easter plays as well.[16] On one side we find its defenders—for the most part members of the lower clergy—for whom it is an indispensable means of waking up a sleepy congregation or else, more generally, regard it as an opportunity to put jest in the service of doctrinal teaching. Taken alone, such arguments are easily seen to be secondary justifications of a custom that can all too easily be abused and that was subjected to heavy criticism. These "Easter tales" could be closely connected with the sermon (amusing representations of the descent into hell, entertaining stories about the disciples at Emmaus), but they could also be aimed at well-known weaknesses of certain parishioners, who consequently saw them as a reason for leaving the church or who never came at all.

However, Easter laughter arose primarily from obscene farcical motifs—which were occasionally made understandable by mimicking them. Complaints about obscenity run through all the ecclesiastical protests, from Oecolampadius's polemical *De risu paschalis*, through Geiler von Kaisersberg, and up to Erasmus. The evidence cited by individual critics must be given differing weights, since in the sixteenth century the *risus paschalis* was drawn into the Reformation controversies, in Oecolampadius for example,

and served to disqualify "papist clerics." However, even a man like Geiler
not only urges moderation but offers a fundamental warning against "lis-
tening to tales and fables and funny stories. As the old preachers did, the old
roosters, who told a fable on Easter day and made an Easter play."[17] That
should provide very firm proof that the funny stories and tomfoolery in the
sermon constitute the same phenomenon as the comparable outgrowths of
the Easter play and indeed that these may have received a decisive impetus
from the sermon custom. At the very least, they are the same phenomenon
in principle, and criticism of one is relevant to the other. That is precisely
why the *risus paschalis* attested to by this highly controversial debate is so
valuable in our context. Scholastic theology, on the basis of which people
sought in subtle ways to justify the comic elements in the plays, does not
recognize the *risus paschalis*. Where it enters into the theologians' pur-
view, it is criticized. Easter laughter appears in a perspective "from below."
Stumpfl's conjecture that it is a pre-Christian form of the boisterousness of
the pagan festival of the dead is once again a hypothesis that prematurely
resolves the problem.[18] There can be no doubt, however, that Easter laughter tends to paganize Christian Easter joy. For the time being, this joy has
nothing to do with laughter and hilarity. The play may be conceived as a
"merry figure," as "bringing salvation," the visualization of the Easter event
that announces the certainty of the Resurrection—but wherever it admits
the *risus paschalis*, it is no longer concerned with the glad tidings so understood, and the kerygmatic *surrexit* celebration is once again played back into
an archetypal dimension, into an archaic "laughing ritual."

IV

The *risus paschalis* has the character of a reply: it derives its life from fear
overcome. In this aspect it is far removed from the ridiculousness of the sort
of immoderate provocation that makes up the "comic conflict" in F. G.
Jünger's sense. Nevertheless, this conflict is by its nature also involved in
religious drama. It is as if structures alone could ground neither comedy nor
laughter, or more precisely, it is as if there were no structure of a comic
object in itself, as if on the contrary the object first emerged beyond its
structure, namely in its particular perception as "laughable." In this respect
it seems tempting to analyze the reply-character of Easter laughter a little
more closely, and there is reason to think that such an analysis will prove
useful for our systematic approach.

"Laughter is absolutely proper to human existence, and that means that it is part of our specificity." Starting from this proposition, J. Ritter many years ago set forth a theory of laughter whose resources have still not been exhausted and which can be connected with the drift of our argument in a most welcome way.[19] It is one of the most important correctives to two traditional explanations of laughter: the centuries-old theory of contrast or incongruity and the theory of degradation represented in particular by Bergson. In opposition to both these explanations, Ritter can show that laughter did in fact result from a contrast in representation and apparently also, as Bergson would have it, judges in the name of the dominant norm, in the name of comprehensibility; but he also shows that this norm is thereby itself implicated at the same time. For what stands in contrast to it, what is excluded from it as negative, inessential, and ridiculous is not merely negative but only something that the particular normative seriousness cannot entirely do away with and that belongs to the whole of life just as much as what counts as positive and essential. Ritter maintains that in laughter the secret appurtenance of the excluded, the void, to the whole of life is made visible. Laughter, "seen from within and as expressive, is in no way connected with the feeling of emptiness, but rather with the positive, affirmative states of joy, pleasure, enjoyment, and happiness."[20] And thus it transfers the negative itself into its own positivity. It retains what seriousness has excluded, holds it fast, confirms it in its positive appurtenance to the whole of life, and acts it out against the normative reasonableness. The norm itself is at stake, while laughter reveals it in the narrowness of an exclusive principle.

Thus a model can be developed from the theory of laughter that coincides precisely with the schema of exclusion and inclusion that underlies our analysis of the ambivalence of kerygma and myth in general. It is as if this ambivalence, along with the *risus paschalis*, found its confirmation in the Easter play—indeed, as if it found there its most significant expression. It is no accident that Ritter also illustrates the reply-character of laughter by means of an ambivalent phenomenon: the ambiguity of puns. Here, an apparently harmless and respectable realm of meaning is invaded by another that is excluded from it, and in such a manner that the excluded appears wearing the mask of the respectable and permitted. The comic thus emerges in a double movement: "first, by going beyond the given order into a realm excluded from it, and second by making this excluded realm visible in and through the excluding realm itself."[21] The latter is implicated as what counts as respectable and thus as normative. Laughter affects and destroys its object only superficially. In reality it unmasks the norm itself, it reveals it in the narrowness of an exclusive principle. The norm is involved, insofar as laughter once again invokes what it has set aside. There is hardly a more striking example than the ridiculous devil. It is one thing to say that this ridiculousness targets an unfounded claim to mastery, an immoderate provocation, to use Jünger's terms, and another to see in this laughter the confirmation of a secret appurtenance of the excluded, that is, of the dualism, to the whole of the lifeworld. The excluding norm, that is, the monotheistic dogma that evil is merely tolerated, is the implicit target of laughter.[22] What theology represses returns in laughter at the ritually conquered unconquerable.

V

With this formulation we are no longer operating with Ritter's terminology but rather with Freud's, which does not come up here accidentally. For Freud also describes laughter—as Wolfgang Preisendanz has already pointed out—as a way of positivizing something excluded but in a way not foreseen by Ritter, in which what is brought in appears in the mode of a "return": as a gain in pleasure against "the challenge of critical judgement," against "the repressible activity of civilization."[23] Ritter's apology for laughter is dependent on the premises of the Romantic theory of the comic. To play with the norm is for him to be beyond reasonableness, to act out infinity in opposition to it. However, it can just as well mean to go back before the norm, to tap sources of pleasure that reasonableness has closed off. Only when it is read in Freudian terms does Ritter's model come into full congruence with our formula of playing the kerygma back into myth and only then can it open up the special ritual moment of the *risus paschalis* as well. For if this laughter lives on anxiety overcome, then that means, interpreted in Freudian terms, that it draws its increase in pleasure from "an economy in expenditure on inhibition or suppression," from the anxiety cathexis that here, in the ritual victory over the unconquerable, can be done away with.[24]

Spared anxiety cathexis also indirectly frees up the comic element in the *visitatio* sequence. As an immediate source of pleasure there appears in addition what can be explained in Freudian terms as a comparison of two cathexes that takes place in the preconscious—in accord with the model of the de-sublimation of the sublime Freud himself described:

When, therefore, the procedures that I have discussed for the degradation of the sublime allow me to have an idea of it as though it were something commonplace, in whose presence I need not pull myself together but may, to use the military formula, "stand easy," I am being spared the increased expenditure of the solemn restraint; and the comparison between this new ideational method (instigated by empathy) and the previously habitual one, which is simultaneously trying to establish itself—this comparison once again creates the difference in expenditure which can be discharged by laughter.[25]

Making kerygmatic seriousness itself available for such a comparison seems at first glance no more within the horizon of Christian Easter joy than the naturalistic-sexual boisterousness into which this seriousness deteriorates: in the *risus paschalis* what is repressed by Christian happiness returns. Nevertheless, this comedy is triggered by elements that are already present within the Christian realm: the figure of the ointment-seller, Jesus as *hortulanus*, the disciples. Without these starting points, without the "glad tidings" incarnated in these figures, what we earlier described as the carnivalization of religious consciousness becomes unthinkable. One is reminded here of the mechanism of intensified pleasure-development that Freud describes as the "principle of assistance":

A possibility of generating pleasure supervenes in a situation in which another possibility of pleasure is obstructed so that, as far as the latter alone is concerned, no pleasure would arise. The result is a generation of pleasure far greater than that offered by the supervening possibility. This has acted, as it were, as an *incentive bonus*; with the assistance of the offer of a small amount of pleasure, a much greater one, which would otherwise have been hard to achieve, has been gained.[26]

The announcement of the "glad tidings" is the point at which the kerygma offers itself as a trigger for potential quests for pleasure. The "glad tidings" themselves release what they repress—and it is precisely thereby that they are revealed as repressive—and yet the Christian Easter goes on as though the springtime celebration alluded to in its very name did not belong to the whole of the lifeworld.

Thus it is once again precisely the ambivalence of kerygma and myth that must be detached from Stumpfl's substantialist conception of a self-maintaining substratum. Just as in the case of the Devil a pagan ritual figure is not brought into a Christian play but rather the dualism becomes visible in the—officially merely "tolerated"—Satan of Judeo-Christian tradition, in that of the *visitatio* sequence as well no Christian Marys play is interpolated into a ritualistic physician's play, but rather the kerygma is played back into the myth it has itself negated. If we now apply this to the comic, we find that in laughter the naturalistic *ōstarūn* is seized and played into the Christian Easter play. With this modification, Stumpfl will have to be protected against Bausinger's criticism, to which I now return. In the questionable scenes, he says, "a comic element asserts itself, an expressly anti-ritualistic tendency which is, it is true, very quickly 'ritualized,' just as—thus far one could go along with Stumpfl—in traditional plays. But Stumpfl rejects this basically theatrical element from the outset."[27] The impulses leading to such secondary ritualizations are not indicated; what on the contrary clearly suggests a primary ritualization of the kerygmatic, namely the massively imported naturalistic themes, is not mentioned. Bausinger is thinking here only in terms of the opposition between Christian and worldly, and consequently everything that cannot be accounted for theologically is seen as theatrical elaboration, "secularization," as it is put explicitly.[28] If this comic element belonged to the secular, the theatrical, then it would have to remain vital today. However, it has become foreign to us, dead, and precisely because laughing depends upon "the order, out of which and by means of which the material becomes laughable, being effective with regard to life."[29] The effectiveness with regard to life of the *risus paschalis* was grounded, however, far away from any secular theatricality, in its ritualistic reply-character, in its embedding in a mythical-archetypal experience of the Resurrection of God.

This laughter reveals itself as a ritual laughter also and precisely at the point at which the comic appears to go beyond the mystery of salvation, and even to use the salvation-history event as a pretext in order to receive from it an entry into a purely worldly scene. The tavern brawl in the Emmaus play can serve as an example. In a detailed study, Gustave Cohen many years ago attempted to show that this scene was already embedded "embryonically" in the Gospel of St. Luke, had continually "evolved," and had taken on an increasingly "secular" character.[30] However, as always happens in explanations conceived in evolutionary terms, the impetus that sets the whole process in motion remains unexplained. For this reason it is now important that the *dum fabularentur* (Luke 24:15) become, in a free interpretation of the biblical context, one of the most important triggers for Easter tales and thus for the *risus paschalis*. This Easter laughter might then have taken over the whole Emmaus story; that is, the inn does not need to have been first a discovery of the play but can already have been present in the Easter Monday sermon. It is certain, however, that it was present in the overall context of the continuing holiday. For this day was the day of the journey to Emmaus, which began with the visit to churches and cemeteries and ended in the tavern. Here was recuperated what had been forgone during Lent, just as in the Sterzing Friar play, where after the disappearance of the Lord, Luke and Cleophas get drunk, beat up the innkeeper, and shout at his wife when she interferes:

> Ich geb dir eins an die rotzen,
> Und tanz dir um auf der votzen. (p. 51)

> *I'll lambaste you on the snout,*
> *And dance you around on your cunt.*

Again, this kind of comedy is not acted out with the aesthetic distance of the theatrical but rather with carnivalesque boisterousness, ritual laughter in Bakhtin's sense. What is invoked in it is not simply worldliness but a very specific domain of life, the one that is repressed during Lent. And once again it is made visible in and through the excluded domain itself. After the disciples have left the inn, they discuss the experience they have had. Cleophas convinces the doubtful Luke, and as if to strengthen their conviction, together they drink the rest of the wine and eat the rest of the Easter eggs, which in the Middle Ages, precisely because the church required that they be forgone during Lent, had lost none of their pagan, fertility-magic significance. And it is out of just this ambivalence that Peter asks that the concluding, common *Christ is risen* be sung.

It is true that the Sterzing Friar play is an extreme, just as is the Sterzing Easter play, but we must pay attention to extremes if we want to grasp in all its clarity the impetus behind processes of so-called secularization and literarization. The comedy of the Easter play has its ritualistic "place in life" in a still preliterary institution. It brings into the ecclesiastical realm what the latter excludes. This excluded element is not secular worldliness but simply what stands in opposition to religious seriousness, and is not for all that nonreligious. I return once more to Ritter: the essence of seriousness requires half of the lifeworld to exist in the form of the opposite and negative, "not because man lives in two worlds, but because, in Platonic terms, in order that something may be posited as existing essentially, something has to become non-existent as its other."[31] Laughter in religious drama does not distinguish the ecclesiastical from the secular; rather, it essentially transcends the identification of the religious with ecclesiastical seriousness. Since it brings into this seriousness another kind of religiosity that was excluded from it, it lends the play a broad inclusiveness that can be seen in its popularity and through which alone this popularity can be explained. Herein lies its proximity but also the difference already mentioned with regard to the Shrovetide play, with which the Sterzing Easter plays in particular show an unmistakable relationship. Independently of the question of source and influence, we must remember that the comedy of the Easter play is distinguished from the carnivalesque exclave of the Shrovetide play in that here the excluded element itself is involved.[32] Hence the religious drama Bakhtin ignores is precisely the place where the "ancient ritual orientation of laughter toward the most lofty" is more clearly demonstrable than anywhere else.[33] Carnival laughter draws its life from the benevolent tolerance on the part of that world of seriousness from which it is excluded. In religious drama, on the other hand, it is ignited by this seriousness itself and in the process positivizes what the latter negativized.

PART 2

The Inferred Beginning: The Adam Play

CHAPTER 5

The Fall in the Ambivalence of Dramatic and Substantial Dualism

I

The Old French *Ordo representacionis Ade* is the oldest extant vernacular play.[1] Its first two parts, the fall into sin and Cain's fratricidal murder of Abel, have no prototypes in the liturgical tradition. They nevertheless take off, like the celebration, from the *responsoria*, and the way in which they do this once again makes the distinction between the liturgical and vernacular traditions visible at its central point. The scaffolding for both scenes is provided by the *Sexagesima Responsoria* in the Gregorian *Liber Responsalis*.[2] The play deviates from this sequence in two cases. The first involves an abbreviation: the passages relating to the creation of Eve are omitted, because in the play Eve appears as already created. The second deviation is more important. The sixth *responsorium* contains the divine prohibition, the seventh the return of the God who punishes. The Gregorian sequence thus leaves out the fall proper. The play, however, clearly focuses precisely on the fall. Of the 590 verses in the first part, 273 (113–386)—more than half—are devoted to the temptation. The deployment of the vernacular tradition thus already occurs against the background of this event, whose differing variations we have been able to follow in the Easter play and which can be reduced to the formula of exclusion on the one hand and inclusion on the other. For with the temptation scene, the *responsorium* sequence is not merely supplemented; rather, the play takes up something the liturgical presentation had excluded. A central interest of the play is thereby disclosed and will become even clearer in the amplifications that this inclusion bestows upon the biblical presentation.

The biblical account refers only to Eve and the serpent and not to the scenes with the Devil that in the Adam play precede the temptation proper.

In the play, a swarm of demons appears immediately after the divine prohibition, and as the first rubric indicates (following 122), they first indulge in mischief through provocative gestures *per plateas*, hence evidently amid the audience, and only then approach paradise, in order to point out to Eve the forbidden fruit. Their leader soon emerges from the swarm, tempts Adam, fails, returns to the gate of hell, seeks advice from his fellows, takes another turn through the audience, and then undertakes a second attempt (following 172). Again he fails, returns to the gate of hell, and moves among the spectators again before finally approaching Eve (following 204). After he has gotten her ear, he withdraws again before returning as the biblical serpent and completing his seduction of Eve (following 292). However, his role does not end there. He bestows thorns and thistles on the couple driven out of paradise (following 518; the biblical presentation leaves this up to God's announcement of this punishment), and assisted by his fellow demons, he finally leads them chained and fettered into hell (following 590). Soon thereafter the swarm of demons reappears among the spectators in order to indicate in advance that the second part, the fratricide, should be seen as the Devil's work as well. Consistently, this second part also ends with Cain and Abel being led off to hell (following 744).

The identification of the serpent with the Devil is not, of course, original with the Adam play; it has been shown to be already present in the New Testament, and thus a consequence of the salvation-history interpretation of the Old Testament.[3] The originality of the play consists in the way it makes dramatically exciting material out of this identification. While in this case the serpent merely completes what the Devil, in repeated attempts and making use of all sorts of persuasive arts—often praised for their psychological subtleties—has already begun, in the figure of Satan the play constructs a dramatic-dualistic counterpart to the divine *figura* of the initial and concluding scenes. This structure is possible only in the play, not in the celebration. The latter can admit—and does so with considerable hesitation—representatives of the pagan counterworld, such as the ointment-seller and the grave watch at the tomb, but in the consecrated space of the church there is no room for the lords of this counterworld. Not until the play was moved outside was the Devil set free and a dramatic counterpart thus made available, and this freedom was made use of everywhere. In this way the procession of the prophets in the Adam play continues the dualistic stylization of the first part, in that each prophet is led away to hell immediately after he has made his prophecy. This procession is something invented by the play for which there is no model in either the extant versions of the liturgical *Ordo prophetarum* or in its source, the pseudo-Augustinian *Sermo contra Judaeos, Paganos et Arianos de Symbolo*.[4] A very similar example is found in the *Sponsus*, which also dates from the twelfth century, where it is only in the final vernacular versions that Jesus, in contrast with what we read in Matthew 25:1–13, is not content with the *vos ignosco* but explicitly condemns the foolish virgins to hell (*En enfern ora seret meneias*), and this judgment is immediately carried out by the demons: *Modo accipiant eas Demones, et precipitentur in infernum.*[5] Devils are not only required when it is a question of carrying off the dead so that the play can move on. They may do this, but their function is never limited to mere stage technique. It fulfills a basic requirement of dramatic illustration, and hardly any of the plays forgoes the opportunity to bring hell into the work for this purpose.

Since M. Sepet's discussion of "semi-liturgical drama" scholars have considered the liturgical substratum of the Adam play as proof of its "transitional character" and thus implied that the celebration continues to develop organically.[6] In the process it is ignored that the celebration did not move beyond—but rather preserved and handed down—a particular stage, and that on the other hand, the play from the outset manifests a level of quantitative and qualitative elaboration that cannot be derived in evolutionary terms from contemporary liturgical forms. In his critique of evolutionism, Hardison pointed to the differing character of the two traditions but saw this difference only in external matters such as length and techniques of versification and staging and sought to explain it only in a chronological manner: "a strong vernacular tradition existed in Norman England in the twelfth century. This tradition undoubtedly was a branching off from the liturgical tradition, but the branching must have occurred before liturgical drama developed its typical complex forms. After the branching, the vernacular drama followed a course of development quite different from that of the Latin drama."[7] Hardison did not see, or did not wish to see, that this difference is not quantitative but rather structural in nature. The recognition of a structurally grounded discontinuity between the two traditions is incompatible with the emancipation model borrowed from Murray, by which Hardison links himself to the Darwinian evolutionary school that he criticizes in the person of Chambers. Herein lies the chief contradiction in his allegedly "archetypal" approach, which causes him to fall back into an evolutionary way of annexing the play to the liturgical tradition and to overlook the obvious. That the difference between celebration and play does not involve quantitative matters alone but also structures is shown not only by the Adam play but also, as we mentioned earlier, by the *Seinte Resurreccion*, which also dates from the twelfth century.

Barring the discovery of new texts from an earlier period, the fact that these twelfth-century plays represent a starting point need not be put in question. The high level of elaboration in the very first vernacular texts, which is striking in comparison with the stagnating celebration, can to a large extent be balanced against their other possibilities. Along with the figure of the Devil is made available the whole counterworld he represents, and in religious drama this counterworld is that of the Jewish people. The difference between the celebration and the play is once again typical. The liturgical *Ordo prophetarum* goes at most so far as to allow some Jews and a couple of pagans to appear in the middle of the church's nave; both groups are urged by the *vocatores* to lend their belief to the prophecies.[8] The Adam play is the first to pick out a particular representative of the synagogue who enters into a debate with Isaiah and makes fun of the sprig that should bear a blossom (833 ff.). This scene, in which the previously mentioned *Sermo contra Judaeos* and a *Dialogus de altercatione ecclesiae et synagogae* (also pseudo-Augustinian)[9] are contaminated, returns a few centuries later in the *Disputatio ecclesiae et synagogae*, a broadly acted-out call for conversion that is particularly typical of the German Passion plays but which also degenerated into a wholly un-Christian call to wreak vengeance on those who had killed the Christian God.[10]

The *Seinte Resurreccion* offers an entirely similar picture. It ends with the deployment of the grave watch, which Caiaphas himself leads to the sepulcher, where a Levite priest makes them swear on Moses' Law to arrest anyone who approaches the place—which soon thereafter happens, with the arrival of Joseph of Arimathea. It is precisely this arrest of Joseph that makes it possible to reconstruct with certainty the progress of the Jews play, since it seems possible to explain the inclusion of this scene only if later on use is made of a corresponding episode from the *Gesta Pilati*. In the latter the guards return at just the right moment with the bad news for the high priests, since the latter are already worried about Joseph's miraculous disappearance from the prison and therefore inclined to buy the soldiers' silence with gold.[11] We can thus assume that the early *Seinte Resurreccion* already had a developed Jews play and thus anticipated the German Easter plays by two to three centuries in this respect as well (this is shown by the fact that Caiaphas and the Jewish council, the request to Pilate for a grave watch at the sepulcher, and also a guard scene between the Resurrection and the descent into hell are constants).

Having completed this excursus on the history of the genre, let us now return to the systematic approach. What has to be excluded in the liturgical framework is included by the play. Visualization of salvation history as a drama of salvation first becomes possible in this way, and the Adam play posits—as it immediately seizes upon these possibilities with its emphatic dualistic stylizing of the story of the fall—the programmatic starting point of the vernacular tradition. It presents salvation history as a drama of salvation, or more precisely, it presents the beginning of this history as the first act of a drama. However, does this drama still remain truly a salvation-history drama?

II

The biblical narrative of the fall is an etiological saga, which with the figure of the serpent points to a mythological substratum. The latter has a broad spectrum that reaches from the serpent of original chaos as far as the original serpent in its double meaning as a power that both creates life and devours it. Nowhere in the ancient East is any literary parallel to the biblical narrative to be found. However, there is no doubt that with the serpent the Yahwist is alluding to non-Jewish myths according to which gods of chaos in the form of serpents and dragons were engaged in a battle against creator gods.[12] He brings them in to distinguish Jewish belief in the almighty creator from those ancient Oriental ideas. On the other hand, however, precisely the allusive character of the serpent inevitably poses difficulties for any interpretation that sees in the serpent no more than a "requirement of visualization" for events that take place within human beings.[13] Certainly Genesis 3 is concerned with man and his guilt, but this guilt remains connected in a veiled way with "a power opposed to God, which played a part in man's falling away from God, and mortally threatens human life in all times."[14] The fact that God damns the serpent makes all the more urgent the question as to whether he, the Almighty, has allowed the serpent to do his unholy work: this damnation is unable to bring the story out of the dualistic twilight. If we want to reconcile its etiological telos with the monotheistic premise, something previously known and previously believed must be brought into it and maintained in opposition to its graphicness.

At first glance it seems as if the Old French Adam play has it easier in this regard. It no longer reads the biblical account as a saga about the origin of the hardships of human life but rather as the beginning of a history of salvation. The serpent no longer signals a broken myth; instead, it is a mere metamorphosis of the Devil, and even if at first this Devil is allowed to succeed, Adam and Eve already know about the progress of salvation history and thus about their future redemption: in the moment of the fall this redemption is already figurally present (333 ff., 383 ff., 587 ff.). What the Devil can and may do is determined by God. The Devil is God's creation, and his function is to put men's obedience to the test. That the play develops him into a dramatic dualistic counterpart entrusted with this task seems theologically not only legitimate but even necessary: God has given Satan full power to carry out this test.

However, all these theological justifications precede the play as premises but are not also convertible into its graphic nature. The fact that the victor is himself overcome later on does not yet prove that only a dramatic and not a substantial dualism is involved here. Ultimately God has to put quite a lot of things to work in order to avoid the consequences of what is supposed to be a test he himself has set up. That the represented dramatic dualism does not in fact reflect a substantial dualism is not something the play teaches and demonstrates but rather something that is once again brought into the play beforehand as a paradox of belief and that must be maintained against its graphic nature, or more precisely, it should have had to be brought in and maintained. For it may be doubted that the audience adhered to the premise rather than to what was shown, and what is shown is the dualism, immediately comprehensible and plausible, whereas the premise is simply incomprehensible.

We must however go further and ask whether this ambivalence first becomes virulent in the perspective of the audience and its reception or whether the author and the production are already affected by it. Certainly moral and theological interest in the depiction of human sinfulness and the play's specific interest in the Devil's arts of temptation coincide. However, the whole functions once again only on the assumption that evil is merely tolerated. Since the symbolization of this assumption is omitted, the act of setting free the Devil's wiles becomes theologically ruinous. What is decisive is not the happy ending but rather the question as to why it ever started, why the Almighty gave evil such a free hand that he later on had to sacrifice his own son in order to put everything back in order—in short, why, given the assumption of omnipotence, salvation had to have a history at all. Myth also has stories that end well. Thus it is not the conception of the end but rather that of the beginning that must distinguish the unique salvation history from the plurality of mythical histories. That is precisely the point of the doctrine of the fall, with which evil is brought into the world out of the dimension of a cosmic power and is supposed to be transformed into a historical beginning, whereby this beginning is situated in the disobedience of the humanity that was created free by God.

If this beginning of salvation history is to be transferred in a theologically conscientious way into visibility, the possibility remains of making the Devil at most into a quasi-allegorical figure, and this change was in fact attempted. In a Spanish *aucto del peccado de Adan*, for example, the Devil appears accompanied by his helpers Gula and Avaricia, who carry out the temptation of Eve and thus at the same time deliver the moral lesson. However, there is a reason that this play represents an exception that is late, and so far as I can see, limited to Spain.[15] For what was gained here theologically was lost dramatically. The intercalated allegories deprive the play of the intimacy of Eve's encounter with the Devil and thus of the most fascinating moment in the whole episode. In general the vernacular plays acted out this encounter not indirectly through allegorical means but rather directly, and in this the Old French Adam play remained an unsurpassed model.[16]

The tension is increased here through a series of attempts. Twice Satan tries in vain to get Adam to listen to him. He first succeeds with Eve, to whom he subtly presents himself as simultaneously enlightening and tempting. He is concerned about Eve's benefit and honor (207), and if Adam does not see to these, then he, Satan, must do it. Eve is fragile and delicate, fresher than a rose, brighter than crystal, and moreover much cleverer than Adam (224 ff.); in short, she could be the mistress of the world (255) if she were to put an end to the great deception (*grant engin*, 213) God uses to keep them in slavish dependency. God as a wily oppressor—Eve is not up to dealing with this wiliness in one who is full of wiles. However, before the disaster occurs, still another dialogue is inserted as a retarding phase in which Eve tries to persuade Adam. The Devil senses that things will go no further in this way, and in the middle of their conversation he approaches Eve in the form of a serpent, whispers his counsel in her ear, takes the apple, and confronts Adam with the *fait accompli*.[17]

These events are handled far better and in a more fascinating way than in the aforementioned Spanish play with the allegorically disempowered Devil. Nevertheless here as well what is gained on one side is lost on the other. What this play teaches visibly, and that means without the invisible premise, is a perfect dualism that to a large extent releases the oppressed from their moral responsibility. To be sure, the Devil's most subtle tricks remain merely tolerated by God, but they are seen through only by one who is already a believer anyway, and not, in contrast, by anyone who still stands on the other side of the central, decisive paradox of this belief. It cannot be claimed that in the author of this play the interest in dramatic effectiveness was stronger than the sense of the economy of theological arguments. However, one may wonder whether the interest in the lamentations of the fallen Adam and Eve (from 315 on) is identical with the interest that stands behind the dramatic representation of the fall itself. Blake's conjecture that Milton secretly stood on the side of the Devil is meaningful for the authors of the religious drama as well, at least in the sense that they very probably recognized in this figure a means of making their plays produce an effect on the audience. The power of these plays consists, as we will often have the opportunity to observe, in the way they were able to use theological justifications to conceal entirely different interests, but also in the ambivalence of their didactic function.

Seen from this point of view, the moment when the Devil outwits Eve takes on a special meaning. We have seen how much dramatic tension the Adam play derives from this outwitting. As the villain's mode of operation, cunning is a eminent dramatic category. In the play, the villain is in every case fascinating, even when one knows how harmless he "actually" is, and he first becomes really fascinating when he is so clearly and in such a masterly fashion raised and elaborated into a dramatic counterpart as he is in the Adam play. To be sure, his outwitting of Eve occurs within the monotheistic framework, and the Devil's cunning is also merely tolerated, but anyone who sought to argue in this manner would already no longer be grounding the beginning in salvation history. For it is precisely the moment of outwitting that confuses the moral dimension of the event and frees the person outwitted from moral responsibility.

Cunning is an authentic dualistic category of myth, and it bears an explicit "mythological stamp."[18] When the seducer in the Adam play describes the divine prohibition as a great deception, this description is not perfidious at least in the sense that it blames God for something that He is in principle incapable of doing. At any rate, gnosticism seriously raised precisely this objection. In the ophistic exegesis, the serpent's work is the salvation of the anti-demiurgic power that frees humanity from the worldly imprisonment in which it is kept by the creator god.[19] The author thus has the Devil bring in a dogmatically embattled position of the myth at the same time—a technique that Northrop Frye has described, with regard to comparable phenomena in modern literature, as "demonic modulation":

> The qualities that morality and religion usually call ribald, obscene, subversive, lewd, and blasphemous have an essential place in literature, but often they can achieve expression only through ingenious techniques of displacement.
>
> The simplest of such techniques is the phenomenon that we may call "demonic modulation," or the deliberate reversal of the customary moral associations of archetypes.[20]

Naturally, in our example this intention is not already the tendency toward the revolutionary that Frye sees signaled in the guiltless serpent in Shelley's *Revolt of Islam*. In religious drama demonic modulation, of which further examples come to mind, is as it were produced by itself out of the problem of visualization. Even though dogma has moved beyond them, dualistic images of myth retain their fascination here because as images they are more comprehensible than the unreasonable demands of belief. Wherever the latter are brought into the picture, they give the impression of being stopgaps. They appear unambivalent when viewed in the perspective of the Devil's cunning deception, that is, when they are viewed negatively, but one must not forget that summoning up such images at the very least confuses reflection on the theologically decisive issue.

Cunning is thus a signal of myth, and makes the Devil into a dualistic counterpower opposing God, a power that has a very specific interest in the temptation. This interest precedes the salvation history beginning and thus the fall as a causal determination, and it connects the historical grounding of evil with the competing mythological grounding:

Il vost traïr ja son seignor
E soi poser al des halzor.

Tel paltonier qui ço ad fait
Ne voil que vers vus ait nul retrait! (Adam play, 289–92)

He wants to betray his lord,
And raise himself to the heights.
What a rascal who did such a thing
I don't want him to approach you again!

When Adam warns his companion in this way, the play moves beyond the horizon of the biblical presentation. For the mythologeme of the fall of the angels is not found in the canonical books but only in the Apocrypha (Slavic Book of Enoch 29:4 ff.; *Vita Adae et Evae*, 12–16), which are first cited in two passages in the New Testament (Luke 10:18 and Apocalypse 12:7–9). Religious drama, however, made great use of it. As early as 1195 a no longer extant *Ordo creacionis angelorum et ruinae Luciferi et suorum, et creacionis hominis et casus et prophetarum* was staged in Regensburg.[21] With only a few exceptions, later plays, wherever they reach back into the most ancient history, insert the fall of the angels before the fall of man, thus acquiring a dramatic polarity. Thereby a shift in the structural sequence of the story is produced that recalls the Easter play. A salvation-history "cardinal function" is once more brought into an oppositional schema and thus becomes part of the "narrative sequence" of myth: God overthrew Lucifer and created man as a substitute—but Lucifer avenged himself by seducing Adam and Eve. That the mythologeme of the fall of the angels remains connected with the created nature of the Devil does not alter the fact that in this narrative sequence salvation history is mediated. It does not fade, as does the Resurrection in the Easter play, into a mere catalyst; it remains a cardinal function but now in a history that is essentially a history of gods not a salvation history.

Salvation history is thus mediated, inferred, both in its beginning and in its development. The overthrown power's act of revenge must be countered by a corresponding divine act of revenge, as it is already announced by the Adam play apropos of the damnation of the serpent:

Femme te portera haïne:
Oncore te iert male veisine.
Tu son talon aguaiteras,
Cela te sachera le ras.
Ta teste ferra de itel mail

Qui te ferra mult grant travail.
Encore en prendra bien conrei
Cum porra vengier de toi.
Mal acointas tu sun traïn;
Ele te fra le chief enclin. (479–88)

The woman will hate you:
She'll be a bad neighbor to you.
You'll catch her heel,
She'll crush your head.
She'll beat your head with a mallet,
Which will cause you great pain and woe.
And still she'll consider well
How she can take revenge on you.
Too bad you met up with her;
She'll make you bow your head.

What this revenge will be like, Adam himself tells us. God will come and through his might he will set free those imprisoned in hell: *Gieter nus voldra d'enfer par pussance* (590). Thus in this first vernacular play we already find the mythical narrative sequence, stretching from the beginning of the dualistic conflict to its resolution, that will be the object of the great cycles of the late Middle Ages. Just as in the case of the Easter play, in that of the Adam play we must demonstrate the ritual that corresponds homologously to this narrative sequence—a ritual that can first of all characterize the sequence as mythical.

CHAPTER 6

Figural Events in the
Locus and Archetypal Events
on the *Platea*

I

When in the year 1500 people wanted to put on a Passion play in Amiens, the petition submitted to the authorities included the request "to have the devil-characters run around" (*faire courir les personnages des diables*). This request probably referred to a practice that had been explicitly forbidden a few years earlier and that has also been shown to have existed at Chaumont. In the latter place it was customary to allow the devils and the Saracens belonging to Herod's entourage to advertise the play during the preceding three months. They ran through (*parcourir*) the town and the surrounding countryside, and this activity led to dreadful disturbances.[1] The devils indulged in extortions that produced such considerable revenues that this function of the advertisers, which was at first disdained, soon became highly sought after. Stumpfl believed that he had found in this tradition evidence that "very clearly proves that the devil-play in religious drama served to amalgamate pagan-ritualistic demon-processions."[2] At first glance, nothing seems to support this hypothesis more than the fact that such a ritualistic substratum can be discerned in the vernacular tradition from the outset, that is, in the French Adam play. In the latter we read in the first rubric that Paradise should be built *loco eminenciori*, on a more elevated place. This *locus* must have been immediately in front of the church door, so that God could come out of the church and return to it.[3] Where the opposing pole, hell, was localized and how it looked can be inferred only indirectly from the rubrics. The demon's path leads to Paradise, as we already saw, *per plateas*. The Devil's *discursus per plateam* is a *discursus per populum*, wherefrom it follows that *platea* or *plateae* simply indicates the square in front of the church, where the spectators have assembled.[4] Hell must be situated in the foreground, off to the side. The demons swarm out of it in order to approach *per plateam* the elevated paradise, and they return to hell, whether seeking further counsel or with triumphal shouts. While Adam and Eve are being led away, heavy smoke is supposed to arise, and kettles and pans are to be loudly beaten upon, so that it can be heard outside (following 590). Whether this hell was a simple hole or, as first appears in later times, a spring, tower, or fort; how it was closed off, whether with a door, a railing, or a curtain, or whether it was constructed, as also happened in the late Middle Ages, as an infernal maw that opened and closed—all this can no longer be determined.[5] However, it seems beyond doubt that already in the Devil scenes of this early play elements of the pagan demon-procession were included. These elements are indicated not only by the *discursi per populum* with which the devils preface their attacks but also especially by the noise they make with cooking pots and metal tubs in hell. We will not go far wrong in assuming that they already have, at least externally, the typical appearance of the medieval stage devil, that therio-morphic form in which the pagan residues are most evident: masks, animal skins, goats' ears, horns, tails, horses' or goats' feet, etc.

The fact that Stumpfl does not examine this early bit of evidence does not necessarily mean that he was ignorant of it. His central postulate cannot be proven by the Adam play. As we have seen, this postulate is already invalidated by the liturgical celebration itself, for whose nucleus, the Marys scene, no clear pagan analogue can be found. It is invalidated again by the beginning of the vernacular tradition, where the latter finds not its first but surely one of its first manifestations in a play that is thematically far re-moved from pagan springtime and initiation rites. The play's subject is the beginning of Christian salvation history, and its model is the biblical ac-count. Here, in this Judeo-Christian tradition, the priority and central impulse are determined.

If Stumpfl's approach may thus be due to a specifically German per-spective that sees the vernacular tradition as starting with the fourteenth-century Easter plays, it is nevertheless impossible to overlook the fact that already in the Adam play the Christian tradition is not represented purely. The Christian-figural level of what takes place in the *loco* is associated with a pre-Christian ritualistic element on the level of what takes place in the *platea*, and at least on this point the defenders of a Germanic dramatic continuity can confidently take their stand. And all the more so that the doubling of *platea* and *locus* does not remain a peculiarity of the Adam play but is repeatedly visible—with differing degrees of density and clarity—in the subsequent tradition. Religious drama makes it possible to recognize in manifold forms a ritualistic "protection"[6] of the site of the play, even if this protection of the already constructed stage was only simulated or aimed only at the spectators crowding forward, who were threatened with being hauled off to hell:

> Ir lieben mentschen alle,
> swiget nu und lat uwer kallen;
> ich wyl uch vorkundigen eyn gebott,
> das der her schultheys thut:
> wer da betredden wirt in dissem kreyß,
> er sij Heyncz adder Concz adder wie er heyß,
> der do nit gehoret in dit spiel,
> (vor war ich uch das sagen wel!)
> der muß syn buße groiplich etphan:
> mit den tufeln muß er yn die helle gan!
> . . .
> her schultheyß, macht ir den slagk,
> do sich eyn iglicher nach richten magk,
> nu wyt gnung wol umb
> die wyde vnd auch die krumme,
> die lenge und auch die ferre!
> uns sal nymmants irren!
> mer woln ungedrungen syn!
> ir hot wol gehoret der herren pynn,
> die der schultheys hot gethon:
> darumb rument unß dissen plann![7]

> *Dear people all,*
> *be quiet now and leave off shouting:*
> *I want to inform you of a commandment,*
> *that the mayor here makes:*
> *anyone who comes within this circle*
> *whether Heinz or Karl or whatever his name,*
> *who does not belong in this play*
> *(I want to assure you of this!),*
> *must repent enormously:*
> *he'll have to go with the devils to hell!*

. . .

Here, mayor, strike them a blow,
so they'll all move the right way,
now all around
the straight and the crooked,
the long and also the short!
let there be no mistake!
we don't want to be pressed in upon!
you've heard the punishment
that the mayor has ordered:
so clear this square for us!

The Alsfeld mayor's blow that clears the play's arena makes it possible to recognize with unusual clarity the archaic heritage of the ritual magic circle (Alsfeld Passion play). Only the Middle English theater in the round, which was common throughout Cornwall and probably beyond it as well, is comparable to the Alsfeld play on this point. On the continental manor-house stages only expressions such as *parc* or *champ* still refer to the protected space of the ritualistic play.[8]

More clearly than the site of the play, the event itself allows us to discern a ritualistic "continuity," and again this is clearest in the masks of the devils. What in the Adam play still appeared against the background of a relatively minor *discursus per populum* grew, in the later Passion play, into a full-scale "deviltry" that was now separated from the audience but still took place in the *platea* near the audience. In this case, Lucifer holds council in front of the hell constructed at the front of the stage, assigning tasks and praising, scolding, and punishing those who return. The ritualistic-mythological attributes are manifold: they are found in the external appearance of the Devil, in the cleverly set up mouth of hell, in the wild ring-dance performed by the minor devils around their lord enthroned on the *dolium* or Devil's barrel (Alsfeld Passion play, following 138).

II

We have already seen how much this kind of elaboration of the dualistic counterpart is already called for by dramatic visualization, and this interest peculiar to drama demands a careful and differentiated assessment of what a certain kind of folklore studies has seen as manifestations of Germanic continuity. Even if we abandon the postulate of the general priority of pagan ritualistic plays and their simple "amalgamation" by the Christian play and agree to limit ourselves to the thesis regarding the secondary "break-through" of the "popular," the dilemma that already affected Stumpfl's physician play remains in full force: namely, that the "Germanic conti-nuity" has to be inferred almost exclusively from the Christian play. In contemporary folklore studies' own critical reflections on the concept of continuity, the central point is the postulate of the "unbrokenness" of a tradition. If we apply this criterion of Bausinger's to religious drama, and particularly to the Devil scenes, we see that a continuity so conceived can be attributed only to the play, not to the "heritage." The part of this "heritage" that can be connected with something comparable is highly discontinuous and occurs (as is shown by Stumpfl's previously mentioned proofs of ritu-alistic deviltry, for example) at a time when deviltry in religious drama was already in full bloom. To be sure—and Bausinger himself points this out—large gaps in the evidence can also result from inadequate sources: "The burden of proof for the explanation of a gap still lies with its full weight on research—inadequate sources alone do not produce continuities."[9]

In view of the blemishes put on Germanic folklore studies by the Vienna School, this kind of self-examination and critical reassessment is certainly necessary and fully comprehensible in its radicality. However, the apologetic element in such an undertaking can easily lead to falling into the opposite extreme. That Bausinger seems to have been exposed to this peril is shown by the Easter play, in which the material collected by Stumpfl does not support the underlying thesis but is probably still sufficient also to invalidate Bausinger's counter-thesis of a "theatrical element independent from the outset."[10] Much the same can be said regarding the criterion of "unbrokenness." If on one hand it shows where it is meaningful to speak of continuity, it nevertheless must not lead to a positivistic backsliding that merely ignores pre-Christian or extra-Christian substrata. There is still less reason to do so in the measure that religious drama itself points to un-mistakable manifestations of this substratum. This was already seen in the presence of the pagan ōstarūn in the Christian Easter play, and it is now con-firmed anew by the Devil's plays in the ritualistic platea. With the protected play space, with the mouth of hell (now and then explicitly termed "chappe d'hellequin"[11]), with the devils' masks, with their names[12]—with all these characteristics, the pagan element, no matter how discontinuous, is visible in the Christian play itself.

There can thus be no question of getting rid of the ritualistic sub-stratum by making use of the criterion of unbroken continuity. As was already shown in the case of the Easter play, it has only to be brought into the proper perspective. It then emerges that the role of this "heritage" in Christian drama is basically much more exciting than the champions of "Germanic continuity" imagined: this heritage is not undermined, amalgamated, or defused; rather, religious drama provides it with the dramatic continuity that the Vienna School or Chambers and his followers postulated for the substratum. Like the Christian Easter rites and the pagan rebirth rites, the Satan of Judeo-Christian tradition assigns the pagan demons a place within a comprehensive myth from which they draw a new lease on life. In the masks of the devils in the play, something emerges to live in broad daylight and in the public square, if not in the church itself, whose existence in "folk drama" (according to Chambers) was suspected by the church and can now be inferred only from ecclesiastical permissions and prohibitions. Also, the demons in the Adam play scamper about in front of the church door in their ritualistic *discursi per populum*.

III

The twelfth century is the period of the most creative development of typological thought.[13] The Adam play can vouch for this. The fallen Adam and Eve proclaim, in the midst of their laments, the redemption that God will one day grant them:

> Mais neporquant en Deu est ma sperance.
> D'icest mesfait char tot iert acordance.
> Deus me rendra sa grace e sa mustrance;
> Gieter nus voldra d'enfer par pussance. (587–90)

> *But nonetheless I put my hope in God.*
> *Redemption for this crime will cost dearly*
> *God will give me back his grace and presence;*
> *He will pull us back from hell through his might.*

The fall into sin is a *figura* of the victory over the Devil during the descent into hell. The fulfilled grace, "albeit a thing of the future, and even of a specific historically identifiable part of the future, is nevertheless included in the present knowledge of any and all times. For in God there is no distinction of times since for him everything is a simultaneous present, so that—as Augustine once put it—he does not possess foreknowledge but simply knowledge."[14] Thus if in the play Adam and Eve already know about their future redemption, although in itself such knowledge belongs only to God himself, then this is a didactic accessory, a salvation-history interpretation of the nonetheless unique story of the fall. Of this much there can be no doubt; indeed, a proclaiming as well as a fulfilled *figura* first appears as such in what Auerbach calls a vertical relationship to divine omniscience, in which there is no *differentia temporum*; but also in this divine panorama the historical uniqueness of salvation-history events is not abandoned but rather bases the nonmythical self-conception of this history precisely on this uniqueness. As Paul and Peter emphasize, the death of Christ is not a repeatable event (*pollakis*) but rather a unique one, a redemption accomplished once and for all (*hapax, ephapax, semel*; Hebrews 9:12 and 26–28; 1 Peter 3:18). Salvation-history uniqueness is thus the unalterable correlate of omnitemporality.

Since Auerbach himself stressed the full historicity of the figural pole, it is surprising that he also uses the concept of figural omnitemporality where its problematic character becomes unmistakable. In the play not only do the figure and the fulfillment coincide, but also both coincide with the here and now of the play itself. And the "transfer of the event into a contemporary environment, which strikes us as anachronistic"—the description in the Adam play of the fall as a breaking of the feudal bond, for instance—is also for Auerbach a manifestation of "figural omnitemporality."[15] One has to do a lot of constructing to build this actualization as well into a figural structure, something like this: the fall as a figure, the descent into hell as redemption, and the present of the twelfth century as a new high point, from which in the consciousness of a redeemed time the unredeemed time is retrospectively seen, or rather both are seen together. However, the play closes—in its original form—with the procession of the prophets, which points forward figurally to Jesus, and the first part ends with the laments of the repentant sinners (523 ff.). These laments thematize, along with the figural sense, the *sensus moralis*: to the figural overview of the fall and the redemption corresponds, on the moral-tropological level, the coalescence of the old, fleshly Adam and the new, redeemed Adam. It is as though the coincidence of figure and fulfillment with the here and now of the play could also be made clearer on this tropological level than on the figural level, to which intensification, not repetition, is essential. It would thus be in the sense not of a figural but of a moral omnitemporality that Adam's fall is the fall of all of us and that the redemption promised him is ours as well. The second redactor who added the *Quinze signes* to the original play thus has the whole of the *sensus moralis* of the first part in view: on the last day, a terrible judgment will be passed on all those who have not overcome the old Adam within themselves.

Admittedly, the figural and moral readings do not coincide but rather compete. The moral interpretation is a timeless conjunction of elements that are separated in the horizontal dimension as proclamation and fulfillment, it does away with the "concrete historical reality" [*Innergeschichtlichkeit*] that is essential to the figural. Auerbach's introduction of the concept of figural omnitemporality in his essay "Figura" allows us to see clearly what end it is to serve: the ahistorical conjunction of figure and fulfillment *sub sensu morali* is supposed to be established as a divine overview and therefore brought back into historicity—precisely because omnitemporality in God does not cancel this historicity. What is at issue is thus saving the "living figural interpretation" from being vitiated by the "pure abstract allegory" of the doctrine of fourfold sense: "for while the adherents of this doctrine recognize the literal or historical sense, they sever its connection with the equally real prefiguration by setting up other, purely abstract interpretations beside or in the place of the prefigural interpretation."[16]

However, whether this abuse was actually helped along by Augustine must remain questionable. Even if in his interpretation three of the four senses are conceived concretely in terms of events, the *sensus tropologicus* remains ahistorical, and while the main evidence for a figural omnitemporality (*De div. quaest. ad Simplicianum* II qu. 2n. 2) does have to do with the supratemporality of divine knowledge, it is not, as Auerbach himself admits, expressly connected with figural interpretation.[17] In the Middle Ages the latent conflict between typological thought and the doctrine of fourfold sense noted by Auerbach was not reflected upon as such and is probably first discernible in the hermeneutics on which Auerbach's whole work is based. The figural conception of history was not so innerly historical as Auerbach wanted it to be. *Sub sensu morali*, it could repeatedly develop into an ahistorical standstill, in which its historicity encountered an inalterable boundary.

Religious drama is the best proof of this possibility. It presents salvation history—in itself figurally constructed—less in figural omnitemporality than in the ahistoricity of its moral sense. That is the first major reduction of the historical dimension. It is, however, only the precondition for a second one. Like the Easter play, the Adam play allows us to see clearly that its atemporality is not dissolved into the *sensus moralis* but is rather the atemporality of a ritual play that, with the liturgical choral responses and the pagan-ritualistic demons' *discursi per populum*, once again appears against the background of the ambivalence of kerygma and myth familiar to us from the Easter play. Hence we find ourselves back at our starting point: with the mythological stamp of the Devil's cunning, with the mythical narrative sequence in which the play situates the fall as an inferred beginning, and with the search for the homologous ritual. Such a search may seem superfluous to someone who relies on figural interpretation and the fourfold sense alone. However, anyone who proceeds in this way is interpreting as a didactic image what is in truth a ritual play. For this play, however, there is something decisive that no interpreter of the Adam play has so far noticed: the doubling of what takes place in the *locus* and what takes place in the *platea*, whose constitutive significance, as we saw, is not limited to the Adam play but which here makes visible with unusual clarity the interlayering of the kerygmatic and mythical-archetypal dimensions of what takes place.

For this reason I must return once more to the heart of the temptation scene and to one detail in particular that has been previously overlooked, if I am not mistaken: the Devil's temptation is carried out in three phases. The first two are directed at Adam and fail; the third is directed at Eve and succeeds. We thus have here another case of "three with emphasis on the end" (*Achtergewicht*), the play-form of the triplet, with which we are already familiar and which is moreover found in later plays as well. Thus in the Künzelsau Corpus Christi play the attempts are specifically numbered: *Sathanas secundo temptans Euam*, or *Sathans tertio temptans Euam*.[18] In the Vienna Passion play it even appears twice. The Devil approaches Paradise with a thrice-repeated *Bistū dō inne, Eua?* (Are you in there, Eve?), and after she has answered him, the temptation is once again carried out in Lucifer's three speeches.[19]

Just as in the Easter play, however, this kind of triplet is in each case more than a mere play-form. Here again it has the function of qualifying the occurrence. It is explained first of all as genuinely figural: as an Old Testament type that finds its antitype in the failed temptation of Jesus in the wilderness. In this Adam-Christ typology the threefold temptation of Jesus, generally interpreted as a temptation of the *gula*, the *vana gloria*, and the *avaritia sublimitas*, was included only rarely, since it required putting pressure on the text of Genesis 3:1–6, where there is no mention of three attempts. It was possible,[20] however, and in the case of the Adam play it must be presumed, because it is the best explanation for the fact that the author, deviating from the biblical model, has the Devil turn first to Adam: the Adam-Christ typology is more rigorous if Adam and not Eve at first appears to be the object of the temptation. On the other hand, the fact that a typology that was burdened with such obvious difficulties and was so seldom referred to by exegetes nevertheless found its way into the play cannot be explained by typological interest alone. We may suggest that in the temptation of Jesus what attracted the author was not primarily the antitype but rather the triplet. Thus a latent function is hidden behind the manifest one, as we have already seen in the Easter play, and as we will have occasion to see in detail in the Passion play. When our author sets the three unsuccessful temptations of Jesus in the wilderness in parallel with the three—ultimately successful—temptations in Paradise, he acquires from typology a tension-increasing and structure-building element. As such, however, it appears in the perspective of the pagan-ritualistic goings-on in the *platea*, out of which the tempter emerges to approach Paradise. The figurally derived triad is inserted as a ritual triplet, and as such it signals an ambivalent figural understanding of the temptation. Whereas in the failed temptation of Jesus the magic number three is denied as such, its point is restored in the Adam play, in which the whole event is played out of the moral dimension and ritualized.[21]

Thus precisely where scholars have thought they could discern most clearly the psychological realism that would serve "to make the fall comprehensible in its historicity and human necessity"[22]—precisely here nests a ritual element that can be accounted for neither figurally nor morally and allows us, on the contrary, to see in it a mythical-archetypal understanding of this salvation-history beginning. What happens in the *loco* and what happens in the *platea* are bound together in a unity in which the figural overview, the moral unification with the here and now of the play, and the ritual representation of a foundational beginning pervade each other inseparably. If we consider in addition that the whole fills up the gaps left behind by the *responsoria* sequence, then we find fresh proof that the play does not receive its rite in advance from the liturgical substratum but has to achieve it in opposition to the conscious exclusions of this substratum itself.

If we now glance back at the mythical narrative sequence, it becomes clear how little dramatic dualism can be considered simply the unavoidable price to be paid for graphicness. Neither could it be objected, therefore, that we argue here on the basis of a theological rigorism that cannot be maintained in any form of visualizable didactic communication. Religious drama is not concerned simply with graphicness but with acted-out images, and this interest, which goes beyond the mere visibility peculiar to the play, dualistically weakens the lesson in a way that remains very foreign to the sermon, for example. Precisely because sermons and plays have not only been compared but have sometimes also been genetically related, we must state very clearly that the sermon narrates salvation history while the play acts it out and that the importance of this distinction and its consequences cannot be too highly stressed. The influence of the sermon may be very evident, particularly in the late cycles, but it cannot be shown to be the central impetus for religious drama in general.[23] The playing out of opposition and the sinking of the figural occurrence in the *loco* into the ritual occurrence in the *platea* is borne by an interest specific to the play and is foreign to the sermon. Homiletics keeps the model of the biblical story in the dimension of moral *imitatio*, whereas in contrast the play presents the exemplary and binding character of this model only in the mode, which is specific to the play, of identical repetition in another perspective. Nowhere in the history of religious drama is there more insistent moralizing than in the Old French Adam play, and not only in the procession of the prophets and in the concluding *Quinze signes* but also at the end of the first part, in the laments of the fallen Adam and Eve (from 315 on). However, it is also true that nowhere is the temptation preceding these laments performed in a more masterly fashion. It takes up, let us recall, more than half the first part of the play, and here the biblical cunning excluded from the *responsoria* sequence is not only brought into the picture but played out in the mythical-archetypal manner analyzed above.

The attraction and the significance of the Adam play are not exhausted, however, by the fact that here, right at the beginning of the vernacular tradition, the ambivalence of a "Christian" ritualistic play comes so clearly into view. They acquire their full vividness against the background of a development in the history of dogma, which took a decisive turn precisely in the twelfth century.

CHAPTER 7

The Play's Dualism and
Dogmatics' Exclusions: Anselm of Canterbury's
Cur Deus Homo

I

The last quotation given above from the Adam play, the proclamation of divine wrath, is a paraphrase of the prophecy in Genesis 3:15, which since Irenaeus had been a constant component of the so-called recapitulation theory. This theory constructs a typological-figural relation between Adam and Christ in such a way that Christ as the new Adam takes up human history on a higher level and leads it to a good end. Drawing on the key passages in Paul (Romans 5:18–19 and Corinthians 15:44–49) it is possible, as J. Daniélou has shown, to deduce in accord with this thesis an exegesis of two central categories: the opposition between sinners and the righteous and the progress from the fleshly to the spiritual man. According to Daniélou, the emphasis could be put on either the former or the latter, although the latter was supposed to be more important, since on it the specifically Christian schema of typological intensification was based.[1] He leaves undecided what happens when the other case occurs, that is, when the opposition is emphasized at the expense of the progress. With regard to this question the inclusion of Eve, and thus the parallel Eve-Mary, is highly informative.

One of the earliest documents is found in Justinian. Jesus, it is said in the *Dialogues*, was born of a virgin, so that the disobedient end up just as they began: just as Eve was a virgin, whom the serpent's word impregnated and who gave birth to the disobedient ones, so the virgin Mary was impregnated by the word of God and gave birth to the obedient one.[2] This explanation is a rigorous reconciliation, on the Pauline model of opposition and salvation-history progress. Things look somewhat different in Irenaeus's perspective; for him, the Adam typology has shaped the concept of *re-*

capitulatio. He cites, and thus we come back to our reference to the Adam play, the prophecy in Genesis 3:15, and goes on, in contrast to Justinian, to include the serpent within the oppositional schema. Since Jesus has re-capitulated everything, he has also recapitulated the temptation, and in such a way that he has challenged to battle and conquered the enemy who has kept humanity imprisoned since the fall. However, this victory would not have been easily possible had not the victor been born of a woman, since it was also a woman who was to blame for the original defeat.[3] In Justinian, the serpent produced disobedient man who, by Jesus' obedience, received a salvation-history compensation. In Irenaeus, the serpent gains victory and lordship, and Jesus' *recapitulatio* is consequently annihilation and libera-tion. Thereby, however, the essentially imageless salvation-history opposi-tion between sinners and righteous, between obedient and disobedient, develops into a dualistically structured image. Salvation history no longer occurs in direct correlation with divine will and human obedience but rather by way of the detour through the authority of the Devil. The latter requires "mythological complications" (*mythologische Umständlichkeit*)[4] on both sides: like the Devil's victory, the divine revenge also relies on cun-ning—this time a pious cunning, a *pia fraus.*

The so-called Redemption theory, according to which Christ's blood and life is a ransom paid to the Devil and to which he is thus entitled, works with a whole catalog of images of cunning.[5] Had the Devil seen through the divine plan, he would not have entered into the deal. However, he thought-lessly takes the bait of human nature and is caught on the hook of the Godhead concealed within it, as if it were a fishing pole. This image of the fishing pole can be replaced by another, such as that of a sling, a net for catching birds, or a mousetrap. The images of battle, of cunning, of victory, and of fettering also already had a long tradition when the vernacular play lent them not only new life but in addition a broader effect than they had previously had. In this renaissance was taken up and perpetuated, however, what the history of dogma had just put behind it. For the specific theologi-cal problematic of the dualistic images is the subject of an early Scholastic treatise that had a lasting effect on medieval soteriology. This treatise ap-peared in 1098, that is, a good half-century before the first extant vernacular plays: Anselm of Canterbury's *Cur Deus Homo.*

In the very first chapter of this work appear some of the topoi of recapit-ulation theory familiar to us from Irenaeus and also from the Adam play, for instance the argument that since the cause of our damnation was a woman, our Savior must also be born of woman, or again the argument that the Devil, since he defeated humanity with the help of the fruit of a tree, must also be conquered through the suffering of a man on a tree trunk. However, such images (*picturae*), Anselm lets his dialogue partner Bosco object, can give only a highly imperfect impression of the divine plan of salvation:

> B. Omnia haec pulchra et quasi quaedam picturae suscipienda sunt. Sed si non est aliquid solidum super quod sedeant, non videntur infidelibus sufficere, cur deum ea quae dicimus pati voluisse credere debeamus. Nam qui picturam vult facere, eligit aliquid solidum super quod pingat, ut maneat quod pingit. Nemo enim pingit in aqua vel in aëre, quia nulla ibi manent picturae vestigia. Quapropter cum has convenientias quas dicis infidelibus quasi quasdam picturas res gestae obtendimus, quoniam non rem gestam, sed figmentum arbitrantur esse quod credimus, quasi super nubem pingere nos existimant. Monstranda ergo prius est veritatis soliditas rationabilis, id est necessitas quae probet deum ad ea quae praedicamus debuisse au potuisse humiliari; deinde ut ipsum quasi corpus veritatis plus niteat, istae convenientiae quasi picturae corporis exponendae.[6]

> B. *That is all very fine and can be grasped through pictures. However, if there is not something solid there for it to rest upon, it is not enough for the unbelievers to see why we must believe that God wished to suffer all that we said. Now whoever wants to make a picture chooses something solid on which to paint, so that what he paints will endure. For no one paints on water or on air, since no trace of the picture remains there. Thus when we present these convenient reasons to the unbelievers as pictures of an event that has occurred, they think, because they imagine it, what we believe is not an event that has occurred but rather an invention that we have, so to speak, painted on clouds. Therefore a solid underpinning in accord with reason is first to be demonstrated, that is, the necessity that proves that God must or could condescend to what we proclaim; then, so that the body of truth itself may shine forth more clearly, these convenient grounds for belief such as pictures are to be represented.*

Thus the goal of the following argument is indicated: the mere *convenientia* of the images must be supplemented by the *necessitas* of rational proof, in order to arrive at new images—that is, as is explained in later passages, images that are in accord with reason (*picturae rationabiles*, 2: 8). However, this path can surely not pass by way of the doctrine—and here Anselm indicates his chief dogmatic opponent through the character of Bosco—that sees Jesus' death as a ransom paid to the Devil and thus not by way of the so-called Redemption theory of Origen and Irenaeus. For this doctrine of salvation, which gives the Devil a necessary role in its fundamental system, comes into conflict with the omnipotence of God and makes things easy for the unbelievers (1: 6–7). Man is not indebted to the Devil but rather to God. His honor is injured through the fall, and this injury demands either satisfaction or punishment (*satisfactio aut poena*, 1: 15, 13). Punishment would, however, disturb the harmonious achievement of the divine plan for creation, since human beings are meant to replenish the choirs of angels decimated by Lucifer's fall and thus to collaborate in the completion of the *civitas caelestis*. However, if human beings can become angelic only through complete satisfaction, they are incapable of producing this satisfaction by themselves, because it must be in proportion to the magnitude of infinite guilt. Only God can produce this infinite satisfaction. However, if humanity must give something that only God can give, it follows that only a God-Man is capable of meeting the requirements of this satisfaction. Hence he sacrifices himself, he gives the maximum that man is capable of giving, and since he gives the maximum that man alone could give only as *debitum*, gives it freely and blamelessly, from his suffering emerges a gain through which the whole of sinful humanity can be redeemed: *Illo vero sponte patri obtulit quod nulla necessitate umquam amissurus erat, et solvit pro peccatoribus quod pro se non debebat* (2: 18).

We can for the time being make do with this very crude sketch of the so-called doctrine of satisfaction, which nevertheless already is sufficient to indicate its theological interest. The Christian doctrine of Redemption, as we read in the initial quotation, is supposed to be founded on a *soliditas rationabilis* and to do away with the accusation of mere invention through the rigor of conceptual deduction. The starting and ending point of this deduction is the concept of God's honor. It is injured, it demands satisfaction, and it determines the scope and performance of this satisfaction. The legal claim, which the Redemption theory accorded the Devil, has entered into God's *justitia*. The work of Redemption has become a matter that the trinity settles, as it were, by itself.

Without exception, specialized theological studies on Anselm rightly emphasize this systematic exclusion of the Devil as the bottom line of the doctrine of satisfaction. In actuality this exclusion is typical of its place in the history of dogma. While it no longer makes the Redemption pass by way of the Devil's authority, it dismantles the "mythological complication" characteristic of the Redemption theory. From this point of view it can be regarded as the endpoint of a centuries-long effort to extricate the doctrine of incarnation from the spell of dualistic images such as ransom or battle, cunning and victory. Nevertheless, even Anselm's dismantling of this complication has to come to a halt before one boundary: before the fact of the existence of evil, which salvation alone first forces to have a history. At this point the conceptual deduction in the *Cur Deus Homo* is linked with the premise of the *credo quia absurdum,* or as it is called here, *incomprehensibilis sapientia,* of which it is postulated that it also governs evil (1: 7) but which cannot be further questioned as to why it allowed evil at all. And it is precisely at this point in the system, which is no longer covered conceptually, that the mythological images break in once again. Not only is the mythologeme of the fall of the angels mentioned as an explanation of evil, but also the Redemption as a whole is connected with this mythologeme through the restitution and completion of the *civitas caelestis* demanded by the *honor dei.* On account of this intended function of man the Devil is consumed with envy (*accensus invidia*), avenges himself through the temptation, and is conquered anew by Jesus (2: 19).

The fact that Anselm's *Cur Deus Homo* shows, in addition to the force of conceptual deduction, a sort of force of the image, is an outcome that theological discussion in every way plays down, when it does not ignore it altogether, but which nonetheless becomes important in the context of the question with which we are concerned here. Anselm himself was clever enough not to attempt to simply set the concept against the image. As the initial quotation shows, for him it was rather a matter of achieving in the conceptual deduction the *corpus veritatis* that was supposed to make the traditional images of the recapitulation theory immune to the objection that they were a mere *figmentum.* However, among these new images to be acquired in the form of *picturae rationabiles* was also that of the victory over the Devil. Since it cannot be necessary that an omnipotent God descend from Heaven in order to do battle with the Devil he has only allowed to exist (1: 6), this image as well must be understood in terms of the satisfaction of the exigent *honor Dei.* It is not incumbent upon God to take up this battle but rather on men, who injured God through the fall and must make satisfactory amends through a countervictory over the seducer (2: 19). This countervictory has to be as difficult as the Devil's victory was easy, indeed it must be, as a victory for God's honor, of the greatest possibility difficulty: *iustum est ut homo satisfaciens pro peccata tanta difficulatate vincat diabolum ad honorem dei, ut maiori non possit* (2: 11). The hardest and most difficult thing man can offer for the honor of God is to die voluntarily: *Victoria vero talis debet esse, ut ... per mortis difficultatem vincat diabolum* (1: 22). Jesus has taken this death upon himself and in doing so has won the victory that humanity owed to God.

That the humblest of all deaths should thus represent a victory is of course an image that unbelievers will again accuse of being a mere *figmentum.* In addition to the many inconsistencies within the purely conceptual deduction itself discovered and discussed by theologians, particularly since Harnack's polemic,[7] another emerges from the competition between concept and image we examine here. Anselm begins with the intention of convincing unbelievers of the *soliditas rationabilis* of Christian images, but with the end product of his argumentation—namely the *picturae rationabiles*—he no longer addresses unbelievers but rather, as he repeatedly stresses, those who are already believers and who will rejoice in the *ratio certitudinis* of their belief (1: 25; 2: 15). In actuality, the *soliditas rationabilis* referred to here is hardly apt to persuade the unbeliever; it is for its own part grounded in a highly irrational manner, namely in the aforementioned belief in the *incomprehensibilis sapientia* of the divine work of salvation. If this belief must be brought into the proper understanding of the *picturae rationabiles,* then the question as to the prospects of these images arises all the more urgently if they are brought back into the dimension of what can be perceived with the senses, and above all, if they are acted out.

Anselm's soteriology radicalizes the basic Christian striving to ground salvation history as a history that, structurally speaking, does not interpret the syntagmatic opposition between the old and the new Adam, between fallen and redeemed humanity, as mediating a paradigmatic opposition, for it is precisely in the repression of the paradigmatic that the desired uniqueness of this history in contrast to mythical histories consists. The play, however, draws its life from just this kind of mediation of paradigmatic oppositions. It cannot make the Devil stand in the corner, as Anselm would have it do, and let the event of Redemption pass him by, as it were. However, if it posits him as an opposing player who brings about Jesus' death, then the victory in the Passion undeniably becomes a phase of his outwitting, and the incarnation slips into the twilight of a merely supposed appearance of corporeality—in short, the moral impetus of the doctrine of satisfaction is once again disturbed by everything that is supposed to have been overcome by it. Therefore the dilemma of the Passion play is already adumbrated. At first, however, the play stubbornly defended its interests against the markedly hostile conception put forward by Anselm. Hence before turning to the Passion play itself, we need to return once more to the Adam play and the Easter plays, since the theological problematics of the *descensus* first acquires its full vividness when it is seen against the background of the reception of Anselm.

II

Of course, we must not project the Adam play, which appeared some 50 years after Anselm's *Cur Deus Homo*, back onto the doctrine of satisfaction. What it shows first of all is only that a position that must be regarded, in terms of the history of dogma, as having been abandoned is taken up in the play and perpetuated by it. Let us emphasize this fact, in order to avoid misunderstandings on this important point. We are not talking about causalities such that the play might be claimed to deny a dogmatic position intentionally and thus take on a heretical character but rather about divergent tendencies that can be explained on the basis of their peculiar interests and constraints. The play is constrained by its dramatic images of defeat and revenge, and in this drama of salvation the cross at first has no place. God himself announces his *vengeance* in condemning the serpent, and Adam, along with the prophets in the third part, already know wherein it will consist. Abraham speaks of a someone who will come later and hold the Devil's fortresses and castles in his hand (761 ff.); from Aaron's line will come a scion who will do damage to Satan and release Adam from prison (777 ff.); Jeremiah prophesies that the Lord will live on earth as a mortal man and give his body as ransom (*rançon*) for the prisoners (870 ff.), and Nebuchadnezzar promises to those thus released from punishment a return to Paradise (926 ff.). All these prophecies thus explicitly cite the motif of the descent into hell, which neither the liturgical *Ordo prophetarum* nor its source, the pseudo-Augustinian *Sermo contra Judaeos, Paganos et Arianos de*

Symbolo, connects with the Redemption. Only twice are the Passion and the cross alone mentioned, whereas on six occasions the Redemption is associated with the descent into hell,[8] and on one of these, as we just saw, Jesus' death is expressly referred to as ransom in the Redemption-theory sense.

This marked alignment with the *descensus* casts doubt on the hypothesis that the Adam play is a fragment of a cycle that had already represented the whole New Testament salvation history in the manner of the cycles found in the late Middle Ages. The description of the fifteen signs of the Last Judgment, with which the manuscript of the play concludes, are surely secondary additions.[9] However, if in its place something other than the procession of the prophets originally followed, then it would probably be not a Passion play—which first appears in the vernacular in the fourteenth century—but rather the Resurrection play alone, that is, an Easter play with a descent into hell. That such a coupling of the fall and the Resurrection, which itself still eschewed the mediating procession of the prophets, was possible, is shown by the first complete extant French Easter play, the *Résurrection Notre Seigneur* in the fifteenth-century St. Genevieve manuscript. Here a Resurrection play beginning with the guard-scene immediately follows a first part with scenes depicting the creation, the fall, and Adam and Eve being led off to hell.[10] This sequence is, so far as I can see, unique in the history of the Easter play, but it only makes clear what is also valid for the other Easter plays that first really flourished in Germany around this time, that is, from the fifteenth century on: namely, that here a conception of salvation history emerges that is wholly organized by the victory over the Devil, not on the cross but in the descent into hell, and that connects this victory with revenge for the defeat in Paradise. What is striking about this is not the conception in itself but rather the fact of its late flourishing. For now, in the fourteenth and fifteenth centuries, this conception can be seen against the background of the full reception of Anselm and of the doctrine of satisfaction. The Easter play completely falls out of this reception, and if one asks what gave it the strength to assert itself against this reception-history, we must refer to the image of the descent into hell from which it draws its life and which typically does not appear at all in Anselm. In fact, it has no place in his system, and yet the point of his system is to construct a way of conquering of the Devil in which the Devil is, so to speak, bypassed.

In striving toward this goal, Anselm joins theologians who did not agree with him in many other ways, for example his contemporary Abelard, who sees in the *descensus* merely a graphic expression of the meaning of another event, namely the Crucifixion. The *Descendit ad inferos* formula in the apostolic *symbolon* is supposed to show only that the righteous of earlier times participate in the effects of the Passion.[11] Similar tendencies are manifest in Petrus Lombardus, Durandus de Sancto Porciano, and Duns Scotus.[12] These writers were obviously trying to get rid of dogmatic-history ballast. The doctrine of Christ's descent into hell had long since lost its original function.[13] It was from the outset a product of the delay of the Parousia, which was supposed to offer a new answer to the Pauline discourse on Christ's victory over supernatural powers opposing the divine. For this doctrine, the Crucifixion became "simply the gate through which Christ passes in order to actually encounter in the underworld the forces he has to overcome."[14] At the same time it raises a second problem that comes up in the course of developing an eschatology: how the righteous of pre-Christian generations can participate in salvation. According to the new doctrine, Christ appeared in Hades between his death and his Resurrection in order to preach to those imprisoned there and to offer the sacrament of baptism. The increasing problematization of both motifs in the course of constructing early dogmatics cannot and need not be pursued here. The doctrine of Christ's descent into hell survives less in the history of this motif than through its establishment in the apostolic *symbolon*, which itself has a complicated history that is not very relevant to our purposes here. The Middle Ages finds itself led to discuss the *descensus* chiefly by the *symbolon*. This approach is already evident in Abelard, and it is particularly clear in Thomas Aquinas, whom I must discuss briefly, since in his work the previously traced divergence of interests between play and dogmatics seems at first to have disappeared.

Thomas maintains that the descent into hell is a salvation-history reality. However, it must not be overlooked here that his whole argument seeks to prove not the *necessitas* but only the *convenientia* of this event. While the forty-sixth and the fifty-third questions (*Summa Theologica*, III) deal with the "necessity" of the Passion and the Resurrection, the fifty-second question deals solely with whether it was "appropriate" that Christ went down into hell. In Thomas, this kind of *convenientia* argument has a defensive interest, as we will see again later in another connection: it rescues traditional positions from their theoretical, even if not always expressly acknowledged, lack of necessity. The *symbolon* with the *Descendit ad inferos* formula nonetheless appears as such a traditional position in the fifty-second question. Thomas shows it to be *conveniens* by means of a typological retro-projection onto the Old Testament. However, it remains clear that the suffering on the cross is the central act of salvation as opposed to the *descensus* justified in this way. Christ's soul goes down into hell immediately after his death (*statim, Christo morte patiente, anima . . . ejus ad infernum descendit*, 52, 5) and frees, in virtue of his suffering (*in virtute suae passionis*) the righteous of earlier times who are held there solely because of original sin. Consequently, the *descensus* is in the first place not a central and thus not a "necessary" event in salvation history; rather, it is an episodic, even if "appropriate" event; and secondly, in this episodic status it remains plainly connected with the Crucifixion. This connection provides an excellent confirmation of our structural description of salvation history as a solely syntagmatic opposition between fall and Redemption. The paradigmatic opposition of the *katabasis* mythologeme appears as merely *conveniens* in Thomas. In contrast, *necessitas*, as a "cardinal function," is attributed solely to the Crucifixion and the Resurrection, which in their consequences do in fact produce a syntagmatic opposition but are not integrated into a paradigmatic opposition.

Precisely the opposite is the case in the Easter play. Here the salvation-history "cardinal function" of the *surrexit* announcement is not only de-functionalized, as was shown in the first part, while the Resurrection is aligned with the victory over the Devil in the *descensus*. Rather, as can now be seen in Thomas, the "cardinal function" of the Crucifixion is itself challenged by the mere fact that the Easter play includes the descent into hell at all and thereby brings it into the Easter event. The Jesus of these plays customarily observes that his death has given him the power to break through the gate of hell, and even, as in the Redentine play for example, binds Lucifer with his wounds (567 ff.). However, this moral identification of his act of liberation competes with and goes behind the mythological attributes of the accompanying angels and of the *Canticum triumphale*. The bearer of this attribute is then also no longer the soul of the man who has just died a mortal death but rather the resurrected and powerful God who storms hell. Herein lies the theologically problematic step that the play takes beyond its liturgical analogue, the ceremony of the *Elevatio Crucis*. For here the crucified man remains the symbol of the Jesus who pounds on hell's gate, despite the clear connection between the *descensus* and the Resurrection celebrated in the following matins. The Easter play, on the other hand, makes Jesus rise from the grave and storm hell after he is already resurrected, whereby what Thomas tried, by means of the emphasis of the word *statim*, to weld together as closely as possible, is completely cut off. Thus both the play and the *Elevatio* preserve an emphatic Easter theology that had been surpassed by Anselm, but the play now does so in the pronounced manner of a complete abandonment of the dogmatically decisive point: the epiphenomenality of the *descensus* as opposed to the genuine saving act of death, and more precisely the death that Jesus died as a man in order to redeem men's sins. Thereby the Redemption is in large measure detached from its specifically Christian background. The cardinal function has passed from the moral event of the Crucifixion to the mythologeme of the descent into hell.

J. Kroll, to whom we are indebted for a highly informative study of the history of the *descensus*, rightly points out that this motif's chance lay first of all in being able to make the story of Christ's suffering, which by including Crucifixion and humiliation runs completely counter to ancient thinking, acceptable to Hellenism at all, since the idea of *katabasis* was thoroughly familiar to the latter.[15] However, this probably held true for periods other than just the Hellenistic. It seems that later on, the vitality of the representation of the *descensus* should be sought as well in its indissoluble, tense relationship with the Pauline doctrine of the cross and more precisely in the sense that it lifts the burdens put on belief by Paul's notion of victory through death. In this respect the play does not line up with the broad area of medieval religious and didactic literature that was strictly controlled by dogmatics.[16] More than almost any other example, it can clarify the price paid for visibility in this area and by this salvation-history position. Here the constraint and the logic of graphicness are brought to bear on the original interests proper to the play itself. Here a position that had long been abandoned by theologians is not merely maintained but is elevated to become the whole's vanishing point. The binding force of the wounds, invoked only through memory, could not compete with the forcible fettering of Satan acted out before everyone's eyes. Here lay the high point of the play and here at the same time the paradoxes of belief were dissolved in the plausibility of mythological visibility. In this way both the authors' dramatic needs and the audience's demand to see were satisfied, and since what is posited by the scene, namely the myth of Jesus' descent into hell, was at least verbally identified as an event proceeding from the Crucifixion, both authors and audience could indulge in the illusion that they had before their eyes an image of the salvation-history event.

III

The Easter play flourished at the same time as the Passion play. Only a single Latin Passion play survives from the twelfth century, and although it was published in 1936, it received little attention.[17] The two thirteenth-century Benediktbeurn plays, also in Latin, are better known.[18] It was probably in the same century that the vernacular tradition also admitted the representation of the Passion story. The existence of vernacular Passion plays from the fourteenth century on has been established.[19] While the Easter play asserted itself and developed in opposition to the reception of Anselm and his doctrine of satisfaction, the emergence and flourishing of the Passion play not only parallel this reception history quite closely but also become understandable precisely as parts and results of the latter. For as we have shown, with Anselm's treatise the motif of the divine nature of men as a consequence of the Incarnation, which is central to the whole original and early Christian tradition, is replaced by the idea of a substitute performance of penance through the Crucifixion, in which the satisfaction of the injured divine honor takes place. The meaning of Christ's Resurrection as assurance of the divine nature of men thus yields precedence to the significance of his death for salvation. While the old tradition lived on in the Easter piety of the Eastern Church, the cross was henceforth central to the Western Church's soteriological interest. This new conception became pervasive from the twelfth century on, through Bernard of Clairvaux and the Victorine school, and in later medieval treatises and summas as well as in the broad area of edifying literature. It was well established in the thirteenth century—that is, at precisely the time of the first proven performances of Passion plays.

This coincidence, no matter how striking it might be, has nonetheless up to this point received no attention in research on the early history of the Passion play. This lack of notice is undoubtedly the result of an organic-evolutionary conception of the ways in which the history of genres unfolds, a conception that prevents one from seeing that the vernacular play is not only discontinuous with the Latin liturgical celebration but also developed heterogeneous traditions within its own domain. Just as the liturgical Easter celebration did not "evolve" into the vernacular play by including the chronologically prior *descensus*, neither did the Passion play emerge simply as an outgrowth of the Easter play. The Benediktbeurn *Ludus breviter de passione*, cited in particular by H. Craig in support of his evolutionary "principle of dramatic growth," proves very little.[20] The last rubric in this play suggests that it was moved forward in the Benediktbeurn Easter play, but the latter's first rubric clearly connects it with matins, so that the coupling with the Passion play must be considered secondary.[21] Thus only questionable evidence for the organic hypothesis remains, namely the performance of the Passion in Padua in 1243 or 1244, but it cannot be determined whether this was in fact followed by a Resurrection scene, and the so-called Sulmona fragment, which Craig classifies as early, is nonetheless first extant in a fourteenth-century manuscript and moreover ends with the setting up of the watch at the sepulcher. Even Young does not consider this evidence sufficient to justify adopting Meyers and Creizenach's strained evolutionary hypothesis.[22] It never occurred to Craig that if we take these facts into account, the secondary insertion of a Passion play that emerged independently can just as well also be associated with the old Easter play tradition, even though this supposition is supported by sound evidence, namely the independent Passion plays of the thirteenth and fourteenth centuries. In fact nothing is more obvious than that a Passion play was first performed on Good Friday, to be followed by a Resurrection play on Easter Sunday, and that the two were brought together only in the course of the development of cycles and the parallel detachment of the performances from the holy days.

How the development of the Passion play proceeded in detail, whether through direct dramatization of the gospel accounts or through the detour of the *planctus Mariae* (Mary's lamentation) or reading descriptions of the Passion, seems to be a question of little importance. For what matters is not these possibilities themselves but only the impulse behind them. Craig reduces the latter to an already existing potential, whose realization was attached to an "accidental quality": "medieval people were not deterred from dramatizing such a subject as the Passion by any unwillingness to present sacred subjects. Indeed, the impulse would be quite the other way. They would, and later actually did, willingly stress the subject of the most moving, central horror. The play of the Passion simply was not invented until late."[23] Here the kind of renunciation of knowledge that accompanies an organic conception of genres becomes quite clear. In such a perspective, the conditions under which changes in the structure of genres occur are not even an issue. Thus although Craig discusses in connection with the great Benediktbeurn Passion the alternative hypothesis of a development independent of the Easter play, in this case as well he is interested only in the search for an organic kernel that he thinks he has found in a liturgical office devoted to Mary Magdalen and Lazarus.[24] To be sure, in criticizing evolutionary thinking one must take care not to fall into the other extreme and simply deny in principle any sort of development from a "kernel" to a "whole." However, as in the already cited hypotheses concerning origins (*planctus Mariae*, readings of the Passion), in such a perspective it is also and especially important always to inquire in each case regarding the impulse that is at work in what is only apparently a blind organic development. And here one must not overlook the fact that the Passion play is driven by a soteriological impulse different from that behind the Easter play tradition. The latter is situated in an emphatic Resurrection theology. For Amalarius of Metz the central mystery of salvation was not what happened on Good Friday but what happened on Easter Sunday. However, the decisive theological turning point marked by Anselm comes precisely between the tenth and the thirteenth centuries. The Western Church is henceforth characterized by an equally emphatic theology of the cross, and it is within the latter that the Passion play finds its place.

At the same time, it cannot and need not be denied that the Passion play alone, independently of a following Easter play, apparently was not shaped by a peculiar tradition. The texts from Monte Cassino and Benediktbeurn are the only ones that could be cited in this regard, and there is no reason to postulate such a tradition by referring to other texts that might have been lost. It is obvious that the Passion play was very quickly set ahead of the Easter play, but the descent into hell remained the dramatic climax that the play could not give up without denying its own interests. In actuality it can be clearly seen that the representation of the Passion also drew its dramatic power from the *descensus*: Jesus' concluding victory over the Devil was preceded by suffering and death as a battle with his opponent. However, the Passion play, which drew its vitality from the soteriological impulse of the doctrine of satisfaction, thus became at the same time a test of the latter's antidualistic strategy. The Adam play and the Easter play could avoid the problem, but the Passion play had to deal with it. What will become of Anselm's *picturae rationabiles* when both the cross and the *descensus* are graphically represented? With this question we leave the excursus on the history of dogma and the history of genres and resume our systematic approach.

PART 3

The Archaic Middle: The Passion Play

CHAPTER 8

The Passion Play Between
Mythologeme and Theologumenon

I

The first complete vernacular play extant is the fourteenth-century Old French *Passion du Palatinus*, whose action stretches from the Last Supper to the Marys scene.[1] The representation of Christ's suffering is more than twice as long as the concluding Easter segment. With its elaborate scourging and Crucifixion scenes and the legend—characteristic of the French Passion play—of the smith who made the (blunt) nail for the cross,[2] it lies wholly within the mysticism of the Passion that had been flourishing since the twelfth century. It ends with a *planctus* in which Mary and John both take part and is followed immediately by a descent into hell.

The sequence here is striking. In the Easter play the *descensus* does not appear in its usual place, that is, in the framework of a play about the watch at the sepulcher, but even before the entombment, to which the Easter play goes back in every case, as the Anglo-Norman *Seinte Resurreccion* shows. Thus our thesis regarding the discontinuity of the development of the Passion play is confirmed, since this text clearly does not indicate a Resurrection play that was supplemented by the story of the Passion. No extant Easter play has a tomb-guard play that includes not the *descensus* but only an eight-line Resurrection scene in which Jesus refers to the descent into hell that precedes the Easter play itself (1722).[3] The hypothesis that a *descensus* originally placed here was given priority must be excluded because precisely this peculiarity of the play is present in the prototype common to all the French Passions of the thirteenth and fourteenth centuries: the twelfth-century epic *Passion des jongleurs*, where we read:

> Lor(e)s enclina son chief (en) jus,
> (Li esperis) s'en est issus.

Issus en est, il le voloit
A ynfer est alés tout droit. (1551–54)[4]

Then he lay down his head,
His spirit left it.
It left, he wished it
To hell he went straightway.

So in the Palatine Passion play as well it is not the risen Christ of the German Easter play but rather "Esperiz Jhesu" (Jesus' spirit) that goes from the cross down into hell.[5] This appears at first to be in full harmony with the demands of dogma. However, the writer cannot make one element follow the other nearly so quickly as they do in the epic prototype. In the latter, Jesus' spirit went "straightway" ("tout droit") to hell—which corresponds to the Thomistic *statim,* though naturally there is no direct reference to it— but in the play this "straightway" is spread out in a characteristic manner. Our author first makes the Crucifixion conclude with the usual *planctus,* as we have already mentioned, and he then opens the descent into hell with a dialog between Satanas and Enfers in accord with the model of the Gospel of Nicodemus.

Thus the mythological has marked the whole course of events from the outset. What is broadly acted out here, in the dialogue between a Satan innocently boasting about his success and an Inferus who suspects what is about to happen, is the outwitting of the Devil through the death on the cross.

Voëz le mort a grant viltance
Entre deux larrons crucefiez,
Et par les mains et par les piez,
Plus vilment que nul autre lerrez, (1244–47)

See here the dead man scornfully
Crucified between two thieves,
Crucified by the hands and feet,
More shamefully than any other thieves,

thus Satan brags about the man hanging on the cross. He claims to have made the blood stream out of Jesus' body, and should Jesus nonetheless dare to show himself in hell, he vows to take care of him; but Inferus suggests that he should look over on the other side, where the liberator has just appeared:

> Tornez vous, resgardez avant!
> Veez ci venir le sodeant,
> Plus blanc que nule fleur de lis.
> Ne sai comment il est revis.
> En sa main porte nostre mort,
> La croys ou il fu mis a tort. (1363–68)

> *Turn around, look ahead!*
> *See the redeemer coming here,*
> *Whiter than any lily.*
> *I don't know how he returned to life.*
> *He bears our death in his hand,*
> *The cross where he was wrongly put.*

The gnostic light-symbolism, on which the Gospel of Nicodemus lays such stress, may here be represented only by the white of Jesus' robe, but the dialogue that introduces this event verges on a mythological dimension that also marks the greeting of the liberator by the suffering souls:

> Glorieux pere debonaire,
> Vous irez d'enfer vos amis traire;
> Roys et sire de paradis,
> Vo cors a esté en croys mis,
> La deité le puet bien faire. (1386–90)

> *Glorious, noble father,*
> *You shall go to release your friends from hell;*
> *King and Prince of paradise,*
> *Your body was put on the cross,*
> *The deity can surely do it.*

These lines are spoken at a point when Jesus is still hanging on the cross (where he remains until the entombment after the descent into hell), simultaneously visible on the adjacent stage. Thus the undramatic, invisible image of the victorious sufferer competes with the powerful liberation carried out by the *roys de gloire* (1395), and against the background of these competing images the quoted lines become doubly problematic. For since they explicitly assert that God the Father himself was crucified, they do not adopt the key idea of the doctrine of satisfaction, and thus they draw attention neither to the Jesus hanging on the cross nor to the suffering man but rather to the merely supposed corporeality of the Godhead involved in the outwitting of Satan. We see what sort of victor emerges from this kind of competition between images. Here the Passion is pushed into a docetic twilight by the mythological visibility of the *descensus*, and the descent into hell itself raised to the status of a genuine act of salvation.

This perspective first emerges, as we have said, with the *descensus* and with hindsight from its point of view. It collides with the central interest in the Passion that is borne by the whole first part of the play, and in this sense it is corrected by Jesus himself when, keeping in mind inter-trinitarian differentiation, he instructs the wretched souls:

Je vieng de la destre mon pere
Pour vous sauver ai mort sofferte (1432–33)

I come from my father's right hand
To save you I suffered death

The fundamental dilemma of the Passion play is nevertheless not thereby overcome: it refuses to deny itself as drama, and if it wants to maintain the battle in hell as the climax and turning point in this drama, then it must accept a dissociation of this central moment from the act of dying, which is central from a salvation-history point of view. The move from death on the cross to victory in hell results from images that are inconsistent because they are incommensurable. The play cannot escape the tension that distinguishes the visible image from the one directed to the eyes of belief, that is, the tension between mythologeme and theologumenon.

II

Here we shall not pursue the question as to how this dilemma is worked out in particular phases of the history of the Passion play. We will take up the story at the point where the Passion clearly turns in the direction of the doctrine of satisfaction, and we will try to see how the now explicit claims of the theologumenon can be reconciled with those of the mythologeme. The Arras Passion, which is attributed to Eustache Mercadé, is the first that seems informative on this point. It is framed by the so-called Trial in Paradise, a great debate among the four daughters of God—Justitia, Misericordia, Veritas, and Sapientia—in which the divine plan of salvation, which the mystery play thereafter brings into the picture, is discursively developed. This allegory, which goes back to one of Bernard of Clairvaux's sermons on the Annunciation,[6] was a topos of medieval homiletics, from which it found its way into many Passion plays. It is well known that there were close relationships between religious drama and homiletics. These relationships consisted first of all in the inclusion in the performance itself of themes and motifs taken from sermon literature, and then in sermonlike commentaries on what was represented, which were found in prologues, epilogues, and in the course of the play. These commentaries are usually considered unproblematic, as indeed they were intended to be; they are seen as explanations and warnings intended to promote edifying reflection on what was represented. However, the most striking thing is thereby overlooked: the fact that they are present at all and that they expand in proportion to the increasing scope of the plays themselves. Thus they obviously suggest that the events represented are in great need of commentary; the self-evidence of these events is not taken for granted. This need for commentary becomes particularly clear in the case of the Trial in Paradise. To be sure, the Trial's popularity may be based above all on the fact that the allegorical conflict offered a first opportunity for a dramatic representation of the act of salvation, but for the performance, an allegorical double would have been dispensable. Nonetheless, the Trial developed into an independent framing play, prelude, or interlude alongside the prologue and epilogue, grew in the French Passion plays to more than 1,500 lines, and provided Greban, as we shall see, with an opportunity to make major theological corrections in its prototype.

In what follows we will seek to discover how this programmatic introductory section operates in relation to an exposition in the play itself. Here we must first observe that the Trial in Paradise already represents a specific product of the reception of Anselm. It makes the specialists in dogmatics uncomfortable, since there appears in it what Anselm himself sought to derive by force from the concept of the *honor dei*, as a solution to the embarrassing dilemma of a God who was not identical with himself. For example, J. Rivière emphasizes that this latent anthropomorphic conflict among the divine attributes is "eccentric" and a product of the reception of

Anselm that is found in the works of only second-rate theologians.[7] However, here something is assumed as a premise that cannot be regarded as proven, as the reception history of Anselm up to the present day clearly shows: namely, that the concept of *honor dei*, as it is developed in *Cur Deus Homo*, is bound up with the divine benevolence and thus can be neither reduced to nor made equivalent to the concept of justice. A juristic schema of equivalence is no doubt present in Anselm and cannot be set aside as a theologically marginal phenomenon.[8] No wonder then that the allegory that strikes specialists in dogmatics as "eccentric" finds its theological place in homiletics, which is central for communicating salvation, and Bernard of Clairvaux, Innocent III, and Peter of St. Victor all make use of it. However, a theology that obviously could be communicated only with a loss of substance may describe not only the subject addressed but itself as well. For one thing, it should have questioned its own activities when it formulated its self-understanding on a level of reflection that remained inaccessible to those for whom this self-understanding should have been most important. For another, and this has to do with the problematics of self-understanding, we must ask whether the price that had to be paid for visible communication did not throw a subversive light back onto unresolved difficulties within the conceptual system.

Harnack put together a catalog of these difficulties: "the mythological concept of God as a powerful private individual who is raging against tarnished honor and will not abandon his wrath before he has received at least an equally great equivalent; the whole gnostic tension between justice and benevolence, insofar as the Father is righteousness and the Son benevolence; the frightening idea (in contrast to which the views of the Fathers of the Church and the Gnostics are greatly to be preferred), that mankind is freed from a wrathful God, (. . .) the dreadful thought that God has the hideous prerogative over men that he cannot forgive out of love, but always requires payment."[9] This criticism may be specifically Protestant, an issue decided in advance by the theology of suffering as punishment. However, its central idea is unmistakable: the retrospective connection of the Redemption with God's injured honor has not overcome dualism. What Anselm in fact has achieved is not the elimination of an authority but merely a change in the occupation of "places" in the system: Justitia henceforth replaces the Devil as the dominant authority. Without such an authority the sacrifice of the Son cannot be conceived, and if the Devil is not to figure as the receiver of atonement, then God must take over his function as well and demand this sacrifice. The dualistic splitting of divine authority into a will to salvation and a will to justice can be concealed by Anselm only by connecting the divine will to salvation not primarily with a humanity in need of redemption but rather with the *civitas caelestis* to be completed: God needs mankind in order to fill out the decimated choir of angels and to expand it still further in accord with the original plan. However, this concealment is possible only conceptually, that is, through subsumption under the concept of *honor dei*. Each form of visualization, including the allegorical one, lays this dualism bare. The Trial in Paradise thereby acquires an explanatory function: its supposed anthropomorphism in actuality brings to light the dualism of Anselm's conception of God.

This revelation is, however, followed by another. Anselm's subsumption of the will to salvation under the concept of honor and the resulting extreme mediation of the Redemption is the inhumane element—pointed out by Harnack, among others—with which this soteriology skirts the edge of self-betrayal. However, it no longer has any alternative. Anselm's anti-dualistic strategy necessarily leads him not to let hell, much less Jesus' descent into hell, appear in view at all; the image of the heavenly city must remain the keystone of the system. For wherever the will to salvation is not connected back to God's honor in this way but rather, as in the Trial in Paradise scenes, thematized as *misericordia*, the focus shifts back to those suffering in hell as the object of this sympathy. However, insofar as hell and the Devil come back into view, the shift in the occupation of "places" carried out by Anselm becomes itself thematic, that is, the "place" in the system is no longer unequivocally but ambivalently occupied, precisely through God's justice *and* the Devil's "right." Here lies the deeper ground for the fact registered, with perceptible discomfort, by Rivière: the traditional images of the Devil's right did not simply disappear in the wake of the reception of Anselm's work but instead, as the object of a permanent denial, remained components of writing in the didactic and edifying domain as well as in the domain of dogmatics. The point that historians of dogma of all stripes repeatedly trot out with satisfaction, namely that the Devil's claims are rejected, primarily indicates that it is precisely in these denials that the dualism is perpetuated. It is the provocative plausibility of its answer with regard to the meaning of the loftiest of all sacrifices that assures it this vitality and from which even the scholastic summas were unable to tear themselves away. Their denial of this plausibility was however once again possible only on the level of conceptual distinctions and could not be translated into visible comprehensibility. The Trial in Paradise scenes not only extend Anselm's concept of honor to a dualism of justice and compassion that still remains within the monotheistic framework but also reveal, by evoking the image of the souls suffering in hell, the ambivalent status of Justitia, since they do not commit themselves with regard to whether God's justice or its systematic competitor, the Devil, must redeem mankind.[10]

Precisely this ambivalence comes to the fore in the Arras Passion play.[11] There, the archangel refers, wholly in Anselm's sense, to the abandoned *beaux sièges celestiaux* (fine celestial seats, 717), in order to move God to undertake the Redemption in the interest of his own honor:

> Salve ta haultene equité
> Et l'honneur de ta deité. (813–14)

> *Save your lofty equity*
> *And the honor of your deity.*

This appeal succeeds, however, only after Sapientia has shown the disputants a way out, through the planned incarnation, and she justifies this plan less by reference to the uncompleted heavenly city than by reference to the emphatically conjured up image of the hellish prison. The ambivalence of this justification corresponds to the ambivalence of the concept: satisfaction is not mentioned but rather redemption (*rachat* or *racheter*: 600, 960, 966, 970, 24798). Concerning this redemption, it is clearly stated only that it consists in death on the cross (959–70, 24797–800), without the recipient of the "payment" (599, 24790) being named. Where redemption is mentioned, Lucifer is not, and vice versa. Typically, in Sapientia's justification the plan seems hardly a compromise. If she at first describes it (588–600) as a liberation from the bonds of the prince of hell (1331–38), then even if the concept of the *rachat* does not disappear here, Lucifer is still more clearly implied than Justitia, about whom nothing at all is said. Only in the conclusion of the trial, after the play, does the pendulum swing back in the opposite direction. Here it is Justitia who is satisfied with the sacrifice of the Son (although she even now does not explicitly claim the payment for herself, 24785–804), and what is more important, the liberation of Adam from Lucifer's prison (*prison Luzifer*, 24821) is here not connected with the descent into hell but rather identified as an automatic result of the Crucifixion. Jesus shows God the Father the wounds with which he has rescued mankind and then continues:

Et apres celle griefve mort
Que j'ay souffert sur terre a tort,
Au tiers jour sui resuscité,
Et puis je sui es cieulx monté,
Et sui revenu en mon estre
Ou tu m'as fait sir a ta destre. (24625–30)

And after that painful death
That I wrongly suffered on earth,
On the third day I rose from the dead,
And then ascended to heaven,
Where I resumed my true being
And you seated me at your right hand.

It is as if the author afterward wanted to distance himself from his own play. For what he has Jesus completely fail to mention here is the descent into hell, which in the play itself was the central event of the fourth day and the dramatic climax of the action as a whole.

III

It will now be interesting to trace the way in which this obvious dilemma, which the author indirectly acknowledges, is worked out in the representation itself. The play consists of four days and contains some 25,000 lines. The first day includes Jesus' birth and childhood, the second his public life up to the point where he is taken prisoner, the third the condemnation and Crucifixion, and the fourth the descent into hell and the Resurrection. However, the *descensus* is no longer inserted abruptly, as in the Palatine Passion play, but rather prepared for at length. From the first day onward, the wide-sweeping performance is carried out by means of devil scenes and thus structured in a dramatic and dualistic way. It could be assumed that here would be dramatized the claim that the Satan of the Palatine Passion play, drawing on the Gospel of Nicodemus, first raised with retrospective reference to the suffering on the cross—namely, that the Crucifixion was his work. However, on closer inspection we can see that in the Arras Passion play precisely this aspect of the Passion is avoided.

The scenes in hell on the first two days take place against the background of the weakening of Satan's power that gradually becomes perceptible with Jesus' arrival and action on earth. These events begin right after the annunciation to Mary. Satan reports a secret angelic mission, and the troubled Lucifer sends him back to earth, commanding him to now fill up hell with victims (1111–213). After the birth of Jesus, Satan returns to hell with only a single witch, and this result seems to Lucifer decidedly meager for a year's residence on earth (2393–3456). The dark soul of Herod, who has the murder of 14,000 children on his conscience and because of the loss of his own son has taken his own life, rejoices all the more (5073–144; 5452–534). Satan claims to have incited Herod, who feared for his throne, to carry out the massacre but characteristically only with the goal of doing evil (*mal faire*, 5088) and thus not as a result of recognizing that the young child (*jone enfant*, 5090) represents a threat to hell itself. After his failed attempt to tempt Jesus (6809–7056), Satan gives up that approach and tries instead to get the Jews to put him to death. After even the woman of Canaan, whom he had counted on having as his victim, is saved, Lucifer goes on the defensive:

Tost, tost, bien tost, frumez nos portes!
C'est Dieu le pere qui revient. (7909–10)

Hurry, hurry, close our gates!
It's God the Father who is coming.

However, the danger that is at first averted returns. The moment of the outwitting of Satan through the Crucifixion does not become thematic, but the figure of Jesus is nonetheless mythified through the anticipation of the descent into hell. He appears from the outset as the invisible power threatening Lucifer's realm. Its dramatic interest consists less in the fact that God becomes a suffering man than in the fact that this man nevertheless remains a powerful God and acts as such.

A detail central to the third day of the Passion play shows that there is no way of bringing together the mythologeme of the battle in hell with the kerygmatic and nongraphic image of victory through suffering. Here only one devil scene makes preliminary reference to the Crucifixion, and in it

Lucifer does not seek to cause Jesus' death but rather to prevent it, foreseeing what is to come. Satan is supposed to suggest to Pilate's wife, in a dream, that she should encourage her husband to set Jesus free (14096–207). This scene, which draws on Nicholas of Lyra's commentary on the gospels,[12] became a permanent part of the Passion play, yet in it still another biblical episode (Matthew 27:19) is dualistically stylized. This scene is particularly interesting for us because in it the dilemma we are examining becomes tangible. The writer has carefully avoided the (mythological) motif of the outwitting of Satan by giving him the "bait" of the cross, but in order to do this, he has to abandon the dramatic sequence of action that leads to the mythologeme of the battle in hell. Protecting the opponent in this way represents an unsuccessful attempt to integrate the Crucifixion into the phenomenality of a drama of salvation, and this attempt reveals the fundamental inconsistency of the image.

This dilemma is repeated at the end of the third day, which closes with the announcement of the descent into hell and the entombment. As Satan is arguing under the cross with the archangel Michael regarding the soul of the good thief, he is informed about what is to come:

Leur dis et fais sont acomplis,
Car le filz de Dieu de lassus
A esté en croix estendus
Pour racheter l'humain linage
Qui dedans le limbe en servage
Ont esté en captivité,
Tantos en seront hors jetés
Et mis en consolation. (17616–23)

Their words and acts are accomplished,
For the son of God from on high
Was hung upon a cross
To redeem the human race
Held in limbo
in captive serfdom,
Soon they will be delivered
From there and consoled.

Here we find once again the concept of Redemption with the ambivalence we recall from the Trial in Paradise. To be sure, here as well the Crucifixion is not interpreted as ransom paid to the Devil. Nonetheless the retrospective reference to the cross has less to do with the satisfaction of justice than with the act of liberation that is "soon" (*tantost*) to occur. When shortly thereafter Lucifer, informed by Satan, calls for an extensive fortification of hell, the worst sinners are mashed into cannon fodder and others are burnt into sulfur (18162–231). Then the focus is no longer on the man Jesus and the moral worth of his suffering but rather with the divine conqueror of the prince of hell. Even if Jesus goes down to hell as a spirit (following 20898), the acting out of the *descensus* on the fourth day leaves no doubt that it is inserted not theologically, as an epiphenomenon, but rather dramatically, as the climax of the action.

IV

The greatest and best-known French Passion play is by Arnoul Greban. He wrote it when he was still only a *Magister artium*, that is, before or just at the beginning of his theological studies, but the future *Baccalaureas*'s dogmatic conscientiousness is already clearly discernible in it. This becomes particularly evident when his play is compared with its model, the Arras Passion. Even more clearly than his predecessor, Greban considers the event in need of a preliminary allegorical explanation. His Trial in Paradise is not only a good three hundred lines longer but also far more rigorous theologically. The most striking mark of this is the systematic use—so far as I can see, the first such in the history of the Trial in Paradise—of the concept *satisfaction* or *satisfaire* (2357, 2529, 2556, 2763, 2917, 2962, 3038, 3168, 34230, 34234, 34285, 34314, 34403, 34472). Thus the ambivalence of the concept of Redemption, as it appears in the Arras Passion, is set aside. Whereas in the Arras Passion we find that God had to become a man

> Pour faire et payer la grant somme
> Dont l'homme sera racheté, (599–600)

> *In order to make and pay the great sum*
> *With which mankind will be redeemed,*

Greban leaves no doubt that it is Justitia who has demanded the *grant somme en reparacion* ("the great sum to be paid as reparation," 34221) that is paid to her and thus is supposed to bring about the satisfaction (34234). The Devil is mentioned only insofar as it is explained why mankind and not he is to participate in Redemption (2620 ff.). The description of this act of Redemption excludes him, or more precisely, it attempts to exclude him, and this attempt is not wholly successful here, either. The passage requires a more detailed analysis.

As Justitia sees her position increasingly shaken by the reference to the remorse of fallen mankind, Sapientia comes to her aid with a comparison drawn from the *cause civille* (2913), that is, from criminal law: remorse, she explains, is of no more help to mankind than to a lawbreaker confined in a royal prison; the latter cannot be saved from a deserved death by all the tears and laments in the world. Greban's purism here makes use of a highly subtle argument. For what is passed off as a comparison with criminal law is at the same time a weakening of the idea of hell. For the *prison de roy* ("royal prison") spoken of here stands for the *prison Luzifer* (24821) in the Arras Passion, whereby Lucifer is now no longer even conceived as God's prison warden. Hell no longer appears as an independent reality but only as a mere image dispenser. By means of this correction, Greban obviously believes he has simultaneously gotten rid of the descent into hell. He lets Truth take up the image introduced by Sapientia and exploit it for her own purposes:

Voire, més, en bonne equité,
autre voye y fault esgarder
et encores me vueil fonder
sur la similitude bonne
que dame Sapience donne.
Car, posé que le malfaiteur
qui est en chartre habitateur,
ne puist satisfaire a son mal,
neantmoins, par don especial,
le roy le puet permetre vivre
ou force vient, qui le delivre,
le prince de celle cité,
qui oncques n'y avoit esté.
Sy vueil a ce point pervenir
que tel prince pourroit venir
en humaine habitacion,
qui en prenroit compassion
en baillant bonne delivrance. (2937–54)

Here indeed, in all fairness,
another way has to be considered,

and yet I want to base myself
on the good comparison
made by Lady Sapientia.
For supposing that the criminal
who dwells in prison
can do no satisfaction for his crime,
nonetheless, by a special gift,
the king can let him live,
or a force may come to deliver him,
the prince of that city
who never had been there.
Thus I want to arrive at this point,
that such a prince could come
into the dwelling place of men,
who would take pity on them,
and give them good deliverance.

Here as well the mythologeme is present only as an image dispenser. The *descensus* is not a special phase in the work of Redemption; rather, it is to provide a schema for the visualization of this work as a whole: the dungeon is not associated with hell but rather graphically represents the situation of fallen mankind, and the liberation does not refer specially to a descent into hell but rather to the presence of the prince of heaven in a place where he had previously never been and thus to the incarnation (*en humaine habitacion,* "in the dwelling place of men"). What is presented as moral and juridical allegory is in fact an allegorization of the mythologeme.

However, even an allegorically interpreted mythologeme is not yet a theologumenon. On the contrary: this insistence on the king as the prison warden makes all the more urgent the question as to why this all-powerful monarch cannot simply temper justice with mercy. Greban invokes this possibility by referring to a "special gift" (*don especial*) made by the king but then draws back with the treacherous "or a force may come to deliver him" (*ou force vient, qui le delivre*), leaving it unclear why this princely liberator had himself to die the most humiliating of all deaths. The image of the princely liberator does not incorporate the idea of a substitute satisfaction for a mankind that is itself incapable of providing satisfaction. Moreover, the allegorization cannot incorporate the cross, either. Instead, this special kind of Redemption has to be added to the picture as an obvious contradic-

tion. First of all, Sapientia continues, a prince must be found who is "powerful" enough for this task (2973–80). An angel is out of the question because
he would have only finite power (*puissance finie*, 1998). The infinite injury
done to God, on the other hand, can be made good only by an infinite
power (*puissance souveraine*, 3049) and thus only by God himself. The
concept of *puissance* becomes a kind of instrumental construct, and it is
easily discernible that its purpose is to make possible the transition from the
representational realm of a powerful liberation to the abstract realm of
moral magnitudes as conceived by the doctrine of satisfaction. However,
even this bridge collapses halfway to its goal. When Sapientia explains why
the Son, not the Father, must make "the great journey," she makes no
reference to the "powerful prince" of the allegorization:

> S'est ainsi que l'omme a failly,
> Si fault qu'il treuve homme pour luy
> qui porte la peine et martire,
> puisque de soy n'y puet souffire. (3064–67)

> *Thus it is that man fell,*
> *Hence he must find a man*
> *to bear the pain and martyrdom,*
> *since he cannot do it himself.*

If we now consider the Arras Passion play from this point of view, we see
something else: Greban is obviously trying to remove the ambivalences in
his model in accord with a strict doctrine of satisfaction. However, insofar
as this purist tendency is extended to the traditional dramatic-dualistic
images as well, the inconsistency of the conceptual and the visual presentation of the working of salvation appears in an even more acute form. Still
more striking than this inconsistency that already exists within the Trial in
Paradise is, however, the inconsistency between the allegorical frame and
the play proper. For the frame does not lead us to expect that this play more
than almost any other makes room, in the devil scenes, for the dramatic-
dualistic counterpart.

V

In contradistinction to the Arras Passion play, Greban puts the whole salvation history on stage. His play begins with a prelude that includes the

creation and the fall of the angels and thus has in Lucifer already achieved the dramatic opposite pole that henceforth keeps things moving forward. The fall is preceded by a more extensive scene in hell, in which Lucifer rages against the fact that humanity is to receive the heavenly seat from which he and his followers were ejected (661–66). Satan is supposed to thwart this divine plan. Thus an argument with which we are familiar appears in a completely altered context. In Anselm, the heavenly city was a metaphorical attribute of the *honor dei.* The point was the necessity of its completion and the consequent necessity of the work of salvation. The play's scene, in contrast, is presented from the point of view of the one who put the choir of angels in a condition requiring restitution and who is now preparing to prevent this restitution. Anselm's metaphorical visualization of a moral category is thus brought back into the mythologeme, and in advance, this mythologeme now inversely moves the subsequent fall out of the moral dimension: Satan does not appear as the incarnation of the evil in men but as the executive organ in a conflict whose antagonists bring mankind into their dispute only indirectly. Anselm's argument first appears with its original function only in the Trial in Paradise at the beginning of the first day of the play, but as one might expect, Satan, who has already successfully battled the divine plan, will not remain inactive in the second phase either.

In fact, Greban's Passion play already shows how the immanent logic of the dualistic image can develop a force and a fascination that not only leave the genuine, very conscientiously formulated program behind but can also seek to surpass the model at the very point where it hesitated for obviously theological reasons. This development is already evident in the scene in hell after the Annunciation, that is, in the first scene that has a counterpart in the Arras Passion play. In Greban's play, it has greater weight not only because of its length (273 lines versus 102 in the model) but also because from the outset it targets Lucifer's strategy, which is immediately conceived in full awareness not only of what he has lost but also of what he has retained:

> ne demeure que mon orgeuil
> qui ne s'est mué ne changié
> en moy depuis qu'il fut forgié
> lassus au pardurable empire,
> si non que toujours il empire,
> sans soi diminuer en rien. (3718–23)

only my pride remains,
which has not altered or changed
in me since it was forged
up there in the perdurable empire,
except that it grows constantly worse
without diminishing in any way.

Along with this enduring pride, Lucifer has also retained a pale reflection of heavenly omniscience. Anticipating what is to occur, he sends Satan to earth to see if perhaps someone might be born there who through his perfect virtue could make good on Adam's failure. If such a person appears, he is to be corrupted and thereby made "unworthy of providing satisfaction" (*indigne pour faire satisfaction*, 3942). However, Lucifer's foresight is limited. If he knew wherein the planned satisfaction consisted, he would have to do everything he could to prevent Jesus' death, and that is just what he does not do—at least not for the time being.

The divergence from the Arras Passion play is first discernible in the massacre of the innocents. As we have seen, in the Arras Passion the scene in hell came after the massacre, and Satan was therefore less interested in the child than in Herod's soul. Greban moves this scene forward (7259–424). Satan reports the rumor that a virgin has given birth to a son who is to redeem mankind and simultaneously announces the imminent massacre, which he has incited Herod to carry out. The massacre thus appears to be a strategic countermeasure intended to kill the opponent. Lucifer praises this plan in the strongest terms and sends Satan back to earth to carry it out. Hence now for the first time the doubling of the opposing power in Lucifer and Satan—which Greban took over from the model—is put into service: just as God sends Jesus to earth, Lucifer sends Satan to destroy the opponent who is threatening the infernal city.

Greban also supplements his model by making a scene in hell, in which Lucifer assigns Satan this special task, precede the temptation of Jesus (10417–539), and this shows clearly the care he takes to fit the action into this perfect symmetry of dualistic authorities. With regard to the salvation of the woman of Canaan, Fergalus complains:

ce Jhesus qui regne sur terre
nous maine la plus forte guerre
qu'oncques fit homme en ce party. (12301–3)

this Jesus who reigns over the earth
is making mightier war on us
than ever did any man in these parts.

Everything is in fact modeled on war, far more explicitly than in the Arras Passion play, and with a far more extensive elaboration of Lucifer's strategy. Thus Greban adds to the scene of Lazarus's awakening from the dead a concluding scene in hell (15061–166), in which Lucifer first has the gate to hell barred, so that such slip-ups won't happen again, and in which Satan then decides to approach the Jews in order to bring about Jesus' death. Lucifer adopts this plan a little later on (17284–423), when he sends Berich to the Pharisees and Satan to Judas—still another significant alteration of the model, in which the remorseful Judas first summons the devils who bring him, at Lucifer's behest, the rope with which he hangs himself and then carry his soul off to hell (13065–187). Greban consequently does not hesitate to make his Satan appear at the Last Supper and remind Judas of their contract (18208–13).

While Greban develops the dualistic image more consistently than did his predecessor, in his play the incarnation slips into exactly the latent docetic perspective of the outwitting of the Devil through Jesus' merely supposed appearance of corporeality that was deliberately avoided in the Arras Passion play. Greban himself recognized this danger. In the case of Pilate's judgment, he follows his model, at the price of an obvious inconsistency: the same Lucifer who had first sent Satan to destroy their opponent, now gives him the assignment of using Pilate's wife to prevent Jesus being condemned. At the same time, however, he once more has the gate of hell shut tight (23233–371). In this latter regard the logic of the image can be maintained, but this means that the dramatic action now moves not primarily toward the cross but once again toward the *descensus*. Immediately before the Crucifixion, the conflict appears with utter clarity. Here Greban has once again supplemented his model. First he has God the Father explain beforehand that Justitia will now be satisfied (24409 ff.). Then follows a scene in hell in which Satan reports his failure to persuade Pilate's wife and Lucifer has the gate of hell locked up again: even before the Crucifixion the action skips over the cross and moves toward the descent into hell—in which Greban's Passion play also finds its dramatic climax (26081–283).

Even the Crucifixion itself is already seen against the background of this impossibility of visually representing the doctrine of satisfaction. When

Satan appears under the cross only to discover with resignation that something is happening there that exceeds his understanding (24885 ff.), the demands of the theological interest are apparently met: the Redemption is carried out by eliminating the dualistic counterauthority, thus directly relating the achievement of satisfaction to God. The defeat of the infernal powers becomes an automatic consequence, as it were, of an event that sidesteps them. However, from the Devil's point of view, which Anselm had very wisely not considered at all, the whole matter remains in the (mythological) dimension of cunning. This becomes evident when Satan waits by the cross, hoping to seize Jesus' soul (24915 ff.), but then has to recognize that what he wanted to carry in triumph off to hell is apparently well on its way there already

> pour rompre portes et verroulx
> et nous destruire et pillier tous. (25872–73)

> *to break through the gates and locks*
> *and destroy and pillage us all.*

Other plays make explicit the mythological character of this scene. In the Alsfeld Passion play, for instance, Satan climbs up the left side of the cross while an angel climbs up the right side; naturally, the angel wins out, and Jesus' soul flies off in the form of a white dove (following 6267). Satan is driven away by another angel with a sword and has moreover to endure being accused of stupidity by his master. The death on the cross is explicitly described as a trick:

> Sathanas geselle, was stundestu dan do?
> nach der sele dorfft dir nyt weßen go,
> want du bist eyn rechter geck:
> die sele is langes hene enwegk!
> ich focht, mer syn daran betrogen:
> sie ist eyn ander wegk gezogen! (6304–9)

> *Satan, my comrade, why did you stand there?*
> *you shouldn't be eager for the soul,*
> *for you are a real clown:*
> *the soul is long gone!*
> *I fear we are thereby tricked:*
> *it has taken another way!*

The genuinely dualistic character of the outwitting is here brought immediately into the image and at the same time brought to the concept, so to
speak. Lucifer's reference to trickery is another very good example of Frye's
"demonic modulation": the dogmatically scarcely tenable formula of God's
pia fraus comes back linked to the Devil's perspective. What is characteristic
here is the source from which religious drama drew this scene of Satan at the
cross: in this case as in others, the apocryphal tradition provides the out-
moded dualistic images with a continuing life that is not disturbed by
developments in the history of dogma.[13]

Greban's Passion play is so informative because in it the dramatic interest in such images comes repeatedly into conflict with dogmatic consciousness. Thus on one hand it cannot forgo the scene with Satan at the cross—
again in opposition to its model, the Arras Passion play—but on the other
hand it still does not go so far as, for instance, the Alsfeld play, which shows
hardly any dogmatic inhibitions. The care with which Greban deals with
the subject of the *pia fraus* is typical. It is hardly noticeable when Satan after
the presentation of Jesus in the temple and Beelzebub after Lazarus is raised
from the dead realize that they have been deceived (7107, 15063). No mention is made of fraud and deception in connection with the death on the
cross. Only in the descent into hell does it appear indirectly and in an out-
of-the-way place. When Cerberus considers complaining about the illegiti-
mate abduction of the souls just freed by Jesus, he is warned by Lucifer:

Ton appel riens n'y pervendroit:
Jhesus, qui la chose a bastie
il seroit la juge et partie. (26203–5)

Your appeal would come to nothing:
Jesus, who performed the act,
would be both judge and adversary.

What Greban cites here in the mode of "demonic modulation" is none
other than the widespread late medieval tradition of the *Processus Belial,* the
trial of the Devil in which the plan considered by Cerberus is staged and
hell's representative has to experience exactly what Lucifer prophesied.[14] In
this mediated way Greban has brought in the *pia fraus.*

One may wonder why he was prepared to do so at all. One may only say
that for Greban the fate of Lucifer, who has been defeated through trickery,

was part of the figure of the prince of hell, which he no doubt found fascinating. Precisely at the point where the fascination becomes particularly clear, theological consciousness also appears no less clearly. For like his predecessors, Greban distanced himself from the descent into hell as a whole. In the prologue and epilogue to the third day there is no reference to this dramatic climax of the whole play. And in the Adam-Christ typology in the concluding Trial in Paradise, the cross stands right in the middle, whereas the descent into hell is mentioned only in passing in a single verse (*mettre mes amis a delivre*, 34233). All these elements cannot, however, conceal the fact that the attempt made in the introductory Trial in Paradise to reinterpret the descent into hell as an allegorization of the whole event of salvation not only fails at that very point, as we already saw, but also and primarily in the play itself. It collides with the indispensability of the Devil as a dramatic counterpart and hence with the succession and competition of incommensurate images. Because of the dualistic description that already began on the first day, the action depends so heavily on the antagonism between Jesus and Satan that the central act of salvation necessarily appears to be the (visible) defeat of the opponent, that is, the mythologeme, and not the (invisible) moral achievement of the suffering man Jesus.

However, in this way the central interest of the doctrine of satisfaction is put in question. The latent Docetism, which Greban first takes into account (with regard to the Massacre of the Innocents) and then avoids (in the scene with Pilate's wife), acquires a new actuality in the scene where Satan appears at the foot of the cross. The moral worth of the Passion becomes implicitly, and occasionally also explicitly, a phase of the outwitting and is thereby made usable for the mythologeme. If this idea is regarded from the point of view of reception, then we perceive very clearly the theologically ruinous ambivalence: the spectacle of the Passion is supposed to turn our eyes back to man's guilt, but such a pious reflection is also constantly disburdened through the projection of just this guilt onto the original enemy, who is powerful elsewhere but defeated in the play.

VI

In the late medieval Passion plays a problematics thus returns that first manifested itself at precisely the point where Christian salvation history was conceived as "drama": in the second-century apologetics that made recurrent use of mythological and particularly gnostic forms of thought. Clement of Alexandria was the first to speak of a Christian "drama of salvation."[15] Salvation history becomes for him a "salvation theater" comparable to Euripides' *Bacchae*, which is played out among Adam, the serpent, and God. It is interesting that since here the incarnation is seen as the putting on of a dramatic mask, the Passion once again becomes a phase in the outwitting of the Devil. Both the conception of the Redemption as a "drama of salvation" and the notion that the redeemer "outwits" the demiurges by taking on a merely apparent corporeality are common ideas in gnostic thought.[16] However, just as already in Paul himself the gnostic way of speaking about the outwitting of the rulers (1 Corinthians 2:6 ff.) remains unconnected with the word of the cross (1 Corinthians 1:18 ff.),[17] so Clement was also unable to integrate the suffering Jesus into the graphic nature of the "drama":

> When the first man played freely in Paradise, he was still the child of God. However, when, giving himself over to pleasure (because it creeps on its belly, the serpent signifies allegorically the worldly vices that devote themselves to matter), he allowed himself to be seduced by his desires, the child grew up disobedient. Man, who was not yet bound to his innocence, found himself bound through sins. The Lord wanted to free him from his bonds, and imprisoned in flesh (this is a great mystery) he overcame the serpent, subdued the tyrant death, and—this is the most extraordinary thing—showed by his outstretched hands that man, who was bound to death, is liberated. What a mysterious wonder! The Lord lay stretched out, man is resurrected, and man, who fell from Paradise, receives an even greater reward, heaven, for the faithful.[18]

The cross is mentioned twice in this passage. First, it appears in connection with the outstretched hands, which indicate the liberation of mankind, and thus as a symbol of the victory of Christ, who—once again, in mythological discourse—"imprisoned in flesh . . . overcame the serpent." Immediately thereafter the death on the cross is evoked by the reference to Jesus stretched out: the graphicness of the gnostic "drama of salvation" cannot be maintained when it has to be made commensurable with the Christian-Pauline conception of the Redemption.

Centuries later, when attempts were made to bring the drama of salvation directly into the picture, failure recurred under more acute conditions. For the position reached at this point in history was no longer open to accommodation but was rather at right angles to phenomenalist Christology of the gnostic type. It is highly significant that in Anselm's *Cur Deus Homo* the gnostic passage in 1 Corinthians 2:8 appears in a surprising context, namely in response to the question as to whether Christ's death also affects the sins of those who killed him:

> A. Hanc quaestionem solvit apostulus qui dixit, quia *si cognovissent, num-quam dominum gloriae crucifixissent* (1 *Cor.* 2:8). Tantum namque dif-ferunt scienter factum peccatum et quod per ignorantiam fit, ut malum quo numquam facere possent pro nimietate sua, si cognosceretur, veniale sit, quia ignoranter factum est. Deum enim occidere nullus homo um-quam scienter saltem velle posset, et ideo qui illum occiderunt ignoran-ter, non in illud infinitum peccatum, cui nulla alia comparari peccata possunt, proruerunt. Nam non consideravimus eius magnitudinem ad videndum, quam bona esset vita illa, secundum hoc quod ignoranter factum est, sed quasi scienter fieret, quod nec umquam fecit aliquis nec facere potuit (II, 15).

> A. *The Apostle resolves this question, saying, "None of the rulers of this age understood this; for if they had, they would not have crucified the Lord of glory." Knowingly committed sins are so clearly distinguished from those com-mitted in ignorance, that the evil they could never do on account of its excess, had they known it, can be forgiven, because it was done unwittingly. For no man can knowingly or even willingly kill God, and for that reason those who killed Him unknowingly did not fall into that infinitely great sin, to which no other sin can be compared. In order to see how good this life is, we have ac-cordingly not considered the magnitude of the sin with regard to whether it was committed in ignorance, but rather with regard to whether it was com-mitted knowingly, which no one was ever able to do and never will be able to do.*

The passage is thus not connected with the "rulers of this world," as it is in its biblical context but rather with the men who, not knowing Jesus and his divinity, killed him, that is, with the Jews. Redemption is available to them if only they want it—in contrast with the Devil, concerning whom it is explicitly said in the next to last chapter that he cannot possibly be recon-ciled. Thus once again Anselm's antidualistic strategy is manifest. Whereas he relates ignorant killing to men and thus excises the Devil and his outwit-ting, he removes the isolated statements in 1 Corinthians 2:8 from the context of the mythologeme and makes them a point in his moral argumentation. The play, however, is thus overloaded. It has to hold fast to a phenomenalist Christology and in reality presents the gnostic model, whereby we mean by gnostic a type most clearly seen in religious historians' reconstruction of a gnostic redeemer myth, and not, of course, the reception of such a myth itself: the celestial redeemer is sent by God the Father to earth, where he battles and conquers the Devil and then returns to his heavenly home. While all this draws on and carries out the doctrine of satisfaction set forth in the Trial in Paradise, it lays bare the aporias of this doctrine, which are concealed conceptually only with great difficulty. The shift into visibility moves the conception of God in Anselm and in Scholasticism back into a mythological dualism, into a "drama of salvation." Frye says at one point that "the crudest of Plautine comedy-formulas has much the same *structure* as the central Christian myth itself, with its divine son appeasing the wrath of a father and redeeming what is at once a society and a bride."[19] For Frye himself this sort of homology is a kind of resultant; as we now see, it should have been a heuristic fiction serving as a starting point for functional-structural analyses of the type we have undertaken here in relation to Anselm's refutation of such a "nuclear myth."

No matter how valuable Greban's Passion play may have been for this purpose, it is not enough to consider religious drama and in particular the Passion plays wholly in terms of the price to be paid for visibility alone. For from this point of view the play always appears merely as a derivative, a byproduct, a compromise between the strength of the concept and the limits of the image. However, what we showed earlier with regard to the Easter play and the Adam play is also valid here: that these images were acted out and ritualized in this kind of play. Thus in the Passion play the doctrine of satisfaction is not primarily threatened by the fact that the cross cannot be integrated into the oppositional structure of the dualistic image. The ambivalence of this Passion is far more a product of the identical repetition of the Crucifixion in the play. In this way become visible, as we shall soon see, impulses that can no longer be reconciled with the moral interests of the doctrine of satisfaction but instead shift the historical sacrifice out of the kerygmatic dimension and into the archetypal dimension of a ritual sacrifice.

CHAPTER 9

Jesus As Scapegoat I:
Compassio and Ritual Graphicness

I

In the first chapter of her book on Shakespeare, which is devoted to the late medieval Passion plays, A. Righter cites a passage from Thomas Beard's *Theatre of God's Judgment* (1631) reporting a performance in which the actor playing Jesus was fatally wounded by the centurion's sword-thrust.[1] Righter does not merely see in this kind of occurrence an error in performance but rather tries to discern in it the "awesome immediacy" and the "curious sense of violence" of a stage on which play and reality were inseparably interwoven. In actuality, the plays must have presented martyrdom with an intense and unmediated ferocity and graphicness that strike us as eerie. On the basis of the slightest references, often only allusions in the gospels, thousands of verses that filled two or more days were studded with unequaled cruelties and performed before crowds that could number ten thousand and more. If one wants a more detailed account of the extent of these cruelties, one must turn once again to Arnoul Greban's Passion play. This play and the Passion by his successor Jean Michel, whose scenes of torture are closely connected with it, are surpassed by hardly any other play of the late Middle Ages in their extensive and detailed representation of the martyrs.

Greban's Passion illustrates in an exemplary way not only the whole spectrum of the cruelties that characterize these plays but also their theological problematics, and I shall begin with the latter. This problematics consists in the fact that the doctrine of satisfaction, which enters the tradition precisely in Greban's play, does not require this kind of graphic elaboration on martyrdom. In fact, in Anselm we read that the Devil is to be conquered with the greatest possible difficulty, but Anselm refers to giving up one's life voluntarily.[2] The interest of his argument is directed to the voluntary death of the innocent God-Man—not to the detailed circumstances of this death, a focus that first really appears in the medieval reception history of this doctrine. Even if the *neccessitas* of Christ's death is not questioned, at least its detailed circumstances are, and people limited themselves to referring to mere *convenientia*. This argument no longer starts out, as did Anselm's, from the plan of salvation—in order to derive from it the necessity of Jesus' death—but rather from the biblical fact of the Crucifixion, which is now taken to be the most appropriate kind of redemption. As the decisive relevant passage in Thomas Aquinas (*Summa theologica*, III, *quaestio* 46) shows, this kind of reference has an express defensive interest: the biblical details of the most humiliating of all deaths are, so to speak, rescued (for the most part through typological projection back onto the Old Testament) from the theoretically acknowledged possibility that a *minima passio* would have been sufficient to redeem all the sins of mankind. Nevertheless: *secundum convenientiam, sufficiens fuit quod pateretur omnia genera passionem* (46, 5). Thomas counts among these kinds of suffering those involving individual limbs of the body. These include all the tortures reported in the Bible but no more than these. Thomas's interest is in the assignment of the individual pains to the various limbs and senses but not in depiction and detailing. And in that respect his interest is most clearly different from that of the plays, which in every case go beyond the synoptic gospels.

This difference becomes fully evident if we contrast them not with the Scholasticism of the high Middle Ages but rather with the contemporary nominalism. In the latter this very *convenientia* reappears in the free and arbitrary *acceptatio* of the sacrifice by the sovereign divine will, which nonetheless could just as well have declared the death of an angel or of a *purus homo* who had remained free of earthly sin to be an adequate satisfaction.[3] No path is marked out in advance that leads from this nominalist *satisfactio secundum acceptationem* to the graphicness of martyrdom as it is presented in the plays. The formula "nominalistic naturalism," to which H. Kindermann in his *Theatergeschichte Europas* sought to reduce the Passion plays, is a short-circuit.[4]

Greban confirms this idea. The prologue to the third day allows us to recognize a model for the presentation of martyrdom that is heterogeneous with respect to the dogmatic tradition: the mysticism of the Passion. For its part, the latter draws its essential impulse from the interest in Jesus' Crucifixion implicit in the doctrine of satisfaction but does not direct this interest back toward the injured honor of God but rather—at least primarily—to the sympathetic observer. The central concepts of *contemplacion* and *compassion* appear right at the beginning of the prologue (19915, 19908), at whose midpoint the familiar mirror metaphor then appears, according to which the Passion is supposed to make it easier for the reverent observer to bear his own suffering:

> Ainsi va ses dueulz moderant,
> en ce mirouer considerant,
> ou tout cueur, pour son dueil mirer,
> se doit parfondement mirer.
> Et, affin que vous y mirez
> et doucement la remirez,
> ce devost mirouer pour le mieulx
> vous ramenons devant les yeulx,
> senssiblement, par parsonnaiges.
> Mirez vous si serez bien saiges,
> chascun sa fourme y entrevoit:
> qui bien se mire bien se voit
> Dieu doint que si bien nous mirons
> que, par mirer, nous remirons,
> après ceste vie mortelle,
> la puissant essence immortelle
> qui regne sans jamais tarir. (19948–64)

> *Thus he moderates his pains,*
> *by looking into this mirror,*
> *where every heart, to see its sorrow*
> *ought to profoundly consider itself.*
> *And so that you might see yourself there*
> *and gently look at it,*
> *this pious mirror for your own good*
> *we bring before your eyes,*
> *in visible form, with characters.*
> *Look at yourself, if you are wise,*
> *each of you sees his form there:*
> *Anyone who really looks will really see himself.*
> *May God grant that if we look at ourselves,*

by looking we may perceive,
after this mortal life,
the powerful immortal essence
that reigns inexhaustibly.

What Greban does here can be seen as an exemplary articulation of the theological and official self-conception of late medieval visual representation of the Passion. The mirror stands metaphorically for the *imitatio Christi* and also appears with this meaning in the writings of the mystics. Thus Johannes Tauler commends "the change in the images of our Lord," in order to order life "in mirror-fashion," following the model provided by Christ.[5] Although in the passage quoted the reference is to correctly hearing and understanding (19932), this statement reminds us of the mystical preachers who sought to bring before the inner eye the Passion that the play now presents "visibly" (*sensiblement*), "with characters" (*par parsonnaiges*). On the other hand, what distinguishes the play from mysticism and makes it apparently more theologically acceptable is the strong emphasis on the didactic element and the accompanying omission of all the tendencies specific to mysticism, such as separation, retreat, isolation, and a personal search for salvation outside of ecclesiastical or institutional mediation. The mystical schema of levels, which leads from *contemplatio* through *compassio* to *unio*, is taken over by the play in a reduced form focusing on the moral worth of emulating Christ, wherein it approaches other forms of meditative-didactic Passion literature (history, treatise, sermon, elaboration of a legend).[6]

Nevertheless, in presenting martyrdom the plays also draw on motifs that have to be considered specific products of visionary and ecstatic Passion mysticism. These sources have been frequently (but not up to this point systematically) collected, without however making clear the central problem that concerns us here. As so often happens, it was apparently believed that the matter was cleared up once an "influence" had been named. However, "influences" can divert our attention from the difference between completely heterogeneous functions. For the graphic details of the mystics, because they are represented *in vivo*, not only acquire a renewed unmediated intensity and urgency but also are acted out to an extent that can be explained only by an additional interest specific to the play. Bonaventura's *Itinerarium mentis in Deum*, Jacopo of Milan's *Stimulus amoris*, and especially the *Meditationes vitae Christi* also produced by Italian Franciscans, the Cistercian-influenced apocryphal writings such as the so-called *Dialogus beatae Mariae et Anselmi de passione domini,* or the *Liber de passione Christi et doloribus et planctibus matris ejus,* and finally the visionary nun-mysticism like that of the *Revelationes* of St. Bridget of Sweden—all these documents distinguish themselves by offering more and more precise information about the Passion than do the synoptic gospels, and yet their detailed description of the martyrs and their suffering is far surpassed by the plays. For example, the motif of Jesus being spat upon, which is not elaborated in the Gospels (Matthew 26:67, 27:30, Mark 14:65, 15:19) is initially intensified in the *Dialogus beatae Mariae et Anselmi*: "consputus fuit quod quasi leprosus apparebat."[7] However, the stakes and the goal are incomparably more graphic in the Arras Passion, which even Greban could not take over in this detailed form:

> A no roy fault porter honneur,
> Il a son musiel tout honny,
> Je feray une roye cy,
> Pour ce que d'eaue point n'avons,
> Laver lui fault de racquellons,
> Cellui qui mieulx le racquera,
> Ung lot de vin il gaignera,
> Mais racquier faulra ou moillon.

> LE IIe DE JHERUSALEM
> Esse salive ou moucquillon
> Qu'on racquera empres son nez?

> LE PREMIER DE SIDON
> Racquiez lequel vous volez,
> Le plus ort est tout le meilleur.

> LE PREMIER DE JHERUSALEM
> Je croy qu'il y ara pieur,
> Avisez lequel, Jacopin.

> LE IIE DE THIRY
> Tu as locquiet un beau loppin,
> Mais il va trop devers l'oreille.

> LE IIIE DE JHERUSALEM
> Racquons d'accord, je le conseille.

> LE V^E DE SIDON
> C'est bien dit, nous sommes d'accort,
> Ve la et la j'ay sur le bort.

LE IIE DE JHERUSALEM

Ve la es dens et sur la joie.

LE PREMIER DE SIDON

Racque plus hault, je te le loie,
Racque fort, fiers en la narine,
Que Dieu lui envoie mal estine,
Il sera bien appareillié.
Avise la.

LE IIE DE SIDON

   C'est bien alé,
Il est entre l'oeil et le nez.
Or avisez la, avisez,
L'ay je assis sur le menton!
J'ay racquiet de bonne façon,
S'il fust plus hault, j'eusse le pris.

LE IIIIe DE SIDON

Il me semble qu'il en a ris.
S'il ny a meilleur, je l'aray.

LE Ve DE JHERUSALEM

Or avise droit la, je l'ay,
J'ay racquiet droit ens ou mouillon.

LE IIIIe DE JHERUSALEM

T'as passé la roye.

THARE

   Ça mon,
Il nous convient recommencier. (14610–47)

Our king must be honored,
His face has been dirtied,
I'll make a rule here,
Since we have no water,
we'll have to wash him with spit,
the one who spits on him best,
will win a jug of wine,
but he must spit right at the middle.

SECOND MAN FROM JERUSALEM
Is it slime or snot
We'll spit at his nose?

FIRST MAN FROM SIDON
Spit whatever you want,
The more disgusting the better.

FIRST MAN FROM JERUSALEM
II think there'll be something worse;
Look and see, Jacopin.

SECOND MAN FROM TYRE
You've picked off a big piece,
But it's going too far toward the ear.

THIRD MAN FROM JERUSALEM
Let's spit together, that's my advice.

FIFTH MAN FROM SIDON
Right, we're in agreement there,
see there and there, I've got the side.

SECOND MAN FROM JERUSALEM
See there, on the teeth and cheeks.

FIRST MAN FROM SIDON
Spit higher up, I tell you,
Spit hard in his nostril,
Let God send him the worst,
He'll look nice.
Look there.

SECOND MAN FROM SIDON
             That's good,
It's between the eye and the nose.
Look out now, look out,
I've put it on the chin!
I've spat the right way,
If it were higher up I'd have won the prize.

FOURTH MAN FROM SIDON
It seems to me he laughed at it.
If there's nothing better, I'll get it.

THE FIFTH MAN FROM JERUSALEM
Now look right there, I've got it,
I've spat right in the middle.

FOURTH MAN FROM JERUSALEM
You've gone too far.

THARE

Well,
We'll just have to start over.

The source says nothing at all about the interest that lies behind this elaboration. By itself, it explains neither why it was taken over nor why it was developed into just such a nasty kind of "play." Mysticism for the most part omits such action.[8] It focuses on the martyred Christ and his wounds and thus the *compassio* is always simultaneously thematized through Mary's perspective. A typical example of this type of description can be found in St. Bridget: Christ, covered with blood flowing from the wounds made by the crown of thorns, has to wipe his eyes in order to see his mother.[9] The plays explode this perspective, even where the pious women accompany Jesus on the entire way to Golgotha, as for the most part in the French tradition, which is marked by the pseudo-Bonaventuran *Meditationes.* The action elaborated at each of the stations of the cross goes far beyond the direct or indirect *compassio* demands of the Marys scenes that are repeated in each case. If in addition figures like Pilate or even the torturers are made to express compassion, these are secondary moments of compensation, between which an action takes place that is no longer oriented toward moral transposition at all.

Hence we should not allow ourselves to be misled by such pseudo-didactic indications, trying to interpret solely as moral *imitatio Christi* what is based on altogether different interests. The availability of official opportunities for compensation still does not explain why they were used in just this way. The identity of particular Passion motifs provides evidence for a relationship between Passion mysticism and drama, and at the same time for a discrepancy between self-understanding and its undiscovered impulses. We need not go into here the kind of impulses that were behind mysticism—and in particular behind certain forms of visionary and ecstatic mysticism and especially female mysticism.[10] In any case the plays received their graphic details from an interest that could also no longer be contained morally, and this interest peculiar to the play will be investigated in the following analysis of Greban's Passion.

II

The first crucial scene to be examined is Annas's interrogation of Jesus. Biblically, this interrogation is based solely on an unclear passage in John 18:12 ff., which was nonetheless already widely interpreted in patristic writings as suggesting that Jesus was indeed first taken to Annas but only later on interrogated by Caiaphas.[11]

However, Greban does not allow the opportunity to begin with the martyrdom to go unexploited (as it does in most of the German plays), locating it right at the end of the second day and at the same time anticipating the third day. Since the interrogation itself to a large extent coincides with Caiaphas's later questioning, Greban's interest was not in the interrogation itself but rather in the first torture scene that follows it. In fact, the slap with which the biblical scene concludes (John 18:22) is here only a beginning. Since Annas can no longer consult his colleagues, because of the late hour, he has the prisoner bound to a column (19582 ff.) and guarded by his men:

ANNE
Venez ça, mesgniee mauvaise,
ouez que je vueil proposer:
je m'en vois ung pou reposer
tant que l'aube du matin viengne.
De cest homme icy vous souviengne
tant que vous aymez vostre vye,
gardez le bien qu'il ne s'enfuye,
veillez le icy toute la nuyt
et, affin qu'il ne vous ennuyt,
esbatez vous a quelque jeu.

ROILLART
Nostre esbat est ja tout pourveu:
a riens ne nous voulons esbastre
sinon a le torcher et batre
si nous en mocquer entre nous. (19728–41)

ANNAS
Come here, you evil troop,
hear what I have to say:
I am going to rest a while

until the morning sun comes up.
Keep an eye on this man here
As you value your lives,
make sure he doesn't get away,
watch him all night here
and, so that you don't get bored,
amuse yourselves with some game.

DIRTBAG
We've got our sport already:
We don't want to play at anything
Other than tormenting and beating him
And thus mocking him, all of us.

Jeu ("game," "sport") and *esbatre* ("amuse") are the key words in what follows here and in later scenes on the third day. Jesus, bound firmly to the column and motionless in his exhaustion, has to be "awakened" (19757 ff.). Lots are drawn to see who will have the pleasure of striking the first blow. Dentart wins, but he is not content with a single blow and gets into a fight with the other men:

DENTART
As tu ce malice advisé?
Martin voit pres, le diable y court.

ROILLART
C'est a tromperie et a tort.
Comment n'entens tu point le jeu?

DENTART
Le coquin pour qui je l'ay eu,
le comperra ou je fauldray.
A quel costé luy asserray
une broignie sans farser?

GADIFFER
Ha, que voulentiers le verray!

DENTART
A quel costé luy asserray?

ROILLART
Dela, et je luy donrray
une deça pour redresser.

DENTART
Tien, va jouer!

ROILLART

> Tien, va dancer!

GADIFFER
An dea, mon tour garder vouldray.
Il me fault ung petit penser
a quel costé luy asserray
une broignie sans farser.

DENTART
Or, tien, vela pour toy armer.
Je te donne ceste huvecte. (19792 ff.)

BUCKTOOTH
Did you see that trick?
Martin's looking, the devil's at it.

DIRTBAG
It's cheating and wrong.
Don't you understand the game?

BUCKTOOTH
The rascal who did it to me
Will pay for it wherever I want.
Where should I hit him
a good one, no joke?

TOSSPOT
Ah, I'd like to see that.

BUCKTOOTH
Where should I hit him?

DIRTBAG
On the other side, and I'll hit him
On this side to straighten him up again.

BUCKTOOTH
Take that, now go play!

DIRTBAG

> *Take that, now go dance!*

TOSSPOT

Ah, gad, I'd like to keep my turn.
I have to think a little:
Where should I hit him
a good one, no joke?

BUCKTOOTH

Here, take this to protect yourself.
I'll give you this helmet.

What Greban has composed here is a rondeau with the rhyme scheme ABaAabbabAB, that is, an extended "rondeau triolet" with a one-line internal refrain and a two-line concluding refrain. The rondeau, which was from the outset a dance song, is a lyrical genre whose first representative is Adam de la Halle. With the fourteenth-century *Miracles de Notre Dame* it also found its way into religious drama and developed—in the form of the so-called "dramatic rondeau"—its own tradition, whose impulses then had an effect on the lyric. The functions of the rondeau in religious drama are manifold. It serves as a hymn to the Godhead, as prayer and song of praise, as pastoral song, as lament of the fallen angels, as a battle or attack song, etc.[12] Greban's Passion represents a high point in the history of the rondeau, with regard to both the formal variations he developed and the density with which he inserts it into the action. Frequently striking, and occasionally following one another, the rondeaux appear where their function seems at first not clearly determinable: in the central scenes of martyrdom. A first aid to understanding is provided by O. Jodogne's observation that the "dramatic rondeau" reflects "the agreement of some secondary characters with the movements of the group."[13] In actuality this observation seems to me applicable to the key scenes in the Passion. The refrain here connects the torturers to a play that is cruel, this time, and precisely the passages that are apparently highly literary become an indication of a preliterary dimension in which these plays still move: the "dramatic rondeau" structures a ritual.

In the same way, in the hearing before Caiaphas the biblical gesture of the rending of garments (Matthew 26:65, Mark 14:63) is underscored by a rondeau. The thrice-repeated *Ostés, ostés/il est coupable de mort griefve* ("Stop, stop,/he deserves death," 20742 ff.) becomes a prelude to a large-scale ritual whose individual phases (spitting, abuse, beating) are stressed by additional rondeaux (20799 ff., 20815 ff., 20853 ff.). The whole performance is once again characterized as *esbas, jeu* (20833, 20816, 20953)—as a play that horrifies the tormentors of the meanwhile wholly undone victim. In order to be able to continue anyway, they discover, again drawing on the synoptic gospels (Matthew 26:67–68, Mark, 14:65, Luke 22:63–64), a new game. They cover Jesus' head, striking him and letting him guess who has dealt the blow, the biblical *crucifige, crucifige eum* returning in another rondeau and, with still another, ending a first phase of the martyrdom:

MALCUIDANT
Or, prophetize maintenant
qui t'a baillé ce horïon.

DRAGON
Tu est tant saige et advenan:
or, prophetize maintenant.

GOULU
Je sçaray tout en ung tenant
se son sens vault ung porïon.
Or prophetize maintenant
qui t'a baillé ce horïon.

BRUYANT
Il nous songe cy le moron;
noz faiz ne luy semblent que truffes.
Resveillons le!

ESTONNÉ
        De quoy?

BRUYANT
              De buffes,
tant que nous pourrons ramonner.

MALCUIDANT
Pour raplastir ces grosses buffes,
resveillons le!

DRAGON
        De quoy?

MALCUIDANT
            De buffes.

DRAGON
Et dea, Malcuidant, tu te truffes:
tu ne fais point tes coups sonner.
Resveillons le!

GOULU
> De quoy?

DRAGON
> > De buffes,
> tant que nous pourrons ramonner. (20931–48)

DISBELIEVER
Now prophesy to us, you Christ!
Who is it that struck you?

DRAGOON
You're so smart and attractive:
Now prophesy.

LOUT
I'll find out once and for all
If his head is worth a leek.
Now prophesy
Who struck this blow.

LOUDMOUTH
He thinks we're fools here;
What we're doing seems to him mere mockery.
Let's wake him up!

SCATTERBRAIN
> > *What with?*

LOUDMOUTH
> > > *With blows,*
> *as many as we can lay on him.*

DISBELIEVER
To tamp down this heavy breathing,
let's wake him up!

DRAGOON
> > *What with?*

DISBELIEVER
> > > *With blows.*

DRAGOON
Hey now, Disbeliever, you're kidding around:

you're not making your blows resound.
Let's wake him up.

LOUT

What with?

DRAGOON

With blows,
As many as we can lay on him.

The scourging continues. From the biblical *crucifige* (Matthew 27:23, Mark 15:13–14, Luke 23:21, John 19:6) comes the rondeau *Porte, porte, porte au gibet/et sur piéz le nous crucifie!* ("Take him, take him, take him to the gibbet,/and crucify him by the feet!" 22631 ff.). Pilate has Jesus tied to a column and stripped, then hands him over to the scourgers with the rondeau *Frappez fort, frappez ribaudaille/Homme ne se mecte en oubly!* ("Hit hard, hit him, you rascals!/May no one fail to strike!"). The gathering of the rods is accompanied by another rondeau (22769 ff.), until the whipping begins (22795 ff.). Pilate again eggs on the tormentors, and with the beginning of a particularly clever rondeau refrain arising out of the specific ritual moment, the scourging reaches its apex:

BROYEFORT

Que plaidez vous?
Voicy quanque vous demandez.

PYLATE

Avant, garsons, vous vous rendez!
Reprenez alaine et vertu
et le me rendez tant batu
de tous lez qu'il n'y ait que batre.

GRIFFON

Empreuf.

ORILLART

Et deux.

BROYART

Et trois.

CLAQUEDENT

Et quatre
et le cinquieme de surcrois.

GRIFFON
Telz metz faut il a ung follatre.
E m p r e u f.

ORILLART
      E t d e u x.

BRAYART
           E t t r o i s.

CLAQUEDENT
                E t q u a t r e

BROYEFORT
Griffon, tu comptes sans rabatre:
pour ung coup tu en frappes trois.

GRIFFON
Quand ce sont dix, fais une crois:
je ne le fais que pour esbatre.
E m p r e u f.

ORILLART
      E t d e u x.

BRAYART
           E t t r o i s.

CLAQUEDENT
                E t q u a t r e.
E t l e c i n q u i e m e d e s u r c r o i s,
qui luy donrra?

GRIFFON
        Se tu m'en crois,
baille luy hardiment la touche. (22798–815)

TROUBLEMAKER
        Why are you complaining?
Here's as much as you want.

PILATE
Come on, boys, you're giving up!
Catch your breath and take heart,
beat him up for me so much
that there's nowhere left to hit.

ROWDY
Here's number one.

BIG-EAR
                    And two.

BRAYER
                                        And three.

CHATTERTOOTH
                                                            And four

and number five to boot.

ROWDY
That's the kind of dish to serve a fool.
Here's number one.

BIG-EAR
                    And two.

BRAYER
                                        And three.

CHATTERTOOTH
                                                            And four.

TROUBLEMAKER
Rowdy, you're counting without letting up:
You're striking three blows for every one.

ROWDY
When it gets up to ten, mark it down:
I'm only doing it for the fun of it.
Here's number one.

BIG-EAR
                    And two.

BRAYER
                                        And three.

CHATTERTOOTH
                                                            And four.

And the fifth one to boot,
who's going to give it to him?

ROWDY
>   *Take my advice,*
>   *and hit him a good one.*

After Pilate, who has been so cruel but now suddenly feels sympathy, has tried to call a halt to the beating, the royal ritual begins with the putting on of the tattered purple robe and the crown of thorns—which is interrupted once again by people spitting on Jesus. The crown, whose thorns are so sharp that it can't be held in the hand, is jammed on with big sticks *jusques au fin fons du cerveau* ("right down into the brain," 22936). However, even when homage is paid to Jesus with blood streaming down his body, the cruel play does not come to an end. A final *jeu* follows (22953, 22963), in which the tormentors compete in tearing out the victim's beard. The winner is supposed to be the one who can pull out the biggest handful. Big-ear is the best at this:

> Je l'ay ja si ferme empoignee
> que la char est venue apres
> et le cler sang. (22957–59)

> *I grabbed it so hard*
> *the flesh came along with it*
> *and the bright blood.*

Greban seems to have sensed that here he had arrived at the limit of what was possible, for almost as soon as it has begun, he allows this last scene to be broken off by Pilate's reference to *Ecce homo* (22971 ff.). The Jews nevertheless go on relentlessly. The large-scale ritual began with a rondeau framing the biblical *crucifige*, and it ends with another such: *Il faut qu'il soit en croix pendu/ou nous ne sommes point contens* ("He has to be hung on a cross/or we won't be satisfied," 22995 ff.).

The path to Golgotha begins with the ripping-off of the purple robe, which has stuck fast to the wounds and now opens them up again (23824 ff.). Chanting the rondeau *Si luy fault donner du remis/d'un baston travers ses costéz* ("We'll have to get him going again/with a stick across his ribs," 24187 ff.), the tormentors goad Jesus, who under the burden of the cross is not moving forward. When they arrive at the place of execution, Jesus' clothes are removed and he is laid upon the cross and attached to the wood with blunt nails. Since the holes have been bored too far apart, his arms must be pulled apart with heavy rope by three finger-lengths, *jusqu'aux nerfz desjoindre* ("to the point of separating the ligaments," 24700), and this again takes place in a rondeau form:

GRIFFON
Or, tirez fort, fort, ribaudaille!
La main y vient ou pou s'en fault.

BROYEFORT
Il n'est pas besoin que je y faille.
Or, tirez fort!

BRAYART
       Fort, ribaudaille!
J'ay paour que le cueur ne luy faille
au tirer.

CLAQUEDENT
Mais, que nous en chault?
Or, tirez fort!

GRIFFON
       Fort, ribaudaille!
La main y vient ou pou s'en fault. (24705–12)

ROWDY
Now pull hard, hard, you rascals!
The hand almost reaches.

TROUBLEMAKER
I don't need to fail at that.
Now pull hard!

BRAYER
       Hard, you rascals!
I'm afraid his heart will fail
with all this pulling.

CHATTERTOOTH
But what do we care?
Now pull hard!

ROWDY
       Hard, you rascals!
The hand almost reaches.

After what happened with the arms has been repeated during the nailing of the feet (24725 ff.), each of the victim's bones can be counted, as a tormentor gleefully observes (24763–64). When they attempt to pull out his teeth as well, Greban has Pilate once again call a halt and order the cross erected, and therewith—in another clever use of the refrain technique—the ritual reaches its climax:

PYLATE
Prenez moy lances et paffus,
juisarmes, picques, estendars,
eschelles, pavillons et dars;
chascun saudars la main y teingne
et chascun son cousté soustiengne
de bonne puissance et rëalle.
A m o n t!

GRIFFON
    A m o n t!

CLAQUEDENT
        H a l l e b o i s!

ORILLART
            H a l l e!
S o u s t e n e z l a!

BRAYART
      M a i s s o u s t e n e z.
Tous le faiz dessus nous devalle.
A m o n t!

BROYEFORT
    A m o n t!

GRIFFON
    H a l l e b o y s!

CLAQUEDENT
        H a l l e!
Oncques je n'euz charge si malle:
je me romps se vous n'y venez.
A m o n t!

ORILLANT
    A m o n t!

BRAYART

        H a l l e b o y s!

BROYEFORT

                    H a l l e!

S o u s t e n e z l a!

GRIFFON

M a i s s o u s t e n e z! (24779–92)

PILATE

Take lances and swords,

flails and scourges, pikes, standards,

ladders, flags, and arrows;

Let each guy put his hand to it

and each do his part

with good real strength.

Up!

ROWDY

    Up!

CHATTERTOOTH

       Haul on the wood!

BIG-EAR

               Haul on!

Hold it up!

BRAYER

      Hey, hold it up.

All the weight is on us.

Up!

TROUBLEMAKER

    Up!

ROWDY

       Haul on the wood!

CHATTERTOOTH

            Haul!

I never bore such a terrible weight:

I'm going to collapse if you don't help.

Up!

BIG-EARS

Up!

BRAYER

Haul on the wood!

TROUBLEMAKER

Haul!

Hold it up!

ROWDY

Hey, hold it up!

III

It is not only in France that the tormentors make everything into "play," using Jesus as a sort of "toy." In Germany the Eger Corpus Christi play is a particularly informative example. Here too Annas's men begin immediately with their "merry play." It is called *puczpirn* (4517), "pear-shaking": they all form a circle around Jesus, who stands *in medio*, and then they all run at him, shaking, hitting, and shoving him. Caiaphas goes further:

SEYBLEIN DICIT:
Herr, gib uns in ein weil her
Und las uns spiln nach unser beger.

CAYPHAS DICIT:
Nempt in hin den ungelencken
Und spilt mit im, was ir kindt erdencken.

HELFLEIN DICIT:
Rattet irn herrn mit ganzen sinnen,
Was spil wel wir mit im beginnen?

SCHLEM DICIT:
Ich rat mit ganzen treuen,
Das alt spil wel wir wider verneuen.

MAGOCK DICIT:
Ich weis kein pesser kurzweil neicht,
Wir spilen mit im kopauff ins licht. (4694–703)

SEYBLEIN SAYS:
Lord, give him to us for a while
and let us play the way we want to.

CAIAPHAS SAYS:

Take that broken man there
And play with him however you wish.

HELFLEIN SAYS:

Men, rack your brains and advise:
What game do we want to play with him?

SCHLEM SAYS:

I advise with all sincerity
That we renew our old play with him.

MAGOCK SAYS:

I can think of no better pastime
than playing blind man's bluff with him.

In the Hegge, Wakefield, and York cycles, English variations on "blind man's bluff" appear,[14] and here, with regard to the English cycles, a ritual character is for the first time expressly attributed to this cruel play. Thus J. Speirs made the excellent observation that in the Gospels Jesus' stubborn refusal to respond to any of his tormentors' questions or jibes has a moral dimension, whereas in the plays it becomes a ritual symptom: "in these episodes of the Mystery cycle, Christ has something of the mysterious impersonal or non-human quality of the sacrificial victim, something even of the passivity or immobility of a masked figure or of a sacred doll or puppet, image of god. Thus the Buffeting is, it seems, essentially a rite."[15] A. P. Rossiter speaks similarly of the cruelties of the Passion as the pagangrotesque side of a "Gothic" drama, characterized by the "presence of two rituals at once, of which the one is the negation of the faith to which the piece is ostensibly devoted."[16]

It is no accident that such attempts at ritualistic interpretation emerged in English scholarship. They are the product of a folkloric tradition that is comparable to the Vienna school's but that was not subjected to comparable tests of endurance. Of course, they do not escape the fundamental problematics of any approach seeking to establish a popular continuity. Rossiter is in Chambers's tradition. His history of English drama is a prehistory of Elizabethan theater, and like all prehistories, it is obligated not only to produce what is attributed to the period itself (i.e., the opposition between sublime and grotesque) but in addition—and here Rossiter is comparable to Stumpfl—to assume a dramatic continuity in performance and folklore tradition that cannot be proven.[17] Speirs fails in a similar manner when he draws directly on the Cambridge School tradition in connecting religious drama in a completely unmediated way with an archetypal king-ritual on the model of A. M. Hocart's *Kingship* (1927) and Lord Raglan's *Hero* (1937), which is supposed to have endured as a sort of substrate. His description of the cycles—in itself correct—as a drama that is not didactic but instead still extensively ritualistic thus goes along with the thesis of a "parallel between the ritual origins of Greek drama and those of English drama," whose hastiness we have already demonstrated in the first part of our study.[18]

With regard to such attempts, we will thus need to make a hermeneutically enlightened archetypal criticism fruitful in the same way as we did with regard to Stumpfl and Hardison in discussing the Easter play. In the former case we were concerned with the archetype of the rebirth of the god, as in Frye's system, and thus with *anagnorisis*; here, it is a question of the *pathos* and *sparagmos* phase, of the god's sacrifice as a *pharmakos*, as a scapegoat.[19] According to Christian doctrine, however, Jesus did not die as a ritual *pharmakos*—even if, as Frazer suggested in an appendix to *The Scapegoat*, he was killed by the Jews within the framework of an annual Haman ritual.[20] What Jesus was to the Jews, according to Frazer, he is not yet for Christians. Seen in this way, however, the question as to whether or not Jesus was killed by the Jews as a ritual victim is far less important than another of Frazer's references to the Christian interpretation of the festival of Purim. For Christians, in this case there was in fact a connection: for a long time they had seen in the ritual destruction of the image of Haman a blasphemous parody of the Crucifixion of Jesus and tried to put an end to this Jewish custom. Although the Codex Thedosianus already made practicing this custom a punishable offense, it continued, as Frazer observed, into the eighteenth century.[21] It was, however, particularly controversial in the late Middle Ages and may be regarded as one of the chief grounds for the inflammatory accusations that Jews practiced ritual murder.[22] It seems entirely possible that these accusations also played a role in the elaboration of the Passion play. Thus it is perhaps no accident that Greban has the martyrdom begin with a scene (once again in rondeau form) with Annas's retinue where secrecy is stressed:

DENTART
Puisqu'il n'est ame qui nous voye,
pour la doubte du sommillier,
il le fault ung pou resveillier.

GADIFFER
Il y convient dresser la voye
puisqu'il n'est ame qui nous voye.

ROILLART
Comment?

DENTART
　　　De torchons a montjoye
dont il ara plus d'un millier.

GADIFFER
Et, fust il filz de chevalier,
puisqu'il n'est ame qui nous voye,
pour la doubte du sommillier,
il le fault ung peu resveillier. (19756–66)

BUCKTOOTH:
Since there's no one to see us,
for fear that he might be sleeping,
we'll have to wake him up a bit.

TOSSPOT
We should tie on his burden
Since there's no one to see us.

DIRTBAG
How?

BUCKTOOTH
　　With lots of rags,
he'll have more than a thousand.

TOSSPOT
And, even if he were a knight's son,
Since there's no one to see us,
for fear that he might be sleeping,
we'll have to wake him up a bit.

These and the following cruel "games" are thus supposed to constitute a play within the play, a Jewish ritual within a *historia passionis* seen in Christian terms, blind brutality compensated in the *gloria passionis* of which the observer is at all times aware. The question is whether such explanations suffice, indeed whether they are not more likely to obscure a far more important problematic: the possibility of latent functions that may be concealed behind manifest rationalizations and justifications of these cruelties.[23] Let us not forget that the elaboration of the Passion play, as it is carried out by mysticism and *a fortiori* by the drama, is not called for theologically. What we have before us is rather a gigantic inclusion of something that is biblically and theologically excluded, and hence what must first claim our attention is the impulse behind this inclusion and not the immanent theological justifications of what is included.

IV

This question regarding the impulse that lies behind this opening up to extreme cruelties is probably the most stimulating one that the medieval Passion plays pose for us. A first answer can be given with the help of Frye's "demonic modulation": the victim can be harassed in this way because the devil and his Jewish helpers are officially to blame for it; this answer allows people to represent what they themselves would secretly like to do to the victim. This could thus be described as a classic case of psychoanalytic projection. Freud himself suggested this interpretation, in connection with his explanation of the tragic hero's guilt, in the course of which he also mentions the Passion plays. The relevant passage from the final chapter of *Totem and Taboo* reads:

> However, why had the Hero of tragedy to suffer? and what was the meaning of his "tragic guilt"? I will cut the discussion short and give a quick reply. He had to suffer because he was the primal father, the Hero of the great primeval tragedy which was being re-enacted with a tendentious twist; and the tragic guilt was the guilt which he had to take on himself in order to relieve the Chorus from theirs. The scene upon the stage was derived from the historical scene through a process of systematic distortion—one might even say, as the product of a refined hypocrisy. In the remote reality it had actually been the members of the Chorus who caused the Hero's suffering; now, however, they exhausted themselves with sympathy and regret and it was the Hero himself who was responsible for his own sufferings. The crime which was thrown on to his shoulders, presumptuousness and rebelliousness against a great authority, was precisely the crime for which the members of the Chorus, the company of brothers, were responsible. Thus the tragic Hero became, though it might be against his will, the redeemer of the Chorus.

> In Greek tragedy the special subject-matter of the performance was the sufferings of the divine goat, Dionysus, and the lamentation of the goats who were his followers and who identified themselves with him. That being so, it was easy to understand how drama, which had become extinct, was kindled into fresh life in the Middle Ages around the Passion of Christ.[24]

Here the scapegoat no longer appears in connection with a specific Jewish ritual but rather in the dramatically constitutive function of a "substitute construction" related to the original killing of the father. In one respect the attractiveness of this interpretation can certainly be granted. The fact that the killing of the scapegoat was set up as the doing of the Devil and the Jews surely offered an ideal opportunity for the projection of one's own aggressivity, and in this sense we can speak of a "subtle hypocrisy" not only with regard to the ancient chorus but also with regard to the lamenting women and, in an extended sense, to the whole audience of the Passion plays. However, this kind of projection merely offers a reception-psychology possibility. In contrast, Freud understood the "subtle hypocrisy" at the same time in a very specific genetic context, as a "substitute construction," as "a tendentious repetition of that great original tragedy" on which the overall structure of *Totem and Taboo* and *Moses and Monotheism* depends. However, to the extent that we consider Freud's interpretation in this comprehensive context, it cannot be adopted without critical examination. Malinowski mercilessly indicated the historical determination of the whole construction: "It is easy to perceive that the primeval horde has been equipped with all the bias, maladjustments and ill tempers of a middle-class European family, and then let loose in a prehistoric jungle to run riot in a most attractive but fantastic hypothesis."[25] Like others before and after him, however, Malinowski also pointed to the circular logic of the construction itself, which tries to explain the origins of culture through a process that already assumes human beings that experience remorse and mental conflict and therefore presupposes that they are cultural beings and no longer anthropoid apes.[26] One of the most recent critics is Claude Lévi-Strauss, who considers Freud's theory untenable even if we abandon, as A. L. Kroeber sought to do, the postulate of an aboriginal patricide in favor of an atemporal drive that is supposed to stand behind repetitive phenomena such as totemism and taboo.[27] According to Lévi-Strauss, what is crucial is not this alternative but rather the question whether drives and emotions or fear can be seen as the origin of institutions.

He answers this question with a firm negative, and in doing so he agrees with Malinowski and his judgment that "the word 'complex' carries with it certain implications which make it altogether unsuitable."[28]

Our initial question, however, did not in any way concern the origin of the Passion play but rather the impulse that stood behind a particular development. For this question we do not need to adopt Freud's own genetic construction, particularly since it can be shown to be false in purely historical terms: medieval drama was not reignited by Christ's suffering but rather by his Resurrection. The greatest obstacle to a Freudian approach is constituted not by this construction (which is, as we shall see, dispensable) but rather by a certain kind of rationalization of the cruelties and brutalities that led us to Freud. We will first discuss these rationalizations, against which we will have to develop our thesis that the scapegoat ritual is the latent function of the Passion play.

CHAPTER 10

Jesus As Scapegoat II:
Typology As Desymbolized
Pseudocommunication

I

The motif of pulling out the beard is among the most brutal moments of the tormenting of Jesus. The authors themselves seem to have sensed that here they had arrived at a limit of what was possible. They avoid lingering on this episode, quickly breaking it off. There is no reference to it in the synoptic gospels, and consequently it appears as a very extreme exploitation of an aggressivity liberated by "demonic modulation." On the other hand even this extreme appears not to depend upon the alibi of modulation, since it is professed in the songs about the suffering servant of God in Isaiah:

> I gave my back to the smiters,
> and my cheeks to those who
> pulled out the beard;
> I hid not my face
> from shame and spitting. (Isaiah 50:6)[1]

In the synoptic gospels striking and spitting are in fact mentioned but not the pulling out of the beard. Thus the play goes further, but it uses the same source: the Old Testament figure of the Passion of Christ. Even more important here than Isaiah 50 is Isaiah 53:

> As many were astonished at him—his appearance was so marred, beyond human semblance, and his form beyond that of the sons of men. . . . He was despised and rejected by men; a man of sorrows, and acquainted with grief. . . . But he was wounded for our transgressions, he was bruised for our iniquities; upon him was the chastisement that made us whole, and with his stripes we are healed . . . and like a lamb that is led to slaughter,

and like a sheep that before its shearers is dumb, so he opened not his mouth. . . . And they made his grave with the wicked. . . .

A similar typological potential was offered by the psalms of complaint. Thus, to mention only one detail that hardly any play eschews, the motif of the dislocation of the limbs during the Crucifixion goes beyond the already quoted *Dialogus beatae Mariae et Anselmi* back to the psalm Jesus cites on the cross: *Postea pedes funibus traxerunt, et clavum acutissimum incutiebant, et adeo tensus fuit ut omnia ossa sua et membra apparerent, ita ut impleretur illud. Psalmi: Dinumeraverunt omnis ossa mea* (Psalms 22:17).

We are indebted above all to F. P. Pickering's vast erudition for our knowledge of the most important Old Testament sources used to enrich the *historia passionis* with this kind of detail. In a series of investigations into what he called "the common fund of Passion history in the Middle Ages"— in essence he is concerned with the previously mentioned mystical texts, which also served as sources for the play—he convincingly demonstrated that typological grounds could be found for all the cruel details of the Passion. Typological "elaboration" can be traced back into patristic writing and, as Pickering suggests, it finds one of its most important justifications theologically in Christ's statement that he must fulfill what has been said about him since Moses and the Prophets and in the Psalms: *necesse est impleri omnia quae scripta sunt in lege Moysi, et prophetis, et psalmis de me* (Luke 24:44). Thus behind the gothic realism of the late medieval crucifixions we should seek less a specific development of "religious feeling" than the obligation, expressed in one of Christ's own statements, that people tried to fulfill through ever more subtle discoveries of typological models of the *historia passionis*.

Now typology is a method that was from the start developed with regard not to the New but rather to the Old Testament in order to make the latter's history readable as salvation history as well. It could then provide a way of interpreting certain New Testament events that thus became meaningful for the first time. This was the case, for instance, with the early Christian "rescue" of Jesus' initially catastrophic end, through a retroactive relationship with the servant of God, that is, through the scriptural evidence in Isaiah. Finally, it could serve to show that New Testament events that, from a particular dogmatic point of view, seemed to be unsaturated if not superfluous in terms of salvation history were at least "appropriate." As we have shown, this idea can be illustrated by the Thomistic *convenientia* interpretation of the Crucifixion. However, the play, like its models, has no antecedent "given" that can be brought into typological harmony. Instead, it acts out typology as the models had "elaborated" it, and within the immanence of simple "verbal traditions" little can be discerned about the interest concealed in this kind of amplification of the biblical *crucifixerunt eum*.[2] The actuality of such traditions depends upon a specific reception interest that first "ignites" them and cannot itself be derived from them. It is true that many cruel details of the Crucifixion can be traced back to patristic writings, but they first appear *en masse* in the late Middle Ages and thus at a time when the essentially apologetic interest of patristics is dying out. Regarding the crucial question as to what interest takes its place, Pickering has little to say. Typological "justification" does not seem to me to be the primary problem but rather the impulse that stands behind the "innovations."[3] That statement is particularly true in cases in which the exegetical relationship was obviously no longer known. Thus Pickering himself notes with regard to his main discovery, the harp and bow comparison, that toward the end of the Middle Ages "only the result of the analyzing comparison, namely the verbal sequences 'like an arrow' or 'like a bowstring,' was truly understood."[4] This is confirmed by Jean Michel's Passion play, which Pickering cites. Only the tormentors speak of the strung bow (27296 ff., 27340 ff.); no exegetical clue is provided from the words spoken by either God or St. Michael (27024 ff., 27104 ff.) or from those spoken by the pious women (27180 ff., 27136 ff.). The most interesting aspect in this connection is that the *Passion du Palatinus* contains the legend of the smith who makes the blunt nails (787 ff.)—which Pickering associates etiologically with the image of the harp—but it does not mention the holes that are bored too far apart, which—according to Pickering's persuasive explanation—must also be genetically derived from the harp image.[5] The etiological telos of the legend—if it ever had one—thus has no equivalent in the cross and can therefore hardly be considered a motive for its inclusion in the play. On the other hand, Jean Michel's Passion play has the blunt nails and the pre-bored holes, but the only image mentioned is, as we already saw, the bow, not the harp. In such cases it becomes clear that the relevant traditions survive or are received entirely independently of their exegetical background. This kind of ignorance of the exegetical "origins" nevertheless makes the search for the impulses behind reception and further "elaboration" all the more urgent.

Here Pickering's most recent article on this problem seems to me still not sufficiently decisive: the "false paths" taken by medieval historiography remain unexamined as such. Nevertheless, what to Pickering at first seemed justified as a pious task is now explicitly problematized, and indeed one of his proofs can also be seen as a welcome confirmation of our own approach to the question: the opposition between Rupert von Deutz's typological mania and typological restraint of Petrus Comestor who, in commenting on Luke 24:42 in his *Historia Scholastica*, clearly does not cite the *omnia* . . . *de me* as part of a concealed polemic.[6] Petrus expressly excludes, we might say, what others include, and therefore this evidence once again lays bare the problem that is always threatening to recede from view under the exuberances of typological elaboration: these elaborations are not theologically required, no matter how immanently justified they may seem.

The authors themselves were apparently not aware of this contradiction, even when they were as theologically reflective as was Greban, for example. This fact becomes particularly clear in the scene in which Jesus bids his mother farewell in Lazarus's house in Bethany. The original form of this description is found in Bonaventure's *Meditationes*, from which it spread to countless Passion stories, treatises, and plays.[7] The object of the latter is to provide a foundation for the work of salvation, which is established by means of four requests made by Mary, wherein the theses of the Scholastic doctrine of satisfaction appear in popularized form. Jesus could, according to these requests in Greban, redeem mankind without taking it upon himself to die, or else, if that is not possible, he could die without suffering.[8] If this option too cannot be avoided, Mary wants to die first, or else, if this alternative is also denied her, to become as insensible as a stone (16484 ff.). Jesus' answer to the first question goes like this:

> mourir me convient par Envye
> en adverissant Ysaÿe
> qui, en ses saintismes devis,
> a dit de moy: *Sicut ovis*
> *ad occidendum ducitur.* (16511–15)

> *It is fitting that I die willingly*
> *thereby verifying Isaiah*
> *who, in his most holy verses,*
> *said of me:* Like a lamb
> that is led to the slaughter.

And to the second question, which concerns the extent of the suffering, he replies:

> car comme tous ceulx d'Adam néz
> ont pechié jusqu'a vous et moy,
> je, qui humanité reçoy
> pour tous les humains delivrer,
> doy sur tout mon corps endurer
> excessive peine et amere.
> Oez Ysaÿe, ma mere,
> et vous confortez a ses ditz.
> Dit il pas: *A planta pedis*
> *usque ad verticis metas*
> *nun est in eo santitas?* (16526–36)

> *for since all those of Adam born*
> *have sinned, down to you and me,*
> *I, who have taken on humanity*
> *in order to deliver all mankind,*
> *must endure in all my body*
> *extreme and bitter pain.*
> *Hear Isaiah, mother,*
> *and take comfort in his words.*
> *Does he not say:* From the sole of the foot
> even to the head,
> there is no soundness in it?

Both of the mother's questions are directed to the necessity of death and suffering, and in both cases there follows, as in the example mentioned in Thomas himself, a justification by simple *convenientia*, which again in both cases is provided by typological recourse to Isaiah.[9] With a little exaggeration one can thus say that Greban formulates the problem with which we are concerned without himself recognizing it as such. A certain tradition not only continues on blindly—that is, even after the original motivation has faded away—but also first produces, hundreds of years after its theologically problematic nature was recognized, its most luxuriant flowers.

II

In his first study on the *Gotisches Christusbild* (*The Gothic Image of Christ*), Pickering identified this process of "desymbolizing" and thus held in his hand at least a conceptual key to solving the real problem. For him, desymbolization is a procedure "in which an original symbol of the Crucifixion is treated as if it were the *comparatum* in a comparison: Christ on the cross is like a harp, like a bow. It would nevertheless be hasty to speak of a 'decline of symbolism' as soon as a comparison appears, for Augustine had already been driven by his heretical opponents to resort to this procedure of the analyzing comparison. The method worked out in controversy must also have been used in the training of the clergy. The substitution of 'is like' for 'is' did not at all necessarily lead to a full desymbolization. However, the passage in the Psalms about 'counting the bones,' now understood historically, definitely brought these two symbols, the harp and the bow, along with it."[10] Here it becomes once again clear to what extent Pickering from the outset approaches the problem within the immanence of the exegetical tradition: the suggestion regarding the training of the clergy provides no bridge between the apologetically motivated situation of Augustine and the unmotivated typological mania of late medieval authors.

Things look different, however, if we understand desymbolization in the sense of what A. Lorenzer described, in his studies preliminary to a meta-theory of psychoanalysis, as desymbolized pseudocommunication. Desymbolization here means a process, carried out through repression, in which conscious representants ("symbols") regress into unconscious representants ("clichés"). This regression is—still according to Lorenzer—marked by the dominance of a scenic-situative aspect that absorbs the object and takes its symbolic setting from it. Where there were situations that were reflectively controlled, there now appear scenes in which repression has shattered entirely a situation that was originally symbolically mediated, in order to desymbolize the elements of this situation that were frowned upon. To this first aspect of desymbolization corresponds a second, a peculiar "destruction of language." Since symbolically mediated action presupposes the possession of a system of significant gestures, that is, a language, behavior determined by clichés can also be described as "exclusion from speech communication."[11] This exclusion does not entail an absence of language, however, but rather a distortion of language, pseudocommunication. Behavior determined by clichés is never carried out in an unbroken way but is constantly bound up with symbolically mediated elements. It is both distorted and concealed by them, and observation, and first of all self-observation, is made impossible:

> The relationships are similar, to make use of a somewhat crude comparison, to those between an account falsified in masterly fashion in an enterprise of embezzlement, in which the embezzler succeeds in constructing the balance on both the credit and the debit sides such that the falsification cannot be discovered within the system. The comparison has two limits: one is that an embezzler—the patient—is himself the one defrauded, the falsification being carried out behind his back; and the other is that neither of those involved can simply get out of the system: language cannot be transcended. Only the consequences, the real outcomes, can make the unbalanced books recognizable—but even then, not transparent.[12]

It seems that we have come a crucial step closer to our problem. We can now surmise that the "elaboration" of the *historia passionis* is also this kind of masterly falsification carried out behind the backs of those involved. This falsification is made transparent only by its result, the inordinate cruelty of the way in which it kills the object of its love, Jesus Christ. It cannot be discovered within the system; that much is shown by the authors and their later interpreters, including Pickering. What makes it undiscoverable within the system is the complete veiling of the regression. Even the most extreme cruelties appear in the garment of typological—that is, as we now see, pseudosymbolic—disguise. This concealment remains the only function of typology, which is no longer symbolically mediated but continues on blindly, unaware of its own tradition. The late medieval *historia passionis* is thus not a typological "elaboration" in the sense of a task set by Jesus himself but rather a series of scenes that are not grasped conceptually, and the "understanding" that was established concerning them was pseudocommunication, "participation in a sequence of actions, that is, in a scene, in which the play is performed over the heads of the individuals."[13]

Lorenzer's concept of "scenic understanding" cannot, of course, be simply transferred from psychoanalytic hermeneutics to a hermeneutics of the plays. In psychoanalysis itself the experience of evidence is connected with a repertory of images and models of interaction that are shared by the analyst and the analysand and that make it possible to recognize the different experiences as expressions of one and the same scenic—that is, cliché-like—arrangement.[14] These models of interaction have to be verified in the analysis itself: in the exchange of transference and countertransference, in the identification and directed regression of the analyst, in his participation in the primal scene, and in the reconstruction of the original event to be formulated in biographical terms. In dealing with this "scenic understand-ing," metapsychological explanation by means of constructing hypotheses must, according to Lorenzer, be restricted to heuristic functions—a postu-late that can be maintained only so long as the psychoanalytic conversation itself is achieved. This accounts for the well-known sterility of a literary hermeneutics that attempts to proceed psychoanalytically, insofar as it by-passes the texts in order to take the authors as the object of its analysis: without the metapsychological hypothesis of the Oedipus complex, such attempts collapse or indeed are never realized at all.

The object of our analyses, however, is not authors but rather institu-tions. Therefore we do not need to abandon Lorenzer's concept of desym-bolization but only to transform it in functionalist terms. If in psycho-analysis desymbolized pseudocommunication indicates a distorted private language and thus the neurotic patient's social disintegration, in the case of religious drama we can see it as one of the "techniques" by means of which, as Pierre Bourdieu has shown, institutions strive to conceal their own true nature and which ultimately all belong to the "logic of concealment": "The relationships and real configurations are to a certain extent lost, dissolved, submerged, annulled, and transfigured in the toils of false relationships."[15] However, this interpretation suggests that the conception of a masterly falsification could be extended beyond the Passion play to the whole phe-nomenon of "religious drama," thereby making it possible to connect our formula of the playing back of the kerygma into a mythical/archetypal dimension with Lorenzer's concept of desymbolization. This gives us the key to a controversy that is as old as religious drama itself. Desymbolized pseudocommunication, masterly falsification, now proves to be responsible for the apparently insoluble question as to whether these plays were con-cerned with the church's interests or not. This pseudocommunication ex-plains why the plays seem in fact superficially harmonizable with church doctrine and why it requires laborious analysis to understand the falsi-fication. What actually happened here was "performed over the heads of the individuals," and was apparently not evident to the authors, the audience, or the ecclesiastical authorities. It took more than five centuries, from Florus of Lyons to the Council of Trent, before what was really being acted out here was seen through.

If we now return once more to the Passion play, we must ask wherein we can discern the "real configurations" (Bourdieu), the "cliche-like models of interaction" (Lorenzer), or, as we can now put it, the latent functions that are concealed behind the veiling typology of the *historia passionis*. We have already noted that institutions are not products of fear, but at the same time they are, as Gehlen says, a response to terrors from which they liberate themselves through representations. This liberation can, however, be described by means of Freudian concepts insofar as these are detached from their dogmatic foundations and especially from their oedipal background. Thus Gehlen himself explained the category of "stabilized tension" with the aid of the Freudian concept of ambivalence.[16] In the same way, the reception of Freud by the social sciences, and in particular by social psychology, makes it clear that even without Lamarckian phylogeny and the attribution of a dominant function to the sex drive within affectivity, Freud's central discoveries such as identification, ambivalence, repression, and substitute objects retain their relevance.[17]

In the same way, a "scenic understanding" of the Passion play can refer to models of interaction that may similarly be kept independent of metapsychological hypotheses, as Lorenzer himself attempted to do for psychoanalytic interpretation. Among recent systematic approaches in social psychology that are indebted to Freudian psychoanalysis, P. R. Hofstätter maintains that the substitutive affective cathexis, in other words, the scapegoat mechanism, deserves special emphasis.[18] Thus we do not need to adopt Freud's own hypothesis concerning the original patricide in order to recognize this mechanism, this cliché, in the late medieval Passion play. The theologically unrequired and to that extent unmotivated cruelties acted out in these plays have the latent function of a scapegoat ritual that doubly disguises itself in the most subtle way: first through projection onto the Jews who superficially carry it out and secondly by providing typological cover for even the most brutal details. The interest in this kind of "elaboration" of the *historia passionis* is thus not historical but ritual in nature.

Thus the Passion plays prove to be particularly informative. As we saw in the preceding chapter, they go beyond literary and also graphic representations of the Passion, not in their key motifs but rather in the way in which they are acted out. If they are seen in their particularity, as we have tried to see them here, then they can at the same time shed a brilliant light on the late medieval "realism" syndrome, of which they are generally regarded, and in particular by Pickering, as being merely one symptom among others. For then it emerges that the play reveals a virtually unequaled degree of brutality because through these elements is fulfilled a ritual interest in the sacrificial death of Christ that is concealed behind typological cover. In the kerygmatic interpretation, the sacrificial death of Christ is a unique, representative self-sacrifice on the part of God, through which, whether conceived as a punishment or as a meritorious achievement, an equally unique salvation history event, namely the fall, is morally compensated for. This compensation is prolonged in the *pascha perpetuum* of the sacrifice of the Mass. This perpetuation of the redemption can be conceived anthropologically and in this way described as a more or less specifically Christian institution that proves the historical character of the origin it establishes insofar as it repeats it not identically but rather "bloodlessly" and in fact repeats it on a daily, not a periodic, basis. Over a few centuries of the Middle Ages, however, there competed with this institution another one, namely an acted-out ritual that repeated the same event as the Mass did, albeit in a different way: not strictly periodically but nonetheless in many cases annually, and in every case not merely commemoratively but identically. At the center of both institutions stood the divine scapegoat. In one case he was sacrificed bloodlessly, in the other in a bloody manner; here the archaic substratum came back "into play," and was "acted out" to the point of *sparagmos*. Indeed, the ritual character of the Passion play first attained its full vividness against the background of this competition between two institutions.

III

In the sacrifice of the Mass, the invocation of the Lamb of God simultaneously alludes to the archaic scapegoat and—in a salvation-history interpretation of this sacrifice as a perpetuation of the unique self-sacrifice of God—negates it. However, if this salvation-history grounding ever became problematic, it was in the late medieval practice of the Mass. The grace-theology premises of the doctrine of transubstantiation could only be maintained at the elevated level of reflection and in the strict conceptuality of Scholastic *quaestiones*, and even here a Thomas Aquinas labored mightily to guarantee the integrity of salvation-history uniqueness to the sacrificial death of Jesus.[19] However, among the lower clergy and in the daily celebration of the Mass that was for the most part incumbent upon them, a misunderstanding of the idea of transubstantiation, together with snares of the allegorization of the Mass, led to a magical degradation of the Eucharist. In the twelfth century there began to appear reports of miracles related to the host, whose bearers tried to see the Lord's body in place of the image of the bread. From Innocent III on, regulations proliferated regarding what should be done in case of possible *pericula* or *defectus* during the celebration of the Mass, for example, in the event that Christ appeared in *specie carnis vel pueri*. The late medieval "fruits of the Mass" ultimately have the effect of a parody of what Florus of Lyons had once seen as the *fructus spiritualis* of the sacrifice, whereas in contrast the work of the allegorists remains recognizable in even the most deplorable outgrowths of the demand for visibility: the sight of the elevated host was considered the central salvation moment; people ran from one church to another in order to participate in it as often as possible and fought over the places from which one had a clear view of the altar.[20]

Up until the Council of Trent, Scholasticism clearly remained without influence on the liturgy and the interpretation of the Mass.[21] We cannot and need not say here who is responsible for this lack of influence, whether Scholasticism itself, in which dogmatic purism and an express depreciation of the credulous crowd often went hand in hand,[22] or the church, which finally decided under the pressure of the Reformation to explicitly adopt the Thomist doctrine of the sacraments and whose need to catch up is evident in the history of post-Tridentine theories of the sacrifice of the Mass.[23] It is important for us to recognize the connection between these so-called "misuses of the Mass" and the phenomenon of the Passion play. The essential ritual features of the plays must be seen against the background of an understanding of the Eucharist that had deteriorated and sunk to the level of a kind sympathetic magic. The Passion play also alludes to the scapegoat in its Last Supper scene, either by referring to the blood shed for the many, which points back through Mark 14:24 to Isaiah 53[24] (thus for example Greban, 18080 ff.; the Eger Corpus Christi play, 4109 ff.), or by referring to the *lamlein, Das die sund der welt auf im trait* ("the little lamb, who carries the sins of the world on him," Wackernell, 299; cf. Hegge cycle, 255, 692 ff.). Whereas the liturgical rite's central passage, the transubstantiation, continued to be associated with the Last Supper and not with the Crucifixion,[25] in the play the Last Supper is only a transit station, so to speak, on the way to a ritual that crystallizes precisely the motif that the liturgy excludes.

No matter how much the allegorization that dominated medieval understanding of the liturgy after Amalarius of Metz had enriched the Mass with symbols of Christ's death,[26] before the sixteenth century, when the so-called "mactation" theory emerged, there is no reference to the motif of "slaughter," at least in the Western Church. The play, on the other hand, once again includes what the liturgy excludes; we might also say that once again it segments differently. It does not see the cardinal function in the performative *Haec quotiescumque feceritis, in mei memoriam facietis*, but rather in the constative *crucifixerunt eum*, upon which the Bible characteristically elaborates just as little as does the liturgy. Thus we have here again a shift in emphasis that reminds us of the one in the Easter play. Just as the latter acts out the *descensus* ritual in opposition to the exclusions made by the liturgical *elevatio* and the Bible itself, here the "slaughter" is dramatized in opposition to the implicit or explicit exclusions made by the Bible, the liturgy, and dogmatics. It appears with a graphicness that brings back into the limelight the archaic substratum so subtly repressed in the Mass and thereby makes the *historia passionis* verge on the ritual killing of the divine scapegoat. Here a mythically/archetypally oriented interpretation of the sacrifice of the Mass is "acted out."

This consequence can only be denied by anyone who considers Mass and play as incomparable phenomena and thereby overlooks how much the play itself is related to the Mass and sees itself as a continuation of the latter. Attending a play, like hearing a Mass, is a religious act, for which indulgences are promised in countless prologues and precursor speeches. Concerning Zuckmantel in Silesia, where Passion plays were performed well into the second half of eighteenth century, we know that traditionally the play began inside the church itself after the Mass was over and went as far as the Crucifixion. Then the latter took place in the nearby Rochusberg, to which the players and the audience went on a great Passion procession.[27] This kind of tradition is a particularly significant proof of the regression into archaic ritual we are examining here. However, it only makes explicit what the play's borrowing of liturgical formulas and prayers itself implies.[28] If the martyred Christ calls from the cross for reverent memory of his sacrificial death, then in these *improperia* (Jesus' complaint) not only is the Mass's "memory of sacrifice" brought to an end but at the same time the archetypal function of sacrifice, which is negated and overcome in the bloodless "commemorative sacrifice" of the Mass.[29]

We must not here draw back before the consequences and treat as merely an edifying play something that drew its life from its moral appeal only in the realm of manifest functions, whereas in the realm of latent functions it drew its life from the archaic impulses of *sparagmos*—from the event of annihilation or dismemberment of the victim by which the God-head is supposed to be led to restore the uninterrupted relationship to the sacrificial community.[30] This *sparagmos* is a phase in Frye's "quest myth," which we find once again structurally in religious drama: Jesus battles the Devil (*agon*), and is then killed as a scapegoat (*pathos/sparagmos*), mourned by the pious women (*threnos*), and thereafter celebrated as a gloriously resurrected God (*anagnorisis/theophania*). However, as already in the *agon* and *theophania*, we now find in the case of the *sparagmos* as well that Frye's archetypes, understood as elementary patterns that structure a literary universe conceived as autonomous, remain functionally questionable. So long as we take an interest in the mere reference to recurrence, we must also inquire into the function of such a recurrence, and this question can be answered, as we can see in Frye himself, only in a substantialist manner.[31] If we abandon this interest (as we had decided to do), then it is necessary to dissolve, by means of functional comparisons, the concept of the archetypal, in the sense of a universal structural model: the decisive difference proves to be whether the *agon* takes place in the *descensus* or on the cross, whether the *theophania* is seen with the *oculi cordis* or visibly staged, whether the *sparagmos* is merely mentioned or actually played.

In such comparisons of functions, Frye's patterns can be made problematic, and thus the concept of the archetypal shifts from a structural description to a functional description. It is no longer directed toward structural recurrence, invariance, or universality but rather toward what is in a Christian perspective an archaic function of certain structural images: archaic in relation to the "absolute cultural threshold of monotheism," beyond which religious drama falls back as a monumental "transcendence in the immanent."[32] Thus the Passion plays present a hermeneutics of latent functions as precisely the model case. They can show what harmonizing interpretations cannot perceive. For anyone who sees in these plays merely the edifying mirror they claim to be fails to recognize the characteristic archaic "graphicness of the translation of an idea in the results, that is, in the actions."[33] The Mass abandons this graphicness, it commemorates. The play acts.

V

Thus the play also sometimes concentrates on the action of sacrifice alone, omitting the *descensus* and the Resurrection. The exemplary French case is that of Jean Michel's Passion play, which makes Greban's second and third days into its fourth, and has the fourth day end with the sealing of the tomb. Comparable examples exist in Germany. Thus the Frankfurt and Heidelberg Passion plays also confine themselves to Jesus' earthly existence and death. The synchronization of the performances of these plays with the events of Easter week or with other cross festivals has not been established. We must therefore assume that here an original, independent Passion play tradition was not maintained, but instead a dissolution of the cycles took place. This assumption has been occasionally contested,[34] but it seems to me no less likely in the aforementioned German plays than in that of Jean Michel. There is no reason to deny this kind of abscission of the Passion from a more comprehensive play, and in fact it can be supported theologically. For the withdrawal of the Resurrection behind the event of the death is, as we have shown, characteristic of the dogmatic tradition in the Western Church, in particular since Anselm, in whom the God-Man, to borrow Harnack's phrase, "only had to die."[35]

In Michel the concept of satisfaction is found no less often than in his predecessor Greban (532, 551, 566, 574, 577, 7722, 17998, 19992, 27040), and so we may well say that here Scholastic Christology is pursued in the most consistent manner. In fact gaining theological correctness by emphasizing the moral aspect constitutes one of Michel's chief concerns. Among his additions to the model are not fewer than three sermons by Jesus, including the Sermon on the Mount (8946 ff., 10655 ff., 16795 ff.). He also expands by more than half its length the prayer in the garden at Gethsemane that introduces the Passion and has as its object the *débat* between the obedient spirit and the body sweating with fear (Greban 18739 ff.; Michel 19929 ff.). This expansion indicates a further insistence on the core idea of the doctrine of satisfaction, namely the suffering of the man Jesus who, precisely as human, also knows fear and trembling. However, just as striking is the fact that the emphasis on the moral dimension is not accompanied by a downplaying of the graphic nature of the martyrdom. On the contrary: in the *flagellatio* Greban's four whipmen are, at Pilate's behest, supplemented by a fifth drawn from Annas's entourage (24907 ff., then after 24926), Greban's *He salut, rex Judeorum* (22891) is transformed into the ritual rondeau offered just here: *Hee, ave rex Judeorum, / roy des Juifz, je vous salue* (25011 ff.), and the same thing happens again a little later in Greban's *Et vive nostre roy nouveau* ("And long live our new king," 22937), from which Michel repeats the refrain with only a single alteration: *Hee, vive nostre roy nouveau* (25071).

Thus Michel's Passion play appears against the background of an escalation of both moralizing reflection and ritualistic graphicness; the latter is, I repeat, not required by the doctrine of satisfaction and thus also cannot be motivated by it. In actuality, in the ritualistic graphicness a primary interest also manifests itself that already characterized the Passion play before Greban's adoption of the doctrine of satisfaction, and if Michel isolates the Passion and presents it in expanded form over four days, then in such a play this interest is primarily isolated and brought to an end. The built-in reflections on the moral achievement of the martyrdom may indeed control this primary and play-specific tendency, but they cannot direct it back into the kerygmatic dimension.

VI

The Corpus Christi cycles show a play that consciously tried to break out of this kind of ambivalence. Of all the religious dramas, these plays exhibit by far the most extensive evidence of theological self-control. Like the Passion plays, they are a response to believers' demands for visibility, to the late medieval, epochal desire to see the host (*Désir de voir l'hostie*, as E. Dumoutet entitled his important study on this subject)[36]—but a response that turns out quite otherwise and whose theological implications become immediately evident in the context we have just discussed.

I will forgo reference to the often-told history of these cycles in order to proceed immediately to the key difference. Whereas it was shown that the Passion play tends to precipitate out the sacrifice, the Corpus Christi play always presents the whole of salvation history from the Creation to the Last Judgment. Thus it very consistently translates the theological definition of the Eucharist into visible terms, for this definition essentially includes the future fulfillment. In enumerating the different meanings of the Eucharist, Thomas Aquinas explicitly refers to a *significatio . . . respectu futuri*.[37] For Thomas, as we showed in the first chapter, the Eucharist is a pledge of redemption, a *pignus futurae gloriae*.[38] This inclusion of the future end contrasts very sharply with the premature end of the Passion play in the *descensus*, and in fact this difference between the overall arrangement of the two play forms has consequences that have still not been defined and evaluated for either of them, because a comparison has never been systematically carried out.

No doubt the most important of these consequences consists in the fact that the Corpus Christi play presents a history that has not yet come to an end, and therefore it eludes the kind of mythical type of identical repetition that characterizes the Passion play. Like the Corpus Christi play, the Passion play may also move forward the creation and the fall, but the response is then once again—as we saw in Greban's play—a model of the gnostic type, ending with the redeemer's return to his heavenly homeland. While the Corpus Christi play opens this model to the future *parousia*, it represents a history that is in part over but in part remains to occur, and in the future part takes on a pronounced fictional character. Any study of the Corpus Christi play has to begin by asking to what extent this fictional end retroactively affects the overall arrangement of the cycles. The latter are in theory far more clearly supported by a theological didactics than are the Passion plays, and in this sense they are "more literary." However, what is crucial here is the already quantitative balancing of the individual images. The climaxes are denied demarcation and elaboration, or to put it more precisely, they are no more and no less demarcated than the preceding and following images. Seen from the point of view of salvation history, everything is of equal importance and not only what is acted out in paradigmatic oppositions.

The character of the cycles is revealed most clearly at the key point in their theological logic: the situating of the Last Supper within the framework of the central scenes of suffering—that is, the scourging and Crucifixion scenes—that surround this eucharistic celebration. The practice of representing not the Last Supper but rather—as for example in the Hegge cycle—a celebration of the Mass in which Christ becomes the priest consecrating the host and the apostles become the faithful taking communion is a clear expression of the didactic intention, and it is also found in the continental Passion play.[39] However, no Passion play contrasts, as Hegge does, an extremely broadly structured Last Supper scene (242 ff., 411 verses) with scenes of scourging and crowning with thorns, which end with a brief "dumb show" after no more than two verses spoken by the Jews and are then immediately connected with the pious women's verses of lament in the *compassio* perspective (294, following 675). The Crucifixion is just as remarkably brief; although it includes the motif of the tearing apart of Jesus' limbs, it brings the whole to an end in 27 verses. Chester offers a very similar picture. Here as well an elaborate Last Supper scene (265 ff., 264 verses) is juxtaposed with a relatively short scourging (293 ff., 48 verses) and an equally short Crucifixion (304 ff., 40 verses). The eucharistic thematics is broadened to include scenes that were originally alien to it. Thus in the *visitatio* the resurrected Christ turns to the audience to deliver a long speech that is nevertheless related not to the Passion that lies behind him but rather, once again, to the eucharistic bread and its dogmatics (337–38, following 154). It is 32 verses long.

The later Towneley cycle is entirely different in this regard. Jesus' speech to the audience, which is borrowed from the Chester *Visitatio*, has here swollen to 108 verses. Then fifteen stanzas describe the suffering on the cross and its redemptive effect on mankind (313 ff.), and only following this pious image come two concluding stanzas again dealing with the eucharistic bread.[40] Two interests are clearly competing here: the kerygmatic-symbolic interest in the Eucharist as the bread of life and the mythical-archetypal interest in the redeeming blood of sacrifice. And in the Towneley cycle as well the foregoing events stand against the background of this competition, which in purely quantitative terms already gives the cross a far broader scope. Whereas in the Hegge cycle the conspiracy is made part of a broadly structured Last Supper scene, now the Last Supper is incorporated into a broadly structured conspiracy and also given an appropriate content: the paschal lamb is eaten, and without bread and wine being in any way mentioned, attention is focused on the traitor Judas (214 ff.). Clearly here the sacrificial meal, completely omitting the eucharistic thematics, is a mere way station leading to the central ritual: the tripartite sequence of "buffeting, scourging, and crucifixion" that reminds us of the continental Passion plays.[41] To mention only a single concrete example, this sequence contains, from the victim's fastening on the cross to the raising of the cross, 143 verses

(261 ff.), as opposed to 27 in the Hegge cycle and 39 in the Chester cycle. The York cycle, which is related to the Towneley cycle, offers much the same picture. Here we also find no reference to the Eucharist in the representation of the Last Supper. In the framework of the Corpus Christi play this is a very remarkable phenomenon, which up to this point has not been noted. The tendency of the older Chester and Hegge cycles, which is so clearly different, makes it possible for us to see how later the didactic phase and therefore the opening of the Passion story onto a kerygmatically defined future effect passed increasingly out of view.

Possible but unlikely is the explanation that this omission of reference to the Eucharist was the result of theological conscientiousness, that is, of anxiety that the eucharistic mystery might be profaned in being transposed into the play. This kind of anxiety was obviously a factor in the German Corpus Christi play from Künzelsau, but in this case not only the Last Supper but also the Crucifixion and—in the first version—the *visitatio* were omitted.[42] This omission of the central mystery of salvation bespeaks a theological conscientiousness that reminds us of the liturgical celebration's reservations about opening itself up to the *Christophania*. Here as well, we may assume, the presence of the sacrament itself has an inhibiting effect on visualization, although the play as a whole apparently strives to commemorate visually the *waren leichnam in des brattes schein* (the true body/corpse of the Savior in the appearance of bread) and elsewhere also constantly makes the relationship to this its thematic occasion.

In Germany, where in contrast to England and France both types occur, the divergent tendencies of the Passion and Corpus Christi plays become clearest. The crucial factor is not the didactic references to the Eucharist itself, since in every case the German Passion play also includes them, even if in less detail. More essential is the overall arrangement of the Corpus Christi play, that is, the sequence of the images from the Creation to the Last Judgment and above all the constant presence of the *rector processionis* who comments on them. Here the Künzelsau play is once again the clearest example. Crowning with thorns, scourging, and Crucifixion are reduced to the appearance of a *Salvator cum corona*, then a *Salvator cum statua*, and finally a *Salvator cum cruce* (in each case, accompanied by two soldiers), with the *rector* directing his demands for *compassio* to the people (3672 ff.); no bawling torturer, no blows with the fist, no blood flowing from scourging, no rope pulling the limbs apart, no hammer blows are to disturb the remembrance of suffering experienced with the inner eye alone. No greater difference is possible between memory-images internalized in this way and the *meng schön andächtig figur* (45) of the Donaueschingen Passion play, where, to give a completely contrary example, Christ's mistreatment at the hands of the tormentors takes place with a dull brutality unrelieved by any distancing speech by the *proclamator*. A naive interpretation thought it recognized in this the danger that the "historical event of the Passion" might carry away the spectator, "without his having received sufficient encouragement to see the salvation event behind this painful occurrence."[43] In reality we are no longer concerned with a historical event that has to be reformulated in terms of salvation history. What is behind this kind of graphicness is a conception of sacrifice that has fallen out of the kerygmatic back into the archetypal. According to Gehlen, such "paths leading away from an achieved high point are always the natural ones, to assert this is always improbable, but the point is not to explain these deviations, but rather on the contrary to explain how the rite could be maintained in its purity at all."[44]

CHAPTER 11

Jesus As Scapegoat III:
"Nominalist Theater"—Archaic Sacrifice Play

I

An analysis of the latent functions of the Passion play need not be limited to the *historia passionis* itself. To the extent that these functions allow us to probe behind the apparent rationalizations offered by theology for the graphic representation of the Passion, they can also resolve the structural incommensurability of the death on the cross and the preceding descent into hell that interested us in the first chapter. To this end I must return once more to the "comic" Devil. E. G. Jünger took care not to apply his model of the "comic conflict" to the Christian God and his opponent, but he nevertheless roots the superiority of the victorious party "in the aesthetic category itself: it has to do with the fact that the superior party responds in an appropriate way to an inappropriate provocation."[1] In religious drama, where the response passes by way of an archaic sacrifice ritual, there can obviously be no question of such aesthetic appropriateness. Therefore the Passion play, which presents this conflict in toto, confirms what became evident in the Easter play: that in applying apparently "suitable" models or theories of literary comedy we risk misunderstanding, precisely as literary comedy, what in fact still lies in a preliterary ritualistic dimension.

In actuality, if we look more closely, it becomes evident that there is a very particular reason for the comic nature of the Devil in the late Passion play. As already in a preliminary manner in the Easter play, here too it is not God's true opponent—that is, Lucifer, the Lord of hell himself—who is made risible but rather Satan, his emissary on earth. Lucifer is in general described as one who foresees the future, has an inkling of the coming defeat, and refuses to surrender afterward. In Greban he immediately thinks of the two pawns whose capture seems to him more important than bewailing all the losses incurred:

Ce qui est perdu est perdu,
mais penssons tous au residu,
de le saulver mieulx qu'i pourra (26268–70)

What is lost is lost,
But let's all think about what's left,
and save it as best we can.

He has had to absorb a blow, but he is going to continue, true to the confession with which he introduced himself at the start:

ne demeure que mon orgeuil
qui ne s'est mué ne changié
en moy depuis qu'il fut forgié
lassus au pardurable empire,
si non que toujours il empire,
sans soi diminuer en rien. (3718–23)

only my pride remains,
which has not altered or changed
in me since it was forged
up there in the perdurable empire,
except that it grows constantly worse
without diminishing in any way.

If we add to this the even later remark about Cerberus—that a complaint for illegal abduction of those in hell would lead to nothing, since Jesus would be both judge and party (26203 ff.)—then Lucifer loses all comic traits in this sober self-assessment. He is cheated, and therefore not laughable.[2] It took a ruse—seen from the divine point of view, it is a "pious trick," from Lucifer's point of view, a simple infraction of the law—in order to bring off the redemption. The party defeated in this way is no dull-witted comic villain, who can only be outplayed through the cunning tricks of superior rationality, but rather a dualistic counterpart who also possesses angelic rationality, who has been circumvented only through the intention of a mystery that has never before occurred and that escapes all understanding.

Satan, on the other hand, is deliberately constructed as a ridiculous figure. He leaves hell bragging about himself, and he has to see his usual successes becoming rarer and rarer. Whenever he returns to hell empty-handed, he himself is meted out the same punishments for which he sought victims among men. These punishments of Satan by his own comrades are important in the context of our inquiry. Medieval descriptions of hell are notoriously inexhaustible in inventing the most extraordinary torments. What distinguishes the play is their application to Satan himself. What he has to endure counts, along with the details of Jesus' suffering, among the cruelest moments in the plays, and these tortures also share with the Passion an unmistakable ritualistic character. Satan is bound with red-hot chains and beaten, immersed in molten lead, and subjected to other torments that are traditional motifs. All this torture becomes in the play a *diablerie*, a hellish ritual Lucifer commands the minor devils to inflict upon Satan. This ritual is shown in the most striking way by a detail again found in Greban. As an example I take the first great scene in hell after the birth of Jesus. Satan is reporting on the presentation at the temple and incurs Lucifer's wrath by announcing the redemption to come:

> Suz, Belzebuth, viens si le lye
> devant moy de chaines de fer
> emflambeez du feu d'enfer,
> plus ardant que feu de tempeste,
> et le batez par tel moleste
> qu'il soit brullé de part en part. (7345–50)

> *Come, Beelzebub, tie him up*
> *before me with iron chains*
> *sizzling with hellfire,*
> *hotter than thunderbolts,*
> *and beat him mercilessly*
> *so he'll be burned on every side.*

The following ritual, just like that of the scourging of Jesus, takes the form of two extensive dramatic rondeaux—further evidence of the fact that apparently highly literary passages can indicate the preliterary dimension in which these plays still move:

SATHAN
A, mercy, maistre!

BELZEBUTH

 C'est trop tart.
vous arez ung *pugnivimus*
sur vostre groing, villain sauldart.

SATHAN

A, mercy maistre!

ASTAROTH

C'est trop tart.

LUCIFER

Chauffe il?

CERBERUS

 Mais demandez s'il art
comme brandons au vent remus?

BERITH

Voicy le galant bien camus:
je croy qu'il en a bien sa part.

SATHAN

Ha, mercy, maistre!

LUCIFER

    C'est trop tard;
vous arez ung *pugnivimus*
Rifflez dessus, grans et menuz;
le ribault est habandonné.

BELZEBUTH

Les deables l'ont bien ramené
pour nous rapporter tel langaige.

LUCIFER

Sathan, comment te va?

SATHAN

     J'enraige.
Helas, maistre, misericorde!

LUCIFER

Joues tu la ton parsonnaige?
Sathan, comment te va?

SATHAN

     J'enraige.

ASTAROTH
A dueil, a passion, a raige
convient qu'on le tue et descorde.

LUCIFER
Trainez le d'une grosse corde,
tout partout l'infernal mesnaige,
affin que plus ne s'i admorde.

CERBERUS
J'ay si grant paour qu'il ne me morde
que je y prens bien envis vinaige.

SATHAN
Je meurs, je forsene en couraige;
il n'est ame qui s'en recorde.

LUCIFER
Sathan, commant te va?

SATHAN
                        J'enraige.
Helas, maistre, misericorde! (7351–79)

SATAN
Ah, mercy, Master!

BELZEBUTH
It's too late;
you'll get a pugnivimus
on your snout, vile ruffian.

SATAN
Ah, mercy, Master!

ASTAROTH
                        It's too late.

LUCIFER
Is he getting hot?

CERBERUS
            Ask rather if he's burning
like firebrands in the wind?

BERITH
Now the rogue's about done for:
I think he's gotten what he deserved.

SATAN

Ah, mercy, Master!

LUCIFER

It's too late;
you'll get a pugnivimus
Flay him, large and small;
the scoundrel is abandoned.

BELZEBUTH

The devils have punished him well
for giving us such reports.

LUCIFER

Satan, how do you feel?

SATAN

I'm in torment.

Alas, Master, mercy!

LUCIFER

Are you playing your role?
Satan, how do you feel?

SATAN

I'm in torment.

ASTAROTH

With pain, suffering, and torment
it's fitting that he be killed and dismembered.

LUCIFER

Lead him with a large rope,
All through the infernal realm,
so that he never does this again.

CERBERUS

I'm so afraid of him biting me
That against my will I'm taking vinegar.

SATAN

I'm dying, I'm going mad;
no one seems to notice.

LUCIFER

Satan, how do you feel?

SATAN

> *I'm in torment.*
> *Alas, Master, mercy!*

It is as if in such scenes Greban had offered an interpretation of his "comic" Devil. In the doubled pair of Lucifer and Satan he simultaneously separates the figure on one hand into the terroristic background as it is manifested in Lucifer's persistent pride and on the other into the relieving function of the ritual of punishment that the minor devils carry out on the very one who, as Lucifer's emissary on earth, represents the earthly embodiment of the omnipotence and omnipresence of evil. The ritualistic character of the so-called "Devil's comedy" could not be more obvious, and thus its latent relation to the ritualistic graphicness of the crucifixion also becomes evident. Structurally speaking, the two images cannot be reconciled: as we have seen, the cross does not fit into the dualistic narrative sequence in the dimension of latent functions. However, they become reconcilable in the identical aggressivity of the punishment ritual that is carried out on Jesus Christ and Satan as substitute objects. The cathexes point here to a unity that can be conceived only functionally and no longer structurally.

In this perspective of affective cathexes, it is easy to add the great Passion plays to the late medieval syndrome of collective neuroticization. The flourishing of these plays coincides with the period when the obsession with witches began to spread from a few strongholds to the whole of Europe. The church itself, first in Rome and later among fanatic Lutherans, regulated this obsession. Toward the end of the fifteenth century it was institutionalized: in 1484 the Bull *Summis desidereantes affectibus* appeared, in 1486 the *Malleus maleficarum*. W. E. Peuckert put this "witch-hammer" at the center of his study on the "apocalyptic century" and also demonstrated in it particularly the discrepancy between ecclesiastical dogma and ecclesiastical practice. In the theological explanation, evil remains merely tolerated, but against this tolerance stands the "practice of those years and the Dominicans' *malleus*. In the latter evil is autocratic in its embodiment in the Devil, fallen angels, demons, and the natural world. They act wholly on the basis of their own peculiar wills—the just mentioned reservation is only theoretical, and is every day forgotten and ignored in behavior."[3] The Passion play as well must be seen against the background of this kind of contradictoriness. No sharp distinction can be drawn between what it teaches (the metaphysical impotence of the Devil) and that from which it draws its life (the obsessively experienced omnipotence of the Devil). For the doctrine of the Devil's impotence is presented in acted-out rituals that in themselves already implicitly deny, and in their popularity completely deny, this very doctrine. Their popularity is that of an institution that provides exoneration, but everything for which it provides exoneration remains at the same time immanent in it. The exorcism of the Canaanite woman performed by Jesus brings into the picture what never could become visible in any real exorcism. Here, in the play, it can be shown that the Devil escapes from the potential witch and flees to hell surrounded by smoke and thunderclaps, as a rubric in Jean Michel's play explicitly indicates (following 8368). The emotional power of the scourging could be equally immanent in the play. This suggests that the flagellation phase, on which all the Passion plays lingered, was in terms of reception psychology invested in a similar way to that in which the equally public scourging ceremony was invested up until the movement was forbidden.[4]

However, the pathological addiction characterizing that desolate epoch is immanent above all in the scapegoat. H. R. Trevor-Roper has rightly emphasized that behind the late medieval obsession with witches and hatred of Jews stood the longing for a scapegoat.[5] Peuckert also devotes an entire chapter to those who were deemed the "guilty ones" in the "apocalyptic century": the heavenly bodies, the pieces of silver, the false king, and especially the Devil and the Jews.[6] It can be said that religious drama set up the last two for the tribunal. However, it did so in a very particular way. Its most original contribution to the late medieval search for "guilty ones" is precisely the sacrifice of the innocent one, the divine scapegoat Jesus Christ. However, this sacrifice of the innocent Christ also implicated those who were its superficial executors, the Devil and the demonized Jews,[7] and this increased relieving effect makes the Passions not considered by Peuckert probably the most striking of all the testimonies to an epochal longing for scapegoats.[8]

II

The elaboration of what is immanent in the Passion play—a degraded understanding of the Eucharist, the late medieval atmosphere of penitence marked by collective neurosis, a pathological obsession with "the guilty ones"—all these elements should have made it sufficiently evident that these plays are certainly not a theater that brings nominalist theology into the picture. If from this result I once again return to Kindermann's formula of "nominalistic naturalism," it is not in order to make Kindermann the "scapegoat" of the thesis developed here but rather because this formula, like Kindermann's talk about "gradualism" and "nominalism" in general, is exemplary of all attempts at an explanation in intellectual history terms of the phenomena that are here analyzed as eluding any such explanation.

For Kindermann himself the whole matter is very simple. Nominalism teaches that concepts lack any metaphysical reality and therefore relieves the historical and individual of the gradualistic mirror-function and establishes the "isolation of the body," the "triumph of the corporeal," the "victory of the impulsive, the uninhibited." Like the great popular preachers of the time, religious dramas seek control over this "impulsive desire for life," seek "to arouse the conscience," precisely with "the naturalistic means that alone retain respect in this nominalistically determined world." Not only the "naturalism" of representations of the Passion, in which the "*compassio*, the almost bodily sympathy of the spectator is the aim," is nominalistic, but also everything that stands in contrast to the holy, thus including the "typically nominalistic" comedy and especially the demonic counterworld: "the satanic element that now appears in all the descent-into-hell scenes as the opposite pole of the divine shows the yawning abyss of the new, difficult to bridge over dualism between the newly exposed devilish danger and divine salvation. Man, abandoned in the middle of these two fields of tension: that is now, in the age of nominalism, the whole problem of religious theater and certainly not only of its texts, which merely provide the score, but also and especially of its staging and its art of representation."[9]

There is a great difference between describing the way religious drama looked in the so-called age of nominalism, and speaking, as Kindermann did previously, of the nominalistic foundation and determination of these plays. As we have shown, dualism initially has nothing to do with this determination. It points to an interest specific to the play already in "gradualistic" times. To be sure, this dualism in late medieval drama is more marked than ever, and we can certainly agree with Kindermann that "the nominalistic age is no longer unequivocally theocentric."[10] However, what the nominalistic age was not, nominalism itself certainly was: unequivocally theocentric.

In a highly relevant chapter of his book *The Legitimation of the Modern*

Age, Hans Blumenberg has spoken of a "theological absolutism" as the epochal signature of nominalism.[11] In this concept he sees the endpoint of a development in intellectual history that began at precisely the point where we first found not a harmonizing but rather a latent relationship of tension between religious drama and the dogmatic tradition: in Anselm of Canterbury's doctrine of satisfaction. Blumenberg analyzes the medieval reception history of this doctrine to show that the retroactive relationship between the work of redemption and the demand to satisfy God's injured honor set in motion a process in the course of which the Christian doctrine of salvation was subordinated—abetted particularly by the reception of Aristotle—to a speculative theocentric omnipotence and ultimately absorbed by it. What was at first equivalent to a final victory over the "gnostic trauma" came in medieval nominalism to be a new chasm between the world and an omnipotent God whose behavior toward it consisted only of arbitrary acts. Blumenberg develops this equivalence of voluntarism and gnosis in terms of the history of ideas or problems. As a dualistic counterauthority there develops what he calls "human self-affirmation," or in concrete terms, modern philosophy. The dualistic counterauthority of the play, in contrast, does not lie in the dimension of intellectual history. It is not rationally but rather terroristically cathected, and therefore it is at most interpretable as a perspective "from below" on the radically theocentric character of nominalism: Lucifer becomes the true master of a world under the sign of "gnostic" abandonment.

Herein lies a fundamental divergence between the play and the tradition of intellectual history. The difference is shown by the figure of Jesus. Nominalistic theocentrism, with its interest in the predicates of omnipotence and infinity attached to its conception of God, is directly and irreconcilably opposed to the play's interest in the God of salvation. For this God of salvation is no more a part of the development of a nominalistic "gnosis" that remains within the dimension of intellectual history than is the Devil. At most we should ask whether the so cruelly martyred victim in the plays, who is in this respect comparable to the Devil, does not also throw a similar light "from below" on divine omnipotence and arbitrariness. For surely nominalism played a role in constituting the need that found in these cruel plays a response that was clearly adequate to it. This response can be interpreted as direct or indirect. Direct, in the sense that the ritualistic graphicness remains related not to "nominalistic naturalism" but rather on the contrary to "theological absolutism" as a function providing exoneration. I am deliberately formulating this not as an assertion but as a suggestion in order to show how the archaic nature of these plays could be connected with positions in intellectual history. The people's yearning, documented by the popularity of the Passion plays, to have God made visible and, if one wants, "punishable," is perhaps not adequately explained so long as this distant God who abandons the world to the Devil is not taken into account as a historical premise and provocation.

This premise is at least valid, and thus I come to the indirect response-character of the plays, in the sense that the age of nominalism is identical with what Peuckert called the "apocalyptic century," that is, with the epoch in whose manifestations religious drama seamlessly joined and which shows most acutely in these manifestations how nominalistic speculation withdraws from responsibility to the world. Far from being a nominalistic theater, these religious plays prove to be based on the dualistic sense of the world to which nominalist theocentrism represents the clearest imaginable antithesis. Hence they are not in any way the powerful instrument of church propaganda that has been seen in them but rather a very specific product of the lower clergy from which their authors came and which stood much farther from the dogmatic claims of university theology than from the rather mythical religiosity of their bourgeois clients. That the plays were written primarily for brotherhoods and guilds and had to submit to the censure of ecclesiastical authorities gives us the best indication as to where they should be situated. The frequent anonymity of their authors does not make them into "folk poetry" but rather suggests that they were a product of a popular piety that was largely theologically unenlightened and in which both author and audience participated.

Obviously, the official diocesan authorities allowed the performance of these products, and to this extent the Protestant polemic was not unjustified when it counted the plays among the "guilty" and added to them the "chief guilty one": the church itself.[12] This polemic did have consequences, as we know. To what extent the prohibitions of the plays should be attributed directly to Protestant influence, to what extent they may have forestalled such criticism, or to what extent, entirely independently of them, misgivings on the part of the Catholic Church itself may have led to them, can only be decided case by case and even then only with difficulty. Even if one considers Protestant influence to be as strong as does H. C. Gardiner, the fact remains that the Catholic Church separated itself with marked celerity and willingness from this heretofore only half-heartedly accepted product of popular piety. The plays counted among the positions that could not be held and that the church had no interest in holding. What is documented by their prohibition is the acknowledgment of a failure: the failure of a theological reformulation not only of the omnipotent creator God but also of the God of salvation. It may be that Blumenberg's expression, "theological absolutism," does not make the anthropological components of Scholastic speculation sufficiently clear.[13] An adequate institutional anchoring of Christian salvation theology was in any case not available in the time of nominalism, and this fact alone is decisive in the context under discussion here.[14] For the epochal significance of the Passion play lies precisely in the fact that it occupied this institutional, salvation-history vacuum and that those who took on this vacuum took salvation history into their own hands.

III

This metaphor raises problems. For the institution "religious drama," which appears as a result of this "taking into one's own hands," was, in contrast to traditional ecclesiastical institutions and in particular the Mass, no longer the genuine product of a Christian anthropology; it did not fill in gaps left elsewhere but rather grew out of an impulse that was heterogeneous with respect to the doctrine of original sin and the need for grace and which, seen from an anthropological point of view, can be best construed as self-preservation, as *conservatio sui*. It is this sort of self-preservation that appears under the rubric of "undetermined obligation" in Gehlen's theory of religion.[15] Only an anthropology that makes self-preservation in this sense its foundation, that conceives man as a defective being reduced to instinct, and that has to learn and act if it wants to survive can provide grounding for ritual representation and then for imitation in general as a systematic fundamental category, as an act leading to the first institutions. Only such an anthropology can explain how the rite, in consequence of its institutionalization and representation shares the fate of all institutions, that is, how it shares in the "exoneration from the actuality of the initial position—it does not survive the self-intensification but precisely thereby gains the power and freedom for elaboration, for enrichment in motifs, for working out in detail, and for the liberation of the genuinely dramatic element."[16]

The rite that thus exonerates itself is not—and this was our starting point—already given along with the Christian liturgy: for the latter, the path to the dramatic is blocked. The play must thus go back beyond the kerygma, so to speak, in order to acquire its rites and only to the extent that it then acts them out is the archaic process of the liberation of the dramatic described by Gehlen repeated. Whereas, this process can be only hypothetically developed and reconstructed in relation to ancient drama, it is now repeated—and therein lies the uniqueness of religious drama—in historical time and under the more restrictive conditions imposed on it by the Christian anthropology that was initially opposed to it: the liberation of the dramatic took place in the mode of "playing backward."

The external history of the plays and their immanent theological self-control first gain their full vividness against this background. In both is manifested Christian theology's age-old mistrust of plays, even if they are religious plays; and no matter how much they emphasize that they are performed in honor of God, the God they honored was no longer unequivocally the Christian God of Grace. They were plays honoring God insofar as institutions could not be imagined otherwise than as established by God or directed to Him. This introduction of God conceals, as Gehlen demonstrated, the hiatus between the necessity and the reality of institutions, but that is a specific solution of the myth that finds its anthropological explanation in the category of "undetermined obligation." Thus the institution of the Passion play is also a play in honor of God, but what matters genetically are archaic impulses (Gehlen's *Appeldaten*) such as hunger, war, plague, the Devil, and belief in astrology. This is why these plays only become comprehensible in relation to an external world that is not conceived as monotheistically weakened and neutral with regard to salvation but rather as an effective presence of horrors.

This subject can be clarified by reference to W. Pannenburg's attempt to make Gehlen's category of "undetermined obligation" fruitful for a specifically Christian anthropology as well. The latter would then be characterized by the fact that the chronically needy human being does not first become ritually active and make himself a religion under the pressure of his excessive drives but rather in his "infinite dependency always already presupposes a correspondingly infinite, not finite, transcendent counterpart."[17] This kind of openness to the world is supposed to indicate a trusting self-opening to this divine counterpart and no longer the mere reassuring religiosity of archaic cults. With a view to this alternative between "assurance" and "trust,"[18] religious drama should, however, be for the most part put on the side of assurance and not of trust: although conceived as an institution if not instituted by God, at least in His honor, it secretly drew its life from its ability to offer such assurance. As a vow, it retains, to quote Gehlen once again, something of the "most naive and indestructible social figure it represents, that of a gift and the expectation of receiving something in return."[19] Thus the most fundamental ambivalence of these Christian *ludi* is probably that of their archaic element itself: they are, compared with Christian anthropology, a regression, a degradation, an externalization. On the other hand, they gain precisely through the antithesis to this anthropology a characteristic pathos of the "nevertheless." Whereas in the self-restrictions of the liturgical celebration the devaluation of any "transcendence in the immanent" that came in along with monotheism becomes obvious, this kind of devaluation is absent in the vernacular play. What is brought into the picture in this tradition, in opposition to theology's exclusions, produces highly ambivalent results: "Christian" ritualistic plays in which, on this side of the "absolute cultural threshold of monotheism," the legacy of the archaic "transcendence in the immanent" returns.

IV

Here as well the commandeering of religious drama by the historians of the theater has a misleading result. Naturally, the splendid productions on the continental and especially on the French manorial stages are theater-history documents of the first order, and at first sight baroque plays seem in fact to already be anticipated in the late Passion plays. On the other hand, however, the grandiose scale of these productions makes the concept of theatricality appear inappropriate. The audience that flocked to these plays was in reality not yet an audience in the sense of a theater community. Rather, the Passion plays bound the whole city and its surroundings together in a single festive community. The whole life of the community was concentrated on these plays: work stopped, the churches remained empty.

These festive communities must have been enormous, if the documents are to be believed. During the whole of a weekday-long Passion performance in Reims in 1490, the 16,000 spectators said to have attended were provided by the city with wine and pastries.[20] The chronicle of La

Rochelle for the year 1492 reports on the most marvelous Passion play that was ever performed there: "it lasted more than a week, with as much joy and amusement as satisfaction for everyone, and a large number of musicians played constantly, day and night, to entertain the people, so that most of the nights that week were spent in all sorts of diversions for visitors as well as for the residents."[21] The testimonial value of such documents is completely misunderstood if one sees in them a secularization that turns religious into bourgeois drama, or, as Weimann suggests in discussing the pastoral scenes in the English pageants, into plebeian self-representation. To be sure, the pleasure taken in costumes and plays has to be considered at the same time, and it is clear that the plays were performed for an audience, but in general this audience did not have to pay to attend, precisely because it was not yet, as Kindermann thinks, a "real theater audience" but rather a festive community that came together to witness an acted-out sacrifice ritual.[22] One thing must never be forgotten, precisely because it is never explicitly mentioned: the occasion for all the festivities so proudly reported by the chronicles is the representation of Christ's Passion. It was the cruel play about the bloody sacrifice of God that was celebrated, with wine and pastries, music and entertainments. And thus we break through the magnificent productions that already seem baroque to find once again the archaic sacrificial play, in which people experience unity with the divinity and boisterously celebrate this bond.

It appears that it is in this dimension that all the consequences of H. Brinkmann's observation that "the reality of medieval drama [resides] solely in its performance" first become visible.[23] To this reality in performance also belong the already-mentioned deaths, which were more and something other than mere stage accidents, and also the "scandals" reported by the chronicles, which were also more than mere breakdowns in performance. Thus among the documents unearthed by Petit de Julleville we find a report of a Passion play performed in 1551 in Auxerre that lasted 28 days, after which the cemetery where it took place was declared to require purification and reconsecration, and the bishop of Bethlehem made use of the opportunity thus provided to explain the mystery of the Passion "in its pious truth," as the archival source puts it.[24] Certainly one must not rely too heavily on such testimonies. However, it is striking that the organizers were repeatedly urged by ecclesiastical or communal authorities to avoid "scandals,"[25] and even if we assume that the cases we know about were only worthy of notice because they were exceptional, still it is necessary to recognize the dimension in which they became possible at all. What Luis Vives once explicitly lamented, namely that the performances of the Passion reminded him of the "old stage-plays of the pagans" (*vieux jeux scéniques des Paiens*),[26] can also be in part reconstructed from the plays themselves, as for example in the appeals for the audience to be still, to be quiet and watch reverently, which run through all the prologues and precursor speeches and which can be explained only against the background of an entirely different audience mood. Vives's comparison with the pagan *circenses* is found again elsewhere, in England, for instance. For the Dominican John Bromyard, the plays are simply *nova spectacula*, for William of Waddington, a "manifest folly" (*folie apert*), and in the Lollardist *Tretise of miracles pleyinge* they are described as an opportunity for gluttony, drunkenness, and lust. Even someone basically well disposed toward the plays such as the Minorite William Melton complains that in York both local and visiting spectators had degraded the plays through "revelings, drunkenness, shouts, songs, and other insolences, in no wise attending to the divine offices of the said day."[27]

Much the same can be said of Italy and Spain. In 1565 Archbishop Borromeo of Milan held a diocesan synod dealing with the decisions and guidelines issued by the Council of Trent. One of its results was a strict and total prohibition of religious plays:

> Quoniam pie introducta consuetudo representandi populo reverendam Christi Domini Passionem et gloriosa Martyrum certamina, (. . .) hominum perversitate eo deducta est, ut multis offensioni, multis etiam risui et despectui sit, ideo statuimus ut deinceps Salvatoris Passio nec in sacro nec in profano loco agatur, sed docte et graviter eatenus a concionatoribus exponatur (. . .) Item, Sanctorum martyria et actiones ne agantur, sed ita pie narrentur, ut auditores ad eorum imitationem excitentur.[28]

According to Gardiner, this rejection is comprehensible only against the background of a rapidly growing and menacing Protestant infiltration of the archbishopric, though in more peaceful times the tendency was always to condemn errors and misbehavior but not the plays themselves. In Milan at this time this cautious way of proceeding was no longer possible, the plays already being, Gardiner suggests, exposed to the *risus*, *despectus*, and *offensiones* of the Protestants in particular. This reference to Protestantism is, however, not at all convincing. There was also trouble in Spain, where according to Gardiner's own admission the Protestants couldn't touch the plays,[29] and where nonetheless the *Examen sacrum* put on in the sixteenth century by the Jesuits of Salamanca scolded the spectators for having come only to laugh, *a sólo reir*.[30]

In fact, if we also include the non-Italian documents, we can assume that the behavior of the audience Borromeo complained about was largely characteristic of the atmosphere of late medieval performances of the Passion plays. People laughed, and this laughter went beyond the tolerated exclave of the *risus paschalis*. People laughed, as the passage from Luis Vives proves, during the Passion and thus against the intention of the play itself. It would be pointless to discuss which particular passages might have elicited this laughter. More important is the insight that this laughter was once again aimed at the very holy seriousness with which, expressed in terms of Ritter's answer-model, an anarchic and excessive festive joy was brought into the holy play about the sacrifice of God. Freud described very well the connection between the sacrificial rite and excess:

> A festival is a permitted, or rather an obligatory, excess, a solemn breach of a prohibition. It is not that men commit the excesses because they are feeling happy as a result of some injunction they have received. It is rather that excess is of the essence of a festival; the festive feeling is produced by the liberty to do what is as a rule prohibited.[31]

Admittedly, with the single exception of the *risus paschalis*, these excesses in religious drama were not a liberation in this sense but rather products of a performance reality that revealed its true impulse behind the official self-concept of these plays. And so instead of this kind of liberation from what was otherwise forbidden, the plays themselves were prohibited.[32] These late medieval prohibitions constitute a historical confirmation of what the preceding investigation sought to demonstrate.

Conclusion: "Play"
As a Class of
Functional Equivalents

I

A "little like contraband" (*un peu comme contrabande*): that is how the Romantic writer Léon Gautier suggested that tropes made their way into Christian liturgy[1]—tropes from which, to be sure, nothing further "evolved" but which nevertheless clearly reveal the impulses that religious drama as a whole carried within it. The present work has not been satisfied with official explanations, whether these are offered by the plays themselves or by their harmonizing interpreters. It has looked carefully and brought much to light that was undeclared, far more than the substratum-researchers were able to make out of pagan relics. For these relics, brought into the play and broadly acted out in good conscience, nonetheless turned out to be clues or traces leading to the most important and at the same time least obvious contraband: the latent mythical-archetypal presence of salvation history itself. In the preceding analyses, this ambivalence of kerygma and mythos proved to be so complex and multifaceted that any attempt to summarize its results is doomed to fail. Indeed, it is to be feared that during the investigation itself a too sharply defined point of view was employed and apparently unambivalent results emerged, whereas our concern is always with their ambivalence. At least the constant intention was not to resolve this fundamental ambivalence of the plays but rather to make it the intersection of all the perspectives.

The basic criteria of selection underlying this work were established at the outset. We need to return to them in one respect. In the foregoing analyses one side of religious drama that yielded little or nothing for our line of questioning is underrepresented. This area concerns the greater part of Old Testament history and also the part of New Testament history that might still most identify these plays as what Walter Benjamin saw in them, that is, as "epic theater" and hence as part of the prehistory of baroque drama.[2] Without excessive simplification, one can say that every attempt thus made to derive modern theater in continuous manner from its alleged medieval prehistory took only this epic side into account. As in all prehistories, religious drama had thus to produce what was seen in baroque theater. For scholars in Romance languages, "the worldliness of Mary Magdalene" in Jean Michel's Passion play became an anticipation of Molière, just as for English scholars the raging Herod or the *Secunda pastorum* anticipates Shakespeare—and at first it was only for this reason that these plays were deemed worthy of attention. But that toward which everything in religious drama tended, that is, the Passion and the Resurrection, was ignored.[3] The omission of the key scenes was the price to be paid for writing this type of prehistory.

Benjamin himself is obviously against this kind of one-sidedness. Although in his philosophy of history, which contrasts ancient tragedy rooted in a ritualistic commemoration of sacrifice to modern drama that takes history as its subject, religious drama appears as the origin of the modern drama, Benjamin has salvation history as a whole in view: for him, the content of baroque tragic drama is a secularized salvation history. But the criteria of "epic theater" cannot be applied without qualification to religious drama. This is already true as long as the dimension we have called here kerygmatic is taken into account. Thus the *fable*, as dualistic, is essentially dramatic. The *hero* appears as a thinker, as a wise man, but he is, although not tragic, nonetheless also the protagonist of the dualistic fable and thus in no way an uninvolved bystander with regard to the events on the stage. The *proclamator* or *regens ludi* who accompanies the play might more appropriately be seen as such a third-party outsider, but this "wise man" is again not identical with the untragic hero himself. Religious drama could also be seen as *didactic play*, but at the center of this didactic play there appears, along with the demand for *compassio*, a moment of thematized empathy. Thus the description of the audience as *relaxed* becomes questionable: the spectator is supposed to be shaken and moved to tears in watching the martyrdom, not superior and relaxed.

Such qualifications become all the more urgent if we view religious drama with regard to the ambivalence of kerygma and mythos, and here begin also the hermeneutic difficulties to which we referred at the outset. It is necessary, according to the passage we quoted from Benjamin, "to become conscious of the critical framework within which precisely this fragment of the past is juxtaposed with precisely this present."[4] Had Benjamin been the Marxist he occasionally thought he was, this postulation would necessarily have led to a critical "sublation" of past art. The prehistory of the epic theater that he sketches nevertheless bears the signature of the preservation and actualization of a "past laden with the present"[5] in which Jürgen Habermas has discerned the essence of Benjamin's "rescuing criticism," of his "conservative-revolutionary hermeneutics."[6] But that precisely the kerygmatic moment in religious drama should be worthy of this kind of preservation will seem obvious only at first glance. To be sure, we can learn to reevaluate an Anselm of Canterbury if we consider the myth into which the Passions played back his doctrine. But conversely, we can also ask whether this return of myth, just at the time when theology had so thoroughly killed it off, does not reveal the limits of those secular efforts we call Scholastic. Those who should have been the special object of these efforts, namely the great mass of the faithful, disappeared from view in the Scholastic concern with pure kerygma, and if this mass of the faithful found in religious drama a substitute that really should not exist, then the existence of these plays makes Scholastic theology appear to have done a poor job of explanation.

It is thus the ambivalence of the "nevertheless" that we emphasized in the preceding chapter, which leaves open what is to be "rescued" here. Behind the de-symbolization of the kerygma is hidden a bit of unreconciled myth. The latter was the latent function from which the play drew its life, and our main interest was focused on this function. It could not be an interest in a "rescue" in Benjamin's sense, nor could it be an interest in an ideology-critical "sublation." For in religious drama myth took over a function for which theology remained responsible, and thus our methodological interest could not lie in playing out or rescuing one in opposition to the other but solely in bringing the functional correlation of both into view under systematic viewpoints. In conclusion, we would like to return once more to the guiding model worked out in the course of our investigation and inquire into the possibilities of generalizing it.

II

Plays are institutions, and as institutions they exonerate. But they exonerate in a special way. H. G. Gadamer, who develops his ontology of the artwork using play as a guide, has defined this exoneration as an excellent form of "self-representation," one that allows an "enduring truth" to emerge.[7] Gadamer calls this "transformation into an object," in which the transformation does not simply intend a shift into another world but rather aims at the autonomy of the object that finds its measure in itself and does not measure itself against anything that is outside its own: "The transformation is a transformation into the true. It is not an enchantment in the sense of a spell that awaits the releasing word that will transform it back into what it was, but rather it itself is the release and the transformation back into true being. In the representation of the play what is comes out."[8] Gadamer sees the prototype of this kind of transformation in the "total communication" of religious truth in ritualistic action and ritualistic drama, where the meaning of attendance is "genuine participation in the event of salvation itself."[9]

If we test this idea by applying it to the religious drama of the Middle Ages, we can maintain the concept of "total communication," defined as the self-sublation of the communicating element as the communicated element,[10] only at the price of desubstantializing it. Our analyses have made it clear that we are in no way concerned here with a "transformation into the true"; rather, the "true" in these plays is juxtaposed with something excluded from it, with the being of nonbeing. That is a functionalist dissolution of the ontology that supports the official self-conception of religious drama and here, in the opening up to another kind of religiosity, lies what is ruinous for the Christian claim to truth. While the play no longer—or at least no longer unambivalently—allows itself to be connected with the Christian kerygma, it proves to be not simply another way of communicating Christian salvation but rather breaks out of a class of equivalences defined as kerygmatic. It is not "total communication" that takes place but rather an inclusion of the excluded, a positivization of what the kerygma seeks to exclude from being as something nonexistent.

J. Ritter has developed such a model of the positivization of the excluded with regard to comedy and laughter. Our analysis of the *risus paschalis* followed his model, but we were also able to apply it to religious drama as a whole. And if Gadamer sees in the "total communication" of ritualistic action or ritualistic drama the prototype of his substantialist conception of play, then it seems tempting to generalize the analyses of religious drama undertaken here into a functionalist conception of play. The latter would overcome not only the substantialism of traditional hermeneutics but also the aporias into which one falls when approaching a new determination of the concept of play from a hermeneutically unenlightened structuralism, as J. Ehrmann recently tried to do. His well-founded criticism of Huizinga, Caillois, and Benveniste reveals their normative procedure, which finds expression in dualisms such as play and seriousness, play and reality, play and the sacred, and allows them to define play itself only privatively, as derived. But according to Ehrmann, these dualisms are valid only in the dimension of conscious social structures, not in that of unconscious ones. For here play proves to be co-extensive with general culture, and it is not derivative but rather a "relocation, redistribution of value in pursuit of the immediate satisfaction of needs and desires."[11] The reference is to Freud's book on wit, or more precisely to the mechanism of psychic *expenditure* of energy and *gain* in pleasure—an example that is known to us. We would, however, have found something quite different confirmed by Freud's theory: a specific way of positivizing the excluded. In fact, in Freud himself the compensatory relationship between expenditure and gain is functionally related to culture's "work of repression." Ehrmann ignores this point and pays a high price for doing so. "To define play is at the same time and in the same movement to define reality and to define culture":[12] we could accept this postulate if it were directed toward a functionalist dissolution of the normative concepts of reality and culture. But Ehrmann argues against making use of hypostatized deep structures; consequently posits that play, reality, and culture are synonymous; and finally has to connect his theory of play with game theory.

Thus Gadamer's and Ehrmann's concepts of play can once again make clear the aporias of a hermeneutics that is not mediated systematically and of a structuralism that is not mediated hermeneutically, but at the same time these concepts also demonstrate the promise of the new, functional-structural concept of play toward which our analyses lead. It appears that only such a functionalist concept of play is compatible with the concept of fiction and is therefore able to close a decisive gap in the theoretical foundation of literary studies. The model of the inclusion of the excluded that underlies our analyses seems to be generalizable for this purpose. It would conceive art as the revelation of other possibilities and to that extent suggest that the "positivization of negativity" be hypothetically postulated as the most general point of reference of a class of equivalences termed "play."[13] Religious drama is *ludus* in that it radically reduces the complexity of the dogmatic system. With the figure of the Devil it brings in and positivizes precisely the dualistic counterauthority that monotheistic dogmatics excludes as what should not exist, and it can do this only at the price of raising the play's own complexity to a high degree. Conversely, one can also conceive a positivization of negativity that is characterized not by reduction but rather by the intensification of its own complexity and a decreased complexity of the environment. The formula seems sufficiently strong to integrate the whole spectrum from art that is still anchored in ritual, through so-called "culinary" art, to so-called "emancipatory" art.

Testing this formula will involve, on one hand, further theoretical reflection on the problem of a system-theoretically posited and hermeneutically mediated concept of meaning that is itself closely connected, as Luhmann has shown,[14] with the question of the function of negativity in meaning-constructing experience. On the other hand, it leads to concrete historical research, that is, to the analysis of historical preconditions for the building of structures and of play-worlds. For this analysis, interdisciplinary dialogue with other social sciences remains indispensable, for only with their help will we be able—and this is shown by the example chosen in this study as well—to determine these preconditions positively. Play itself does not render them, for it remains positivized nonbeing. For precisely that reason, however, play acquires a specificity that shows how illusory it is to think that the problem and the solution can simply be taken over by other social sciences.

Afterword

My interest in the religious plays of the Middle Ages arose in a roundabout way. It was preceded by an interest in comedy and the comedic. Thus I ended up doing a review of a book about the comic elements in religious drama. In it, the author argued that the church had placed certain comic elements, particularly as they appear in the Easter play, in the service of preaching Christian salvation, a preaching intended specifically for the common folk, for the great mass of believers. Indeed, the dramatic stagings of the Passion and Salvation of Christ were in fact meant for and carried on by the folk—starting with the still liturgical *Visitatio sepulchri*, through the vernacular Easter plays, up to the great Passion plays of the late Middle Ages. However, would not the drastic, in fact obscene forms of the comic, as they manifest themselves in the Easter plays, necessarily undermine the Christian message? The comic impulse always brings something into play that official solemnity has no desire to recognize, that it would prefer to brush aside, to exclude. Would it not be more obvious to surmise, behind the comedy of the religious play, an interest that ran counter to the kerygmatic gravity of the salvational message? Didn't it require all too much of an intellectual effort, in order to convey and grasp this message correctly? Had a dogmatically rarified theology not suppressed the forms of an entirely elementary, spontaneous religiosity? How, otherwise, can the genesis of the religious play even be understood? Could one not approach this genesis precisely by way of these supposed excesses, by way of the strange humor of the purchase of the salve, of the hortulanus episode, and of the disciples' race to the grave? Or by way of those unspeakably horrifying tortures undergone by Jesus, which the Passion play never tired of elaborating?

Could the total phenomenon of the religious play not be structurally described using the theory of the comic that Joachim Ritter has expressed in the formula of the bringing into play of the excluded, the positivizing of negativity?[1]

The religious drama never became an institution that could have enjoyed undivided theological approval. On the contrary: from the beginning there was dispute. Amalarius of Metz's allegorization of the Mass, with which everything began in the eighth century, immediately encountered bitter resistance from Florus of Lyons, who could not comprehend making the liturgy into a performance. According to him, only an idiot, to whom Christ is already present in the sacrament, would nonetheless prefer to concentrate on the shadow rather than the substance of the *veritas corporis* already at hand. True, theology desires the body but as a symbolic substance. And as soon as an attempt was made, however circumspectly, to interpret the gestural provisions of the liturgy mimetically—for example, to proceed from the *corpus verum* to an *imaginatio corporis*—dogmatic gravity registered an objection. This was my point of departure, my basic question: On one side, formal dogma's understanding of salvation, fundamentally bound up with imperceptibility and the commemorative recollection of the central events of sacred history, namely God's assumption of human form, the Passion and the Resurrection; on the other side, the flight from these standards, indeed, demands, of faith, into vivid perceptibility, into pictorial repetition, into representation.

I refer intentionally to repetition, because these representations are no longer pure ritual but also not yet pure theater. They have their place precisely on the line where ritual and theater meet. The drastic dimension (*die Drastik*) of the comic elements present in the Easter play, and above all in the tormenting of Christ in the Passion plays, has divested itself of its ritual associations, without however having adopted the "as if" of theatrical mimesis. The religious dramas are highly ambivalent ritual dramas. Their ritual substratum does not consist of ecclesiastical liturgy. It also does not belong to the Germanic cult stagings postulated by Karl Stumpfl.[2] Instead, it belongs much more to those archetypal rites and myths that provide Christianity's own foundation and in the negation of which Christianity grounds its understanding of its own sacred history. The religious dramas—and this is the governing thesis of my book—project the Christian kerygma back onto exactly those ritualized archetypes from which this kerygma had originally emancipated itself. The Easter drama, centered on the *descensus ad inferos*, is a dualistic play with the devil; through the defeat of Satan, it wins for itself the freedom to act out the comedy of the mercator play, the gardener's scene, and the disciples' race. The horrifyingly excessive cruelties attached to the scenes of Christ's torture are functionally superfluous to the commemoration of the *historia passionis*. The explanation that this element is simply about a play within a play, the malevolent play of the Jews within the frame of a Christian *ludus*, is therefore unsatisfactory. The space of religious drama was not demarcated by a stage apron or footlights; the congregation is always a part of the performance. The boundary between the play of the Jews and the Christian *ludus de passione* in which it is embedded collapses; the Passion ends up projected back onto the archaic ritual of the scapegoat. The drama thus in itself constitutes an anthropological refutation of the irreversibility posited by theology's redemptional teleology.

II

The book struck—now more than twenty years ago—the state of unsuspecting positivism in which the scholarship of the era was gently slumbering like a shock. The reactions from the perspective of those bent on preserving ecumenical Christian harmony were correspondingly sharp. The author was charged with applying an ultimately "inquisitorial zeal" to claiming the entire field of religious drama for heresy. I could just as well, so ran the objection, have been satisfied simply to draw attention to the "extensions," the "expansions of the world of Christian Truth."[3] To be sure, the helplessness of such reactions also, and perhaps above all, expressed a helplessness vis à vis the theoretical framework within which I had developed my thesis. My theoretical reference point consisted, for one thing, in the anthropological work of Arnold Gehlen. Gehlen speaks of the transformations in structures of consciousness that manifest themselves in tandem with what he labels the "absolute cultural threshold" of Christian monotheism. These take the form of a "tendency to minimize the role of rites," and of an interiorization that relocates religion's ultimate proofs of certainty within the believer's soul. On the other hand, "when religion becomes spiritualized, the masses do not keep pace, and fall back under the hold of magic." The purity of minimalized rite cannot, in the long run, be retained. As

Gehlen observes, "Once a summit has been arrived at, the paths that permit backsliding from it are always the most natural ones to take, the continued maintenance of this high point is always improbable, and it is not the process of backsliding that needs to be explained but rather the opposite: how it was possible in the first place to hold onto the purity of the rite."[4]

I tried to explain this view with the help of Niklas Luhmann's systems theory. My book was conceived during the same time that the reception of Luhmann's work took off in Germany, during the 1970s, and it is perhaps one of the first attempts to apply the early Luhmann to literary studies. His innovative interpretation of sociological functionalism was especially helpful, particularly his concept of "functional equivalence." According to the premises of systems theory, a comparison does not serve, as Luhmann puts it, "to reduce being (*das Seiende*) to essence, but rather to fix and stabilize being in relation to other possibilities."[5] That was exactly what I wanted to establish: Christian drama as "another possibility" of conveying salvation, and therefore functionally as an equivalent of Christian rite. Naturally, for Christian dogma's concept of truth, this thinking in terms of "functional equivalences" and "other alternatives" is disastrous. Because, to quote Luhmann once more, if "all experience can also be other than it is, then the possibility of its nonexistence cannot be excluded, and therefore the content of the experience becomes ontologically nondefinitive."[6] My critics' suspicions of "inquisitorial zeal" were therefore completely misplaced. I was not interested in orthodoxy and heresy but rather in the fascinating opportunity offered by this concrete material supplied by the Middle Ages to study that relationship between rite and drama for which earlier or other cultures only furnish anthropology a scanty amount of evidence to consider. The theology was handed to me as part of the object of investigation. My real interest consisted of the anthropology of a type of drama that viewed itself as spiritual but drew on a different spirit than liturgy did, addressed different needs than the liturgy did, or to put it better, addressed needs with which the liturgy was also concerned but addressed them differently.

III

If I had to write the book again today, I would probably reflect more explicitly on the relationship between a functional approach and the theory of the social imaginary. In his book *The Imaginary Institution of Society* Cornelius Castoriadis develops a theory of the "radical imaginary," which postulates that a complex of imaginary significations always already underlies all social institutions. He calls this complex "magma": "A magma is that from which one can extract (or in which one can construct) an indefinite number of ensemblist organizations but which can never be reconstituted (ideally) by a (finite or infinite) ensemblist composition of these organizations." In terms of the individual imaginary, this magma does not correspond to a "primal scene," in Freud's sense but rather to a "proto-représentation," a "scène totale" that, existing prior to all specific drive structures, has magnetized the psyche and is the underlying lost origin of all its representations: "The psyche is its own lost object."[7] In terms of the social imaginary, social institutions always therefore evolve simultaneously in two dimensions. The first is that of rational designation, differentiation, construction, and functional interpretation. This is the dimension of the *legein* and *teukein*.[8] The second dimension, inseparably bound to the first, is that of the "radical imaginary," the dimension of a creative dynamic continually generating not yet fixed forms of meaning that point back to the permanently lost unity of the original magma: it is the "open stream of the anonymous collective" in the social-historical realm, the "representative/ affective/intentional flux" for the individual "psyche/soma."[9]

The introduction of a transcendentally conceptualized "radical imaginary" results in a critique of functionalism. Social institutions cannot merely be understood as "answers" to subjective or social situations; rather, this need for "answers" always already contains imaginary components that make a given situation so significant that they elicit "answers."[10] However, it appears to me that Luhmann's functionalism is not affected by this critique. For one thing, unlike for traditional functionalism, for him specific answers are always provided with functional equivalents, which no longer adheres to identitary logic in Castoriadis's sense. For another, he discriminates between "manifest" and "latent" functions. Mental acts of repression and displacement can be exactly what makes action possible: "Human activity has to conceal partial aspects of its own social reality from itself, in order not to lose the capacity for orientation and motivation."[11] Castoriadis emphasizes the institution-shaping role of these partial aspects, Luhmann their integration for the purposes of stabilizing the systemic demarcation of inner and outer. Luhmann may weigh the two dimensions referred to by

Castoriadis somewhat differently, but they are equally co-present elements for him.

IV

Let us return to the religious plays. Understood in terms of functional equivalence, the liturgy and the drama have a common imaginary substratum. What they share is Christ as the imaginary pole of an instituted desire for salvation. The liturgy responds to this desire with the recollection of that historical event that made salvation into a permanent certainty: the sacrificial death and resurrection of Christ. What is to be recalled therefore definitely does not belong to the life story of the individual believer himself. What is to be recalled has only been read or heard. Remembrance is therefore dependent upon imaginative elaboration; *commemoratio* and *imaginatio* alike are liturgically activated. Of course, the theological accent is on the commemoration and the accompanying explicating commentary. In Castoriadis's terms, one could say that the commentary represses the imagination in favor of the essentializing operations of the *legein* and the *teukein*.

Nonetheless, this *legein* and this *teukein* cannot shut down the imaginary. The origin of the paraliturgical ceremony of the *Visitatio sepulchri* testifies to this: the Marys arrive to anoint the body of Jesus but find only an empty grave; the angel announces the Resurrection. According to Michael de Certeau, Christianity institutes itself around the "loss of the body," the disappearance of Jesus' body and, with it, the disappearance of the body of the people of Israel. All of Christianity's institutions and discourses are fill-ins for this initial lack, they are directed toward the substitutive "production of a body."[12] The *Visitatio sepulchri* takes off from precisely this point. Admittedly, it still does not produce a body, but it does direct attention to the phantasm of the empty grave. In the *surrexit* jubilation of the angel, this phantasm gets canceled out, as it were, vanishes. The vernacular drama goes one step further. In the *hortulanus* episode it is compelled to reveal and follow its true inclination, over and against the original biblical source. It cannot leave open the question of why Mary Magdalene mistakes Jesus for a gardener. So it turns him into one, disguises him as a gardener, who jokes around with Mary, carrying it to the point of startling sexual allusions. And yet, here too it limits itself in the dialogue to the vision that the Magdalene can see but nonetheless cannot touch: *Noli me tangere.*

However, the imaginary continues to operate. It wants the body. The liturgy of the Mass presents it, in the form of the Eucharist, in which the *commemoratio* of the Last Supper and that of the Crucifixion coincide. The Mass repeats the sacrifice but bloodlessly. The bleeding body is actually present in the consecration, in the words in which the sacrament is administered. That means, however, to refer back to Castoriadis, that the liturgy seeks to locate actual presence in the *legein* and the *teukein*, blocking out the imagination of the bleeding body. The *corpus verum* is created in the act of transubstantiation, in which the body is present but only symbolically.

And, once again, the productivity of the imaginary resists being brought to a standstill, once again it creates an opening for itself, this time in the paraliturgical devotional exercises for which the meditational tracts on the Passion offer guidance. I drew attention to the close relation between these meditational tracts and the Passion plays in my book, without discussing them in detail. Jan-Dirk Müller has recently covered this topic within the framework of a rich and insightful critical dialogue with my theses. As Müller shows, the goal of the meditative *imitatio Christi* consists of the total imaginary identification with Christ as the Man of Suffering. In the triple phases of *memoratio*, *compassio*, and *conformatio*, imagination is always an express provision and/or prerequisite: *considera omnes gestos suos, maxime contemplans faciem eius, si potes imaginari*. The meditator is urged to follow Christ's suffering, *in sua ymagine ante oculos ponere, tamquam Christum corporaliter videat*.[13]

I would apply Müller's findings to suggest that one could also speak explicitly of an *imaginatio corporis* in connection with the meditational literature. One would however immediately have to add that this imagination by itself was apparently not trusted, that in fact its activity was constantly being monitored and supervised by the theological commentaries, which is to say, once again, by *legein* and *teukein*. Müller demonstrates how the critics of the meditational exercises explicitly attempted to discredit this imaginary "realization" of Christ's body as merely phantasmatic, over and against the truly real sacramental presence. This line of criticism is extremely suggestive. Some sense appeared to exist that the imaginary, once liberated, can no longer be recuperated by the symbolic. The commentaries attempt to anchor *compassio* in the consciousness of moral performance, but in fact they no longer have any control over the forms of affectivity to which the subject surrenders in the process of identifying with the imagined Living Body of flesh and blood.

V

As a representation of the *historia passionis*, the drama has both from the outset: Last Supper and Crucifixion, bloodless and blood sacrifice. It would be obvious to begin by tracing how the drama deals with the Last Supper. I didn't do this at the time, and Müller has since also filled this in. The overwhelming majority of the Last Supper scenes contained in the plays are structured in such a way as to avoid competition with liturgy. The phrases accompanying the administration of the sacrament are avoided or are quoted in the vernacular. "The core scene of the Eucharist," Müller concludes, "appears as a blind spot, which could just as well allude to the proximity as to the distance between liturgy and theatrical mimesis."[14] Apparently this "blind spot" has been so thoroughly appropriated by *legein* and *teukein*, to refer to Castoriadis once again, that the imaginary of the play cannot establish itself here.

However, it does also have a blood sacrifice, and here that activation of the imaginary for which the meditational tracts on the Passion supply training once again comes into play, no longer as applied to individual psychology but rather collectively. The decisive difference, however, is that the public no longer has to imagine the body because the drama has already presented it *in persona Christi* and thus *in vivo*. This change necessarily aggravates the possible confusion of actual presence and merely phantasmatic presence feared by the critics of meditational practice. What is at stake in the play is the imaginary substitution of one real presence for another. In the Mass, the presence of the *corpus verum* is bound to the operations of the *legein* and *teukein*. In meditational practice, the emancipated imaginary is supposed to remain under the control and supervision of the accompanying commentary, except that it cannot be ascertained how far this control still extends. In the play, as well, the level of the commentary is present, but it is clearly subsidiary to the exuberantly proliferating representations of the sacrificial offering.

What qualifies the Passion play as a cult play is, above all, the drastic violence of these elaborated representations. This drastic facet is most conspicuously legitimated by the actions of the Jewish aggressors who kill Jesus as a scapegoat. However, the cult drama has no notion of the play within the play; its essential element is dedifferentiation. Therefore, it appears symptomatic to me that the commentary tends to remain silent exactly on the point where it would be indispensable, namely, when it comes to providing a figural-typological interpretation of the specifics of Christ's torture. Every detail, however horrifying, is of course typologically accounted for, and yet, two observations need to be made. For one thing, the fact that the possibility of a symbolic interpretation exists does not explain why excessive use is then made of the possibility. Secondly, the omission of commentary exactly at this point demonstrates to what an extent the imaginary has displaced the symbolic. This was where I found Alfred Lorenzer's theory of desymbolized pseudocommunication so welcome.[15] Müller would prefer to view only one side, the "false" side of the Jewish torturers, as characterized in these terms, whereas, for the believing Christian, "a more comprehensive 'imputation of meaning' (*Sinnverdacht*), namely one that views what Christ's tormentors inflict as part of the divine plan," would be operative.[16] So here Müller would differentiate, whereas I would continue to argue for dedifferentiation. In my book I referred to the fact that the excessive application of figural typology to the Crucifixion was already considered debatable by theologians in the twelfth century. Apparently they saw the difficulty in making this violently drastic extremity comprehensible in moral terms. For what is at stake here is the effort, fundamental to Christianity, to vanquish transgression once and for all, within the medium of a transgressive sacrificial ritual. This effort already confronts theological rationality with a paradox: morality is to be extracted and refined, so to speak, from blood. Then, however, what becomes of this paradox in the theatrical staging? When even commentary itself is dispensed with, then it appears to me that anything like a comprehensive "imputation of meaning" in the strictly symbolic application has already been lost for the authors.

Hence, I believe that, when it comes to this decisive point, the contemporary interpreter should desire no more than the plays themselves. Certainly the Jewish torturers are agents of the divine plan, which dictates that transgression should occur yet once more. With that they also automatically become the agents of the transgressive imaginary, which wants the body, that bleeding body that the Mass so stubbornly withholds. I will not go so far as to assert that the imaginary has simply canceled out the moral sense here. However I would lay emphasis on the fierce conflict that must have been played out here between morality and the emancipated imaginary. Above all, I would emphasize that, while the inundation of the symbolic by the imaginary is theologically and dogmatically regressive, it cannot on this account simply be regarded as a fall back into meaninglessness. The crucial issue here does not concern an opposition between the comprehensive imputation of meaning and meaninglessness; instead, it has to do with those two levels that I described in my book by reference to Luhmann's differentiation between manifest and latent functions. This differentiation corresponds to the two dimensions within which, according to Castoriadis, social institutions evolve, that of the *legein* and the *teukein* on one side and that of the imaginary significations on the other side. Castoriadis thus allows us to avoid the mistake of assuming that the operation of the imaginary in the plays is to be equated with meaninglessness or chaos. Castoriadis refers specifically to imaginary meanings, that is, to a kind of meaning sui generis, which he credits with exercising a primary roll in the constitution of social institutions and which is never fully subsumed in any process of rationalization.

Lorenzer speaks of a "scenic understanding," the "participation in an actional construction, i.e. in a scene, in which the play itself is carried on and through over the heads of the participating individuals."[17] The concept of the scene is also central for Castoriadis. He differentiates between "constituted/formed phantasms" and "constitutive/forming phantasms-phantasmatization."[18] Magma, the "proto-representation," is, as we saw, a transcendental "scène totale." It is transcendental in relation to all "real" scenes, which the imaginary conjures up, and these scenes are not meaningless, inasmuch as they owe their existence to the imaginary, but rather their meaning is to be sought in the imaginary itself. The question is not—and I want to insist on this—one of meaningfulness versus meaninglessness but rather of an institution that is indebted for its existence to the imaginary and that is never fully integrated within a functionalistic interpretation—unless one functionally equates, as Luhmann does, the act of imaginary instituting with the concept of latency, "the latent function."

It appears to me to be an idle question, where in the performative situation the boundary was located between latent and manifest function, between the dynamic of the Imaginary and moral reflection. To this extent the invocation of the ambivalence present in the religious plays is no evasion but instead the only answer remaining for us to the question of how the

Christian community sought to constitute itself in these dramas. In the Easter play it constitutes itself through banishing the fear of the devil and through a cathartic *risus paschalis*. In the Passion play it constitutes itself oppositionally, in relation to the evil Jews, and identificatorily, in gazing on the blood of Christ's martyred body. The Jews' consciously selected scapegoat is the imaginary scapegoat of the Christian community itself.[19]

VI

In closing, I would like to return again to a concrete example to which I already devoted special attention in my book: the rondeaux of Greban and his successor Michel. They run through the entire drama as a poetic *forme fixe*. We find them on the occasions of the shepherds' adoration, the harrowing of Satan in hell, the miracle of the loaves and fishes, the raising up of Lazarus, the entry into Jerusalem—and naturally also the Crucifixion. In this poetic form of the rondeau, the drama appears to aspire to aesthetic elaboration, to cross the threshold between ritual and theater. Nevertheless, the rondeau, with its structuring repetitions, does appear to possess ritual characteristics, by means of which it integrates itself into the cult play. That becomes especially clear in the scenes of torture. Since the rondeau is ubiquitous within the drama, it cannot, in the case of the Crucifixion, be a matter of a specifically Jewish ritual, staged for a community that, in witnessing this ritual, simultaneously commemorates its moral supersession through the power of Christ's suffering. Perhaps it is precisely these torture rondeaux that constitute the clearest symptom of how, in these plays, spatial, temporal, and also "personal" distances and differences (personal in the sense of the persona represented by the player's masks) collapse. The ritual rondeaux channel the imaginary of the *ludus* itself, and thereby channel, in the torture scenes, a transgressive imaginary, a transgressive desire for the body, which itself can likewise be situated exactly at the meeting place of ritual and theatrical mimesis.

Perhaps one could even speak here, with Georges Bataille, of an eroticized violence, that is, a violence that sacralizes the desired body in ceremonially profaning, defiling, and fragmenting it. Bataille's theory of the sacrifice, which he developed together with Roger Callois and Michel Leiris in the late 1930s at the Paris College of Sociology, starts from the paradoxicality of the *felix culpa* in the Christian conceptualization of sacrifice: "That which redeems us is at the same time that which should never have taken place. For Christianity, the prohibition is absolutely affirmed and the transgression, whatever it may be, is definitively condemned."[20] The moralizing of the sacrifice and the loss of the experience of transgression are two sides of the same coin. The experience of transgression only gets recovered, according to Bataille, in erotic ecstasy, in the eruption of violence into frenzy, in the euphoric convulsions of the flesh: "At the base of eroticism, we have the experience of a flash, of the violence unloosed in the moment of explosion."[21] Bataille speculates that this "interior experience of excess" may in turn have made its way into the mysticism associated with the Passion and thereby into the most radical form of meditative submersion in the way of the Man of Suffering. This interpretation suggests that the *gloriosa passio* of the religious plays can also be considered from this perspective.

The Passion plays celebrate a *gloriosa passio*, even if it is tempting to view them as the gratification of a transgressive imaginary, whose moral and reflective side can at best only be surmised. The Easter plays likewise celebrate Christ's Resurrection, even if one prefers to view the drastic dimension of their comic excesses as a ritual liberation from an overwhelming fear of the devil, rather than falling back, for lack of any alternative, on the explanation of an Easter-inspired exultation that slipped out of control.

The author of this book is Protestant by birth. He did not however write it out of any kind of denominational commitment but rather as a Luhmannian "observer." He was fascinated by the exertions of Christian dogma, but he was just as fascinated by the fruitlessness of these exertions, as documented by the religious drama. And yet, at the same time, he would want to call these dramas Christian—because for him, "Christian" is the collective designation for everything that historically has ever understood itself as Christian.

Translated by CHRIS CULLEN

Reference Matter

Notes

INTRODUCTION

1. E. Prosser, *Drama and Religion in the English Mystery Plays* (Stanford, 1961); G. Wickham, *Early English Stages, 1100 to 1600*, 2 vols. (London and New York, 1959); Hardison, *Christian Rite.*

2. W. Mittenzwei, "Aufgaben und Auftrag des Instituts für Literaturgeschichte," *Weimarer Beiträge* 5 (1970): 20.

3. Weimann, *Shakespeare*, 150.

4. R. Weimann, "Gegenwart und Vergangenheit in der Literaturgeschichte," in *Weimarer Beiträge* 5 (1970): 32.

5. Frank, *Medieval French Drama.*

6. See W. F. Michael, "Das deutsche Drama vor der Reformation," *Deutsche Vierteljahrsschrift für Literaturwissenschaft und Geistesgeschichte* 31 (1957): 106–53.

7. W. Creizenach, *Geschichte des neueren Dramas*, 3 vols. (Halle, 1911; reprint, New York, 1965); for E. Hartl, see the introduction to *Das Drama des Mittelalters*, vol. 1, *Osterfeiern* (Leipzig, 1937; reprint, Darmstadt, 1964), 21–240; for R. Froning, see the introduction to *Das Drama des Mittelalters* (Stuttgart, 1890–91; reprint, Darmstadt, 1964).

8. Brinkmann, "Das religiöse Drama," 257.

9. In 1930, Brinkmann saw the task of historical understanding as consisting in "understanding the past on the basis of its own assumptions and through this devotion to enrich oneself inwardly" (*Studien* 2: 193). However, one has to hermeneutically regain the past in order to be able profit from it. "Devotion" alone is not enough. The quoted introduction to the 1959 article attempts to take this fact into account.

10. *Studien*, 2: 273.

11. Gadamer, *Wahrheit und Methode*, 289–90, 356–57.

12. Benjamin, "Eduard Fuchs, der Sammler und Erzähler," in Benjamin, *Angelus Novus*, 303.

13. Luhmann, *Soziologische Aufklärung*, 14.

14. Gadamer, *Wahrheit und Methode*, 274.

15. I have discussed Hardison at length in a preliminary study for this book: "Ritus, Mythos, und geistliches Spiel," in Fuhrmann, *Terror und Spiel*, 211–39. This study also appeared in *Poetica* 3 (1970): 83–114.

16. Frye's "Littérature et mythe" appeared in *Poétique* 8 (1971): 489–514.

17. J. E. Harrison, *Themis: A Study of the Social Origins of Greek Religion*, *2nd ed.* (Cambridge, 1932), esp. 13, 328, 331. A brief but informative introduction to the Cambridge school and its impact on the field is given in E. E. Hyman, "The Ritual View of Myth and the Mythic," in *Myth: A Symposium*, ed. Thomas A. Sebeok (1955; reprint, Bloomington, 1965), 136–53.

18. G. Murray, "Excursus on the Ritual Forms Preserved in Greek Tragedy," in Harrison, *Themis*, 341–63. F. M. Cornford, *The Origins of Attic Comedy* (London, 1914).

19. J. G. Frazer, *The Golden Bough: A Study in Magic and Religion* (1890; reprint, London, 1966).

20. A very good introduction to this history as well as its problematics is given in R. Weimann, "Literaturwissenschaft und Mythologie, Vorfragen einer methodologischen Kritik," in *Sinn und Form* 19 (1967), Sonderheft I, 484–521; expanded version in Weimann, *Literaturgeschichte und Mythologie* (Berlin, 1971), 364–427.

21. Frye, *Anatomy of Criticism*, 108–9.

22. N. Frye, *Fables of Identity: Studies in Poetic Mythology* (New York, 1963), 120. Cf. Frye, *Anatomy*, 365.

23. Frye, "Reflections in a Mirror," in M. Krieger, ed., *Northrop Frye in Modern Criticism: Selected Papers of the English Institute* (New York, 1966), 136.

24. Brémond's "narrative cycle," Barthes's "functions" and "indices," Greimas's "isotopy," and Eco's "play situations" have a status comparable to that of Frye's "patterns." See the programmatic articles in *Communications* 8 (1966): R. Barthes, "Introduction à l'analyse structurale des récits," 1–27; A. J. Greimas, "Eléments pour une théorie de l'interprétation du récit mythique," 28–59; C. Brémond, "La logique des possibles narratifs," 60–76; U. Eco, "James Bond, une combinatoire narratif," 77–93.

25. On the current situation of research in this area, see W. A. Koch's highly informative review of Tzvetan Todorov's *Grammaire du Décaméron* (The Hague, 1969), in *Poetica* 4 (1971): 565–72; Koch identifies the key issue when he observes that in Todorov's work, "the recapitulation, which is not formalized symbolically, already contains all the selected structures. Who is canonizing here, and how?"

We will have to wait and see what solutions linguistics itself, and in particular so-called text-linguistics, may provide in this regard. The multiplicity of competing approaches and schools that characterizes the current discussion suggests skepticism; it seems likely that this multiplicity proceeds from insufficient epistemological self-examination (see below, Chapter 2).

26. See the articles and bibliography in Krieger, *Northrop Frye*; also J. Casey, *The Language of Criticism* (London, 1966), chap. 7; Geoffrey Hartman, *Structuralism: The Anglo-American Adventure*, in Jacques Ehrmann, ed., *Structuralism*, Yale French Studies 36/37 (New Haven, 1966), 148–68.

27. On the most recent developments, see the outstanding bibliography in Josue V. Harari, *Structuralists and Structuralism: A Selected Bibliography of French Contemporary Thought* (Ithaca, N.Y., 1971); also the older bibliography in G. Schiwy, *Der französische Strukturalismus* (Reinbek, 1969), 232–40. I would like to draw attention to hermeneutically oriented criticism of Claude Lévi-Strauss conducted by Paul Ricoeur and Jacques Derrida. Both authors note a peculiar "subjectless transcendentalism" (Ricoeur, "Structure," 619) in Lévi-Strauss, which they make the object of a hermeneutic examination. Ricoeur distinguishes between two poles of mythical thinking, one "totemic" and the other "kerygmatic," which he tries to use to limit the legitimacy of the structuralist approach to so-called totemic cultures that essentially have no history. He sees the Semitic, pre-Hellenic, and Indo-European cultural sphere as essentially constituted through history and kerygmatic surplus of meaning, that is, through factors incompatible with the structuralist commitment to system and against history. Derrida is more radical. Whereas Ricoeur still wants to accord the structuralist position a relative legitimacy, Derrida seeks to uncover the methodological circle hidden behind the denial of a "transcendental signified," and thereby to undermine hermeneutically the structuralist attack on metaphysical traditions: "This circle is unique. It describes the form of the relationship between the history of metaphysics and the destruction of the history of metaphysics. There is no sense in doing without the concepts of metaphysics in order to attack metaphysics. We have no language—no syntax and no lexicon—which is alien to this history; we cannot utter a single destructive proposition that has not already slipped into the form, the logic, and the implicit postulations of precisely what it seeks to contest" ("Structure," 250). Thus he shows that the concepts of the sign and of structure in particular cannot overcome by themselves the opposition between the sensible and the intelligible, as Lévi-Strauss believes, because complete reduction would require the very opposition they are reducing: "the opposition is part of the system, along with the reduction" (251). If the opposition between signifier and signified, between structure and subject, is abandoned, then sign and structure themselves have to be abandoned as metaphysical con-

cepts. Since Lévi-Strauss simply does not examine this question, his suspicion with regard to history conceals the danger of falling back into an "ahistoricism of a classical type, that is to say, in a determinate moment of the history of metaphysics" (263).

28. Luhmann, *Soziologische Aufklärung*, 114.

29. Ibid., 39, 75, 78, 114.

30. Frye, *Anatomy*, 163–86, esp. 163, 172.

31. Ibid., 115 ff.

32. For Frye's contradictory stance with regard to Jung, see ibid., 112, where the anchorage of the archetypes in a collective unconscious is described as an "unnecessary hypothesis," and 192 n, where, with regard to tracing back the four *mythoi* to a quest-myth, Jung's *Wandlungen und Symbole der Libido* is cited as the chief authority.

33. See esp. Frye, *Anatomy*, 105 ff.

34. See the relevant comments in Hartman, *Structuralism*, 159 ff. (cf. n. 28).

35. See above, note 27.

36. See N. Dyson-Hudson, "Structure and Infrastructure in Primitive Society (Lévi-Strauss and Radcliffe Brown)," in *The Structuralist Controversy: The Languages of Criticism and the Sciences of Man*, ed. R. Macksey and E. Donato (Baltimore, 1970), 218–41. See also E. Leach in Lepenies and Ritter, *Orte des wilden Denkens*, 74.

37. *Mythos und Kult bei den Naturvölkern*, quoted in Kerényi, *Eröffnung*, 269.

38. Malinowski, *Myth in Primitive Psychology* (New York, 1926) and *The Foundations of Faith and Morals* (Oxford, 1936); on this issue, see H. Baumann, "Mythos in ethnologischer Sicht," in *Studium Generale* 12 (1959): 1–17, 583–97; also W. F. Otto, "Long ago, through careful research on religion among primitive and cultured peoples we arrived at the insight that no genuine (original) religion ever existed without myth. Today we must learn that there has never been a genuine (original) myth without religion. Thus they are, in a way that remains to be determined, one and the same." (*Der ursprüngliche Mythos im Lichte der Sympathie von Mensch und Welt*, quoted in Kerényi, *Eröffnung*, 271).

39. Gehlen, *Urmensch*, 115.

40. A. Gehlen, *Anthropologische Forschung* (Reinbek, 1961), 56.

41. Gehlen, *Urmensch*, 10.

42. According to R. G. Collingwood, a text can be understood only when one has reconstructed the question to which it is an answer (*An Autobiography* [Oxford, 1939], chap. 5). Gadamer's elaboration of an approach that Collingwood developed as part of a critique of the logic of propositions suffers from the substantialist twist that he gives it with the thesis that at the beginning

stands not the initial question but rather the question posed by tradition itself to interpreters.

43. For the constitution of meaning through system references, see Luhmann, "Sinn als Grundbegriff der Soziologie," in J. Habermas and N. Luhmann, *Theorie der Gesellschaft oder Sozialtechnologie* (Frankfurt, 1971), 25–100. Luhmann proposes to define the concept of meaning as "primary, that is, without relation to the concept of the subject . . . because the latter, as a meaningful constituted identity already presupposes the concept of meaning" (28). For this subject relationship Luhmann substitutes system references: it is first through "the choice of a system reference that the subject matter described by the concepts meaning, experience, action, etc. becomes a psychological or sociological category" (29). On this basis the concept of a "meaning-constituting system" is developed, in which by "constitution" is meant "the relationship between a selective, dense order and openness to other possibilities," and even "a relationship between the mutually-self-determining and the only-possible-together" (30). Here I explicitly include neither the concepts of complexity, selectivity, and negativity in my argument (although implicit points of contact are present, particularly in the guiding model of the inclusion of the excluded) nor Habermas's critical dialogue with Luhmann. I limit myself to what accommodates my attempt to mediate between structuralism and hermeneutics: the connection between a genetic, phenomenologically and hermeneutically oriented concept of meaning and systems theory. It is clear to me that this kind of attempt demands further theorization. Precisely with respect to what remains here still to be done, it seemed to me nevertheless at least equally important to test theoretical reflections by applying them to concrete analyses and thereby to point out the enticing aspects as well as the desiderata of such an enterprise.

44. Luhmann, *Soziologische Aufklärung*, 129.

45. According to Vaihinger, the distinction between a heuristic fiction and a hypothesis is that "a fiction is a mere helpful image, a mere detour, a mere scaffolding, which will be taken down again, whereas a hypothesis anticipates a definitive establishment." Abandoned and theoretically worthless hypotheses can still do service as heuristic fictions (*Die Philosophie des Als ob* [Leipzig, 1922], 54 ff., 148). The concept can thus very well show that structural-functional hypotheses remain usable as heuristic fictions for functional-structural goals but only as fictions, no longer as hypotheses. After the draft for this book was completed, Umberto Eco's confrontation with "ontological structuralism" appeared; on many points, it supports the present reflections. Eco sees structuralism's ontological error as consisting primarily in the fact "that the presumed constants are selected as the single object and as the final goal of the investigation, as an endpoint and not as the starting point for new doubts. There is no ontological

error in having at hand a hypothesis about the *Identical* in order to arrive at a unified exploration of the *Different*. But there is an ontological error in plundering the storehouse of the *Different* in order to find the *Identical* in it, always, immediately, and with absolute certainty" (*Einführung in die Semiotik* [Munich, 1972], 423). Skepticism regarding a search for structural universals, insight into the historicity of codes, and especially the express inclusion of what he calls "communication situations," defined as "the whole of reality, which the choice of codes and subcodes limits, insofar as it makes decoding depend on their presence" (136), in a comprehensive theory of communication, give this book a leading role in the present discussion of the foundations of literary study.

46. Malinowski, *Myth in Primitive Psychology*, quoted in Kerényi, *Eröffnung*, 181–82.

47. Venerable Bede, in *PL* 92, 593A.

48. Kerényi, *Eröffnung*, 182–83.

49. Gehlen, "Nichtbewusste kulturanthropologische Kategorien," in *Zeitschrift für philosophische Forschung* 4 (1949–50): 321–46. The categories described in this article are further elaborated in *Urmensch und Spätkultur*.

50. Pannenberg, "Späthorizonte des Mythos," 499.

51. Ibid., 500.

52. Auerbach, "Figura," 42, 59–60.

53. Auerbach, "Figura," 42.

54. Eliade, *Kosmos*, 35.

55. See Pannenberg, "Späthorizonte des Mythos," 524.

56. Eliade, *Kosmos*, 42.

57. T. Fry, "The Unity of the *Ludus Conventriae*," *Studies in Philology* 48 (1951): 527–70.

58. L. Gautier, *Histoire de la poésie liturgique: les tropes* (Paris, 1866), 138.

CHAPTER I

1. In its simplest form, it reads:

INTERROGATIO:
Quem queritis in sepulchro, Christicole?

RESPONSIO:
Iesum Nazarenum crucifixum, o caelicolae.
Non est hic, surrexit sicut predixerat; ite, nuntiate quia surrexit de sepulchro.
Resurrexi.

(Troparium Sangallense, tenth century, quoted in Young, *Drama*, 1: 201).

In the following I limit myself to the briefest allusions to the often-described history of the development of liturgical celebration; I refer the reader to Brinkmann, Studien; Young, *Drama*; and especially de Boor, *Textgeschichte*, chap. 1 ("Methodische Erwägungen"). With de Boor (and in opposition to Brinkmann) I speak not of liturgical drama [*Drama*] or liturgical plays [*Spiel*] but rather of liturgical celebration as distinguished from vernacular plays [*Spiel*].

2. Young, *Drama*, 1: 133.

3. J. Schwietering, "Über den liturgischen Ursprung des mittelalterlichen geistlichen Spiels," *Zeitschrift für deutsches Altertum* 62 (1925): 1–20, 3, 7.

4. Brinkmann, *Studien* 2: 168.

5. Ibid., 2: 191.

6. Ibid.

7. Chambers, *Medieval Stage*, 3.

8. See the debate between Stumpfl and E. Scheunemann in *Zeitschrift für deutsche Philologie* 61 (1936): 432–43 and 62 (1937): 87–105, as well as Neil C. Brooks's review in the *Journal of English and Germanic Philology* 37 (1938): 300–305.

9. R. Pascal, "On the Origins of the Liturgical Drama of the Middle Ages," *Modern Language Review* 36 (1941): 369–87.

10. B. Hunningher, *Origin*, esp. 77–80.

11. H. M. Gamer, "Mimes, Musicians, and the Origin of the Medieval Religious Play," in *Deutsche Beiträge zur geistigen Überlieferung* 5 (1965): 9–28. Compare Hunningher, *Origin*, 81 ff.

12. Hardison, *Christian Rite*, vii; Stemmler, *Liturgische Feiern*, 3 ff.

13. No future investigation of religious drama can ignore Hardison's brilliant methodological analyses in Chapter 1 ("Darwin, Mutations, and the Origin of Medieval Drama").

14. Stumpfl, "Der Ursprung des mittelalterlichen Dramas," *Zeitschrift für deutsche Philologie* 62 (1937): 87–95, 88.

15. Hunningher, *Origin*, 116.

16. Hardison, *Christian Rite*, 35–177, or about half the book.

17. See the introductory research review in Kolping, "Amalar von Metz," 424 ff. On "Germanic theology," see ibid., 427, 463.

18. Amalarius, *Liber Officialis*, in *Amalarii Episcopi Opera Liturgica Omnia*, ed. J. M. Hanssens, 3 vols. (Rome, 1948–50), 2: 14; hereafter cited as Hanssens.

19. Ibid., 329 ff.

20. *PL* 119, 75 B.

21. Reprinted in Hanssens, 2: 567 ff.; the quoted passage appears on 2: 576, with similar phrases on 2: 571, as well as on 1: 373 (the *Invectio canonica* was very probably composed by Florus).

22. *PL* 119, 74 D and 71 A.

23. Ibid., 82 D.

24. Ibid., 83 A.

25. Ibid., 83 CD; on the tradition behind this view, see Lubac, *Corpus mysticum*, 23 ff.

26. Lubac, *Corpus mysticum*, 219 ff.

27. *PL* 119, 20 D.

28. Hanssens, 2: 396–97.

29. See J. Geiselmann, *Die Eucharistielehre der Vorscholastik* (Paderborn, 1926), 87 ff.; on Florus's critique of Amalarius's doctrine of the *corpus Christi triforme*, see Lubac, *Corpus mysticum*, 297 ff.

30. The following thorough analysis of the role of the didactic impulse in allegorization of the Mass distinguishes my discussion from that of Kolping. Kolping goes no further than the opposition between sacramental mystery (Florus) and a "liturgical play" directed to the "external manifestation," the "externality" and "superficiality" of ritual (Amalarius); see in particular 433, 434, 442, 553. Kolping's alignment of Amalarius's interpretation of the Eucharist with this kind of overall tendency of allegorization is therefore not convincing (see especially 438–39).

31. *PL* 119, 74 D; Florus refers to *Liber Officialis* 2: 2; I was unable to find the reference to the Sun/Phoebus and Moon/Phoebe in Amalarius; perhaps he himself deleted it in later editions.

32. Hanssens, 2: 570, and *PL* 119, 75 A.

33. Hanssens, 2: 569.

34. *At spiritalia ita: per panem, caritatem; per piscem, fidem; per ovum, spem. Quibus tribus colitur a nobis divinitas* (Hanssens, 2: 181).

35. *PL* 119, 82 D.

36. After the banishment of Agobard from Lyons in 835, Amalarius was appointed the administrator of the archdiocese and used his office to carry out the liturgical reforms that were opposed by Florus. On Amalarius's life, see A. Cabaniss's otherwise run-of-the-mill book, *Amalarius von Metz* (Amsterdam, 1954).

37. *PL* 217, 773–916. A good overview of the further development of allegorization of the Mass is given in Jungmann, *Missarum Solemnia*, 1: 120 ff.; on Innocent III and Durandus, see 147–48.

38. Lubac, *Corpus mysticum*, 314.

39. Quoted in Jungmann, *Missarum Solemnia*, 1: 150.

40. In addition to Florus, also Agobard of Lyons, and in the twelfth century, Aelred of Rievaulx; see Chambers, *Medieval Stage*, 1: 81; Young, *Drama*, 1: 548; and Hardison, *Christian Rite*, 78.

41. Hardison, *Christian Rite*, especially 178–219 ("Early History of the *Quem quaeritis*"), see summary of thesis, 198–99.

42. See de Boor, *Textgeschichte*, 26; in Young there is not a single text that is explicitly identified as Franciscan or Dominican; Cistercians and Carthusians were also opposed to such embellishments of the liturgy.

43. In the interest of brevity, here and subsequently I note not the celebrations but only the page references in Young, *Drama*, vol. 1: *ad imitationem* or *imitari*, 249, 384; *ad similitudinem*, 370, 393, 396; *in significatione*, 241; *in persona*, 317–18, 324–25, 329, 366, 371; *in specie*, 366, 382; *in figura*, 366, 400; *sub typo*, 253, 309.

44. Young, *Drama*, 1: 294 (*tres scolares ad modum Mulierum indutos*), 344 (*more muliebri ornatis*), 290 (*duo pueri . . . admictis paratis*).

45. On this point, see the informative article by W. Lipphardt et al., "Liturgische Dramen des Mittelalters," *Musik in Geschichte und Gegenwart* 8 (Kassel, 1960): cols. 1012–51.

46. *PL* 92, 623 A.

47. Hanssens, 2: 359–60.

48. With the exception of the celebrations at Fleury and Hersfeld/St. Gallen (Young, *Drama*, 1: 393 ff., 666–67). See de Boor, *Textgeschichte*, 244.

49. De Boor, *Textgeschichte*, 166–73.

50. Ibid., 223.

51. See, for example, Young, *Drama*, 1: 371.

52. Hanssens, 2: 161.

53. Florus, *Invectio canonica*, reprinted in Hanssens, 1: 367 ff.; the passage quoted is on 373–74.

54. See Young, *Drama*, 1: 243, 247, 264, 275.

55. See de Boor, *Textgeschichte*, Anhang A, 329 ff. ("Die lateinische Grundlage der deutschen Osterspiele").

CHAPTER 2

1. Hartl, *Drama*, 1: 203–4.

2. E. Scheunemann, "Entgegnung," in *Zeitschrift für deutsche Philologie* 62 (1937): 105, and Scheunemann's review of Stumpfl's book in *Zeitschrift für deutsche Philologie* 61 (1936): 436.

3. The *descensus* is not extant, but it is referred to in the Prologue. See *Seinte Resurreccion*, ed. T. A. Jenkins et al., Anglo-Norman Text Society 4 (Oxford, 1943): 7 ff.; see also Frank, *Medieval French Drama*, 86 ff.

4. *Innsbrucker Osterspiel*, ed. E. Hartl, in *Das Drama des Mittelalters: Osterspiele* (Leipzig, 1937; reprint, Darmstadt, 1964), 136–89; hereafter cited as Innsbruck.

5. *Rheinisches Osterspiel*, ed. H. Rueff, in *Das Rheinische Osterspiel der Berliner Handschrift*, Ms. Germ. Fol. 1219 (Berlin, 1925), 47; hereafter cited as Rhein Easter play.

6. Barthes, "Introduction," 95.

7. Louis Marin, "Les femmes au tombeau," *Langages* 22 (1971): 50. J. L. Austin's conception of performative and constative speech acts (*How To Do Things With Words*, Cambridge, Mass., 1962) was also known to the Paris semioticians, who either added it to the description of one of the different levels of the text or included it among the modes of storytelling. In both cases the integration of "récit" (story) and "narration," or "récit" and "discours" was assumed. Marin shows however that even this assumption cannot be made in dealing with biblical texts. See also Marin's "En guise de conclusion," *Langages* 22 (1971): 119–27, where he again interprets the event-structure of these texts on the basis of the relation between "récit" and "discours prophétique," esp. 123–24, 126–27.

8. See especially Todorov, "Catégories," 125–26.

9. Luhmann, *Soziologische Aufklärung*, 73.

10. In Dilthey, "comparison" is a way of verifying "divination," both of which seek to determine the essence of the individual: "We can never forego a comparative method in relation to the individual" ("Der Aufbau der geschichtlichen Welt in den Geisteswissenschaften," *Gesammelte Schriften*, 5th ed. [Stuttgart, 1959], 7: 226); a functional-structural comparative technique is oriented in precisely the opposite direction: "A comparison does not serve, as Husserl on the basis of older traditions still thinks, the reduction of the being to the essential, but rather its reinforcement in relation to other possibilities. The comparison does not establish the being in itself, but rather determines abstract points of view from which one being can be reflectively or actually substituted for another. The gain in rationality does not consist in the certainty that the being remains itself in certain essential traits; it consists rather in the certainty that under some conditions it is not necessary that the being remain itself" (Luhmann, *Soziologische Aufklärung*, 47).

11. See below, Chapter 7. It would be confusing to bring the theological discussion in at this point, since it was ignited almost exclusively by the question about the relationship between the descent into Hell and the death on the cross. Nevertheless, in discussing the Passion play we will return once more to the analysis of the *descensus*.

12. *Tiroler Passionspiele*, ed. J. E. Wackernell, in *Altdeutsche Passionsspiele aus Tirol* (Graz, 1897), 233; hereafter cited as Wackernell.

13. *Donaueschinger Passionspiel*, ed. E. Hartl, in *Das Drama des Mittelalters: Passionsspiele*, vol. 2 (Leipzig, 1942; reprint, Darmstadt, 1966), verse 45; hereafter cited as Donaueschingen Passion play.

14. For further examples, see W. F. Michael, "Die Bedeutung des Wortes Figur im geistlichen Drama in Deutschland," *Germanic Review* 21 (1946): 3–8. I definitely do not agree with Michael's interpretation of this meaning in the sense of "presentation, play, and ultimately drama" (5), as the following will show.

15. *Redentiner Osterspiel*, ed. W. Krogmann, 2nd ed. (Leipzig, 1964); hereafter cited as Redentine play.

16. *Erlauer Osterspiel*, ed. E. Hartl, in *Das Drama des Mittelalters: Osterspiele* (Leipzig, 1937; reprint, Darmstadt, 1964), 205–60; hereafter cited as Erlau Easter play.

17. See, for instance, L. Wolff, "Die Verschmelzung des Dargestellten mit der Gegenwartswirklichkeit im geistlichen Drama des deutschen Mittelalters," *Deutsche Vierteljahrschrift* 7 (1929): 267–304, especially 294: "on the whole the representation strives to go beyond the individual historical moment toward what is enduring and valid precisely for that particular day." Brinkmann follows him: "The redemption is celebrated, not as a unique historical event, but as a ceremony of timeless return and eternal validity; becoming real again and again whenever its memory is observed." According to Brinkmann, the redemption is "also a historical, unique act. But essentially it is more, it constantly renewed itself in the Mass. It was not unique and past, but rather repeatable, immediate presence. And it was therefore justified to treat it as present in dramatic representation" (*Studien* 2: 198, 218). That is exactly the kind of argument that I am trying to show obscures the problem.

18. Eliade, *Kosmos*, 35.

19. Weinrich, "Structures," 29 ff.

20. Lévi-Strauss, *Anthropologie structurale* (Paris, 1958), 265.

21. Gospel of Nicodemus, 2: 18, 7: 23. (See *Evangelia Apocrypha*, ed. Tischendorf, 422, 428, 429). I have found only two cases in which this demand was made only twice: Augsburg (following 2402) and Chester (17: 145, 177).

22. Olrik, "Epische Gesetze der Volksdichtung," *Zeitschrift für deutsches Altertum und deutsche Literatur* 41 (1909): 1–2, especially 7.

23. See M. Lüthi, *Märchen*, 2nd. ed. (Stuttgart, 1968), 29, 96.

24. Young, *Drama*, 1: 163–64.

25. Ibid., 1: 164 ff.

26. The Würzburg *elevatio* is published in G. Milchsack, *Die Oster- und Passionsspiele* 1 (*Die lateinischen Osterfeiern*) (Wolfenbüttel, 1880), 135.

27. Young, *Drama*, 1: 173–74. The Augsburg *elevatio* is published in Milchsack, *Die Oster- und Passionsspiele*, 127 ff. It is interesting that the Bamberg ceremony does not indicate whether the *aliquis in templo qui diaboli personam simulans* was a cleric. Two *elevatio* texts from Mainz discovered by H. Rueff mention that this person is *plebanus vero vel alius* (Mainz/Liebfrauen) or else "the bell-ringer . . . or someone else who is assigned this function" (Mainz/St. Quintin, Rhein Easter play, 71–74). The *elevatio* from St. Quintin is related to those from Bamberg and Augsburg but nonetheless does not indicate whether the priest knocking on the door has also taken the Blessed Sacrament with him on exiting the church. The Liebfrauen *elevatio* is similar to the one in St. Gallen

previously discussed but in contrast to the latter has the *plebanus* ask the question from within the choir. It should also be noted here that the Blessed Sacrament is not with him in the choir but rather with the one who desires to enter.

28. K. Schmidt, "Die Darstellung von Christi Höllenfahrt in den deutschen und den ihnen verwandten Spielen des Mittelalters"(Diss., Marburg, 1915), 18.

29. Young, *Drama*, 1: 102 ff.

30. Kroll, *Gott und Hölle*, 109 ff., 128 ff.

31. On the sources of the *descensus* scene, see Thoran, "Studien," 132 ff.

32. In defense of Brinkmann's hypothesis "that the descent into Hell was worked out in the Easter play before it developed in the ritual in connection with the *elevatio*" (*Studien*, 2: 189), one can point out that the examples in question (Young, *Drama*, 1: 161 ff.) are very late and contemporaneous with the Easter plays of the fourteenth and fifteenth centuries. On the other hand, however, the basic framework of the *descensus* is retained in the plays as well, mainly in the Latin plays, and this cannot be explained in the absence of at least a secondary influence of the aforementioned church ritual.

33. Brinkmann, *Studien*, 2: 173 ff.; Young, *Drama*, 1: 121–22.

34. This distinction between latent and manifest functions is current in sociology, especially since R. K. Merton's *Social Theory and Social Structure*; see 2nd ed. (Glencoe, Ill., 1957), 60 ff. Conceptually, it follows Freud, without at the same time adopting his metapsychological model. What is interesting is the fact that certain systems respond not only to official but also to unconscious needs and can be fully understood only on the basis of this ambivalence. Luhmann has explained in systems-theory terms the advantage of an analysis of latent functions over the latent causes: "The point of uncovering of such latent functions is to redefine experienced problems in such a way as to make them relatable to the inside/outside difference of social systems" (*Soziologische Aufklärung*, 41, 71). On the retention of the Latin formulas in the play, see the analyses in Thoran, "*Studien,*"chap. B II, especially 135 ff.

35. See above, Chapter 2, part IV.

36. Evidence in Lubac, *Corpus mysticum*, 74.

37. H. Moser, "Gedanken zur heutigen Volkskunde," *Bayerisches Jahrbuch für Volkskunde* (Munich, 1954), 208–34, especially 229.

38. This notion is central in Blumenberg, "Wirklichkeitsbegriff," 23, 34, 49–50.

39. Petit de Julleville, *Mystères*, 2: 144.

40. Young, *Drama*, 2: 524–25.

41. Gehlen, "Über die Verstehbarkeit der Magie," *Merkur* 4 (1950): 409–20, 417.

42. On these categories, see Gehlen, *Urmensch*, 78 ff. ("Stabilisierte Span-

nung") and 14 ff. ("Transzendenzen"). "Transzendenz im Diesseits" is for Gehlen a form of behavior freed from need, which does not "consume" things or living beings in their "existence value," so to speak, but rather confers "self value" on them. This "self value" is brought to ritual representation: "This achievement is already moral, in so far as one compulsively relates something to one's own affects and needs (including fear), yet nonetheless acknowledges it in its independent existence. (. . .) The inhibition, bracketing, reservation, or virtualizing of needs and affects that are related to an objective existent, or putting them under certain conditions, is in the same act a verdict on their peculiar being, and a decision to deal with them on the basis of the latter." In contrast, "transcendence in the beyond" presupposes the one, invisible God, the "absolute cultural threshold" of monotheism. The latter "transfers the ultimate evidence of religion from the support of the external world into the inner, the soul"; thus it is characterized by a "tendency to minimize ritual" and representative behavior in general (57).

43. On the anthropological foundation of representative behaviors, see Gehlen, *Urmensch*, 145–56.

44. Hess, *Romanische geistliche Schauspiel*, 156.

CHAPTER 3

1. Young, *Drama*, 1: 402 ff., 405 ff.

2. Stumpfl, *Kultspiele der Germanen*, 305 ff.; Hardison, *Christian Rite*, 227; de Boor, *Textgeschichte*, 166 ff. (arrival of the disciples) and 361–62 (purchase of the ointment).

3. For details, see Stumpfl, *Kultspiele der Germanen*, 222–43.

4. Thus Young dates the Ripoll play (*Publications of the Modern Language Association* 24 [1909]: 303 ff.). Cf. Stumpfl, *Kultspiele der Germanen*, 308.

5. De Boor, *Textgeschichte*, 359.

6. Stumpfl, *Kultspiele der Germanen*, 260 ff.

7. Ibid., 294 ff.

8. R. Reitzenstein, *Die nordischen, persischen und christlichen Vorstellungen vom Weltuntergang, Vorträge der Bibliothek Warburg* (Leipzig, 1926), 157.

9. Stumpfl, *Kultspiele der Germanen*, 231.

10. Stumpfl's comment is in its very conciseness nevertheless also characteristic of his thinking concerning the Germanic substratum: "The connection between the *Tollite portas* and the descent into Hell scene does not seem to be original" but rather the result of the amalgamation of—once again merely postulated—an "independent play of non-ecclesiastical provenance" (*Kultspiele der Germanen*, 341). Thus the tradition of the Gospel of Nicodemus is completely neglected in favor of a pagan-ritualistic credulity regarding demons and thus neglected in favor of the decisive factor, namely the reactualization of the sub-

stratum within a "Christian" ritual play. On this reactualization, see also below, Chapter 6, part 2.

11. Bausinger, *Formen*, 225 ff.

12. Ibid., 235–36.

13. See especially the characterizations in Erlau, verses 443 ff., and *Wiener Osterspiel*, ed. E. Hartl, in *Das Drama des Mittelalters: Osterspiele* (Leipzig, 1937; reprint, Darmstadt, 1964), verses 722 ff., 742 ff.; hereafter cited as Vienna.

14. Young, *Drama*, 1: 395.

15. Ibid., 1: 409.

16. Ibid., 1: 421 ff.

17. See de Boor, *Textgeschichte*, 254, where only the influence of the Latin Easter play is taken into account.

18. *Sterzinger Osterspiel*, ed. A. Pichler, in *Über das Drama des Mittelalters in Tirol* (Innsbruck, 1850), 152 ff., hereafter cited as Sterzing; Wackernell, 233; *Egerer Fronleichnamspiel*, ed. G. Milchsack (Tübingen, 1881), following verse 7978, hereafter cited as Eger.

19. Young, *Drama*, 1: 398 ff. The complaint *Heu! redemptio Israhel/Ut quid mortem sustinuit* goes back, as de Boor shows, to a three-stanza antiphonal exchange between the Marys on their way to the sepulcher (287).

20. For example, Rhein Easter play, 1145 ff.; Erlau, 1202 ff.; Innsbruck, 1144 ff.).

21. In this regard, Hippolytus also appeals to John 20 but not to the *hortulanus* motif [Hippolytos, *Werke*, ed. G. N. Bonwetsch and H. Achelis, vol. 1 (Leipzig, 1897), 350 ff.]. H. Brinkmann, who refers to this passage, did not check it himself and thus makes the erroneous assumption that the garden motif is a product of the exegesis of the Song of Songs (1959, 268; while Bonwetsch's 1902 edition, which Brinkmann cites but which I have been unable to consult, is not identical with the one I have used, the text should be the same).

22. See W. Stammler, "Der allegorische Garten," in *Hart, warr nich möd, Festschrift für Chr. Boeck*, ed. G. Hoffmann and G. Jürgensen (Hamburg, 1960), 260–69. Even when, and this is rare, the friend's herb garden (Song of Songs 5) is itself interpreted allegorically, it appears as a figure of the heavenly kingdom. Thus in an Old German sermon from the thirteenth century, Mary is compared with the throne that "the true Solomon, our Lord Jesus Christ, put in his wonderfully fragrant herb garden in the eternal kingdom" (Schonbach, *Altdeutsche Predigten* 1: 73, quoted in Stammler, 263). It seems to me clear that this "herb garden" is a quotation from the Song of Songs, though Stammler does not really mention it. This interpretation confirms that the garden always appears in the framework of the love relationship between Christ and Mary, Mother of God.

23. Against Brinkmann's view, which derives the gardener scene from the

Song of Songs alone (1959, 268). The verse cited from the Benediktbeueren Easter play, *Veniat dilectus meus in hortum suum*, thus does not lead to the Easter play *hortulanus*. This verse is not, as Brinkmann assumes, put into the mouth of Mary Magdalene, but rather quite obviously into that of the *Mater Domini*. Mary Magdalen is not even present (see Young, *Drama*, 1: 465).

24. The *hortulanus* greets Mary Magdalene with the words used by Rubin in the Erlau Easter play:

"Meus calvo fier,"
sprach ein ochs zu einem stir.
got gruß euch, ir frauen al vir! (779–81)

"Meus calvo fier,"
Said an ox to a bull.
God's greetings to you, women!

The *hortulanus* in another fragment of the Sterzing Easter play published only "tentatively" by Pichler is even more graphic:

Das ist ein wurzen, die heißt bibergeil,
Ist indert hie ein diernl geil,
Die iren maidtumb hiet verloren
Vor dreien oder vier jaren
Die sol nach der wurzen fragen
Und sol sie in der finster ausgraben,
So wird sie ein maid als ir mutter was,
Da sie des zwelften kinds genas.
Noch hab ich ein wurzen, die heißt nachschaden,
Wolt indert ein maid gemeite brüstel haben,
Die sol machen daraus ein salben
Und damit smiern allenthalben,
So werden sie glatt als ein affen ars
Und hert als ein kraglats glas. (pp. 42–43)

That is an herb, it's called castor,
If there is anywhere here a randy girl,
Who has lost her maidenhead,
Three or four years ago,
Let her ask about these herbs
And dig them up in the dark
And she will be as virgin as her mother was,
Before she had her twelve children.

I have another herb called nightshade,
If any girl wants to have a stout breastplate,
She should make an ointment from it
And smear it all over,
She'll become as smooth as a monkey's ass,
And as hard as [ein kraglats] glass.

25. This passage is cited in W. Ganzenmüller, *Das Naturgefühl im Mittelalter* (Leipzig and Berlin, 1914), 26. Similar examples (though not related to John 20:15) of setting spring and Resurrection in parallel are also found on 44 (Fortunatus), 85 (Sedulius Scotus), 127 (Ekkehard), and 168 (Abelard).

26. H. von Campenhausen, *Lateinische Kirchenväter* (Stuttgart, 1960), 82.

27. A. Bourgain, *La Chaire française au 12ᵉ siècle* (Paris, 1879), 380–81. The homily is not to be found in the critical edition of Anselm's *Opera omnia*, ed. Fr. S. Schmitt (1938–61; reprint, Stuttgart, 1968).

28. Cf. Bede: *hortulanus ille in ejus corde tanquam in horto suo granum sinapis seminabat* (*PL* 92, 919 D).

29. Cf. Blumenberg's assignment of metamorphosis to the "satisfied visibility" of myth ("Wirklichkeitsbegriff," 38–39) and also his comment picking up on Jacob Burckhardt: "Metamorphosis as a category thus is already inherent in the genesis of myth itself, as anthropomorphosis: the gods lose their terrifying quality, because they change their shapes. In this way they ultimately become, for the most part, poetic. Burckhardt introduced his statements about the Greek gods with a passage 'On Metamorphoses'; he did not reflect on the reason why this principle of the stories about the gods 'strikes' us in this way: everything subsequent can be explained by the striving not to be understood as metamorphosis or not to allow such things into the world" (33).

30. H. Lausberg, *Handwörterbuch der literarischen Rhetorik* (Munich, 1960), 586. After Blumenberg's comments cited in the preceding note, there is no need to emphasize that the information gap in this case is still not an aesthetic category but rather constitutes thematically the threshold between "terror" and "play."

31. Ganzenmüller, *Naturgefühl*, 44.

32. The Rhein Easter play has the *hortulanus* metamorphosis but does not present it naturalistically-graphically any more than it does the ointment purchase (following 1108).

33. *Ludus Coventriae (Hegge Plays)*, ed. K. S. Black (London, 1922), hereafter cited as Hegge; *Digby Plays*, ed. F. J. Furnivall (London, 1896), hereafter cited as Digby; *Chester Plays I*, ed. H. Deimling (London, 1892), hereafter cited as Chester; *Chester Plays II*, ed. Matthews (London, 1916), hereafter cited as Chester; *York Plays*, ed. L. T. Smith (Oxford, 1885), hereafter cited as York; *Towneley*

Plays, ed. G. England and A. W. Pollard (London, 1897), hereafter cited as Towneley.

34. For example, A. Greban, *Mystère de la Passion*, ed. O. Jodogne (Brussels, 1965), following 29348; hereafter cited as Greban.

35. *Aucto de la Resurrección de Nuestro Señor*, in *Collección de autos, farsas y coloquios del siglo XVI*, ed. L. Rouanet, 4 vols. (Barcelona, 1901), 4: 66–104. See the analysis of this scene from the other points of view in Hess, *Romanische geistliche Schauspiel*, 124 ff., which brought the play to my attention.

36. Quoted in Harrison, *Themis*, 343–44.

37. Frye, *Anatomy*, 189–90.

38. See Hardison, *Christian Rite*, 229–30.

39. Young, *Drama*, 1: 311, 324, 388, 400.

40. The disciples' race also begins with an explicit wager in the Eger Corpus Christi play (1817).

41. Stumpfl, *Kultspiele der Germanen*, 319 ff.

42. Ibid., 218, 322.

43. Ibid., 320.

44. Ibid., 327.

45. Young, *Drama*, 1: 331, 363.

46. Stumpfl, *Kultspiele der Germanen*, 330.

47. On this motif, see Bächtold Stäubli, *Handwörterbuch des deutschen Aberglaubens*, 5: 976–85. In folklore the liver is a highly invested organ (as the embodiment of the life force, as the site of love, of sensuality, of fertility, as magically warding off harm, etc.).

CHAPTER 4

1. I base myself here on G. Müller's description of Aristophanic comedy: "The unleashed animality is paradoxically the true humanity, whose triumph comedy seeks to abet. Reduced to his most natural drives man becomes reasonable in a fantastic manner, and does what reason had long bid him to do" ("Das Hässliche in Poesie und Poetik der Griechen," in *Die nicht mehr schönen Künste—Grenzphänomene des Ästhetischen*, ed. H. R. Jauß (Munich, 1968), 15.

2. The chief representative of this shallow interpretation of comedy, which Stumpfl opposed, is E. Krüger, "Die komischen Szenen in den deutschen geistlichen Spielen des Mittelalters" (Diss., Hamburg, 1931). On the ridiculous and hence harmless Devil, see again Hess, *Romanische geistliche Schauspiel*, 169 ff. and Kolve, *Play*, 140.

3. Jünger, *Über das Komische*, 15 ff.

4. This statement is particularly true of Hess's interpretation (see my review in *Archiv für das Studium der Neueren Sprachen und Literaturen* 205 [1968]: 245–48).

5. E. R. Curtius, *European Literature and the Latin Middle Ages*, trans. Willard R. Trask (1953; reprint, New York, 1963), 420 ff., "The Church and Laughter." The following medieval examples are borrowed from this work.

6. So Hess, *Romanische geistliche Schauspiel*, 180.

7. *Evangelia Apocrypha*, ed. Tischendorf, chap. 4, 20, 394 ff.

8. A welcome confirmation of this interpretive approach, which is directed against the widespread didactic interpretation, is provided in a little-noticed article by Jean Frappier: "The facts are not easy to interpret, but I believe we will not go far wrong in seeing in them the mark of a liberation, or at least of something resembling an unavowed desire to escape from the fear of the Devil. The weapon employed against the Devil's terrorism was the comic, for this is after all the main point—the Middle Ages created a laughable Devil" ("Châtiments infernaux et peur du diable d'après quelques textes du 13ᵉ et du 14ᵉ siècle," in *Cahiers de l'association internationale des études françaises* [July 1953]: 92).

9. See Bakhtin, *Literatur*, esp. 24 ff.

10. Discussion of Wolfgang Kayser, *Das Groteske*, in *Göttinger Gelehrte Anzeigen* 212 (1958): 99.

11. Bakhtin, *Literatur*, 26.

12. Ibid., 53.

13. Ibid., 28.

14. Ibid., 34.

15. Stumpfl, *Kultspiele der Germanen*, 31.

16. H. Fluck, "Der *risus paschalis*, Ein Beitrag zur religiösen Volkskunde," *Archiv für Religionswissenschaft* 31 (1934): 188–212.

17. Quoted by Fluck, ibid., 196.

18. Stumpfl, *Kultspiele der Germanen*, 156.

19. Ritter, "Über das Lachen," 70.

20. Ibid., 64.

21. Ibid., 74.

22. Here I would like to thank Hans Blumenberg for his very welcome support for this interpretation in a letter to me: "But the attempt to see the attribute of ridiculousness as an instrument of de-demonization within this dualism I consider very decidedly modernist. The history of the interpretation of ancient comedy already offers sufficient warnings in this regard. In the dualistic sense, ridiculousness is a quality of a counter-world, not an index of its weakness. Ridiculousness kills, but whoever manages to survive proves himself to be invulnerable."

23. Freud, *Jokes*, 137, 101. On the comparison of Ritter and Freud, see Preisendanz's essay in Fuhrmann, *Terror und Spiel*, 631.

24. Freud, *Jokes*, 119.

25. Ibid., 201.

26. Ibid., 136–37.

27. Bausinger, *Formen*, 227.

28. Ibid., 229.

29. Ritter, "Über das Lachen," 79.

30. G. Cohen, "La scène des pèlerins d'Emmaus," in *Mélanges de philologie romane et d'histoire littéraire offerts à M. Maurice Wilmotte* (Paris, 1910), 2: 105–29.

31. Ritter, "Über das Lachen," 75–76.

32. The more recent interpretation of the Shrovetide play as "primarily a literary-theatrical phenomenon" (Catholy, *Fastnachtspiel*, 13) is helped along by the attempt to defend the value of this genre against the one-sidedness of a folkloric perspective and to requisition it for literary study. In the process, however, folklore studies are to a large extent equated with the Vienna School and with Stumpfl in particular. Recent folklore studies have for their part already drawn corresponding conclusions, in that they no longer speak of ritualistic but rather of plays rooted in custom and thus seek to do justice to the specific entertainment function of the Shrovetide play (Bausinger, *Formen*, 234 ff.). The concept of a traditional play is rather broadly conceived as the "intersection of religious and worldly elements" (ibid., 230), but so long as it is opposed to the "autarkic theater," it seems to me that the decisive moment in the Shrovetide play is assured: its ignorance of aesthetic distance and the preliterary character that is documented therein. In response to Catholy's observation that "Shrovetide customs were very seldom represented in Shrovetide plays" (*Fastnachtspiel*, 2) it may be objected that the plays themselves represented a Shrovetide custom: "In reality the function of convivial entertainment also plays an essential role in the folk custom" (Bausinger, *Formen*, 235–36).

33. Bakhtin, *Literatur*, 54.

CHAPTER 5

1. *Mystère d'Adam* (Ordo representacionis Ade), ed. P. Aebischer (Geneva and Paris, 1963); hereafter cited as the Adam play.

2. *PL* 78, 748 CD; see Hardison, *Christian Rite*, 259–60.

3. Apocalypse 12:9 and 20:2; on this topic, see W. Foerster, *ThWNT* 5: 80.

4. Young, *Drama*, 2: 125 ff.

5. Ibid., 2: 364.

6. M. Sepet, *Les prophètes du Christ* (Paris, 1867), 224.

7. Hardison, *Christian Rite*, 257.

8. Young, *Drama*, 2: 156.

9. Ibid., 2: 192–93.

10. See Chapter 11, note 7.

11. Chap. 13 in *Evangelia Apocrypha*, ed. Tischendorf, 368 ff. Cf. *Seinte Resurreccion*, ed. Jenkins et al., cviii–cix.

12. For documentation on this archetypal meaning of the serpent, see J. Fichtner in *ThWNT*, 5: 571 ff.

13. For instance, G. von Rad, *Das erste Buch Mose, Kap. 1–12/9* (Göttingen, 1949), 70.

14. J. Fichtner in *ThWNT*, 5: 574. Fichtner points out (n. 93) that von Rad speaks apropos of the same passage of an "opponent of men" who remains "throughout all of history in an enigmatic incognito that is difficult to define." B. S. Childs's analysis seems to me very balanced; he shows that the Yahwist focuses his interest less on the origin than on the nature of sin but on the other hand makes the demonic character of the serpent discernible in the calculated tension of a "broken myth": "The Yahwist retained the demonic character of the snake arising out of the myth, but affirmed that he was a mere creature under God's power. The tension created in the language of this broken myth reflected, although inadequately, the incomprehensibility of a reality denied existence in the creation, yet which was active and demonic in its effect on the creation" (B. S. Childs, *Myth and Reality in the Old Testament* [London, 1960], 48).

15. According to the editor L. Rouanet, the *Codice de autos viejos*, to which this play belongs, dates from the second half of the sixteenth century (introduction to his *Colleción de autos* [Barcelona and Madrid, 1901], 1: xii–xiii). The play itself is in vol. 2, 133 ff.

16. Typically, the Spanish *auto* does not forgo having the Devil disguised as a serpent at first confront Eve directly. He asks her about the reasons for the divine prohibition and only then leaves the temptation proper to the allegories (ibid., 137 ff.), on which he comments from the point of view of an observer (198), and later rejoins his helpers (225 ff.).

17. See Auerbach's fine interpretation of this passage, *Mimesis*, 145 ff.

18. Blumenberg, *Wirklichkeitsbegriff*, 30.

19. H. Jonas, *Gnosis und spätantiker Geist*, 3rd. ed. (Göttingen, 1964), Pt. 1, 221–22.

20. Frye, *Anatomy*, 156.

21. Chambers, *Medieval Stage*, 2: 71 ff.

CHAPTER 6

1. Petit de Julleville, *Mystères*, 2: 77–78, 66, 81–82.

2. Stumpfl, *Kultspiele der Germanen*, 342.

3. See the rubrics following 112 (*Tunc vadat Figura ad ecclesiam*) and 518 (*Figura regredietur ad ecclesiam*).

4. See the rubrics following 112, 172, and 204, as well as the detailed discussion of this meaning of *platea* in R. Southern, *The Medieval Theater in the Round* (London, 1957), 228 ff. I am indebted for valuable suggestions to the fine chapter, "'Platea' und 'locus': doppelbödige Dramaturgie," in Weimann, *Shakespeare*, 121 ff. Nonetheless, my analyses tend to contradict Weimann's. He examines the play as a reflection of contemporary social conflicts. Although it is in accord with this thesis that the increased relation to reality weakens the mimetic component and strengthens the ritual component (109), this seems to me to ignore the fact that in religious drama the relation to reality is already a part of ritual representation. The peculiar anachronism of religious drama, which we will need to discuss in detail later on, includes the allegedly mimetic *loco*-action as well as the ritual *platea*-occurrence, and it is precisely here that Weimann has to connect his analyses with a preliminary decision that leaves its mark: "Naturally the anachronism of the Mystery play is also and above all due to the visualizing transcendence of the liturgical performance; this continuing anachronism of the originally ritual *presentatio Christi* in the history of drama, especially in Reformation England, is not capable of development (and here will be for once bracketed out entirely)" (132). What "above all" grounds the anachronism is bracketed: we see what burdens "prehistories" have to assume when Shakespeare stands at the end of them. In contrast, in this chapter I purposely begin with the apparently figural character of the *loco*-action, in order to then describe, on the basis of the ritualistic *platea*-occurrence, the ambivalence of this figural understanding.

5. On the image of hell in religious drama in general, see details in Cohen, *Histoire*, 92 ff.

6. See the wide-ranging compilation of evidence in I. Seydel, "Zur Hegung des mittelalterlichen Theaters," *Studium Generale* 5 (1952): 18–27.

7. *Alsfelder Passionsspiel*, ed. R. Froning, in *Das Drama des Mittelalters* (Stuttgart, 1891–92; reprint, Darmstadt, 1964), 107–26; hereafter cited as Alsfeld Passion play.

8. See Cohen, *Histoire*, 88–89 and L. Traube, "Zur Entwicklung der Mysterienbühne," in *Kleine Schriften*, ed. S. Brandt (Munich, 1920), 293–330, esp. 299 ff. On the theater in the round, see Southern's monograph *Medieval Theater*, n. 256. It also seems not to have been unknown on the Continent; in 1534 a Passion play was performed in Poitiers "en un theatre fait en rond" (Petit de Julleville, *Mystères*, 2: 123).

9. H. Bausinger, "Zur Algebra der Kontinuität," in *Kontinuität? Geschichtlichkeit und Dauer als volkskundliches Problem*, ed. H. Bausinger and W. Brückner (Berlin, 1969), 9–30, esp. 27–28.

10. See Chapter 3, note 11.

11. See Cohen, *Histoire*, 95.

12. For an extensive catalog of names and bibliographical references, see A. Nicoll, *Masks, Mimes, and Miracles* (1933; reprint, New York, 1963), 188.

13. According to F. Ohly, "Synagoge und Ecclesia, Typologisches in mittelalterlicher Dichtung," *Miscellanea mediaevalia* 4 (Berlin, 1966), 350–69, esp. 368.

14. Auerbach, *Mimesis*, 152.

15. Ibid., 155.

16. Auerbach, "Figura," 36–37.

17. Ibid., 43.

18. *Künzelsauer Fronleichnamspiel*, ed. P. K. Liebenow (Berlin, 1969), following 276.

19. *Wiener Passionsspiel*, ed. R. Froning, in *Das Drama des Mittelalters: Osterspiele* (Leipzig, 1937; reprint, Darmstadt, 1964), 80 ff.; hereafter cited as Vienna Passion play.

20. For example, in a homily of Gregory the Great's on Matthew 4:1–11, according to which the apple signifies *gula, eritis sicut dii* signifies *vana gloria*, and *scientes bonum et malum* signifies *die avaritia sublimitatis. PL* 76, 1136 A; see Duriez, *Théologie*, 78 ff.

21. R. Bultmann (*Geschichte*, 273) sees the question of the temptation story as being what a miracle for Jesus and his flock the one thing in question is: "Jesus is distinguished from a magician and Christian miracle from magic. For magic serves men's needs; Jesus and his flock serve God." Bultmann does not discuss the (magic) number three in this context. It also remains unclear whether in rabbinical debates, to which Bultmann traces the dialogue between Jesus and the Devil, the number three more commonly appears (272). The general affinity between rabbinical style and folktale-like artistic means and motifs, to which Bultmann refers elsewhere (47–48), may also at least be cited in this connection.

22. Ebel, Introduction, 26.

23. In opposition to G. R. Owst, who has most decidedly maintained the sermon's constitutive significance for religious drama in *Literature and the Pulpit in Medieval England*, 2nd ed. (Oxford, 1961), 478 ff.

CHAPTER 7

1. J. Daniélou, *Sacramentum futuri* (Paris, 1950), 22.

2. Justinian, *Dialogues* 50, 45, cited in ibid., 32.

3. Ibid., 32 ff.

4. Blumenberg, *Wirklichkeitsbegriff*, 43.

5. These images are very usefully collected in B. Funcke, *Grundlagen und Voraussetzungen der Satisfaktionstheorie des Hl. Anselmus von Canterbury* (Münster, 1903), 16 ff. Gregory the Great speaks directly of a "pious deception": *Nunquam enim convenientius vincitur, quam quum ejus versutia pia fraude superatur* (*PL* 79, 316; Funcke, *Grundlagen*, 22).

6. *Anselm von Canterbury, Cur Deus Homo* (Warum Gott Mensch Geworden), ed. and trans. F. S. Schmitt O.S.B. (Darmstadt, 1956), 1:4; hereafter cited in text.

7. Harnack, *Dogmengeschichte*, 3: 388 ff., esp. 401 ff. ("Beurtheilung der Anselmschen Lehre").

8. Mention solely of the Passion and the cross, 805 ff. and 835 ff.; reference to the descent into hell, 333–34, 590, 761–62, 875–76, 925 ff.

9. This assumption has been questioned by U. Ebel, who tries to "demonstrate an inner necessity in the sequence of scenes and a possibly more comprehensive original unity" in all four parts, whereby she would interpret, in the sense of a "figural world theater" (Introduction, 30), the procession of the prophets as a typological reply to the fall, and the Last Judgment as a similar reply to the fratricide (22). The main evidence offered is the pseudo-Augustinian *Sermo contra Judaeos*, to which the procession of the prophets goes back, and in whose last part the Sibyl recites the acrostic verses about the fifteen signs of the Last Judgment. Ebel thereby draws on a suggestion Sepet had already made in 1878 but which no one, perhaps for good reason, had pursued further. The thematic correspondence between *Sermo* and play may well explain a secondary annexation of the *Quinze signes* to the procession of the prophets, but it cannot, for lack of work-immanent criteria, be also considered as a primary, original continuation. The figural relationship constructed by Ebel does not become thematic: in no passage of the *Quinze signes* is any direct connection with Cain made. If, following Ebel, we take the *coveitié* (965) as a reference to the fratricide (28), then this apparently poorly constructed relationship has to account for the fact that the serpent, who had been condemned in the first part, is shortly before expressly acknowledged to have loyally carried out his duty (957 ff.). Here we encounter an obvious inconsistency that is not overcome through the secondary addition, and in fact the source can be precisely identified: the whole beginning of the fourth part (945–80) is taken almost verbatim from an Old French Passion epic, the so-called *Passion des jongleurs* (see H. Theben, ed., "Die altfranzösiche Achtsilbner-redaktion der 'Passion'" [Diss., Greifswald, 1909], 1–40; see also Frank, *Medieval French Drama*, 125, n. 1). In addition, the *signes de grant confusion* Adam complains about (543) clearly refer in context to the immediate consequences of the fall (thistles, toil, death) and cannot be interpreted as an announcement of the *Quinze signes* (Ebel, Introduction, 27–28)—not to mention that such an announcement in the sense of a figural reply-schema such as Ebel postulates would belong not in the first part but in the second, in connection with the fratricide.

10. Printed in A. Jubinal, ed., *Mystères inédits du 15ᵉ siècle* (Paris, 1837), 2: 312–79 (for the guard scene, see 325). There is thus no reason to consider the first part an interpolation, as does Petit de Julleville (*Mystères*, 2: 393).

11. *Ad inferos dicitur descendisse quia Passionis illius efficaciam justi senserunt antiqui* (*PL* 178, 626, quoted in Monnier, *Descente*, 165).

12. Ibid., 167, 177.

13. The following is based on M. Werner, *Die Entstehung des christlichen Dogmas* (Berlin, 1941), 238 ff.

14. Ibid., 257–58.

15. Kroll, *Gott und Hölle*, 4.

16. See Schmidt, *Darstellung*, 5 ff.

17. D. M. Inguanez, ed., "Un dramma della passione del secolo XII," *Mescellanea Cassinese* 18 (1939): 25–42.

18. Young, *Drama*, 1: 514 ff. and 518 ff.

19. On unverified statements concerning Italian performances of Passion plays in the thirteenth century, see Young, *Drama*, 1: 697–98. For the thirteenth century we can also add the common pattern Frank postulates for the *Passion du Palatinus* and the *Passion d'Autun*, both from the early fourteenth century (Frank, *Medieval French Drama*, 126).

20. H. Craig, "The Origin of the Passion Play: Matters of Theory as Well as of Fact," *University of Missouri Studies* 21 (1946): 88. Cf. also Craig's *English Religious Drama*, 42 ff.

21. See Young, *Drama*, 1: 516, n. 12, and (on the Easter play) 432 ff.

22. Craig, *Drama*, 46; Young, *Drama*, 1: 537.

23. Craig, *Drama*, 42.

24. Ibid., 44 ff.

CHAPTER 8

1. *Passion du Palatinus*, ed. G. Frank (Paris, 1922); hereafter cited as Palatine Passion play.

2. On the history of this legend in the French Passion play tradition, see E. Lommatzsch, "Die Legende von der Schmiedin der Kreuzesnägel Christi," in *Kleinere Schriften zur romanischen Philologie* (Berlin, 1954), 82 ff. Pickering (*Literature*, 285 ff.) suggests a genetic connection between this episode and the typological relation of the Crucifixion to David's harp (Psalm 56) and Job's harp (Job 30:31): Christ's body is strung upon the cross the way the strings are strung on a harp, and in this interpretation the nails become tuning pegs and thus must be blunt.

3. The *Passion provençale* (Didot) also seems to point to an independent entry of the Passion play and a secondary annexation of an Easter play. In this case the Passion concludes with the ascension of Jesus, who takes the soul of the good thief along with him (ed. W. P. Shepard [Paris, 1928], 1625 ff.). Only then does the Easter play begin with a tomb guard scene and a descent into hell. Since

in the Ascension scene there is already reference to the patriarchs liberated from hell (rubric following 1620), the second *descensus* can only be regarded as an inconsistency resulting from the secondary annexation (on sources, see J. G. Wright, "A Study of the Themes of the Resurrection in the Medieval French Drama" [Diss., Bryn Mawr, 1935], 97 ff.). A more elegant solution of this point is represented by the Passion from Arras, where a substitute for this second *descensus* is created: Jesus liberates the incarcerated Joseph of Arimathea and leads him to the empty sepulcher (following 21660).

4. *Passion des jongleurs*, in Theben, ed., "Die altfranzösiche Achtsilbner-redaktion"; see above, Chapter 7, note 9.

5. This statement is generally true of the French plays. Exceptions are the so-called Zion fragment ("Fragment d'un ancien mystère," ed. J. Bédier, *Romania*, 24: 86–94), the *Passion d'Autun* (ed. Frank [Paris, 1934]), and the Passion in the St. Genevieve manuscript (in Jubinal, ed., *Mystères*; see above, Chapter 7, note 10). In these plays, it is the resurrected Christ who invades hell.

6. On the significance of this allegory for the emergence and structural change of medieval allegorical poetry, see Jauß, *Grundriß*, 158–59.

7. Rivière, *Le dogme*, 309–49; in particular, 310 ff. and 348.

8. See H. Ott, "Anselms Versöhnungslehre," *Theologische Zeitschrift* 13 (1957): 187 ff.

9. Harnack, *Lehrbuch*, 408–9.

10. Highly informative in this regard is a series of hardly noticed German Trials in Paradise (Zuckmantel Passion play, the Vordernberg and Salzburg Paradise plays) collected by Duriez, *Théologie*, 195 ff. In these scenes, immediately after the fall Lucifer himself appears before God with the claim that now man must be damned for all eternity. The actual trial begins right afterward with Justice's explicit recognition that what the Devil has said is true. Here there may already be a retroactive influence of the so-called trials of the Devil that were so widespread and so popular in the late Middle Ages, of which the allegory of the four daughters of God also made use, and in a way that confirms the systematic identity of the Devil and Justice that we propose here. In these trials, which are performed after the descent into hell, an emissary from hell appears before God's throne in order to demand the restitution of what has been illegally stolen. In Jacob of Maerlant's *Merlijn*, an elaborated Dutch version of the French prototype, the devil Masceron is so effectively fended off by Mary, who is acting on behalf of mankind, that he decides put his case in the hands of advocates, namely Justice and Truth, whereupon Mary has Compassion and Peace argue for her. *Justitia* thus no longer appears here as an attribute of God but rather as the Devil's lawyer (on the texts cited, see the otherwise modest study by H. Traver, "The Four Daughters of God" [Diss., Bryn Mawr, 1967], 50 ff.).

11. E. Mercadé/Arras, *Mystère de la Passion*, ed. J. M. Richard (Arras, 1891); hereafter cited as Arras Passion play.

12. Roy, "Mystère," 229–30. On the history of this motif, see E. Fascher, *Das Weib des Pilatus* (Halle and Salle, 1951).

13. On the particular sources (*Transitus Mariae, Historia scholastica*, Vincent of Beauvais, Ludolf of Saxony, et al.) see Duriez, *Théologie*, 98, and Roy, "Mystère," 232.

14. See above, n. 10.

15. I base myself here on R. Herzog's analysis of the introduction to Clement of Alexandria, *Protreptikos* ("Metapher, Exegese, Mythos") in Fuhrmann, *Terror und Spiel*, 157–85, esp. 169–70.

16. See H. Jonas, *Gnosis und spätantiker Geist*, 3rd ed. (Göttingen, 1964), chapter 3, part 2, and 275, 324.

17. On these two key passages in Paul, see J. Taubes, "Die Rechtferigung des Hässlichen in urchristlicher Tradition," in *Die nicht mehr schönen Künste—Grenzphänomene des Ästhetischen*, ed. H. R. Jauß (Munich, 1968), 169–85. Taubes interprets 1 Corinthians 1:20 ff. as "absolutely first-rate evidence of the beginning accommodation of Christian valuation of the Greek world" (177). In the present context we need not decide what role was played in this "accommodation" by the "mythical productivity" of Christianity itself, which W. Pannenberg ("Späthorizonte des Mythos," 518) brought to bear against religious historians' construction of a fully developed gnostic redeemer-myth, to which early Christianity had only to resort.

18. Clement, *Protreptikos*, paragraph 111, 1 (translation based on that of R. Herzog, in Fuhrmann, *Terror und Spiel*, 170).

19. Frye, *Anatomy*, 185.

CHAPTER 9

1. A. Righter, *Shakespeare and the Idea of the Play*, 2nd ed. (London, 1964), 27. For other similar cases, see W. Müller, *Der schauspielerische Stil im Passionsspiel des Mittelalters* (Leipzig, 1927), 136 ff.

2. See above, Chapter 7, part 1.

3. See Harnack, *Lehrbuch*, 540–41.

4. Kindermann, *Theatergeschichte Europas*, 218 ff.; on Kindermann, see below, Chapter 11.

5. J. Tauler, quoted in Zingel, "Passion Christi," 49. On the metaphor of the mirror in religious drama, see also Hess, *Romanische geistliche Schauspiel*, 19 ff.

6. On this "making *imitatio* central" and the associated "watering-down of mystical *unio* (. . .) into mere conformity with Christ," see Ruh, "Theologie," 29.

7. *PL* 159, 227 A.

8. On German drama, see Zingel, "Passion Christi," 64 (Tauler), 68–69 and 77 (Seuse), and also 118, which summarizes: "the Passion event is neglected. If the mystic provides an image of the *passio domini*, Christ stands alone at the center. There is no mention of the actors; the concern is focused on the sufferer. Only Mary has a place in a mystical representation of the Passion." This overshadowing of the event and action is connected, of course, with the fundamental question regarding the function of the image in the mystical imagining of Christ, and its weight depends in each case upon the way in which this question is resolved. On this fundamental problematics, see Ruh, "Theologie," 27 ff.

9. According to Duriez, *Théologie*, 403; Duriez still offers the richest fund of source material for the German plays; no comparable investigation is available for France and England.

10. The plays are indebted to female mysticism primarily in the presentation of the scenes in which Jesus is scourged (see the parallels collected by Duriez, *Théologie*, 399 ff., particularly from St. Bridget's *Revelationes*). E. Krebs has emphasized that Jesus' scourging assumed especially marked forms in nun's visions (*Die Mystik in Adelhausen, Festgabe für H. Finke* [1904], 41 ff., quoted in Zingel, "Passion Christi," 98).

11. Duriez, *Théologie*, 379 ff.

12. On this catalog, see L. Müller, *Das Rondel in den französischen Mirakelspielen und Mysterien des 15. und 16. Jahrhunderts* (Marburg, 1884), 63 ff.

13. Introduction to J. Michel, *Mystère de la Passion*, ed. O. Jodogne (Gembloux, Belgium, 1959), cii.

14. Hegge, 277 (verse 170); Wakefield, 239 (verse 244); York, 267 (verse 358). See Kolve, *Play*, 185–86.

15. Speirs, *Medieval English Poetry*, 353.

16. Rossiter, *English Drama*, 76.

17. See ibid., 56 ff., where it is first claimed that interpretations like that of A. Nicolls (*British Drama*) lead to the absurdity of a "poetry-producing folk-soul," whereas in reality religious drama is clearly controlled by a "theological logic." Then two pages later the traditional cliches are repeated all the more massively: religious drama is once again described, entirely in Chambers's terms, as a "secularized religious drama," an "artwork of the folk-soul," "full of the elementary passions and instincts of a thinly-disguised folklore." On the "legacy" of the *joculatores* and *jongleurs*, see also 80.

18. Speirs, *Medieval English Poetry*, 311 ff.

19. Frye, *Anatomy*, 147–48; in Murray, the *pathos* phase is described as "a ritual or sacrificial death, in which Adonis or Attis is slain by the tabu animal, the Pharmakos stoned, Osiris, Dionysus, Pentheus, Orpheus, Hippolytus torn to pieces" (quoted in Harrison, *Themis*, 343).

20. Frazer, *Scapegoat*, 412 ff.

21. Ibid., 392 ff.

22. See Trachtenberg, *The Devil and the Jews* (New Haven, 1944), and Peuckert, *Die große Wende*, 134 ff., as well as Peuckert in Bächtold Stäubli, ed., *Handwörterbuch des deutschen Aberglaubens*, 7: 727 ff.

23. On the distinction between manifest and latent functions, see above, Chapter 2, note 34.

24. Freud, *Totem and Taboo*, 13: 156.

25. Malinowski, *Geschlecht und Verdrängung*, 165.

26. Ibid., 162–63.

27. Lévi-Strauss, *Totémisme*, 100.

28. Malinowski, *Geschlecht und Verdrängung*, 173.

CHAPTER 10

1. Quoted from the Revised Standard Version.

2. Pickering, "Christusbild," 33.

3. Pickering, *Literature*, 281, 257.

4. Pickering, "Christusbild," 33.

5. See above, Chapter 8, note 2.

6. Pickering, "Irrwege," 276–77.

7. See Ruh, "Theologie," 31 ff.

8. Greban's immediate model was a 1383 Passion in the Bonaventure tradition; the relevant passage is found in Roy, "Mystère," 259–60.

9. See above, Chapter 7, part 2.

10. Pickering "Christusbild," 33.

11. Lorenzer, *Sprachzerstörung*, 90.

12. Ibid., 98.

13. Ibid., 98.

14. Ibid., 89.

15. P. Bourdieu, *Zur Soziologie der symbolischen Formen* (Frankfurt, 1970), 25.

16. Gehlen, *Urmensch*, 78–79.

17. P. R. Hofstätter, *Sozialpsychologie* (Berlin, 1967), 26 ff.

18. Ibid., 29–30.

19. Aquinas, *Summa theologica* III, *quaestio* 83; see Harnack, *Lehrbuch*, 581.

20. On miracles of the host and the demand for visibility, see Jungmann, *Missarum Solemnia*, 1: 156 ff., with references to the most important studies; on the "fruits of the Mass," see A. Franz, *Die Messe im deutschen Mittelalter* (Freiburg, 1902; reprint, Darmstadt, 1963), 37 ff.; on the *pericula* of the celebration of the Mass, particularly in the influential fifteenth-century Bernardus de Parentius, see ibid., 474, 506.

21. This fact is noted by Jungmann, *Missarum Solemnia*, 1: 152, 168.

22. On this kind of depreciation in Albertus Magnus, the critic of allegorization, see A. Kolping, "Eucharistia als Bona Gratia," in *Studia Albertina, Festschrift für Bernhard Geyer* (Münster, 1952), 249–78, esp. 253.

23. See J. Betz, "Meßopfertheorien" in *LThK* 7, cols. 350–52.

24. See J. Jeremias in *ThWNT*, 5: 712–13.

25. See R. Molitor, "Passionsspiel and Passionsliturgie," *Benediktinische Monatsschrift* 5 (1923): 105–16, esp. 111: "Through the holy Mass the liturgy connects directly not with the events on Golgotha, but rather with Christ's Last Supper."

26. Sometimes it was the *fractio*, sometimes the *elevatio* before the Pater noster, sometimes the sign of the cross at the end of the *supplices*, or, even more striking, the kneeling of the priest during the *supplices* as a symbol of Jesus' hanging head; see J. Kramp, *Die Opferanschauungen der römischen Meßliturgie, Liturgie- und dogmengeschichtliche Untersuchung*, 2nd ed. (Regensburg, 1924), 56, and Jungmann, *Missarum Solemnia*, 1: 115 ff.

27. *Das Zuckmantler Passionsspiel*, ed. A. Peter (Troppau, 1868), 11.

28. I am not aware of any systematic collection of cases of this kind of borrowing. Our analyses in Part I should have included most of them in the Easter play. For the Corpus Christi play, refer to Stemmler, *Liturgische Feiern*, 238 ("Borrowings from the Liturgy in the Corpus Christi Celebration"). For the Passion play we should mention above all the initial words in the Passion scenes in the narrower sense (where through the retention of the arcane Latin the liturgical character can be made particularly prominent, as for example in Alsfeld following 3087), and also the *improperien* in the Good Friday liturgy.

29. On this doubling of the "memory of sacrifice" and the "commemorative sacrifice," which determines the Eucharist even in its patristic beginnings, see J. Betz, "Meßopfertheorien" in *LThK* 8, esp. col. 346.

30. Here I follow Lévi-Strauss, *La Pensée sauvage*, 295–302; see also H. Hubert and M. Mauss, *Sacrifice: Its Nature and Function* (London, 1964; translation of the *Essai sur la nature et la fonction du sacrifice* that appeared in the *Année sociologique* for 1898), esp. 44.

31. See above, Introduction, note 32.

32. See above, Chapter 2, note 42.

33. Gehlen, *Urmensch*, 19.

34. So far as I can see, R. Froning's judgment is still valid that the ending of the Frankfurt Passion play with the entombment is incomplete, since the conductor's scroll contains the Resurrection and the ascent into heaven (*Das Drama des Mittelalters* [Stuttgart, 1891–92; reprint, Darmstadt 1964], 334). However, the relationship to a Resurrection play is explicitly established only for the performance of 1498 (543). Froning's association of the allegedly incomplete Kremer

copy with this performance, which took place six years later, remains questionable. Instead of starting from the claim "that there was not enough room left for the rest" (334), one can equally well surmise that the performances based on Kremer's copy included no Resurrection. Witnesses of the 1467 and 1492 performances seem to confirm this: they speak of the *tragoedia passionis* or of the *play about our Lord's Passion* (540 or 542). The same may therefore be true of later performances before 1498, for which we have no witnesses but for which Kremer's copy was probably the basis. It was certainly used for at least one performance (334). Our suggestion is significantly supported by the Heidelberg Passion play, which on one hand also goes back to the conductor's scroll or a copy thereof but on the other hand also does not contain the Resurrection (it closes with the imprisonment of Joseph of Arimathea). In this case it is clear that there was "enough space": the copyist provides his play with an explicit "*finis*. In the year fifteen hundred fourteen this book was written by me, Wolffgang Stüeckh, on the Wednesday after visitacionis Marie virginis" (*Heidelberger Passionsspiel*, ed. G. Milchsack [Tübingen, 1880], 294). That there were also performances in Germany of the Passion without Resurrection and independent of the cross festivals must seem in light of all that more than likely, since the extant texts and the performances for which we have witnesses allow only fragmentary reconstructions. Our interpretation of the Crucifixion in relation to a scapegoat ritual is not bound to such a proof, but it is supported by it. For wherever the representation of the Resurrection is omitted, the kerygmatic perspective is decisively abbreviated in favor of the mythical/archetypal perspective.

35. Harnack, *Lehrbuch*, 408.

36. E. Dumoutet, *Désir de voir l'hostie* (Paris, 1926); see also P. Browe, *Die Verehrung der Eucharistie im Mittelalter* (Munich, 1933), esp. 26 ff.

37. Aquinas, *Summa theologica* III, *quaestio* 73, 4.

38. Above, Chapter 1 (Lubac, *Corpus mysticum*, 83, n. 117).

39. See Stemmler's fine analysis of this Last Supper (240–41), especially with regard to the figure of Judas. Whereas according to John 13:12–26 at this same meal Christ, dipping a bit of bread, uses it to brand Judas as a traitor, the Judas in the play is the person who is unfit to receive communion and thereby damned.

40. See again Stemmler, *Liturgische Feiern*, 243 ff., and also, on the "pious images" in general, J. W. Robinson, "The Late Medieval Cult of Jesus and the Mystery Plays," *PMLA* 80 (1965): 508–14.

41. The studies by Rossiter and Speirs discussed earlier (Chapter 9) are, so far as I can see, the only ones that have thus far dealt with the ritual character of these cruel plays. Rossiter sometimes also refers to ambivalent effects (*English Drama*, 75, 78). If his perspective nevertheless does not converge with our own, that is because his talk about the "uncombinable antinomies" and "immiscible

juxtapositions" conceals a Romantic dualism of the sublime and the grotesque that is projected backward, so that the archetypal-ritualistic significance of this "grotesque" does not come into view: "The very values of martyrdom—of *any* suffering as significant—are implicitly denied by thus making a game of it" (70). All the same Rossiter's interpretation operates at a level that his critic Kolve (*Play,* see esp. 134 ff.) never attains. Kolve's thesis, that the "games" played by the tormentors distance or even aestheticize the horror (189, 199), must be regarded as naive because it does not inquire at all into the impulse that lies behind their graphicness—as if the characterization of the tormentors demanded by the "imitation of a total action" could in fact be taken as a justification for their cruel sport. At the end of the analyses of allegedly aestheticized cruelty we nonetheless find something entirely different: "Not all games are for children, and many of those played by the torturers are full of adult cunning and savagery. And actions shaped like a game, played as though they were game, can in fact be serious and real" (204).

42. See the editor's commentary, *Künzelsauer Fronleichnamspiel,* ed. P. K. Liebenow (Berlin, 1969), 276–77. Last Judgment and Crucifixion were also omitted in the enlarged version. Added were only scenes situated on the margins of the Passion (counsel with the Jews, matters relating to Judas): "The basic concern seems to have been not to represent this high point of salvation history."

43. R. Magnus, "Die Christusgestalt im Passionsspiel des deutschen Mittelalters" (Diss., Frankfurt, 1965), 193.

44. Gehlen, *Urmensch,* 247.

CHAPTER 11

1. Jünger, *Über das Komische,* 26.

2. Against Hess, *Romanische geistliche Schauspiel,* 176: "In religious drama the contrasts between good and evil are realized in a comic way. Evil is not really battled, but merely bruised, and therefore it is laughable."

3. Peuckert, *Die große Wende,* 145.

4. See F. W. Wentzlaff-Eggebert, *Deutsche Mystik zwischen Mittelalter und Neuzeit* (Berlin, 1944), 71 ff., as well as A. Hübner, *Die Deutschen Geißlerlieder* (Berlin, 1931), 6 ff. So far as I can see, the connection with the Passion play has never been noted.

5. H. R. Trevor-Roper, *The European Witch-Craze of the Sixteenth and Seventeenth Centuries and Other Essays* (New York, 1969), 90–192. This study is an extremely informative examination and critical summary of the almost overwhelming literature on this question, which is also distinguished especially by its inclusion of the socioeconomic background of late medieval neuroticization. On the scapegoat see esp. 110–11, 114, 166, 186.

6. Peuckert, *Die große Wende*, 103 ff.

7. Here we must not allow ourselves to be misled by the stereotypes of the *Disputatio Ecclesiae et Synagogae* that are found particularly in the German Passion plays. It is clear that what the plays "show" is the obstinacy of the Jews and the call for their return (especially Longinus). But often this pious intention was only an excuse for hateful accusations. In the Donaueschingen Passion play, for instance, the Jews' "guilt" is transferred entirely from the denial of the confession to the killing of the Christian God:

> nu schwigen still, ir lieben kind, so werdent ir sechen in kurtzer frist, wie
> got von den Juden gemartert ist (1736–38)

> *now be still, you dear child, and in a short time you'll see how God was mar-*
> *tyred by the Jews.*

With these words the *proclamator* opens the second day, which is devoted to the Passion. And it is in just this perspective that Christiana remains after Mary's lament; in contrast to the Ecclesia of other plays, she no longer pursues a longer appeal to her opponent Judea but rather, instead of demanding her return, calls for vengeance:

> O ir fromen christen all,
> die verlorn waren durch Adams val
> nemend mit mir hie ze hertzen
> disen bittern tod und schmerzen,
> den hüt hat gelitten Ihesus Christ,
> der himels und erd ein schöpfer ist:
> die Juden hand im genomen sin leben,
> vmb drissig pfening ward er geben
> von eim, der was der junger sin!
> o ir schwester und brüder min,
> helffent mir rechen diese tat
> and dem falschen judischen rat,
> die in so schantlich getötet hand!
> pfüch, ir Juden, der grossen schand,
> das ir vff erd ie wurdent geborn:
> des müssent ir ewenclich sin verlorn! (3616–31)

> *O pious Christians all,*
> *who were lost through Adam's fall,*
> *take to heart with me here*
> *this bitter death and pain*

that Jesus Christ today has suffered
he who created heaven and earth:
the Jews have taken his life away,
for thirty pieces of silver he was betrayed
by him who was his disciple!
Oh, sisters and brothers of mine,
help me avenge this deed,
on the false Jewish council,
who put him so shamefully to death!
Fie, you Jews, what a scandal,
that you were ever born on earth:
for this you must be lost forever!

It is very typical that here two phases of theological unreflectedness come together: first intertrinitarian differentiation—that is, the key to the Christian concept of redemption—is ignored, and secondly, in a similar way the central paradox of this conception, namely that Jesus was indeed killed, but he had to die, is one-sidedly resolved. There remains the appeal for revenge on those who killed the Christian God. This polarization had already begun in the liturgical celebrations that brought in the Easter sequence *Victimae paschali: Credendum est magis soli Mariae veraci quam Judaeorum turbae fallaci* (see Young, *Drama*, 1: 273). Christian truth vs. Jewish betrayal—that is the opposition that runs through the whole of religious drama and with the Passion play ends up in an explicit demonization. The play's demonization of the Jews is the mythical-archetypal counterpoint to Anselm of Canterbury's effort, precisely through disassociating the Devil and the Jews, to strongly emphasize that the latter could be redeemed, whereas the former could not, and to ground their indispensability kerygmatically in the plan of salvation. Whereas Anselm said that the Man-God had caused himself to be killed by his own people, Greban has the mother of God berate this same people as sycophantic traitors:

> Pervers Juifz ou rain de mort repose / traistres chiens, contre vous je m'oppose, / vallez vous huy d'abandenner tel chose? (15345–47)
>
> *Perverse Jews where the reign of death reposes / treacherous dogs, I oppose myself to you, / are you worthy to abandon such a thing today?*

Even for these Jewish "dogs," Psalms 22:17 and 21 offers a typological "justification." Concerning this, Pickering ("Christusbild," 21) writes: "That is what is primary from the point of view of textual history; anti-Semitism is secondary—without, however, repressing the old characterizations and epithets."

Why should it, since it found such epithets very welcome? Here we see once again the problematic nature of the thesis "that 'religious feeling' (. . .) for its part was largely evoked through a verbal tradition that was ultimately based on biblical and ecclesiastical authority" (ibid., 17).

8. That Peuckert does not consider these Passions is typical of the exclusiveness of his perspective. Were the "apocalyptic century" in fact so uniformly apocalyptic in the narrower sense (that is, referring to the end of time) as *Die Große Wende* [*The Great Turning-Point*] makes it seem, then there would be no mythical return to the origin, there would be no ritualistic plays. Pronounced expectations regarding the end of time therefore remain bound up with sectarian movements and can only occasionally gain an influence over larger groups that nonetheless just as quickly ebbed. Here Peuckert's perspective needs to be complemented by that of intellectual history, for which we have to go back to the still-unsurpassed study by R. Stadelmann, *Vom Geist des ausgehenden Mittelalters* (Halle, 1929). There it is demonstrated that the countless visions, laments, and prophecies of the period do not bear their specific eschatological element within themselves but rather derive it from a metaphysics of history that is indebted to the decade-schema of the *triplex discessio*: "Just as the Empire had seen its glittering epoch under Octavian, so must the Church regard the contemporary moment of the birth of Christ as its apex. The further development of both realms is a debasement (not continuous but rather gradual), the breaking-away of individual cities from the Empire paralleling the breaking away of churches from the apostolic see, and as a consequence of their apostasies, shortly before or contemporaneously with the arrival of the Antichrist the faithful will also fall away from the true belief" (229). Stadelmann goes so far as to suggest that the specific eschatologically marked pessimistic observations on the century should be associated with a "dogmatic history of pessimism" rather than with a "history of the belief in pessimism." Thus the ineluctable accordance with the law is indeed recognized in principle, but it is "nonetheless played with and broken apart by activist attempts to ward off disaster, in the course of which ills that can be remedied are pointed out (. . .) The striving to prevent the catastrophe turns eschatology into polemics" (230–31). In the context of our discussion, an especially important observation is "that the figure of the Antichrist rapidly gains greater scope precisely in the late Middle Ages, whereas the idea of the end of the world constantly recedes further" (ibid.). An interpretation of the Antichrist plays, which are commonly too hastily construed as indices of eschatological expectations, should and could start from this observation; for no one who actually believes that the end of time is imminent puts on plays. The question dealt with by the present study has not required an analysis of the Antichrist play. Our thesis is not endangered by them. They celebrate in the ritualistic play the

defeat of the more powerful and thereby produce the same effect of exoneration as does religious drama in the narrower sense. Peuckert's *Die Große Wende* is largely a collection of documents of anxiety. What this collection leaves out, religious drama, shows that the eschatological investment of this anxiety to be partial and secondary. Where ritualistic plays are performed, the world is assumed to be ultimately reliable and ongoing. This is testified to not only by the monumental Passion and Corpus Christi plays but also by the stone monuments of late medieval piety: the major ecclesiastical construction projects that were completed precisely in this "apocalyptic century" (the Sebaldus tower in Nuremberg, 1482; the Frauenkirche in Munich, 1488; the Laurentius portal in Strassburg, 1494; the cathedral choir in Freiburg, 1513).

9. Kindermann, *Theatergeschichte Europas*, 218–20, 284, 220–21. A few further examples of Kindermann's conceptual hypothesis: "nominalistic forms of representation" (273 ff.); "nominalistic marketplace staging" (275, 287, 297); "spiritual nominalism" (287, 293), "nominalistic bourgeois realism" (290); "nominalistic mature development" of the plays (292); "nominalistic simultaneous stages" (304).

10. Ibid., 220.

11. H. Blumenberg, *The Legitimacy of the Modern Age,* Part 2: "Theological Absolutism and Human Self-Affirmation."

12. The crucial documents are collected in Young, *Drama*, 1: 524 ff.; see also 414–15. (*Tretise of miracles pleyinge*, end of the fourteenth century).

13. See W. Pannenberg's review, "Die Christliche Legitimität der Neuzeit," *Radius* (1963): Heft 3, 40–42.

14. That this theology was not available was noted by Jungmann, Missarum Solemnia, 1: 152, 168.

15. Gehlen, *Urmensch*, 136 ff. See A. Jonas, *Die Institutionenlehre Arnold Gehlens* (Tübingen, 1966), 46: "For belief in God he [Gehlen] substitutes a theory of religion that is supposed to make clear what one must believe in. With his category of undetermined obligation and the ritual built on it he goes much deeper than myth, which can only attach itself to this ritual."

16. Gehlen, *Urmensch*, 223.

17. W. Pannenberg, *Was ist der Mensch? Die Anthropologie der Gegenwart im Lichte der Theologie*, 2nd ed. (Göttingen, 1964), 11.

18. Ibid., 22 ff.

19. Gehlen, *Urmensch*, 140.

20. Petit de Julleville, *Mystères*, 2: 57.

21. Ibid., 2: 61.

22. Kindermann, *Theatergeschichte Europas*, 321.

23. Brinkmann, *Studien* 2: 229.

24. Petit de Julleville, *Mystères*, 2: 158.

25. See, for example, Petit de Julleville, *Mystères*, 2: 8 (Bar-sur-Aube), 22 (Beauvais), 125 ff. (Saumur), 165 (Argentan).

26. Quoted by Roy from a translation, "Mystère," 315.

27. Documents in Chambers, *Medieval Stage*, 1: 100 ff., and in Owst, *Literature and the Pulpit in Medieval England*, 2nd ed. (Oxford, 1961), 480 ff.

28. Quoted in Gardiner, *Mysteries' End*, 109–10.

29. Gardiner, 110 ff.

30. Quoted in Hess, *Romanische geistliche Schauspiel*, 159.

31. Freud, *Totem and Taboo*, 13: 140.

32. I do not examine these prohibitions in detail since they have already been exhaustively discussed by Gardiner in *Mysteries' End*.

CONCLUSION

1. See Introduction, note 58.

2. "Was ist das epische Theater?" in Benjamin, *Angelus Novus*, 344–51.

3. Typical of this kind of prehistory is Weimann's work, in which the "gothic naturalism" of the Passion plays is only briefly discussed (136–37).

4. See Benjamin, *Angelus Novus*, 303.

5. Benjamin, "Geschichtsphilosophische Thesen" in *Illuminationen* (Frankfurt, 1961), 276.

6. Jürgen Habermas, "Bewußtmachende oder rettende Kritik," in *Zur Aktualität Walter Benjamins* (Frankfurt, 1972), 173 ff.

7. Gadamer, *Wahrheit und Methode*, 97 ff.

8. Ibid., 107.

9. Ibid., 121.

10. Ibid., 114.

11. J. Ehrmann, "*Homo Ludens* Revisited," in Ehrmann, ed., *Game, Play, Literature, Yale French Studies* 41 (1968); quoted from the Beacon paperback edition (Boston, 1971), 44.

12. Ibid., 55.

13. See my "Komik und Komödie als Positivierung von Negativität," in H. Weinrich and J. Striedter, eds., *Negation und Negativität, Poetik und Hermeneutik* 6 (Munich, 1974), 341–66.

14. Luhmann, *Soziologische Aufklärung*, 144 ff.

AFTERWORD

1. Joachim Ritter, "Über das Lachen" (1940), in *Subjektivität* (Frankfurt, 1974), 62–69.

2. Stumpfl, *Kultspiele der Germanen*.

3. According to Friedrich Ohly, in *Romanische Forschungen* 91 (1979): 111–41, esp. 139 and 114.

4. Gehlen, *Urmensch*, 97, 57, 246 ff. Gehlen is the most important representative of a theory of institutions that proceeds from the anthropological premise of the human being as an instinct-deprived "creature of deficiency" ("*Mängelwesen*"). This being looks to institutions for support and security, and the primordial institution is ritual, as an elementary form for the exorcising of terror. I have presented the principal categories of Gehlen's theory in more detail in my book.

5. Niklas Luhmann, "Funktionale Methode und Systemtheorie," in Luhmann, *Soziologische Aufklärung*, 47.

6. Luhmann, "Wahrheit und Ideologie. Vorschläge zur Wiederaufnahme der Diskussion" (1962) in *Soziologische Aufklärung*, 56.

7. Cornelius Castoriadis, *The Imaginary Institution of Society*, translated by Kathleen Blamey (Cambridge, Mass., 1998), 343, 296–97.

8. See ibid., 221–72.

9. Ibid., 369.

10. See ibid., 115–31 for a critique of functionalism, and 146–64 on the role of imaginary significations in providing "answers" to questions around which social collectivity constitutes itself.

11. Luhmann, "Soziologische Aufklärung," in *Soziologische Aufklärung*, 69.

12. Michael de Certeau, *La fable mystique* (Paris, 1982), 107 ff.

13. See Jan Dirk Müller, "Mimesis und Ritual. Zum geistlichen Spiel des Mittelalters," in *Mimesis und Simulation*, eds. Andreas Kablitz and Gerhard Neumann (Freiburg, 1974), 541–71. The quotes are taken from the Pseudo-Bonventura's *Meditationes Vitae Christi* or, as the case may be, an anonymous meditational manual. Müller cites them from Fritz Oskar Schuppisser, "Schauen mit den Augen des Herzens. Zur Methodik der spätmittelalterlichen Passionsmeditation, besonders in der Devotio moderna und bei den Augustinern," in *Die Passion Christi in Literatur und Kunst des Spätmittelalters*, ed. Walter Haug and Burghart Wachinger (Tübingen, 1993), 175.

14. Müller, "Mimesis und Ritual," 548–49.

15. Alfred Lorenzer, *Sprachzerstörung und Rekonstruktion*.

16. Müller, "Mimesis und Ritual," 565 n. 64.

17. Lorenzer, *Sprachzerstörung und Rekonstruktion*, 89.

18. See Castoriadis, *Imaginary Institution of Society*, 246–47 on "social phantasma" and 284–88 on formations and scenarios of "phantasy."

19. When I wrote this book, René Girard's work was still not widely known in Europe. That was true for *La violence et le sacré* (Paris, 1972) and even more so

for *Le bouc émissaire* (Paris, 1982). The explicit consideration of Girard's theses that is now possible would greatly enrich my arguments. I am thinking in particular of Girard's treatment of the figure of the murdered god and its mythological transformations. My interpretation of the Passion plays is concerned with a similar trope.

20. Georges Bataille, *L'érotisme* (Paris, 1957), 290.

21. Ibid., 103.

Bibliography

Note: The following bibliography is limited to editions cited in the text with verse or page numbers and in the notes with short titles; all works not listed here appear in the notes with unabridged publication information.

A. TEXTS

I. The French Vernacular Tradition

Greban, A. *Mystère de la Passion.* Ed. O. Jodogne. Brussels, 1965.

Mercadé/Arras, E. *Mystère de la Passion.* Ed. J. M. Richard. Arras, 1891 (*Le Mystère de la Passion,* text of MS. 697 in the Arras library).

Michel, J. *Mystère de la Passion.* Ed. O. Jodogne. Gembloux, Belgium, 1959.

Mystère d'Adam (Ordo representacionis Ade). Ed. P. Aebischer. Geneva and Paris, 1963 (Textes littéraires français, no. 99).

Passion d'Autun. Ed. G. Frank. Paris, 1934 (Société des Anciens Textes Français).

Passion du Palatinus. Ed. G. Frank. Paris, 1922 (Classiques Français du Moyen Age, no. 30).

Seinte Resureccion. Ed. T. A. Jenkins et al. Oxford, 1943 (Anglo-Norman Text Society 4).

II. The German Vernacular Tradition

Alsfelder Passionsspiel. Ed. R. Froning. In *Das Drama des Mittelalters,* 567–859. Stuttgart, 1891–92. Reprint, Darmstadt, 1964.

Augsburger Passionsspiel. Ed. A Hartmann. In *Das Oberammergauer Passionsspiel in seiner ältesten Gestalt,* 3–95. Leipzig, 1880. Reprint, Wiesbaden, 1968.

Donaueschinger Passionsspiel. Ed. E. Hartl. In *Das Drama des Mittelalters: Pas-*

sionsspiele, Part 2. Leipzig, 1942. Reprint, Darmstadt, 1966 (Deutsche Literatur in Entwicklungsreihen, Reihe Drama des Mittelalters, vol. 4).

Egerer Fronleichnamsspiel. Ed. G. Milchsack. Tübingen, 1881 (Bibliothek des Literarischen Vereins in Stuttgart, 156).

Erlauer Osterspiel. Ed. E. Hartl. In *Das Drama des Mittelalters: Osterspiele,* 205–60. Leipzig, 1937. Reprint, Darmstadt, 1964 (Deutsche Literatur in Entwicklungsreihen, Reihe Drama des Mittelalters, vol. 2).

Frankfurter Dirigierrolle. Ed. R. Froning. In *Das Drama des Mittelalters,* 340–73. Stuttgart, 1891–92. Reprint, Darmstadt, 1964.

Frankfurter Passionsspiel. Ed. R. Froning. In *Das Drama des Mittelalters,* 379–532. Stuttgart, 1891–92. Reprint, Darmstadt, 1964.

Innsbrucker Passionsspiel. Ed. E. Hartl. In *Das Drama des Mittelalters: Osterspiele,* 136–89. Leipzig, 1937. Reprint, Darmstadt, 1964 (Deutsche Literatur in Entwicklungsreihen, Reihe Drama des Mittelalters, vol. 2).

Künzelsauer Fronleichnamsspiel. Ed. P. K. Liebenow. Berlin, 1969 (Ausgaben deutscher Literatur des 15. bis 18. Jahrhunderts, Reihe Drama, vol. 2).

Redentiner Osterspiel. Ed. W. Krogmann. 2nd ed. Leipzig, 1964 (Altdeutsche Quellen, vol. 2).

Rheinisches Osterspiel. Ed. H. Rueff. In *Das Rheinische Osterspiel der Berliner Handschrift,* Ms. Germ. Fol. 1219. Berlin, 1925 (Abhandlungen der Gesellschaft der Wissenschaften zu Göttingen, philologisch-historische Klasse, NS 18, 1925–26), 1–224.

Sterzinger Osterspiel. Ed. A. Pichler. In *Über das Drama des Mittelalters in Tirol.* Innsbruck, 1850, 143–68.

Tiroler Passionsspiele. Ed. J. E. Wackernell. In *Altdeutsche Passionsspiele aus Tirol.* Graz, 1897 (contains Pfarrkirchers, Amerikaner, Bozner, Sterzinger, Haller Passion, Sterzinger Mischhandschrift, Brixner Passion).

Wiener Osterspiel. Ed. E. Hartl. In *Das Drama des Mittelalters: Osterspiele,* 74–119. Leipzig, 1937. Reprint, Darmstadt, 1964 (Deutsche Literatur in Entwicklungsreihen, Reihe Drama des Mittelalters, vol. 2).

Wiener Passionsspiel. Ed. R. Froning. In *Das Drama des Mittelalters,* 305–24. Stuttgart, 1891–92. Reprint, Darmstadt, 1964.

III. The English Vernacular Tradition

Chester Plays I. Ed. H. Deimling. London, 1892 (Early English Text Society, extra series, 62).

Chester Plays II. Ed. G. W. Matthews. London, 1916 (Early English Text Society, extra series, 115).   .

Digby Plays. Ed. F. J. Furnivall. London, 1896. (Early English Text Society, extra series, 70).

Ludus Coventriae. Ed. K. S. Block. In *Ludus Coventriae or The Plaie called Corpus Christi.* London, 1922 (Early English Text Society, extra series, 120).

Towneley Plays. Ed. G. England and A. W. Pollard. London, 1897 (Early English Text Society, extra series, 71).

York Plays. Ed. L. T. Smith. Oxford, 1885.

IV. Other Primary Texts

Amalarii Episcopi Opera Liturgica Omnia. Ed. J. M. Hanssens. 3 vols. Rome (Città del Vaticano), 1948–50.

Anselm von Canterbury, *Cur Deus Homo* (Warum Gott Mensch Geworden). Ed. and trans. F. S. Schmitt O.S.B. Darmstadt, 1956.

Biblia Sacra Iuxta Vulgatem Versionem. Ed. R. Weber et al. 2 vols. Stuttgart, 1969.

Evangelia Apocrypha. Ed. K. von Tischendorf. 2nd ed. Leipzig, 1876. Reprint, Hildesheim, 1966.

Patrologia Cursus Completus, Series Latina. Ed. J. P. Migne. Paris, 1841–65. [Cited in Notes as *PL*.]

Thomae Aquinatis Opera Omnia. Ed. S. E. Fretté. 34 vols. Paris, 1871–80.

B. SECONDARY LITERATURE

Auerbach, E. *Mimesis: Dargestellte Wirklichkeit in der abendländischen Literatur.* Bern, 1959.

——. "Figura" (1939). Trans. R. Manheim in *Scenes from the Drama of European Literature.* New York, 1959.

Bakhtin, M. *Literatur und Karneval: Zur Romantheorie und Lachkultur.* Trans. A. Kaempfe. Munich, 1969.

Barthes, R. "Introduction to the Structural Analysis of Narratives." In *Image—Music—Text,* trans. S. Heath. New York, 1977.

Bausinger, H. *Formen der Volkspoesie.* Berlin, 1968.

Benjamin, W. "Was ist das epische Theater?" In *Angelus Novus,* vol. 2 of *Ausgewählte Schriften.* Frankfurt, 1966.

Blumenberg, H. "Wirklichkeitsbegriff und Wirkungspotential des Mythos." In *Terror und Spiel,* ed. M. Fuhrmann, 11–66. Munich, 1971.

——. *The Legitimacy of the Modern Age.* Trans. R. M. Wallace. Cambridge, Mass., 1983.

Brinkmann, H. "Das religiöse Drama im Mittelalter, Arten und Stufen," Wirkendes Wort 9 (1959): 257–74.

——. *Studien zur Geschichte der deutschen Sprache und Literatur.* Vol. 2. Düsseldorf, 1966. (Contains: *Der Ursprung des liturgischen Spiels* [1929], 106–

43, and *Die Eigenform des mittelalterlichen Dramas in Deutschland* [1930], 193–231.)

Bultmann, R. *Die Geschichte der synoptischen Tradition.* 7th ed. Göttingen, 1967.

Catholy, E. *Das Fastnachtspiel des Mittelalters.* Tübingen, 1961.

Chambers, E. K. *The Medieval Stage.* 2 vols. London, 1903.

Cohen, G. *Histoire de la mise en scène dans le théâtre religieux français du moyen âge.* 2nd ed. Paris, 1926.

Craig, H. *English Religious Drama of the Middle Ages.* Oxford, 1955.

de Boor, H. *Die Textgeschichte der lateinischen Osterfeiern.* Tübingen, 1967.

Derrida, J. "Structure, Sign, and Play in the Discourse of the Human Sciences." In *The Structuralist Controversy: The Languages of Criticism and the Sciences of Man,* ed. R. Macksey and E. Donato, 247–65. Baltimore, 1967.

Duriez, G. *La théologie dans le drame religieux en Allemagne au moyen âge.* Lille, 1914.

Ebel, U. Introduction to *Das Altfranzösische Adamsspiel,* 7–43. Munich, 1968. (*Klassiche Texte des romanischen Mittelalters in zweisprachigen Ausgaben,* ed. H. R. Jauß and E. Köhler, vol. 7).

Eliade, M. *Kosmos und Geschichte: Der Mythos der ewigen Wiederkehr.* Reinbek, 1966.

Frank, G. *The Medieval French Drama.* Oxford, 1964.

Frazer, J. G. *The Scapegoat* (*The Golden Bough,* vol. 6). 3rd ed. London, 1913. Reprint, London, 1966.

Freud, S. *Moses and Monotheism.* Trans. Katharine Jones. London, 1939. Reprint, New York, 1967.

———. *Totem and Taboo.* In *The Standard Edition of the Complete Psychological Works of Sigmund Freud,* vol. 13, trans. and ed. James Strachey. London, 1955.

———. *Jokes and their Relation to the Unconscious.* In *The Standard Edition of the Complete Psychological Works of Sigmund Freud,* vol. 8, trans. and ed. James Strachey. London, 1960.

———. *Gesammelte Werke.* Ed. A. Freud et al. 17 vols. Frankfurt, 1968.

Friedrich, G., ed. *Theologisches Wörterbuch zum Neuen Testament.* Stuttgart, 1966–79. [Cited in Notes as *ThWNT.*]

Frye, N. *The Anatomy of Criticism.* Princeton, 1957.

Fuhrmann, M., ed. *Terror und Spiel: Probleme der Mythenrezeption.* Munich, 1971 (Poetik und Hermeneutik 4).

Gadamer, H. G. *Wahrheit und Methode: Grundzüge einer philosophischen Hermeneutik.* Tübingen, 1965.

Gardiner, H. C. *Mysteries' End: An Investigation of the Last Days of the Medieval Religious Stage.* New Haven, 1946 (Yale Studies in English 103).

Gehlen, A. *Urmensch und Spätkultur*. 2nd ed. Frankfurt and Bonn, 1964.

Habermas, J. *Zur Logik der Sozialwissenschaften*. Tübingen, 1967 (*Philosophische Rundschau*, Beiheft 5).

Hardison, O. B. *Christian Rite and Christian Drama in the Middle Ages: Essays in the Origin and Early History of Modern Drama*. Baltimore, 1965.

Harnack, A. von. *Lehrbuch der Dogmengeschichte*. Vol. 3. 4th ed. Tübingen, 1910. Reprint, Darmstadt, 1964.

Harrison, J. E. *Themis: A Study of the Social Origins of Greek Religion*. 2nd ed. Cambridge, 1927.

Hess, R. *Das romanische geistliche Schauspiel als profane und religiöse Komödie*. Munich, 1965 (Freiburger Schriften zur romanischen Philologie, vol. 4).

Hofer, J., and K. Rahner, eds. *Lexikon für Theologie und Kirche*. 10 vols. Freiburg, 1957–65. [Cited in Notes as *LThK*.]

Hunningher, B. *The Origin of the Theatre*. New York, 1961.

Jauß, H. R., ed. *Grundriß der romanischen Literaturen des Mittelalters*. Vol. 6. Heidelberg, 1968.

Jünger, F. G. *Über das Komische*. 3rd ed. Frankfurt, 1948.

Jungmann, J. A. *Missarum Solemnia*. 2 vols. 2nd ed. Freiburg, 1952.

Kerényi, K., ed. *Die Eröffnung des Zugangs zum Mythos*. Darmstadt, 1967.

Kindermann, H. *Theatergeschichte Europas*. Vol. 1. 2nd ed. Salzburg, 1966.

Kolping, A. "Amalar von Metz und Florus von Lyon." *Zeitschrift für katholische Theologie* 73 (1951): 424–64.

Kolve, V. A. *The Play Called Corpus Christi*. London, 1966.

Kroll, J. *Gott und Hölle: Der Mythos vom Descensuskampfe*. Leipzig and Berlin, 1932. Reprint, Darmstadt, 1963.

Lepenies, W., and H. H. Ritter. *Orte des wilden Denkens: Zur Anthropologie von Claude Lévi-Strauss*. Frankfurt, 1970.

Lévi-Strauss, Claude. *La Pensée sauvage*. Paris, 1962.

——. *Le totémisme aujourd'hui*. Paris, 1962.

Lorenzer, A. *Sprachzerstörung und Rekonstruktion: Vorarbeiten zu einer Metatheorie der Psychoanalyse*. Frankfurt, 1971.

Lubac, H. de. *Corpus mysticum: L'eucharistie et l'église au moyen âge*. Paris, 1949.

Luhmann, N. *Soziologische Aufklärung: Aufsätze zur Theorie sozialer Systeme*. 2nd ed. Opladen, 1971.

Malinowski, B. *Myth in Primitive Psychology*. London, 1926.

——. *Geschlecht und Verdrängung in primitiven Gesellschaften*. Reinbek, 1962.

Marin, L. "Les femmes au tombeau: Essai d'analyse structurale d'un texte évangélique." *Langages* 22 (1971): 39–50.

Monnier, J. *La descente aux enfers*. Paris, 1904.

Murray, G. "Excursus on the Ritual Forms Preserved in Greek Tragedy." In Harrison, *Themis,* 341–63.

Pannenberg, W. "Späthorizonte des Mythos in biblischer und christlicher Überlieferung." In Fuhrmann, ed., *Terror und Spiel,* 473–525.

Petit de Julleville, L. *Les mystères.* Vol. 1, *Histoire du Théâtre en France.* Paris, 1880.

Peuckert, W. E. *Die große Wende, Das apokalyptische Saeculum und Luther.* Hamburg, 1948. Reprint, Darmstadt, 1966.

Pickering, F. P. "Das gotische Christusbild." *Euphorion* 47 (1953): 16–37.

———. *Literature and Art in the Middle Ages.* London, 1970.

———. "Irrwege der mittelalterlichen Geschichtsschreibung." *Zeitschrift für deutsches Altertum und deutsche Literatur* 100 (1971): 270–96.

Rad, G. von. *Theologie des Alten Testaments.* 2 vols. 2nd ed. Munich, 1966 and 1968.

Ricoeur, P. "Structure et herméneutique." *Esprit* (1963): 596–626.

Ritter, J. "Über das Lachen" (1940). In *Subjektivität,* 62–69. Frankfurt, 1974.

Rivière, J. *Le dogme de la rédemption au début du moyen âge.* Paris, 1934.

Rossiter, A. P. *English Drama from Early Times to the Elizabethans.* London, 1950.

Roy, E. "Le mystère de la passion en France du 14e au 16e siècle." *Revue Bourguignonne* 13 (1903) and 14 (1904).

Ruh, K. "Zur Theologie des mittelalterlichen Passionstraktats." *Theologische Zeitschrift* 6 (1950): 17–39.

Speirs, J. *Medieval English Poetry: The Non-Chaucerian Tradition.* London, 1957.

Stemmler, T. *Liturgische Feiern und geistliche Spiele: Studien zu Erscheinungsformen des Dramatischen im Mittelalter.* Tübingen, 1970.

Stumpfl, R. *Kultspiele der Germanen als Ursprung des mittelalterlichen Dramas.* Berlin, 1936.

Thoran, B. "Studien zu den österlichen Spielen des deutschen Mittelalters." Diss., Bochum, 1969.

Todorov, T. "Les catégories du récit littéraire." *Communications* 8 (1966): 124–51.

Weimann, R. *Shakespeare und die Tradition des Volkstheaters: Soziologie-Dramaturgie-Gestaltung.* Berlin, 1967.

Weinrich, H. "Structures narratives du mythe." *Poétique* 1 (1970): 25–34.

Young, K. *The Drama of the Medieval Church.* 2 vols. Oxford, 1933. Reprint, Oxford, 1967.

Zingel, M. "Die Passion Christi in der Mystik des deutschen Mittelalters." Diss., Berlin, 1956.

Index

In this index an "f" after a number indicates a separate reference on the next page, and an "ff" indicates separate references on the next two pages. A continuous discussion over two or more pages is indicated by a span of page numbers, e.g., "57–59."

Figurae: Reading Medieval Culture